CHRISTINA OF SWEDEN

QUEEN CHRISTINA
Painting by Sébastien Bourdon (1652) in the possession of Freiherr Carl Gripenstedt, Bysta
Photo: Hans Bergman, Örebro

[*Frontispiece*

CHRISTINA OF SWEDEN

by

SVEN STOLPE

Edited by

SIR ALEC RANDALL

THE MACMILLAN COMPANY
NEW YORK
1966

This translation of the abbreviated German version (Königin Christine von Schweden, *Josef Knecht, 1963*) *of the original two-volume work* Drottning Kristina (*Albert Bonniers Förlag, 1960 and 1961*) *was made by* SIR ALEC RANDALL *and* RUTH MARY BETHELL

Library of Congress catalog number 66–15496

The Macmillan Company, New York
Collier-Macmillan, Ltd., Toronto, Ontario

MADE AND PRINTED IN GREAT BRITAIN BY
HAZELL WATSON AND VINEY LTD
AYLESBURY, BUCKS

Contents

Illustrations

Author's Preface to the English Translation

CHRISTINA, Queen of Sweden, daughter of King Gustav Adolf, is undoubtedly the most discussed of all queens in history, second only to Cleopatra. It is hardly too much to say that every year or so a new biography of her is published in one language or another. Generally they are all wrong. They are based on a mass of gossip hostile to Christina, on an abundance of rumour, and on contradictory polemical writing, which began during her lifetime, and flourished especially in the eighteenth century. The Queen of Sweden is presented to the minds of educated people in Europe and America as the prototype of a frivolous and irresponsible woman, avid for pleasure, in that remarkable age of Baroque. Her conversion to Roman Catholicism is dismissed as fraudulent; her entire life is described as given up to vanity and self-gratification.

This picture is a mistaken one. Christina was, before all else, a stoic, a woman devoted to duty, and this was to turn her, in the end, to something like a Christian mystic. She was not free from moral faults, but she was in no way licentious. She was never in intimate relations with a man, and the one man she loved made only a cool response to her infatuation. Her psychology was a highly individual one; she was, indeed, unique among the most famous women of history.

The truth about Christina is to be found by reading her letters, many still unpublished, and examining her other papers and the marginal notes she made in certain books and theological manuscripts that are in libraries in Stockholm and Rome. From a study of this material an entirely new portrait of Christina emerges. It is also important to consider her refusal of marriage against the background of the curious views held during her lifetime about women and child-bearing.

The biography presented here is an abridgment—not an extensive one—of the Swedish original which was published in two volumes in Stockholm in 1960 and 1961. This English version has been translated from the German version. My book on Christina is based on a series of studies, written after much research. As the present book is intended for the reader with a general interest in history I have not encumbered the text with notes and detailed references. It is, however, I hope, made sufficiently clear that the portrait I have tried to give is derived from the study of a mass of original documents, many of them used for the first time. Any new reader who wishes to examine my material for this new picture of Christina is referred to my books, *Fran Stoicism til Mysticism; studier in Drottning Kristinas Maximer* (From Stoicism to Mysticism; Studies in Queen Christina's Maxims), published in Stockholm in 1959, and my *Kristina-Studier* (Studies in Christina), published at Uppsala in the same year.

SVEN STOLPE

Book I

CHRISTINA IN SWEDEN

CHAPTER ONE

The Christina Legend

1. CHRISTINA AND THE LAST JUDGMENT

IN Giovanni Papini's great work, published after his death, *The Last Judgment*, in which mankind is assembled before the eternal judge, Queen Christina of Sweden also appears. The angel says to her:

> People thought you a curious character, Christina of Sweden. You abandoned your father's faith, and struggled all your life long to gain other crowns, but in vain. You abjured your father's religion and attached yourself to the Catholic Church, but you brought shame on your conversion, since a little later you became the lover of a cardinal, and caused the murder of one of your favourites. People were more than indulgent with you, but now it will avail you nothing that you were beautiful, that you were a queen, a scholar and a poet. Now you are to be called to account for your crimes.

Not a word of these accusations by the angel is true. Christina was not the lover of a cardinal, or of anyone else. She never murdered a favourite; rather did she lawfully and rightfully punish a traitor, on whom she was entitled to sit in judgment. She was not beautiful. She could hardly be called a scholar, and certainly not a poet. Papini's account of her shows what influence was exerted on general opinion by scandal-sheets about Christina, and romantic biographies of her.

2. CHRISTINA VENERATED BY HER CONTEMPORARIES

Royalties, of both sexes, have always been the object of servile flattery by their contemporaries. No branch of literature is more worthless and dishonest than the sycophantic scribblings about such persons. It is often painful to observe the contrast, proved by history, between the mediocrity, or indeed the worthlessness, of many royalties and the eulogies of their admirers who were dependent on them.

The case of the young Queen Christina of Sweden was an exception to this rule. There was something special about her, and she was like no other royalty of history. "She has an extraordinarily brilliant intelligence", was the observation of one of her gruff counsellors, Gabriel Gustavsson Oxenstierna. One of the famous, and reliable, reports of the French envoy Chanut to his government, in 1648, when the queen was twenty-two, contained this passage:

> I tremble still when I recall the day when Her Majesty mounted a snow-white Italian horse which was a present from your Eminence [Cardinal Mazarin] out on the plain of Uppland. She was extraordinarily fond of it, and it seemed to know its mistress. She told us to fetch four of the fastest horses from her stables, and challenged us to a race, which she won.

This picture of the young queen in her hunting costume, running a race on her white horse with her favourites and the French Ambassador, on the Uppland plain, which may well have been covered with snow, and triumphantly coming in first, brings to mind a scene from the story of Joan of Arc. The King of France wanted the Duc d'Alençon to bring to him for his inspection the unknown peasant girl who had just come from Chinon with a message from God the Father himself. The duke was out shooting quail. He was called back. After having had breakfast together with the king and Joan, he was so profoundly impressed with the girl that, in his enthusiasm, he presented her with a horse—for out there in the meadows, Joan showed such military qualities that the duke was quite carried away. He later described the incident himself: "After we had eaten the king went riding on the meadows where Joan was riding too, carrying a lance. She handled this weapon with such skill that I gave her a horse as a present."

This scene, as strikingly effective as an extract from the Odyssey's account of life in the land of the Phaeacians* is also in

* See Book XIII of *The Odyssey*.

some respects like the French envoy's description of the young Queen of Sweden. Both were exceptional young women, exercising their horses. They were both called to extraordinary tasks. Both were virgins and were to remain so. They resembled no one else in history.

Of course there is a great difference between the primitive peasant-girl from Lorraine and the cultured daughter of the Swedish King who, as a young girl, had been instructed in literature and politics, who lost her father when she was only six, was parted from her hysterical mother at an early age, and had neither brothers nor sisters.

Chanut reported that Christina had the voice of a young lady, but that it would suddenly—no one knew why—change and become loud, coarse and peremptory, returning just as suddenly to her normal juvenile contralto. Christina was rather short. If she had worn the same shoes as her ladies-in-waiting, this fact would not have been noticed. But in order to make her movements easier as she went about the castle, and walk or ride in greater comfort, she always wore a kind of low-heeled man's shoe.

Chanut continued:

> Monseigneur, I find it hard to approve—if I may use the expression—of the fact that the princess, who speaks excellent Latin* and has mastered French, Flemish, German and Swedish, should now be learning Greek too, though she is making excellent progress. She looks upon all these difficult studies as a kind of recreation. In my view it would be enough if in her leisure time she were instructed by learned persons in the more important achievements of science, and that her mind, so eager to acquire knowledge, should be busied with all kinds of things. But whenever I venture to suggest this to her, she replies that she carries on these language-studies as a diversion during a time which would otherwise be wasted, just as she learnt the game of chess. This did not in the least interfere with her serious studies. She was referring to the *History* of Tacitus; not a day passed without her reading some pages of this work. She is particularly familiar with this Latin writer, who can give matter

* In her autobiography Christina says that before she could read, she had learnt Latin perfectly, but as a girl she could never be brought to speak Latin, though she had a complete command of the language.

> for thought to more learned persons than she. This I should scarcely have believed if I had to rely on reports from other people, or had heard her quote a few sentences at random. But during her last journey to Uppsala she was tired of sitting in her coach and reading, and invited me to get in with her. She then opened this book and I noticed that in difficult passages, to which I had to give much thought and in which I felt some hesitation as to the meaning of the words, she found no difficulty; I quietly admired the way in which she was able to interpret the profound thoughts of the Latin writer in our language, which is not her own.

Chanut added that she often acted as if she understood nothing of the erudite questions which scholars eagerly discussed in her presence, that in many respects she was withdrawn and had an air of mystery. "But it is unbelievable what vigour she displays when she is with her advisers." (Christina noted in the margin: "How amusing he is; he is so badly informed!") He went on to say that she displayed the energy and the sense of purpose which one would expect to find in a young prince. This was because nature had given her all the advantages of a young man. "In the country she is untiring; when she is out hunting she can sit in the saddle for ten hours at a stretch. She is not in the least affected by heat or cold. Her diet is simple, often carelessly prepared and with no refined touches. There is no one in Sweden with a more certain aim when she brings down a hare with the only cartridge in her case."

The concluding part of the characterization has the well-known passage about the queen's piety, her passionate devotion to a life of heroism and virtue.

> Nothing has the slightest importance for her in comparison with her passionate attachment to honour and virtue—*la vertu*. One may say her ambition is more directed to make her name famous by extraordinary merit rather than by conquests; her efforts are aimed more at achieving fame by her own efforts than through the qualities of her subjects.

Chanut's opinion is well worth noting. In another connection he showed himself as remarkably sure in his judgment, without any tendency to exaggeration. All the same, it would seem that in this case he somehow tended to over-rate and romanticize reality. The very sight of this young girl in her twenties, almost absolute ruler over one of the Great Powers of Europe, who pursued erudite studies with remarkable zeal, and at the same time produced such a unique and fascinating effect with her perhaps beautiful eyes and her odd, mannish behaviour, must have been astonishing. An experienced diplomatist, who was acquainted with many highly placed people and had to listen, with an amiable smile, to much foolish talk, was confronted with an exceptional personality, not a half-educated character, not a mere façade, but a real personality, possessed of a firm will and a combination of other qualities. Hence the enthusiasm; hence the exaggeration.

This was the image which came to be generally accepted. There are many examples of the myth-making that soon began, especially from the time when Christina entered into correspondence with scholars, and invited celebrated scientists and philosophers to her court, offering them dazzling rewards—promising them, at any rate. She became the marvel of northern Europe; she was declared to be Minerva in the land of the Scythians; in Paris there was great enthusiasm for her, and from all sides came an abundance of eulogies—one of the most servile from Pascal himself. It was not easy to live up to such excessive praise. Christina was indeed exceptional, but she was not without faults; she was gifted, especially receptive, but not by any means a genius; well-read, but not really what we should call intellectual. During her years in Sweden she never expressed an opinion of her own which had any real interest or value. Her best qualities were different—she had courage and strength of will. She was a born politician and trained to be such—no more.

But the first legend that grew round her person was that she was infinitely gifted, and entirely filled with a striving after virtue and moral achievement.

It was not long before this beautiful legend was reduced to nothing. Perhaps we can say that it survived only in her own country; the romantic ideal lasted long among her loyal Swedish peasants, the middle class and nobility. Abroad an entirely contrary view of Christina soon prevailed. Instead of a stoic superwoman, a gifted young princess of genius, a divine masterpiece, she became in the eyes of the world, by an entire reversal of opinion, a shameless courtesan, a faithless, proud and false woman, the scandal of her century. Giovanni Papini adopted this view of her character.

3. THE ODIOUS CHRISTINA

How did it come about that Queen Christina aroused such extreme hatred, that in later years essays, biographies and articles were published which depicted her as a courtesan, a half-pathological, arrogant, repellent hermaphrodite?

A solitary, proud and provocative young woman in a conspicuous position—perhaps no more than that was needed to put such rumours into circulation, especially in a century when among women of distinction those remarkable for their noble qualities and their modesty were the exception rather than the rule. It all began at a certain point when the queen, without losing her old love for France, took up a new attitude to Spain, France's deadly enemy. By that time the intelligent Chanut was no longer in Stockholm, and the man who looked after French interests in Sweden, the chargé d'affaires Picques, was, though industrious, entirely lacking in judgment. He could never see the queen together with the brilliant Spanish officer and diplomatist Don Antonio Pimentel, without suspecting or at least insinuating an amorous relationship between them. The Danish Minister Juel had an equally lively, not to say degenerate, imagination. Everyone knew of the queen's especial attachment to the beautiful Countess Ebba Sparre—and it was misinterpreted. All the world knew also that the queen had shown remarkable generosity to a succession of young men, members of the nobility. They were rapidly promoted, in particular the elegant and handsome Gabriel de la Gardie and Claes Tott; it is worth-while taking a look at the still extant portraits of the latter. As is well known, the Count de la Gardie was later brought to ruin by Christina, though the account usually given may possibly be not entirely correct. However, there is no reason to prefer uncritically the queen's version to that of de la Gardie himself. The Swedish favourites were succeeded by Frenchmen, especially the witty, somewhat impertinent doctor Bourdelot, who was addicted to gambling. At Christina's court the discontented and those who in their own opinion had been slighted were always more numerous than the favourites. And soon the rumour-mongers were actively at work.

While Christina was in Sweden they kept more or less within the bounds of respectability. But no sooner had the queen left Sweden than scandal-sheets began to be published which were probably political in inspiration. There was a suspicion that Christina's sympathies were still with Spain, and therefore it was a question of reducing her political significance by abusing her morals and dragging them through the mud. Strangely enough, when Chanut's reports were finally printed, they came out together with Picques', so that those who were not in the know saw hardly any difference between them. Chanut, who was highly respected, thus became morally responsible for a mass of gossip which he had never had anything to do with, and of which, in fact, he was unaware. The publication found its way into Queen Christina's hands; we still have her contemptuous comments on it. She saw at once that her old, high-minded friend Chanut could never have been the source of such impudent and false judgments of her.

But the book came out and everyone read it. Under cover of Chanut's name lies were published, and were taken up by a series of writers and padded out, especially in the eighteenth century, when dissolute queens and princesses were a welcome subject for the reproachful writings of many scribblers. Without anyone being able to prevent it, a regular pattern began to be established—the presentation of Christina as shameless, perverted, mendacious, false and blind to all duty. This came to be believed and was the general opinion; indeed, at the time it was part of everyone's common knowledge. Around 1750, people did not hesitate to manufacture pornographic letters which Queen Christina was said to have written to her friend, the lovely Countess Ebba Sparre.

In the development of her evil reputation a not insignificant part was played by the fact that on an occasion that was to become famous, Christina caused a certain Monaldesco, an Italian noble in her service, to be executed. For various reasons she was unable to state what crime he had been guilty of. But public opinion was at once in a position to affirm that Monaldesco was the last in a lengthy list of lovers who had had to be set aside to make room for a new one. All Europe was overwhelmed by a wave of anger and horror at this terrible, inhuman queen. In his book, *Christine de Suède et le Cardinal Azzolino*, published in 1899, Carl Bildt sought the cause of this event in the "ferocity" of the queen, and still in 1959, in such a valuable book as Pierre Frédérix's *Monsieur René Descartes et son temps*, it is stated that Christina had had a succession of lovers, among them Monaldesco, whom she caused to he murdered because she was tired of him.

There are a thousand books, so says one authority, that describe Christina in this fashion. To this day, French writers in particular have tried to outdo one another in depicting her as a shameless, half-crazy murderess; she was, they said, either a wild and reckless courtesan or, to quote the title of one of these books, *chaste et folle* (chaste but mad).

It goes without saying that writers of fiction took up this theme with enthusiasm, and added their contribution; Strindberg's play about Christina is one of the most repulsive examples of this kind of book.

In the eighteenth century a German historian, J. Arckenholtz, assembled in four stout volumes all the material he could obtain. With a loquacity and fussy industry that gets on one's nerves, he produced a theory of his own about the queen. He had, of course, to admit that apparently she had never had any amorous adventures—he saw through the majority of the scandal-sheets. On the other hand he was unable to consider her conversion as anything but a foolish and irresponsible whim, which she is supposed to have regretted in due course. He was of course incapable of judging the murder of Monaldesco correctly, even though he did print Cardinal Azzolino's letter which gave the true explanation. Practically all subsequent writers have based their efforts on this massive and indiscriminatingly accumulated pile of material. There are remarkably few modern, popular accounts which derive from serious research into the life of Queen Christina, yet such research gives an entirely different portrayal of her.

4. GRAUERT AND MARTIN WEIBULL

Objective study began about a hundred and fifty years ago, when an outstanding German historian, W. H. Grauert, in a two-volume book, examined without prejudice all earlier assumptions, and had no great difficulty in discovering them to be largely legends and distortions, although he did not use by any means all the documentary material available. It is curious that Grauert's book is still the best general portrait we possess of Queen Christina; it does honour to German research. What matters is that an extraordinarily competent writer took Christina's conversion seriously, on the whole believed her own accounts of what drove her to this dramatic step, and tried to explain the whole thing by a thorough study of the really important key-documents. But Grauert was unable to stop a further flood of scandal-writings, which went on for a hundred years, notwithstanding the fact that he had, by his book, cut the ground from beneath all malicious insinuations. However, he opened up the great process of rehabilitation; he provided the firm basis from which we could proceed step by step.

The first attempt by a Swede to use really scientific methods was that by Professor Martin Weibull, in 1887–8, with his essay on the so-called "memoirs" of Chanut which have already been mentioned. Weibull undertook the critical study of this book, which perhaps more than any other helped to spread the rumours of Christina's immorality. It was a rewarding task for an experienced analyst of historical documents to prove that all the data contained in the memoirs which may really be traced back to Chanut are reliable, while the utterly unreliable and scandalous allegations are in no way derived from Chanut, but from Picques. Moreover, it was shown that the editor of the memoirs, P. Linage de Vauciennes, had been extremely careless in his handling of the material.

Martin Weibull saw a new picture of Christina emerge from the ruins of the myths. He speaks of what he considers her genuine personality in terms of admiration, one might say affection. According to him she could never have been infected by the atheism of her time; she was a "character"; she had never been capable of lying (though here we must think of her own testimony in a note which has not been printed: "Even the cleverest people were deceived by her powerful imagination.") And if, for example, immediately after her abdication, she used expressions lacking in piety and even dignity, these must be explained as excusable ambiguities, uttered before she could appear with her visor up, so to speak, with the candour she herself always wanted to show. A quotation from Weibull's essay may be given to show how uncritical was his admiration:

> It is Queen Christina herself who is most to blame for the fact that this shadow [suspicion of atheism] fell across her portrait and made a true and just judgment impossible. For she possessed, both in her nature and from her education, even to excess, that relaxed and frank character which marked her people and her family; it was this that made her incapable of suppressing a thought or a word, even if it was to her disadvantage. It was her constant wish to be entirely truthful, and as a queen she considered she could be so. When inner processes of thought, still not completely explained, brought her into that state of unparalleled difficulty—the state of wearing, as a Catholic, the crown of Sweden and of Gustavus Adolphus, she did not resort to untruthfulness, which horrified her. Instead she preferred to entrench herself in ambiguous words, in jokes and at least un-serious tones of irony or satire—double-edged weapons which she could employ with brilliant ability.

No explanation could be farther from the truth. Weibull was so bewitched by Christina that he was incapable of recognizing the facts. Christina was, on the contrary, an adept at dissembling; she boasted of it all her life. "She is 'bilinquis' " (double-tongued) Bishop Terserus once said of her, with perfect truth. She was, as one of her unpublished maxims proves, aware of the fact that people more rarely resemble themselves than they differ from one another, that, in fact, people are constantly changing. She made use not only of ambiguity but of plain lying. During the struggle for the throne of Poland she wrote cynically that people should, if it made things any easier, spread the rumour that she was thinking of marrying; she would have no objection to such rumours, though as a matter of fact she had no thought of marriage. This Macchiavellian characteristic is clearly brought out in Sven Ingvar Olofsson's masterly essay on the queen's policy in her last years in Sweden.

In this way the severe historical analyst, Martin Weibull, who otherwise contributed so much to research about Christina, arrived at an imaginary picture as far removed from the truth as the contents of the scandal-sheets. His naive efforts to whitewash the Swedish queen were due, among other things, to his inadequate knowledge of the world of ideas of that period, the period of French baroque. In the light of his own prejudices all adherents of the Fronde had dubious morals, whereas all Swedes were honest and honourable.

5. CARL BILDT

Towards the end of the last century, Baron Carl Bildt was sent as Swedish Minister to Rome; he was a man with certain literary interests who eventually became a member of the Swedish Academy. It was natural that during his long service in the Eternal City, he should have begun to take an interest in the Queen of Sweden, who had lived there so many years. Moreover, he took an interest in other Swedes who had been in Rome, especially St. Bridget. Over the years his interest in Christina grew, and at length he had the good fortune to obtain practically all the documentary material dealing with the queen; particularly the so-called Azzolino Collection, which is now in the national archives in Stockholm, and the Albano Collection, which is kept in the library of the faculty of medicine in Montpellier. Bildt was an experienced researcher into archives and he recognized the importance of the nuncio's reports. He succeeded in deciphering a number of letters in code, written by the queen to Cardinal Azzolino, for the most part from Hamburg in the years 1666 to 1668. Her other letters to the cardinal, however, so Bildt believed, must have vanished, like the cardinal's letters to her, in accordance with the terms of her will.

Bildt was able to clarify many points. Among others, he succeeded, as soon as he had deciphered the Azzolino letters, in proving that the queen was possessed by an all-consuming, indeed a humiliating, passion for the Cardinal. Bildt had material at his disposal which was far more complete than that available to any of his predecessors, and he was thus in a position to tone down all the shameful rumours about her many lovers, and about her dissolute life in general. Nevertheless he gave a quite untenable portrayal of her personality. Bildt had no understanding for religion. He was a snob who loved to make sarcastic comments on life, and especially on women. His book, written in an elegant style, is in terms of a superiority and contempt for women that we find intolerable today. On the psychological side he understood nothing whatever about Christina. Nor did he understand the age she lived in. He had no idea of the way in which, in the seventeenth century, Stoicism had been replaced by free thought; he knew nothing of the deeper religious currents in the baroque period. A woman who wanted to intervene in world politics, who came into contact with the most famous scholars of her time, who went from one audacious enterprise to another—he quite simply thought her to be hysterical. His final verdict, which unfortunately influenced so serious a historian as Ludwig von Pastor, is as follows:

> When she came to the throne Christina was no Messalina; she was not the helpless slave of her tyrannical temperament. Nor was she another Catherine II, with powerful senses that made many demands. She was a young girl of delicate health who paid no attention to the rules of hygiene, who overtaxed her brain and nerves and directed her energies to the satisfaction of her pride and self-admiration. She was eager for flattery and applause; she exploited her intellectual and material superiority; she was never still; she gave herself to the duties of her position, to her studies and to her pleasures, all at the same crazy tempo. At one moment she would enjoy the intoxication of power; at the next she would be sensible of its bitterness. At one and the same time she was enraptured and weary of greatness, constantly aware of the tyranny it imposed on her. She was a complex, enigmatic creature, lacking a strong hand to guide her in childhood, and in her youth without a loving heart to bring her a modicum of happiness. Her head was

stuffed with knowledge, but no one taught her the lesson of love, and she therefore went through life severe and frigid, with no impulse towards tenderness or kindness or feeling for her native country; in short she was an egocentric neuropath.

Anyone who has had access to the documents which Bildt collected and which he tried, with small success, to reduce to order, will see this characterization to be a crude caricature. Bildt judged Christina with the mentality of the Victorian era. An intellectual strong-willed and energetic woman was to him quite ridiculous. A woman who lived as a virgin was to his cynical mind an object of pity. Christina's whole personality was bound to appear to him psycho-pathological.

The German historian Oskar Wertheimer, who wrote an excellent popular book about Christina, though unfortunately he had no knowledge of the most important documents, was quite right in his remark that Bildt's judgment was wrong in all its details. Although, he said, Bildt had a correct knowledge of her life, he was unable to understand it, and failed to see her true personality, her interior and exterior greatness. Von Pastor, the great historian of the popes, severely criticized Bildt's point of view as being that of a modern man of the world.

An important Swedish literary historian, Heinrich Schück, who based his work on Bildt's portrayal, came to a truly grotesque conclusion. He judged Christina exactly as he judged the women-students of his own time, the eighties of the last century, who had, to his annoyance, crowded into the sacred halls of the Swedish universities, were unable to co-ordinate their thoughts, and lived an irresponsible life in general. Schück had already explained the revelations of St. Bridget as due to her "unsuitable diet". He found the same explanation for the irrational actions of the young queen.

6. CURT WEIBULL—PINTARD

In the thirties Curt Weibull, who was also an historian, succeeded his father Martin Weibull in the role of the queen's champion. In Sweden the school of both Weibulls is considered to be unsparingly critical; its long struggle against the romantic school of historical research, as it was conducted in Stockholm and Uppsala, was finally successful. It is worth noting, however, that in his account of Christina, though the standard with regard to detail was high, Curt Weibull was just as given to romanticizing as was his father. His writing is brilliant; he makes practically no use of subordinate sentences; his style is majestic and crystal-clear. He composed his book as Corneille composed his plays. When he gives an account of the cause of Monaldesco's execution—which Cardinal Azzolino had done already, without giving much emphasis to the story—he accompanies it with such a beating of drums that you might think he was making a communication of world-wide historical interest. Those historians who did not agree with him are treated with contemptuous scorn in condescending footnotes. Curt Weibull considers the lines along which the queen developed to have been perfectly logical; throughout he holds her motives to have been honourable and true to her high character. To him she was a wonderful, single-minded person, who desired nothing that was not just and noble. Once she was entirely convinced of the truth of Catholicism, she had to make the great sacrifice of the Swedish throne, since the laws of the land did not allow her to occupy it any longer. Curt Weibull's narrative is almost devoid of nuances. He writes affectionately and enthusiastically; he is the knight singing the praises of his queen. His book is admirable and indispensable; it is a pity foreign writing about Christina did not pay it more attention. But in its own way it is just as far from the truth as the well-known scandal-sheets. These caused Weibull much annoyance, and he simply went to the other extreme; he can find nothing in Christina that is not completely justified, indeed exalted.

Why did Curt Weibull present us with a picture of the queen that is wrong in almost every feature? The answer is simple, he did not meet the most elementary demands of historical method. He started out from what he wanted to prove, namely, that Christina was a wonderful person. He did not make the slightest effort to provide evidence supporting this view, which he took over from his patriotic, royalist father. He said not a word about other well-known characteristics of Christina—her skill at dissimulation, her deceitfulness in many ways, her inclination to libertinism and her contact with freethinkers. These characteristics conflicted with the opinion he had already formed. He wrote about her conversion without making any enquiry into the question whether, in fact, she had experienced a conversion at all; he said not a word about the circle of French freethinkers by whom she was surrounded at that time and with whom it can be proved she was in sympathy. Curt Weibull had the same peculiar contempt of the Swedish Lutherans as was felt by the Swedish Positivists, and accordingly he produced a caricature of the Lutheran Church and its leaders, reputed to be so contentious and antagonistic to all things of the intellect. He gave no evidence for this, nor for the contrast he set up between this caricature and an aristocratic Catholicism personified by men like Descartes, which is said to have gained Christina's preference. Yet orthodox Lutheranism in no way deserves such contempt, and Christina can hardly be said to have taken her opinions on the subject of religion from Descartes.

In addition, Curt Weibull entirely neglected—and this is his second mistake in method—to consider Christina in the context of the religious tendencies of the time; he merely said a few words about the contemporary cult of virtue. Finally he showed a notable ignorance of Catholicism. Here he was guilty of many disconcerting and important mistakes of detail. For example he did not know the meaning of the Catholic term "confirmation". Whatever the accuracy of his description of the political situation, his judgment is unreliable when he comes to deal with Christina's psychology, her intellectual development and her concern with Catholic belief.

It is true that after the publication of Curt Weibull's sensational and fascinating books it was widely thought that the final history of Christina had at last been written; that is, apart from a few minor additions and emendations. But this idea was entirely unjustified. And now, independently of Swedish scholars, French historians took up Christina and were able to draw on material in French archives, of which the Swedes knew nothing, whereon to base their studies. Especially interesting was the account which

René Pintard, a careful scholar, gave in his book about Christina's scholarly libertinism. Pintard did not know the books of either Weibull, though certain of Martin Weibull's arguments might have been obtained by him from Bildt. He did, however, start out from the assumption that Bildt's psychological interpretation of Christina was correct—which was certainly not the case; and having investigated the archives, he was able to point to many sources that could not be neglected: a mass of letters and other contemporary documents by persons associated with the queen. These documents often show an astonishing agreement with certain features of critical writings about Christina. Pintard said in this connection:

> The fantasy elaborated about Christina in many studies, the pre-formed views about her, the brevity and the inadequate evidence that mark books which are worth attention on this subject, force us to be more cautious in this delicate investigation, where reliable guides are so hard to come by. Nevertheless the light shed by experienced and impartial writers on Christina's abnormal physiology and her odd behaviour leads to the conclusion that many peculiarities, reported by her contemporaries, must be taken as correct. Most of the data about her are to be found in the Arckenholtz collection; they are not interpreted in psychological terms, but they are described impartially. This collection needs to be read in conjunction with the queen's private correspondence.

At times Pintard's sources are obviously inadequate. He relies too much on Bildt's psychological account and takes Arckenholtz to be trustworthy. All the same he comes to an important conclusion: "We can make use of Christina's correspondence as a whole or at least in part, and it does not seem permissible to take no account of the two contemporaries of the queen who were in close touch with her circle—even if they may be charged with excessive strictness in their judgments. At all events it must be said that both knew a great deal and were remarkably correct."

Yet Pintard's story is also incorrect; all he could see in Christina was a shameless libertine; he fails to recognize the seriousness of her attempt to find an adequate explanation of the world and an acceptable faith. In certain respects he relied on old-fashioned accounts of Christina; he had no idea of the way in which she really developed.

7. A NEW PATH

None of the scholars mentioned above, though all made contributions to our knowledge of this mysterious woman, had access to all the material. It is curious that no student of Christina after Bildt seriously examined the Azzolino and Montpellier collections; the first of these is a veritable gold-mine, it contains unknown manuscripts by the queen, maxims, reflections, theological essays, above all important marginal notes on various subjects written in the queen's own hand. Still more important are the foreign archives, in which rich and hitherto unused material about Christina is to be found; the archives of the Inquisition, several of the archives of the Jesuits, the Vatican archives, private collections and German as well as French archives. Once we begin to study this material an entirely new picture of Christina soon emerges, that has little in common with that found in the scandal-sheets or the writing of the eulogists. Perhaps the difficulty is due to the initial assumption that she was a good and loyal Catholic, without any attempt being made to discover if this was so; it was taken for granted that her conversion was due to a decisive spiritual experience, regardless of the complete lack of evidence that she ever really had such an experience: on the contrary, there are many facts to suggest that something altogether different took place.

We can trace the Christina problem backwards, so to speak, and study her Catholic views first: the following account will show that she was not the loyal and convinced Catholic she was supposed to be. As to her conversion, we find there was no profound personal crisis or spiritual upheaval; Christina had quite different reasons for changing her religion. Finally, her abdication, we discover, had nothing to do with her Catholicism. If, as a result, her personality becomes less thrilling, less overwhelming, it gains an inner harmony; the lines along which she was to develop begin to be perceptible.

CHAPTER TWO

King Gustavus Adolphus

I. THE YOUNG GUSTAVUS ADOLPHUS

THE general view of Gustavus Adolphus, shared also by historical scholars, is that he was one of the most balanced leaders in the course of history. This does not mean, however, that he was not in many respects a problematical character, subject, from his youth till his death, to severe tension. This can be shown particularly clearly in two aspects—his religious life and his love-life.

Originally Gustavus Adolphus was brought up in a spirit of toleration by his mother, Christina of Holstein, widow of the man Luther called "the beloved Landgraf", Philip of Hesse. Johann Skytte, a highly cultivated man, distinguished by his intellectual independence, was appointed to be his tutor. All dogma, even the Augsburg Confession, was excluded from his curriculum; his education was chiefly to be based on "the writings of the apostles and prophets". In his youth Gustavus Adolphus read Thomas à Kempis in Latin. Johann Skytte was above all a humanist; he sympathized with Erasmus of Rotterdam, was an adherent of the French humanist Ramée, and detested scholasticism and metaphysics. It may be assumed that his teaching had an influence on the Prince's basic religious ideas; there was no kind of fanaticism about them. The programme he proclaimed at his accession was one of toleration. He firmly decided that he would not give way to the Estates of the realm and persecute the "wicked Calvinists". Adherents of religions other than Protestantism were permitted to reside in the country, provided they did not proselytize or carry on intrigues, "since no authority has the right to control the conscience of others". It seems clear that in this way Gustavus Adolphus sought to protect the Calvinists; his very unattractive father, as we know, had an inclination to their creed. It is said that Gustavus Adolphus also asked the bishops to advise him whether "several religions might not be allowed in the country". At the beginning he was extraordinarily tolerant.

Johann Skytte's influence, however, was before long replaced by that of other men, especially Johann Rudbeckius. Gustavus Adolphus came to look at the situation from the political point of view. He felt himself to be "God's instrument", and he found it natural and right that he should let Catholics be persecuted. He spoke sharply against them at the meeting of parliament at Örebro, in 1617: "This religion, if it can really be considered a religion, is not only idolatrous, it is a merely human construction, contradicting God's Word and the Scriptures, in which lies our way to everlasting bliss; it teaches particularly repellent doctrines: 'haereticis non est servanda fides', that is, there is no need to keep faith with heretics, as they call us."

He spoke of the "devil's brood of Jesuits, who were the cause of horrifying tyranny in Spain, France and other countries. With their Inquisition they stopped short of no one, neither women nor men, lowly or exalted. These murderers have not even spared the son of King Philip II, Don Carlos, who was killed merely on the suspicion that he held the same faith as I do* . . .

In his unfinished autobiography Gustavus Adolphus called the Pope a son of the devil, and the papal legate Malaspina a "Satan's bellows". When he met the Norwegian monk Laurentius Nicolai he abused him, calling him a "hell-hound", asking whether he did not know that hell awaited those who followed such false doctrines. Nicolai calmly replied that it was the Lutherans who could expect this punishment, not his own fellow Catholics. Gustavus Adolphus's increasingly ruthless attitude to Catholics may be seen best in an episode that occurred in the first years of his reign.

2. CATHOLICS IN SWEDEN

On Palm Sunday in the year 1624, Gustavus Adolphus's lute-player, Johann Baptista Veraldi, who, curiously enough, was a

* Gustavus Adolphus seems to have thought Don Carlos was a Protestant.

Roman Catholic, came to his master and gave him some remarkable information. He said there were Catholics in Sweden, perhaps even among the king's councillors. A Catholic priest was guest at that time in the house of one of these councillors; he had the intention of going all over the country, inciting people to become members of the Catholic Church.

It can well be imagined how astonished and infuriated the king was at hearing this. He determined at all costs to get from his lute-player the whole truth about his fellow believers. With a bribe of two hundred thaler he succeeded in making him talk. In the presence of a court-official the lute-player wrote in Italian a letter to the Catholic priest in question, who had gone to Södertälje to celebrate the Easter festival. He was staying with the burgomaster, Zacharias Anthelius, and was given out to be a distant relation of the burgomaster, from Germany. The letter invited the priest to come to Stockholm where, it said, there were a number of hidden Catholics who wished to go to confession.

On 24 April the reply came: "I am delighted that Your Lordship is so helpful to the Catholic religion. I will come as soon as Herre Zacharias Anthelius, at whose disposal I have put myself, finds it convenient for me to leave. I am ready to go to work, even if it means imperilling my life, as I want to win souls for Christ."

This letter, which was addressed to Veraldi, was accompanied by a second one, addressed to Anthelius in Stockholm, where he was staying at the time, engaged in his duties as a king's councillor. This second letter dealt with certain business matters, and mentioned some names. The king saw at once that the traitor's statements were correct. The previous day he had prudently had the councillor Anthelius thrown into prison; the same evening he had the priest brought from Södertälje to Stockholm. The next day he was bound and taken to the king's castle and put in the cell of prisoners condemned to death (*carcer desperatorum*). He had first been stripped of everything, so that he was shivering with cold and to cover his nakedness turned to face the ice-cold prison-wall.

Now the king was to have a second surprise. One of his ablest secretaries, Georg Ursinus (the bear), had fled, taking with him only the barest necessities. On enquiry the councillor Johannes Scutius (Skytte) said he had mentioned to Ursinus that Anthelius had been arrested, and had added: "It will go badly with him. Catholics are traitors to their country and must expect to receive the death-penalty." Further enquiries were made at once and a fortnight later the fugitive was found, on his way to Denmark. He was arrested and brought in chains to Stockholm. Other arrests were ordered by the king.

In the early morning of 25 April Anthelius and Schacht—this was the priest's name—were taken before Gustavus Adolphus who wished to question them himself. At first Anthelius stood alone before the king and the councillor. Then Schacht, who had only just been taken to the prison, was fetched, but Anthelius was kept in ignorance of the fact that his protégé had been arrested. Schacht was kept waiting in the ante-room while the king cross-examined Anthelius.

He had to answer four questions. First, was he a Catholic? He joyfully replied that he was. Second, had he studied with Catholics? He admitted he had. Like many other young Swedes he had studied at the universities of Prague and Ingolstadt, where he had gone over to Catholicism. Not until 1612, when he was thirty-four, had he returned home, and he had then quickly advanced in his career. The third question was whether he had caused the priest to come to Stockholm. This he could deny with a clear conscience, and said that it had been done by Ursinus the king's secretary. The fourth question, whether he knew other Catholics in the city, he refused to answer. He was then led away.

In his cross-examination the priest was treated with the utmost suspicion. He was asked whether he had had contacts with Poles and whether he had received secret instructions from the Pope. Had he wished to murder the king? Gustavus Adolphus promised him his life and honourable treatment if he would become a Lutheran and "confess the truth". He was asked to give the names of his companions, his "fellow-conspirators". It was impossible for the wretched priest to give these. Only non-Catholics were mentioned in the letters that had been taken from him. He was not believed and was taken back to the prison.

His belongings were all carefully examined. A powder he used to wash out his mouth was taken to be a secret poison. He offered to swallow it, but he was not allowed to do so; his captors thought he wanted to kill himself. The king suspected that a small pocket-knife which he had was poisoned; perhaps he was thinking of Ravaillac* and the assassination of Henri IV of France. He also broke a piece of bread to see whether a letter was concealed in it. The priest was regarded as a murderer and seditious agitator, sent by the Pope or perhaps the King of Poland. Twice more the mission-priest was cross-examined by the king, once alone and once in the presence of the chancellor and a notary.

Meanwhile what was happening to Ursinus?

On 5 April he had been traced and shut up in the tower of Stockholm castle. A little later he was questioned by the king. And now the origin and history of the whole "conspiracy" was brought to light. In 1614 Ursinus, who had been educated at a Catholic school in Germany, went back to see a priest there whom he knew. He begged help for the many Catholics in Sweden who were surrounded by non-Catholics, and were without any spiritual ministrations. He had given this priest his address and arranged the code-words *corpus juris*. The two missionary priests who should have travelled with him, however, could not meet him in Lubeck; he had already sailed for Sweden. On 11 April the following year the Congregation of Propaganda in Rome had, at the suggestion of Cardinal Etzel of Hohenzollern, once more decided to send missionaries to Sweden, and allot the necessary money for the journey. Letters imploring help had been received from Sweden, and the two priests, Heinrich Schacht and Theophilus Olaus, could delay no longer. They started on their long journey at the beginning of the year 1623. At first they planned to go from Holland across the North Sea to Sweden, but they found it impossible. They therefore chose the far more dangerous route across the Baltic. Their ship was wrecked, and they were

* François Ravaillac, a fanatic who believed Henri IV of France was going to attack the Pope, assassinated the King on 14 May 1610.

cast up on the island of Lolland. Olaus died a little later. Schacht then tried to get to Stockholm through Malmö, but this proved impracticable. At length he got as far as Helsingborg. Disguised as a pedlar selling mousetraps, he took the road to Stockholm, where Ursinus lived at court as the king's secretary. But in Nyköping Schacht was arrested on suspicion of being a Pole, and was brought before the judges in Gripsholm. The senior master of the court, Theodor Falkenburg, cross-examined him but let him go. Shortly after, Schacht met Ursinus who brought him to Anthelius, in whose house he stayed from November 1623 to March 1624. Then all three were arrested.

Schacht's cross-examination confirmed the statements made by the secretary. He was asked whether the first two missionaries were Poles. He denied it; they were Germans like himself, and had nothing whatever to do with Poland. Their sole purpose was to help Swedish Catholics and assist Protestants to return to the faith of their fathers. Thus full information about the three men engaged in the supposed plot had been obtained. It had also been discovered that of the remaining suspects only two were Catholics. No legal action was taken against them and the public trial of the others could now begin.

On 17 April Anthelius stood at the bar of the court. Next day it was Ursinus's turn. For the priest two days were thought to be necessary. The court met in a large hall and all the members of the city bench were present. In addition to the archbishop, all the bishops and a big crowd of curious onlookers attended. The three accused were examined and condemned. The priest was charged with high treason and incitement to sedition; the two others with high treason only. Since, however, nothing punishable was found about them except their Catholicism and the practice of their religion, Schacht and Ursinus were tortured in an attempt to extract further confessions. Anthelius was spared torture because of his high rank. But none escaped the death-sentence. It was pronounced on 17 April.

Schacht was to be executed as a seditious agitator: "since, though he was aware of the danger, he intended to assemble a papist community, as he said in one of his letters: 'I am ready to go to work even if it means peril of death, and to sacrifice myself, to win souls for Christ's sake', accordingly we decided to punish him as an agitator with death, granting him no pardon, in accordance with the law. Given at Stockholm on 17 April 1624. Gustavus Adolphus Rex."

Nothing more was said about an attempt at assassination.

On 20 April Schacht was tortured again, but without result. No confession could be extracted by this means from Ursinus either. On 12 June all three prisoners were told that they would be executed on 14 June. The execution was, however, postponed, it was thought at the queen's request. On 18 June they were threatened once more and told they would die within two days, but no one came to take them to the place of execution. Meanwhile the rumour had reached Germany that Swedish Catholics had been arrested and Father Schacht cruelly treated. The Elector of Cologne made representations to the King of Sweden. For two more months the prisoners had to stay in their cell, closely guarded, and in a torment of uncertainty. On 1 September, Schacht was given to understand that he must expect to die any day. On 5 September, the warder, a worthy man, asked Ursinus and Anthelius to come together to his room. But his kindness was merely the prelude to a worsening of their situation, for on 6 September both prisoners were told that they would be executed on the 11th; there was no question of further postponement.

The prisoners then wrote some letters, which still exist, among them one to the Congregation of Propaganda in Rome, where the letter was read with deep emotion. "The whole case is remarkable", wrote the representative of the nuncio in Venice, "but it is not suitable to be described in writing." The intention was to introduce forthwith the prescribed canonical cause of the beatification of the two Catholic martyrs, and it was desired that this should not be interrupted by useless gossip. The preparatory cause took place in Liège on 24 and 25 January, and the details given here are taken from the material produced in that connection.

When the scaffold was put up on 10 September, the news of the execution spread like wildfire. Herre Scutius (Skytte) immediately sent his two children, accompanied by a preacher, to his old friend Ursinus, since he knew that the death-penalty had been pronounced solely on account of his friend's religious convictions. Ursinus resisted all persuasion that he should turn Protestant. That the sole crime of the councillor Anthelius consisted in his Catholic faith was admitted even by Gustavus Adolphus on 3 September, when he said that he would forgive him for bringing Catholic priests into the country, if only he would give the names of those who had assisted him. In this case, the king said, his life would be spared. Anthelius replied: "I will give a pledge that I will not leave Sweden. If the king can discover anyone who charges me with treason, he can do what he likes with me."

Then came 11 September. In the documents of the beatification cause at Liège we read:

> Early in the morning both prisoners wrote, in the presence of a witness (Schacht), that they wished to offer up their lives for the Catholic Church. They then waited for the appointed hour, saying prayers. About 9 o'clock executioners and soldiers conducted them to the place of execution. First came Zacharias (Anthelius), then Herre Georgius (Ursinus). When they had reached the place of execution they knelt and prayed for the king, the queen, the state councillors and the lute-player who had betrayed them. They then declared that they were ready to die for the Catholic faith; they embraced and kissed each other; each tried to be the first to be executed. Georgius took off his coat and vest and gave them, with his prayer-book, to Blasius. Then he commended his soul to God and was beheaded.

Meanwhile a Lutheran minister argued with Herre Zacharias and urged that he should abjure his faith. His reply was: "You are not a true priest. How could you give me absolution for my sins and impart to me the body of Our Lord?"

As he said this he saw Georgius's headless body lying on the ground. He clapped his hands and said to the executioner: "Come, let your blade fall on me, for the sake of the Catholic faith."

Then he knelt, lifted up his hands and asked that his head should be struck off at once. The bystanders told him to lower his head; he did so and was then beheaded.

We know all this because Schacht was eventually set free and allowed to leave the country; this is his own description. He further informs us that Herre Skytte and a certain Herre Carolus had the two martyrs buried in the old monastery cemetery in Stockholm. On the tombstone a child shouting for joy was represented and a venerable old man with a candle. Various people, Catholics and Protestants, gave Schacht this information.

3. GUSTAVUS ADOLPHUS' LAST YEARS

No doubt it was a feeling of political responsibility for his country that caused Gustavus Adolphus to increase his pressure on Catholics. He was always convinced that he was right. He regarded it as his most exalted duty, imposed upon him by God, to protect and preserve his kingdom.

War seemed to him a necessary evil, a "malum Dei", an evil permitted by God. Once, he called war not a river or a lake, but a whole ocean of evil. He encouraged his priests to pray constantly for peace. "Peace is, after God's Word, the highest good. A shameful peace is often better than an unjust war." The melancholy he felt after a great victory was a touching feature of his character; after the battle of Breitenfeld he was extraordinarily depressed: "I am not at all easy in my mind. I give myself and my victory over to God's mercy", he said to one of his army chaplains. This remark is one among many that demonstrate the extraordinary moral stature of the king. His interests were emphatically religious. After he had become acquainted with Arndt's *True Christianity** he read it several times. Sometimes he would call his army chaplains to him in the evening, to discuss with them problems of belief. On one such occasion he took the word of *Revelation*, "Blessed are the dead who die in the Lord", and said, "I would rather pray with St. Bernard, 'those who die *for* the Lord'".

We have accounts of his religious practices in the last years of his life. He began the day with prayers in his tent. He always said the war-prayer of Asa in the Second Book of Chronicles (14th chapter), "Help us, O Lord, for we rest on thee". Then the army was called together with drums, cymbals and tambourines. It sometimes happened that the king himself would go with a drum

*Johann Arndt, German Protestant mystic, 1555–1621.

between the rows of tents and call his men. The prayer was always said kneeling, and ended with a hymn. His favourite chorales were "Praised be Jesu's name", "O Lord God of heaven", and "Jesus hanging on the cross". On the day when the battle of Lützen was fought, the soldiers sang the chorale "Fear not, little flock" to the sound of drums and brass instruments. The third verse of this hymn was possibly written by the king himself, at Naumburg, on his way to the battle in which he met his death.

According to the testimony of one who knew him, Henrik Wijmarks, which we follow here, the king's religion assumed eschatological features as time went on. He conversed with that strange Swedish mystic, Johannes Bureus. In his thoughts he was more and more taken up with "eternal blessedness", and he often had premonitions of death. In the summer of 1630, at a meeting with students from Wittenberg, he spoke of his approaching death. At this time he was reading prayers from the Bible every day, which as a rule he did only when he was ill or suffering from wounds—St. John's gospel chapter 17, or the eighth chapter of St. Paul's epistle to the Romans. He had no fear of death; his faith was sure: *Spes mea unica Christus* (Christ is my only hope). He also used to say: "Better a quick death on the battlefield than a long-drawn-out departure in the sick-bed." Another of his sayings, which is found among his daughter's maxims, *Non quali occasione sed quales exeamus* (it is not how we die, but what we are when we die that matters).

This king, so constantly attended by success, who obviously saw himself not only as king of his own country, but as playing a considerable part in international politics, was of an uncommon humility. He was never carried away by his victories, he was always conscious of his weakness and sinfulness. He reckoned with the possibility that his good fortune would change one day and that death awaited him. He spent almost all of his very short life in the field, driven by his sense of duty and his extraordinarily sure political judgment. He hardly ever enjoyed a normal private life, sacrificing himself entirely to his duties.

All he did was done with such calm, such inner serenity and loftiness of spirit that even today the reader can be deeply moved by his words. But he had to pay the penalty—a profound melancholy took possession of him; his victories only increased it and in his later years his thoughts were turned more and more in the direction of a more lofty reality.

4. GUSTAVUS ADOLPHUS' MARRIAGE WITH MARIA ELEONORA

There were undoubtedly several causes for this melancholy and the state of anxiety that afflicted him from time to time. When he died he was still a young man; but what innumerable victories, trials and difficult situations had he not encountered since the day when, at the early age of seventeen, he was crowned king. Not once only, but innumerable times, he was aware of the fact that his own and his country's future was at stake. In almost every situation he had to exert himself to the utmost and conquer, since otherwise all was lost. He might well have said with perfect justice, that he could rest his head in the lap of every one of his subjects—the question arises whether any other ruler of his time could have made the same boast. Yet he knew that he was surrounded by the sons and relations of men whom his father had often treated badly. At times he must have asked himself what was the real meaning of his military and political successes. He defended the cause of Protestant religious liberty, but his victories were praised by the Pope in Rome, and his ally was Cardinal Richelieu.

On the whole the king overcame his scruples. Even if we attribute the descriptions of his harmonious, heroic character to the excessive servility of certain writers, we must admit that his personality was in fact truly harmonious. As an outstanding man of action, he was gifted with the ability to rise above scruples, to avoid making compromises and to follow without swerving from it the straight road of his royal intent.

Yet his melancholy was at times so profound that it could be labelled anxiety. The cause probably lay in his private life, above all in his marriage. Among his closest friends he made no secret of the fact that he regarded his marriage almost as a catastrophe. Again and again he had sought distraction in passing erotic experiences. As a young man he had been sincerely in love with a young lady of noble birth, Ebba Brahe. His mother, the stern Queen Christina, had done everything possible to prevent this marriage, with violent words, a categorical refusal of consent, intrigues, even slapping his go-between herself. When Ebba Brahe married the general Jakob de la Gardie, the mother of Gustavus Adolphus was present at the wedding in triumph, but the young king was not to be seen; he was out sailing on the Baltic. Soon after this he had a liaison with a married woman; there is conflicting evidence about her name. He had a son by her, later the Count of Vasaborg. He tried to forget Ebba Brahe. In a charming farewell letter he wished her a thousand nights of gladness and he enclosed a forget-me-not. He signed the letter "Your faithful and devoted cousin till death, G.A.", twining his initials with those of his beloved. Today we can prove—though it was for a long time merely surmised—that he addressed a love-poem to another young lady of the high-born aristocracy, Margarete Fleming.

Gustavus Adolphus married Maria Eleonora, a princess of Brandenburg, after a short acquaintance, and mainly for political reasons. For a long time German official historians represented this marriage as a happy one. But we are well informed about it by the innumerable letters of Maria Eleonora to Stegeborg Castle and to her German relations, and we know it was quite the contrary. It seems to have given the king neither happiness nor peace. Rather did it add to his cares from year to year; it increased his restlessness and often drove him to utter despair. Maria Eleonora's letters do indeed give a depressing impression. We expect to find bad handwriting and gross spelling mistakes in the manuscripts of the seventeenth century, but the Queen of Sweden wrote like an ignorant house-maid; she had no idea of the logic of syntax, and her letters often reveal a condition of utter mental confusion. After only a short stay in Sweden she became incapable of using even her mother-tongue. The Latin expression *summa summarum*, for example, she wrote as "some somarum". A fine victory she called a fine "fictoriga". She called Gabriel Oxenstierna "Herr Gabergell". Her interests were narrow and on a low level, and revolved mainly around cakes and sweetmeats: in 1622 she sent an apothecary's apprentice from Stockholm to Brandenburg so that he could be taught the "Contitskunst", the art of confectionry, by Christoph Mentzeln of Fürstenwalde, "the best master of his trade". She very much enjoyed the company of dwarfs, an odd taste for which Queen Christina later expressed her loathing. Once, in a letter to Brandenburg, Maria Eleonora said she had had "an uncommon amount of pleasure from these pygmies". At no time in her life was she able to grasp true relations between things; she had no regard for higher aims in life and was never capable of raising herself above her own primitive condition. Even though we are well aware of how uneducated, even vulgar, princesses of the seventeenth century could be, we read Maria Eleonora's letters with a feeling of great embarrassment. So badly brought up was the woman to whom Gustavus Adolphus was bound in marriage. With all this she was highly hysterical, and incapable of self-control or concentration.

However, it should not be forgotten that Maria Eleonora was a handsome and attractive woman. The ordinary portraits give no proper idea of this. In Gripsholm Castle there is a painting that admirably portrays her beauty, before it was ravaged by hysteria and unhappiness. We should also recall a very lively description of the dowager-queen by the French diplomatist Ogier: "We expected to see a distracted widow, overcome by grief. But to our astonishment we found the most beautiful, radiant woman we had ever seen. We were quite dazzled by her beauty. There is nothing that can properly represent her charming features and truly royal figure. The Minister, who was also carried away by her, repeatedly made obeisance to her . . ."

A certain, though not very substantial, interest in art and music may also be counted a positive feature. In 1621 she installed Andreas Düben in the court orchestra; she summoned and employed in her service many artists, for example the Dutchman Simon de Pass. She helped Ehrenstrahl in his career, and once wrote that she would stint herself of food if this could enable him to go and study in Germany and Italy. The Ogier mentioned above, who seems to have been a great flatterer, reported with enthusiasm what he considered to be her well-informed observations on architecture.

Her architectural plans, however, were as a rule extravagant—for example, after the king's death she wanted to build her own "balatium" (palatium, palace) in Sweden or in her own country, to be called Gustavsburg, to keep alive the memory of her husband.

Her feelings for the king were so hysterical that her contemporaries considered her a really pathological case. When she was separated from her husband in 1627, Johann Skytte wrote that no one could imagine the hysterical condition to which her loneliness had driven her. As soon as she had, by her unceasing complaining, persuaded the king to let her go to Germany, she defied his orders, avoided towns where she would have been secure, and wilfully sought out those in which she was exposed to great danger. On one occasion her senseless behaviour seems to have made a difficult military situation still worse for her husband. She was entirely lacking in judgment.

More important than all this was the fact that for many years she was unable to give her husband a son. Her confinements were a long series of mishaps, and indeed disasters. The wedding took place in December 1620; a year later she had a miscarriage and was seriously ill. The king was very depressed and wrote to Chancellor Oxenstierna that he would, he felt, readily understand "how heavily this cross weighs on me. But God, who has cast me down, can raise me up again. To Him be the glory, forever and ever". In 1623 a daughter was born and baptized in the name of Christina Augusta. "The child is getting along well," the queen wrote delightedly, but her small daughter died before her first birthday. In May there was another disaster. The queen had prevailed upon the king to let her accompany him on an inspection of some warships that lay moored off the island of Skeppsholmen, near Stockholm. A sudden gale sprang up from the hills to the south, and the little yacht, with the royal couple on board, nearly capsized. "When Her Majesty returned to the castle", a contemporary recorded, she cried "Jesus, I cannot feel my child", and soon after gave birth to a stillborn son. *O infelix patria, quantum hac turbine concussa est* (O unhappy fatherland, how severely this gale has shaken it). Gustavus Adolphus commented on this occurrence in a letter, dated 21 May 1625, to his brother-in-law, the Elector

Johann Kasimir: "Before I could send off this letter a disaster befell me; my wife brought a dead child into the world. I had not reckoned on this when I began my letter. It is through our sins that it pleased God to do this."

The reader is much moved when, after the clear writing of the letter, he comes to this postscript dashed off in such haste.

We are very well informed about Gustavus Adolphus' opinion of his wife. He naturally kept up a decent courtesy in public, and spoke of her with chivalry and affection. At the beginning of November he spoke about the queen with his advisers, and with an air of desperation begged them to take charge of his beloved wife, if in God's providence some human fate should overtake her. But with his friends and closest advisers he made no attempt to conceal his great disappointment with his impossible spouse, who evidently was incapable even of giving him children who would survive. Not long before his death he spoke about this with Axel Oxenstierna; he called it his *malum domesticum*, his domestic cross. In it he saw a contrast to the success and good fortune he otherwise enjoyed. When he spoke of it with the members of his council, before he left Sweden for the last time, he could not overcome his emotion. He spoke, so it was reported, "in a flood of tears". He desired the council, in the event of his death, to appoint a guardian for his widow, since, "in the words of His Majesty, this most wretched of women" would be in need of one. Axel Oxenstierna says that the king spent a "whole hour" over this question, and tried to bind him to action under oath. The Chancellor at length gave a promise, but he would not take an oath on it. What the king thought of his wife is made clear also by his repeated statement that after his death she was to be allowed no part in the government of the country. His frequent speeches to this effect, his pleading with the councillors "beseechingly" was recalled as a well-known fact by Claes Fleming at a meeting of the council in 1636.

We know that the king planned to pass over his daughter Christina in the succession to the throne after his death. In 1632, so Axel Oxenstierna reported later in much detail, he began negotiations with Brandenburg with the intention of marrying his daughter to the Prince Elector's son, who was not of age at that time. His object was to join up Sweden with Brandenburg and other countries he intended to conquer, so that "the whole would form one *corpus*, and be ruled by one *caput*", with each country retaining its laws and "rights".

When Gustavus Adolphus died the queen lost the last remnant of her self-control and reason. She not only began to squander money without limit, but she wanted the king's coffin put in her bedroom. His heart was enclosed in a case which she wanted to hang on the wall above her head. She had his coffin changed in accordance with her own taste, and decorated it with a wealth of absurd "oval pearls". She persisted in refusing to allow the king's body to be buried. In February 1633, she wrote to von Wolfgast: "Since we, God pity us, were so rarely granted the pleasure of enjoying the living presence of His Majesty, our adored, dearest master and spouse, of blessed memory, it should at least be granted to us to stay near his royal corpse and so draw comfort in our miserable existence." The widow's pathological opposition delayed Gustavus Adolphus's interment until July 1634. Twenty-four hours after this the councillors heard that the queen asked for the coffin to be opened again. Clearly Maria Eleonora was, by this time, of unsound mind.

It is understandable that the austere men of the council, who had been trained in the stoic spirit which prevailed at that time, should have regarded the queen's behaviour with scorn and the utmost alarm. "Her Majesty is weak by nature and prey to her emotions" was what was said in effect in the council. Gustavus Adolphus had considered his wife to be a sick woman. When, in 1632, he was negotiating with the Brandenburg delegate Götze about a marriage between Christina and Prince Friedrich Wilhelm, he said he had given up all hope of further heirs, since his wife was indeed a very sick woman.

CHAPTER THREE

Christina's Birth and Childhood. Christina as a Woman

I. CHRISTINA'S BIRTH

WHAT do we know of Christina's birth with certainty? We have no contemporary account. However, in his correspondence with his relations Gustavus Adolphus made certain observations and gave certain details. We also have the testimony of certain well-informed persons, especially Axel Oxenstierna, who concerned themselves with this delicate question. Lastly, there is Queen Christina herself, who described the course of events at length in her autobiography, one of the most remarkable writings of the seventeenth century.

One might ask whether the queen's autobiography should be relied on. To this day, serious students have always treated it as a reliable source. But obviously the queen may have made mistakes or else, for various reasons, been tempted to touch up the picture she gave of herself. We do not even know exactly when the autobiography was written. From the Christina archives we can deduce that the queen began to think of writing her life-story soon after she arrived in Rome. There is a letter addressed to an ecclesiastic—the name is unknown but we may assume it to have been the future Cardinal Sforza Pallavicino, her biographer—and dated 1658, three years before her arrival in Rome, in which the queen says in fulfilment of a promise, she had begun to write her story in Italian, but that she had met such great difficulties in the language that she found it impossible to continue. She had therefore burnt what she had written, and asked the priest instead to put questions to her about the most decisive events of her life, which she would answer. She said she would place her correspondence at his disposal if he would send her a secretary. It seems there was someone who had asked her to write down the story of her religious life.

We have other indications that the queen concerned herself with her autobiography very early in life. For example, we know she was working on it in 1668, during her lonely and unhappy stay in Hamburg. Her friend Cardinal Azzolino seems to have prompted it, since she informed him that she was very busy with this work.

It is incorrect to say that Christina wrote her autobiography in her old age. When she began it she was probably no more than thirty-two. We know that ten years later, that is, rather more than ten years after her arrival in Rome, she had written at least a part of it.

Since it is hard to understand why Christina should have falsified her recollections, and since we know that she had an uncommonly good memory, we are surely justified in accepting her story as true, with certain reservations. She had, of course, heard many details from others; her destiny as a woman turned out to be so remarkable that she must have repeatedly questioned those who were present at her birth, or had been acquainted with her as a child.

In her autobiography Christina wrote:

> I was born with a caul, and my face was pallid. Only my face, arms and legs were free. My body was entirely covered with hair, and I had a deep, loud voice. This led the midwives attending me to take me for a boy. They filled the castle with shouts of joy, without reason; but for a time the king was deceived. Hope and expectancy combined to lead everyone astray, and great was the confusion of the women when they discovered their mistake. They were at a loss to know how they should convey the truth to the king. At length Princess Katharina, the king's sister, undertook to do so. She showed me to the king, so that he could see for himself what she had not the courage to say. He was thus convinced of the truth. The great man showed no surprise; he took me into his arms, kindly bade me welcome, as if he had been in no way disappointed. He said to the princess: "We thank God, my dear sister. I hope this

> daughter will be as dear to me as a boy would have been. I pray God to protect her, since he has bestowed her on me." The princess wanted to say what she thought he would like to hear, and so, flattering him, she said that he was still a young man, and the queen was young, too, and would soon present him with an heir. But the king replied, "I am content, dear sister. God protect the child." He then sent me away and seemed to be entirely satisfied, to everyone's surprise. He ordered a Te Deum to be sung, and all those signs of rejoicing to be given which were customary on the birth of a male successor to the throne. He showed himself, in brief, as great a man on this occasion as on others. Nevertheless there was a delay in informing the queen of my sex until she was able to bear such a disappointment. I then received the name of Christina.

Finally Christina thanks God for having given her none of the weaknesses of her sex when he bestowed a soul on her; rather He had, in His grace, made her masculine "as was the remainder of my body" (*aussi bien que le reste de mon corps*).

Christina's story clearly shows that the midwives who delivered her—no doubt women of great experience—had taken her for a boy. What she said of her hairiness, the caul and her deep voice is of no importance. It would hardly have been possible to give greater weight to the error about her sex—and we must remember how everyone at the court longed intensely for a male heir—had Christina's later development not shown clearly that her physical and intellectual characteristics were rather those of a man. She was, in fact, so masculine that, so far as we know, she never aroused any erotic interest in a man, but on the contrary, aroused an aversion in many. In later pages we shall come across many examples of her masculine characteristics and physical condition. A medical expert, presented with these facts, and taking into account the process of Christina's birth and the curious misunderstanding about her sex, would hardly hesitate in his diagnosis; she was a pseudo-hermaphrodite (not to be confused with a real hermaphrodite).

And now, bearing in mind the significant error about her sex, and her own statement that the rest of her body, *le reste de mon corps*, was male—we shall take a look at her childhood and youth.

Here the sources of our information are much more reliable, and permit us to draw certain conclusions.

In the first chapter of this book we quoted the account given by Chanut, the French Minister, of Christina's gallop over the plain of Uppsala on Mazarin's white horse. In her autobiography Christina said that she could easily bear heat and cold, take long walks and ride very fast, all without getting fatigued. She was very studious, but devoted equally to hunting, games and sport. She could be the despair of her court, both men and women. She tired them out and gave them no rest, by day or night. When her ladies-in-waiting wanted to reduce the strenuous life they had to live, Christine turned this to ridicule, and said, "If you are sleepy, go to bed. I can look after myself." Her relations with her women companions aroused the astonishment of her contemporaries. In a notable character-study of the queen Chanut wrote in 1648:

> These open-air pursuits and the way she occupied herself indoors differed so much from the things her ladies talked about, that she rarely addressed them, and then only on one particular topic.... She left them alone on one side of her room and went over to talk with the gentlemen, the subjects of her conversation being serious ones of course. She always paid gracious attention to any among them who suggested themes which she thought useful to discuss. But if there were persons whose limitations she knew and from whom she thought she could learn little, she cut the conversation off and continued the talk not a moment longer than was necessary.

Chanut also describes how now and then Christina would put up with the company of her ladies, though often only to irritate them. In a marginal note Christina says that this was correct and gave rise to a great deal of ill-feeling. And on the whole, Chanut continues, living with her was burdensome, as she usually slept no more than five hours a night—the queen altered this to three. On the other hand it often happened, especially in the summer, that she would rest an hour after a meal—"absolutely wrong" was the queen's indignant comment. She paid little attention to dress or adornment; she took only a quarter of an hour to dress—Christina observed that a quarter of an hour was only required for important occasions. Apart from a single comb, a piece of ribbon was all she wore in her hair. She practically never covered her head, either in sun, wind or rain, in town or country. When out riding she wore a hat with feathers, so that no one would suspect its wearer was a woman.

This is a notably trustworthy account. We should, however, remember that Christina—as we shall show later in detail—was very friendly with certain women, her cousin Marie Euphrosine, for example, and the beautiful Countess Ebba Sparre. She was thus capable of making exceptions to her rule of dealing only with men. These two exceptions were on the one hand a woman of remarkable beauty, and on the other a friend of her childhood, a near relation.

The young girl Christina not only showed a marked preference for men's pursuits; she had also, in her own words, "an ineradicable prejudice against everything that women like to talk about or do. In women's work and occupations I showed myself to be quite incapable, and I saw no possibility of improvement in this respect".

2. CHRISTINA IN LATER YEARS

Here we must anticipate and discuss Christina's character as it showed itself in later years. In so doing we should begin by considering such portraits of the queen as have come down to us; in particular that painted by Wolfgang Heimbach in 1667, that is, in her forty-second year. This was evidently not meant to be a caricature; had it been, the face would not have been made so attractive. If this portrait is compared with other similar ones, it will be found that quite early Christina began to look decidedly un-feminine. She looked more like a cavalry colonel than a woman. It can well be believed that no man felt drawn to a person of such a countenance and figure. When she was abroad people always took notice of her. In 1654 someone in Flanders wrote: "She is of medium height, with high shoulders; her eyes are bright, and her nose is a little on one side. She has nothing feminine about her; even her voice is altogether masculine."

An Italian, who knew her, wrote: "Her lips, which were of a fine red colour, might have made a Venus of her, had it not been for so many other details of her physique and her bearing, which would have made one swear she was a Mars."

Another Italian said: "Her skin is swarthy, and very hairy. Her profile shows determination, almost severity. Her eyebrows are marked, her nose too long, her mouth is wide, she has a deep voice, her movements are energetic and abrupt."

A priest wrote: "There is nothing womanly about this princess. Her way of walking, her features and her whole appearance have something masculine about them. I say only what I have seen with my own eyes."

When Christina went on a visit to the French court, she was of course observed with particular attention, since she was so famous and the subject of so much discussion. Many observers wrote down their impressions or conveyed them to others. The Duc de Guise wrote: "Beautiful arms, white, well-shaped hands, but a masculine rather than a feminine impression. A remarkable way of dressing her hair, rather like a man's ordinary wig. Her shoes are like a man's; her voice, too, and her gestures are almost entirely masculine."

The Duchesse de Montpensier, on the other hand, had the impression of a *joli petit garçon*, a handsome boy. The series of descriptions could be continued indefinitely. No one described her as feminine. Yet we know from her doctors she really was a woman; she had, for example, regular menstrual periods, though it should be added that menstruation occurs sometimes with pseudo-hermaphrodites.

3. A "HOT" AND A "DRY" TEMPERAMENT

This is all we can say with certainty about Christina's physical and mental characteristics. It is interesting that she herself complained a good deal about those characteristics. This we discover from statements she made, and they are of especial interest when compared with what the doctors said of her. Emphasis was placed on her temperament, her "ardour".

The seventeenth century had its own special notion of the nature of female sexuality, "heat" and hysteria, a very odd one in modern eyes.

The man who probably knew Christina better than anyone else, Cardinal Azzolino, made some puzzling statements about her in a letter to Marescotti, the nuncio in Poland (on 13 April 1669), relating to her plan of making herself Queen of Poland. He first broached the question of the succession; could it be assumed that the queen would marry and bear children? His opinion was that at her age, forty-two, the possibility could not be ruled out, "for she is still at the height of her powers and we may reckon with some confidence that she will be in a state to bear children for another ten years, whereas perhaps in the earlier part of her life her excessive 'heat' might have prevented it" (*dove prima forse il soverchio calore l'avrebbe impedita*). Baron Carl Bildt commented on this remark in his suave diplomatic style, but although he had discovered hitherto unknown material about Queen Christina, he completely misunderstood her character—as has already been explained in Chapter I (5). He took the view that Azzolino was aware of her bad reputation and was referring to the possibility that her dissolute life had made her incapable of childbearing.

This merely shows how little Bildt understood. He had no idea of what a cardinal could write to a nuncio. He did not understand the way in which a well-intentioned man, wishing to help in a delicate situation, would write to a colleague when it was a question of defending the queen and bringing out her good qualities. He did not grasp at all the nature of Azzolino's relations with the queen, nor did he realize that those relations completely ruled out a cynical attitude. Above all he had no notion of what, in this connection and at that time, was meant by the word "heat".

Renaissance and seventeenth-century medicine was based on that of classical times, mainly Aristotle's biology and Galen's medical works. Well on into the seventeenth century this was the standard teaching, for all its peculiar ideas about sex, childbearing and in particular pregnancy. The views expressed in Aristotle's *De generatione animalium* were still regarded as valid and up to date. A man was "hot and dry", a woman "cold and moist". Aristotle went on to discuss why women were more passionate in summer, while men were more so in winter. He produced similar arguments to explain phenomena such as sexual intercourse between very young or very old people, and he touched on the question of sterility. He came to the conclusion that to obtain good results or any results at all, some kind of equilibrium must be brought about between the basic characteristics of man, heat and dryness, and those of woman, who was regarded as mainly cool and moist. "When there is too much heat, it dries up the humidity; when the hot element is not hot enough, it cannot give the moist element any firm form." For nature to function properly, the two elements had to come together in a satisfactory manner; "otherwise it is like cooking; too much fire burns the meat, too little fails to turn it into food. In both cases the outcome is bad."

According to Aristotle more girls came into the world when the wind was in the north. According to Paulus Diaconus* the cold northern lands were much more apt to foster progeny than the warm and sunny lands; that was why such a prodigious number of people were born at the North Pole.

Hippocrates and Galen held that the human body was made up of four basic elements, earth, air, fire and water, characterized as dry, cold, hot, humid. These characteristics, or "humours", were mainly contained in the bodily fluids (blood, phlegm, yellow bile or choler, and black bile). A system of psychology erected on these assumptions remained valid till the end of the seventeenth century. In Christina's time it was still held that blood was warm and moist, yellow bile warm and dry, black bile cold and dry, and phlegm cold and moist. According to Galen these humours could appear in various combinations, each producing eight different mixtures, or "temperaments". Thus a man with a choleric humour with its bitter yellow bile should possess a warm, dry temperament; the one with a melancholy humour, with its black choler a cold, dry one, the sanguine humour a warm, humid temperament, and the phlegmatic humour a cold, humid one.

On this basis it was possible, not only to determine individual "temperaments", or dispositions, and thus, to a certain extent, to define an individual's outlook on life, but also to recognize certain persons as abnormal or ill. It was held that certain combinations

* Eighth-century Lombard writer, monk at Monte Cassino, important figure in the revival of learning under Charlemagne.

produced people who in various ways were less adapted to ordinary life. This applied to women, too. A work by a French doctor, published in 1573 and widely read all over Europe, *De la génération de l'homme*, by Ambroise Paré, is very informative in this respect. The line of thought it follows was characteristic of the times; as women had a "cooler" temperament than men, they were unable to transform their food into good blood as quickly as men, so that the greater part of it remained undigested and emerged as menstruation. Men had a greater warmth than women.

The man-woman was also described, one in whom menstruation had ceased or had never started, one who might become mannish, strong, bold, superior, with a mannish voice. Such women or girls were naturally more powerful than others and possessed a hot, dry "temperament".

Seventeenth-century medicine insisted that a too-hot woman, one with too many characteristics of the element of fire, could bear children only with difficulty, or not at all. A woman in any case was cooler than a man, hence the connection between digestion and menstruation. But without menstruation no child could be conceived. As a Swedish scholar of those times put it: "The fact that a woman overflows with this humidity is the cause of her humid nature and her low degree of warmth, which is insufficient to transform everything into good blood and bodily substance, for the blood is purified in the blood-vessels of the womb; otherwise it would produce putrefaction and disease in the body." Thus, in order to bear children properly a woman should be dry and cool, possessing only a "low degree of warmth".

Christina herself once spoke of her "violent and ardent temperament, with a slight tendency to melancholy". Such descriptions agree with the medical terminology of the time. The melancholy temperament had an important role assigned to it. Galen, the great authority, taught that persons with an abundance of black bile were melancholy and had a cool, dry temperament. Christina thought she had an ardent temperament, but also a certain tendency to melancholy. She also believed she was choleric, with much bitter, yellow bile, a hot and dry temperament. But she was an exception to the usual pattern, in that she had this tendency to melancholy: according to current opinion this was due to an admixture of black bile. In her autobiography Christina describes herself as impetuous, haughty and impatient, qualities which according to opinion at that time, were connected with yellow bile. She describes how, when a young girl, she had been urgently advised to drink weak beer. "I think this caused all kinds of trouble with my liver. My liver consumed my blood in a remarkable way. I only drank when I was absolutely forced to."

The French doctor Bourdelot, after his arrival in Sweden, wrote a long memorandum on the queen's state of health and her constitution: he thought she was a remarkable case of a person with an "ardent and dry temperament", and "burning hot secretions". Her inborn ardour and dryness, he went on, were intensified by her irrational way of life. "The burning heat of her temperament dried up all the moisture." There is also a memorandum by her Italian doctor, Cesare Macchiati, which says: "Queen Christina's temperament is hot and dry to the utmost degree. . . . She has all the disadvantages and advantages that come from such a hot, burning temperament. She is choleric, proud, arrogant . . . impatient and audacious. . . ." The same memorandum also states that "the original cause of her respect for and devotion to the Catholic faith was her own inclination to celibacy".

During an illness in 1679 Christina wrote to her old friend Bourdelot in Paris that her temperament was "fire and flame". "I think I should have died long ago if I had not been able to adopt a way of life that held in check the burning temperament I had from birth."

She mentioned also her dislike of wine and the trouble with her bile, her oft-mentioned and admitted habit of drinking water, but never, or at least extremely seldom, wine or strong ale. This was in an effort to keep down the heat in her body which strong drink only increased. It may be assumed that the medical knowledge she later acquired encouraged her in her dislike of alcoholic drinks—a dislike which began at a very early age, and was strengthened by the excessive drunkenness she saw round her.

4. CHRISTINA'S CONTEMPT FOR WOMEN. CHRISTINA AND HER MOTHER

In this connection we must mention the contempt she felt for her mother, as wife, mother and regent.

After the king's death it soon became apparent to the councillors that Maria Eleonora's way of bringing up the future queen was fraught with danger, both to the girl herself and to the future of the state. As early as 1636 so much incriminating material had accumulated against the dowager-queen that it became necessary to attempt to keep her in isolation.

In that same year the Council received a remarkable letter from her. As usual it contained a number of demands for money, but then came the odd suggestion that at table Christina should sit between two councillors of the realm, whose duty it would be to pour water into her glass. The Council tried to take a detached view of this proposal, but it is easy to imagine how little they liked it. Axel Oxenstierna was of the opinion that a councillor of the realm should not be required to perform such a menial duty at the royal table, and Jakob de la Gardie (the elder) agreed. It was on this occasion that Oxenstierna raised the question of whether the young princess could properly be brought up by the dowager-queen. On this there was an exhaustive discussion. Axel Banér thought Christina should be separated from her mother, who was totally incapable of educating her; but it should be done tactfully. Åke Natt och Dag declared that the country had the right to see the young queen educated in a befitting royal manner; this was impossible so long as the dowager-queen was with her daughter; therefore the two should be separated. Claes Fleming said he was loath to discuss the matter; but the Council had, after all, waited two years for an improvement, but in vain. Now it was time to take things in hand and counteract the harm that was being done. He recalled Gustavus Adolphus's warning which he gave to the Council, and also in private, that the dowager-queen should on no account be allowed to have any part in the government of the country. Carl Carlsson Gyllenhielm considered that even the best-intentioned parents could sometimes do harm to their children, "like apes with their offspring". Therefore mother and child should be separated, "but in a suitable manner". Jakob de la Gardie held that Christina was being brought up, if not viciously, at least not at all satisfactorily. She was being taught neither to fear God nor to love her country, and she was receiving no training in the art of government. Finally, Axel Oxenstierna, who had just returned from Germany, declared that he would no doubt be blamed if Christina were to die after being parted from her mother, yet the measure proposed was essential. The first approach should be friendly, and if that had no effect, then Christina would simply have to be brought to Uppsala. If Maria Eleonora then tried to follow her there, she should be told that there was no suitable accommodation for her or her court in Uppsala. Later, Carl Carlsson Gyllenhielm had scruples, and declared it ought not to go on record that the dowager-queen was leading her daughter into vicious ways, and teaching her to despise the Swedes. Oxenstierna gave the emphatic reply that if the government had come to so important a decision, it was essential that the true grounds for it should be stated, in order to justify so unusual a measure in the eyes of posterity. And so it was done.

Now at that time it was well known that Queen Maria Eleonora possessed an altogether intractable, hot, hysterical temperament. A stern view was taken of this, in the light of the predominant stoic culture of the day, according to which man was in honour bound to hold his passions in check and keep them under control. But in the light of the prevailing medical and psychological opinions, such a woman was considered in some respects as out of the ordinary, as abnormal. There was also the decisive factor of the queen's obvious difficulty in conceiving children. In fact Gustavus Adolphus believed that, because of her illnesses—he must have meant her morbid "heat"—his queen was quite incapable of bringing normal children into the world. However, there was another theory of hysteria current at the time, namely, that it was a definite disease of the womb, though of a different sort and with other symptoms than those caused by a hot, dry constitution. According to the contemporary view the two theories did not quite coincide in the case of Queen Maria Eleonora. However, this did not prevent the Council and the King entertaining their own explanation of the queen's puzzling and irritating behaviour and her incapacity to give birth to normal children; she was ill, whatever the precise nature of her sickness might be.

As we have seen, Christina was familiar with the medical opinions of her time, and considered herself and also her mother to be "ardent, dry women", who would have difficulty in producing children. She must often have complained about her exceptional physique, and when she was grown up she spoke much about it with her companions. There is a remark of Queen Christina's which, though not fully vouched for, may be mentioned in this connection. After representations had been made to her for a considerable time that it was her duty to give her country an heir, she replied: "I am just as likely to give birth to a Nero as to an Augustus", a monster just as much as a hero. How had she arrived at this idea? Could it not be related to a certain extent to the medical teachings at the time, to the effect that an ardent, dry woman ran the risk of bringing into the world abnormal or deformed children?

One more detail, among her many declarations of opposition to marriage, is worth noting. She had an aversion not only to sexual union and the consequent renunciation of superiority over a man, but she had also a strong repugnance to the very idea of pregnancy and child-birth. Mme de Montpensier related how Queen Christina met the beautiful Mme de Thianges at Montargis and proposed to her in jest that she should leave her husband and go with her to Rome. The best man in the world is of little value—Christina said, according to this source—and it is clearly excusable to run away from a husband. She then "poured scorn on marriage and advised me never to marry; she found it repellent, she said, to bear children".

This morbid reaction was often to be observed in Christina. During the years she resided in her palace in Rome she had with her several strikingly beautiful young women; they attracted attention and one by one got married. When one of her ladies became pregnant Christina refused to see her. If she could not do without her services she would say, "*Faites venir cette vache*," "send me that cow". When another young woman got married Christina said: "It seems you will soon be turned into a cow. Do not, I beg you, come and see me in that condition."

We may here recall that Chanut, as early as 1656, wrote to Mazarin that the queen was aware of the need for her to take a husband and produce children, but she was without the essential "affection".

This picture of Christina includes also her utter contempt for woman as an intelligent being, and especially as a ruler. In a conversation with the English envoy Bulstrode Whitelocke* she gave as one of the reasons for her renunciation of the throne that it was impossible for a woman to be equal to the task of ruling a state. She expressed the same opinion in a series of maxims she composed later on. It was not only women's deficiencies, she thought, but also their good qualities, that made them unfit to rule. This meant that, in her view, a woman, by her very nature, should be subordinate and therefore barred from governing. Christina considered the tale of the Amazons to be a stupid invention. She thought it a good thing that the Salic law excluded women from succession, and she applauded her father for refusing to allow Maria Eleonora to take charge of her education. She felt that it was wrong to entrust the upbringing of a royal child to the mother. The mother, she thought, should have no duty but "looking after the child's health; her authority should be confined to this". Should the king die without leaving a grown-up heir, a council should be established, which should decide everything by a majority. This council should take charge of the education of the young prince. "The first thing is to separate him from his mother, so as to stimulate in him those qualities that made him worthy of his rank, and teach him his duty; the mother could not do this."

There were, of course, many authorities who opposed female succession to a throne. But with Christina there was a complete

* Bulstrode Whitelocke (1605–75) was sent by Cromwell to secure a treaty with Sweden, especially over the dues levied on vessels passing through the Sound. His interesting *Journal of the Swedish Embassy in the year 1653–1654* was published in 1772. He seems to have gained Christina's favour.

denial of the capability not only of a queen, but of any woman, to bring up a son and inculcate in him a sense of duty. This astonishing opinion must have had a cause. Without doubt it was connected with Christina's general contempt for women, and this again depended on her constitution. Her outbursts of temper against her mother prove this.

Christina, indeed, condemned her mother with as much severity as did the national council. "Her Majesty is weak by nature and very much at the mercy of her passions." Christina looked down on her mother's self-abandonment to her passions with all the austerity of Corneille. "Christina knows her mother's faults and often complains about them to her close friends," said Gabriel Gustafsson Oxenstierna in a letter to Axel Oxenstierna. To the talented, precocious young girl her mother was a warning example of inability to control her moods, but she also saw her as an ailing woman. We recall that Gustavus Adolphus before his death gave the ill-health of his wife as the reason why he could not count on having any more children. Later on Christina learned to be milder in her judgment of the passions, for she herself was to be tormented by them for some years. Then her views changed, she drew closer to Racine and his more tolerant conception of human passions. Corneille, a stern judge, would certainly have condemned Maria Eleonora's behaviour with the utmost severity. Racine, on the contrary, did not despise women whose passions tormented them; he might perhaps have seen in Maria Eleonora a sister to his Phèdre.

In her later years Christina must often have been struck by the resemblance between her own life and her mother's. With both of them their departure from their country took place in the deepest secrecy, and when Christina came to love a friend in Italy, she pleaded for his love with the same slavelike humility as Maria Eleonora had pleaded with Gustavus Adolphus. Mother and daughter were equally careless about money. Both of them could hardly bear the dreariness of Sweden. Both were slightly abnormal sexually, though not in precisely the same way.

Christina wanted to be her father's, not her mother's, child. She had, however, inherited much of her mother's weakness. In

1646 Axel Oxenstierna referred to this in a talk with the Brandenburg delegate in Stockholm. His opinion was that the young Queen had brilliant gifts, "high qualities" superior to those of ordinary women; in time, he thought, she would become a "heroine". He mentioned also her remarkable aversion to marriage although she was by then seventeen years of age: she simply dismissed all idea of marrying. This might, he thought, be due to her modesty, or "some other cause", *sive ex alia causa.*

This cautious explanation, *sive ex alia causa*, would lead one to suppose that Oxenstierna had noticed and was aware of the peculiar nature of the young queen which made any marriage impossible for her.

CHAPTER FOUR

Christina and Love

I. INCAPACITY FOR LOVE?

It may be that the foregoing account would lead us to the conclusion that Christina was, physically and emotionally incapable of love. But such a conclusion would be altogether premature. There is no proof of any sort for the deduction given in many popular accounts, as for example the scandalous and vulgar *Vie amoureuse de Christine de Suède, la reine androgyne*, by Princess Lucien Murat, which declared that in reality Christina loved only women, and had an instinctive repugnance to men as such. Christina's relations with her companions of her own sex are, of course, problematical to a certain extent; quite evidently she felt powerfully attracted by beautiful women. But there is nothing to show that she carried this beyond the limits of a certain sentimental attachment, it was an aesthetic admiration, an emotional obsession which in itself, for a young girl brought up in such a peculiar way, had nothing unnatural about it. Christina liked men, she felt drawn to men, and often spoke openly of her desire for men. She once said her temperament would have led her into fearful excesses—*de terribles désordres*—if she had not been born a girl. She also said that she certainly would have married had she not been aware of her power to resist sensuous love. In various passages she gave expression to her cynical view of women's amorous demands: "All women in search of pleasure wish to have a man as a pretext." At another time she said: "If I had been weak, I should like so many others, have known what it is to marry, to give pleasure to myself and enjoy my privileges."

She frankly explained, and emphasized, that if she had been a man she would have abandoned herself to excesses with women (*la débauche des femmes*). Even more, she admits in her autobiography that her hot blood had often brought her near to disaster. What saved her, she said, was, after God's grace, certain claims she made on herself, her good taste, her ambition and her pride, which made it impossible for her to subject herself to any other person—and in the last resort her haughty character which led her "to despise everything and everyone". Her high position, she said, would have made it easy for her to experience *le plaisir*, physical love. There was no man "who would not have counted himself fortunate if she had given him her hand".

From this we may conclude that Christina felt a normal attraction to the handsome and entertaining cavaliers about her, despite her physical condition and her intellectual characteristics, which seem to have frightened men off; despite, too, her repugnance to marriage and sexual intercourse. All this shows how complex her case was; it cannot be dismissed with a few simple medical observations. It is understandable how such a complex case should lead to the most intense strain, and finally to tragedy and catastrophe.

Christina wanted to unite herself to a man, and yet did not want it. There was a deep division in her mind.

2. KARL GUSTAV

The reader of the foregoing chapters will perhaps be surprised to hear that as a girl Queen Christina had for several years experienced a normal sentimental attraction to a young man, whom she, and her court, for a considerable time, looked upon as her future husband. This was her cousin, Karl Gustav, son of her father's half-sister Katharina, and the Count Palatine Johann Kasimir.

This youthful love lasted seven years. Letters are extant from the years 1643 and 1644, which Christina wrote when she was seventeen and eighteen. They abound, of course, in verbose phrases, and are, moreover, written in German, an artless sort of girl's German, with much irregularity of language. (Christina often used to declare that really she knew no other language but French but even in this there were now and then extraordinary deficiencies.

She never made really close contact with either the German language or German culture.)

On 1 May 1643, she wrote that however great the distance between them she could never forget Karl Gustav. On 5 May 1644, she asked him to take certain precautions in their correspondence. She said he must write in code, and mention her name neither on the outside of the letter nor even in the text. His letters should be addressed to "Fräulein Marie", that is, his sister Marie Euphrosine, who later married Magnus de la Gardie. It would be best, Christina said, to delay his courtship a few years, until she had ascended the throne and he had obtained more military experience and authority. It was never too long, Christina added, to wait for something good. No time would be too long to wait for him; he was not, she said, to be worried about the man who was said to woo her, the Prince Elector of Brandenburg. Her devotion was so great that it would end only with her death. Should he die before her, her "affection" for anyone else would come to an end at once; she would meet him again in eternity.

On 16 July 1644 she wrote:

"Since I have no doubt whatever about you, but am completely sure of your fidelity, I will for my part give you the assurance that no length of time and no kind of difficulty will turn me from you."

This letter is very crumpled and seems to have been a long time in the recipient's pocket.

All this is normal, and even moving. But it must be noted that this love came to a sudden end. We do not know exactly why. All we know is that in 1645 the young prince came back home from the "theatre of war", and found that Christina did not love him any more. It never came to a break; we hear nothing about any ill-feeling. She continued to respect him; she remained convinced of his worthiness; later on she had no scruple about nominating him as heir apparent to the throne of Sweden, and often spoke of his unfailing love for her. It is not much to the point to refer to Karl Gustav's corpulence and his inferior intelligence, as was so often done. The prince had had a remarkably good education; he was very knowledgeable and had good judgment.

At that time, moreover, he was not the man of drunken habits that he became later. Rather was he a shy, modest, engaging young man, without much confidence in himself, but with the greatest admiration of and love for the young queen. It was a heavy blow for him when she rejected his love. It is true that he then began to live a really licentious life with various women. He brought a "whore's child" with him to Sweden, and took the precaution of entrusting it to his old teacher, Archbishop Lenaeus, of Uppsala. What impression this made on Christina it is hard to say. At that time people were rather lenient about such erotic escapades; apparently Christina took no offence about the escapades of her father, and was in good relations with her uncle, Admiral Carl Carlsson Gyllenhielm, who was illegitimate. Perhaps we may assume that with her shyness about sex she was repelled by her cousin's lust for life and his excesses. She had no wish to figure among his long series of conquests.

Just at this time, however, something occurred in her life which it is difficult to judge, but its significance should not be underestimated.

3. EBBA SPARRE

At this time a young woman of noble birth, Ebba Sparre, made her appearance at the court. She was born in 1626, the same year as the queen. She was the daughter of Marshal Lars Eriksson Sparre, and granddaughter of Erik Larsson Sparre, one of the leading Swedish humanists of his time, who was executed by Karl IX in 1600. Ebba Sparre came to the queen as lady-in-waiting and struck everyone by her remarkable beauty. This beauty is seen in the portrait which the queen in 1653 commissioned the French artist Sébastien Bourdon to paint; for a long time it was thought to be a portrait of the queen herself. It shows a refined highly-strung woman, and might have come from the salon of one of the *précieuses*. So far as we knew, however Ebba Sparre was never in Paris, where she had a great reputation nevertheless. The French poets and humanists whom Queen Christina summoned to Stockholm in the years after 1650 soon became aware of the beautiful lady of the north. Ebba Sparre was fond of playing the part of Venus in the magnificent ballets that were staged at the Swedish court.

Letters by Ebba Sparre have come down to us; they give an impression of nervousness and insecurity; there is no sign in them of higher education or personal feeling for style. When she was twenty she was engaged to her cousin, Bengt Oxenstierna, later a well-known Swedish statesman. After a few years this engagement was broken off; we do not know the reason. The report that the queen had interfered because of her dislike of the Oxenstierna family, is unfounded. Probably the young woman had merely fallen in love with some other man. Two years later, in fact, she married the brilliant cavalier and knight, Jakob Kasimir de la Gardie. In the amusing gossip diary of a certain Johann Ekeblad we read, under the heading of January 1653, that "yesterday, the 10th instant, the wedding of Count Jakob with the beautiful Sparre was celebrated with much pomp", and the following day he wrote to his brother that "as I write this, Count Jakob is receiving from the red mouth of the lovely Ebba Sparre full recompense for all the torment and anxiety he has suffered for the past three years. Just think of it." This shows that in 1650 Jakob Kasimir de la Gardie had driven the solemn and tedious Bengt Oxenstierna from the field. This sort of thing was unheard-of at the time, and it is probable that relations between the two families became strained. Possibly the queen intervened to smooth things over.

Ebba Sparre's husband rose rapidly in his career; he became a national councillor and infantry general, but in 1658 he was killed in the war with Denmark. "He was shot to pieces by a cannon-shot, which was a cause of grief to many people, above all the young countess, who had come to see him only fourteen days before. There was a general impression that the marriage was not a happy one; in any case relations between Ebba Sparre and her husband's family were not good." Her mother-in-law suspected her of having intrigued against her brother-in-law, Magnus Gabriel de la Gardie, and he seems to have been of that opinion himself. In 1654 he wrote: "What Ebba Sparre, always the bearer of bad news, will do with Her Majesty on their journey may easily be foreseen." He feared her intrigues and was astonished that his brother Jakob had been able to put up with her. "I find it amusing that my brother Jakob allows her to travel. This would not be to my taste, if for no other reason than the gossip to which it gives rise among so many people."

Ebba Sparre had three children, who all died in infancy. She died in 1662. Ekeblad wrote about her death on 26 March: "On the 19th instant the lovely Countess Ebba Sparre died during the night. She had long been ailing. Everyone pitied her and grieved for her."

Magnus Gabriel de la Gardie's allusion to the "gossip" which was stirred up when Ebba Sparre accompanied the queen on one of her journeys probably referred to the malicious rumours which circulated in Stockholm and were industriously spread by the Danish Minister Peder Juel. People noted the evident favour the queen showed the beautiful countess and were scandalized to see this "passion" continue after Ebba Sparre's marriage. Various references were made to the fact, some of them shameful. What was the truth about this "passion"?

Bearing in mind Christina's personality and decidedly masculine characteristics, we are not surprised to find that, when her love for Karl Gustav came to an end, she should have turned in sympathy, perhaps even in a passionate way, to a young beautiful woman. It should, however, be remembered that Christina was otherwise indifferent to young women, and looked down on them with contempt, mostly on account of their intellectual inferiority. She was unable to maintain a conversation with them because of their lack of education. It is impossible that she can ever have been attracted by Ebba Sparre's intellect or education; it was rather her beauty. All her life Christina showed an intense interest in feminine beauty; we may recall the attempt she made to persuade the beautiful Madame de Thianges to leave her husband and accompany her to Italy; she admitted this quite openly. Her admiration for Ebba Sparre is proved: Cromwell's envoy in Stockholm in 1653 and 1654, Bulstrode Whitelocke, gave many interesting details of his talks with the queen, and we owe the following account to him:

The queen was in a very good humour, and taking Whitelocke by the hand, she ledde him to a lady in the roome, whom they called La Belle Comptesse, the fayre Countess, the wife of Grave Jacob de la Garde; the queen sayd to Whitelocke, discourse with this lady, my bed-fellowe, and tell me if her inside be not as beautiful as her outside.

Whitelocke, discoursing with her, found it so; and great modesty, virtue, and witt, accompanying her excellent beauty and behaviour.

The queen pulled off the countesse's gloves, and gave one of them to Whitelocke for a favour; the other she tore in four pieces, and distributed them to Piementelle, to the Italians and to Grave Tott. In recompence of the glove, Whitelocke sent to the belle comptesse a douzen payre of english white gloves, which are in much esteem in this countrey. (8 February 1653.)

It was said that the word "bed-fellow" had an entirely innocent meaning. It signified only that the queen, according to the custom of the time, warmed herself in bed with one of her ladies-in-waiting. But if there is no justification for concluding that the queen had an improper relationship with Ebba Sparre—otherwise she would hardly have mentioned it so freely—the fact was not entirely without significance. We shall see why.

There is another anecdote about the relations between the queen and the countess which should be mentioned in spite of its dubious source. Probably the story was embroidered as it was spread, before it was printed; all the same it has some importance since it shows what people were saying about Christina.

At the Swedish court there was a celebrated scholar named Claude Saumaise (Salmasius),* successor to the famous Scaliger at the university of Leyden. He came to Sweden in 1650, and stayed for only a year. He may be said to have succeeded the Dutch humanist Vossius in the queen's favour. Among many other things he was well known as a commentator on Epictetus. He was an old-fashioned, austere Protestant and detested Rome. "Make the Papacy tremble" was his watchword. To a certain extent he was, however, inclined to the Enlightenment. One of his friends heard

* Claudius Salmasius, Protestant, but famous for his defence of Charles I of England, which provoked a reply by Milton.

him say on one occasion that nothing really proved the immortality of the soul.

This learned man lay one day in bed with a cold, in his room in the palace. Queen Christina went to see him, which would seem to us to be contrary to etiquette, did we not know that she visited her favourite Bourdelot in the same way. She was, as usual, accompanied by the beautiful Ebba Sparre. Salmasius, it is said, made an attempt to hide the book he was reading. "Oh," said the queen, "let me see what kind of book it is. Point out the best passages." She then turned to Ebba Sparre and said: "Come, Sparre, here you have a fine prayer-book called *Moyen de parvenir*. Take it and read this page." Ebba Sparre had not gone far when she was horrified by some of the improper expressions, and blushed and was silent. The queen was doubled up with laughter, and commanded her to read on. Ebba Sparre had to obey.

The book in question was well known, and regarded as scandalous. Its author is said to have been a certain François Béroalde de Verville. He was born a Protestant, but later became a Catholic priest in Tours. His book was usually described as the "Breviary of contemporary scepticism". It appeared between 1606 and 1610, and was notorious for its frankness, its scenes of indecency and its coarse jokes. "The writer put in the mouth of the most serious philosophers the most frightful anachronisms and coarsest of vulgarities." Nowadays we should regard the book as harmless.

The story is probably not entire invention—although told by that malicious man Ménage. We should be careful not to take it too seriously. Yet it is not without interest in view of what we know of the queen's freethinking talk at that time, and her passion for Ebba Sparre.

More important than these two anecdotes is the fact that Queen Christina wrote regular love-letters to Ebba Sparre after she had left Sweden in 1654. Their existence has been known for a long time. They were printed in the middle of the eighteenth century by Arckenholtz, and included in the collection *Lettres secrètes de Christine de Suède*, published in 1761. This correspondence, which served as the source of innumerable romantic accounts of Christina's alleged licentious love-life, is mostly a deliberate forgery. It includes, for example, a love-letter of obvious Lesbian character to a lady called "Madame la Marquise de Grange". Perhaps Madame de Thianges was intended. There are also forged letters from Christina to Descartes, Chanut, Bishop Godeau and others. In one of these fabrications Christina writes among other things of her "supposed conversion". Another letter is a passionate declaration of love: "*Venez, volez dans mes bras désespérés et languissants.*"

Another collection, *Lettres choisies de Christine*, published in 1760, also contains the letters to Ebba Sparre, but with typical additions and distortions. For example there is a severe criticism of conditions in Rome. But if we look at the original letters we find no outbursts against the Catholic Church, nor expressions of Lesbian or otherwise improper character. But really passionate love-letters they most certainly are. They provide an unvarnished portrait of Christina and are worth studying. In the first letter, written in 1655, she says: "How complete would my happiness here have been had it been granted me to share it with you. . . . I swear I should have been fit to be envied by the gods, if I could have had the joy of seeing you. But as I have every reason for doubting such happiness would befall me, you must at least give me the satisfaction of believing me when I say that I shall never forget your services, wherever I may be."

Christina ended by expressing the hope that she would never have the pain of finding herself forgotten by "that person to whom I am most devoted in this world".

The second letter is dated June 1656:

> How happy I should have been, Belle, had it been granted to me to meet you. But I am condemned for ever to love and adore you without being allowed to see you. The envy which the stars have of human happiness prevents me from being entirely happy, for happy I cannot be so long as I am far from you. Do not doubt the truth of my words, and believe me when I say that, wherever I may find myself in the whole world, in me you will find one who is as devoted to you as ever. Is it thinkable that you still remember me? Am I as dear to you as before? Am I wrong to believe that I am the

person you love most in the whole world? If so, do not say it. Allow me to persist in my mistake. Do not grudge me such imaginary happiness as I get from thinking that I am loved by the person most worthy of adoration in the world. Grant me, if possible, this boon; do not let time and distance rob me of the satisfaction of being loved by you. Be assured that, whatever may befall me, I shall never cease from loving you. Farewell, Belle, farewell. I send you a thousand kisses.

The third letter is dated March 1657:

> Since I was permitted to see, in the most beautiful and cultivated country in the world, what our sex could produce in the way of grace and beauty, I can say, with complete conviction, there is no one to measure up to you in the qualities you possess and we admire. Tell me, though, how to find consolation if we are condemned to be parted forever. If I am sure of not seeing you again, I am equally sure of my loving you always. You would be cruel if you doubted this. A friendship which has stood three years of parting, cannot appear false to you if you have not forgotten the right you have over me, you will recall that it is now twelve years since I had the good fortune to be loved by you, and that I, in a word, belong to you in a way that makes it impossible for you to reject me. Only when my life ends shall I cease to love you.

The queen then asks Ebba to make use of "the rights you have over me", if she is at any time in distress. The letter ends: "Farewell. May all go well with you. Don't forget me. I send you a thousand kisses and ask you to assure yourself that I love you from the bottom of my heart."

From these letters it is plain that Christina's love for her beautiful friend was no transient affair, but enduring and sincere. From the correspondence it can also be seen that in 1661 the queen made an attempt to lure her friend to Hamburg. In a letter written by Carl Sparre we read: "I suppose you know that our dear Ebba has gone to Amsterdam. At least it was her intention at the end of this week to sail in a Lübeck boat, and from Lübeck to go to Hamburg along the highway. May God protect her and give her a happy journey."

A year later Ebba Sparre died. Perhaps at the time she was in such bad health that the journey to Hamburg would have endangered her life. In any case all this is a proof that Christina's strong feelings persisted. These feelings, as she herself says in her letters, were to endure literally until death parted them.

Before we give our views on this love between the two women we must—though it is not always easy—deliberately rid our minds of modern conceptions and modern manners of speech. Above all we must always bear in mind that we are dealing with the era before the enlightenment of the eighteenth century. Words then had quite a different meaning from what they have today. We should also remember that the woman to whom Christina wrote was married, and that the expressions Christina used in her letters were not considered in those day to be in the slightest degree compromising. We are faced with a sort of semi-literary passion, which was particularly typical of the time. We shall fail to understand the letters unless we are acquainted with the affected style in which people lived and wrote in the middle of the seventeenth century.

Christina was brought up in a strict, stoic fashion; all foreigners were astonished at the spartan way in which she lived. Not until 1652 did a complete change come over the Swedish court in this respect. Magnus Gabriel de la Gardie's service as minister in Paris from 1646 to 1647 formed the first bridge to the new elegance cultivated in the French salons. De la Gardie returned to Sweden as the first complete cavalier in the new style. Even in 1652 anyone could enter the castle of the Three Crowns; an observer stated that it could happen that the queen, who, in private, had only a bedroom and a closet at her disposal, was besieged before her door by people seeking audience. But from that year, when Bourdelot and Pimentel came to Stockholm, a fundamental transformation took place. Visitors were prevented from invading the queen's rooms; an *antichambre* was made on the model of the imperial court at Vienna. The court attendants were increased in number, new, important official posts were established, and a noble guard was set up to keep watch inside the castle and accompany the queen when she went out.

At the same time a change of taste made itself felt in all kinds of ways—in dress, literary fashion, the theatre and the ballet; all were modelled on foreign patterns. Even the tone of conversation at court was altogether changed.

Far too long have we been accustomed to look upon the "precious" style as something ridiculous, as Molière had treated it in his play *Les Précieuses Ridicules*. In fact it was a really interesting trend of fashion, though it gradually degenerated. "Precious" speech, with its peculiar turns of phrase, was consciously unnatural and mannered and suggests a shrinking from concrete realities; its causes lay deep in people's minds. The dream of a shepherd's life comes back; in literature it is always a sign of a flight from reality. Especially in "precious" poetry, and in the "precious" salons a conception of love prevailed which there is no reason to joke about. Among "precious" women, with several of whom Christina was in regular correspondence, there was an aversion to love and marriage, and the reasons for this must be sought in the wretched conditions under which marriages at that time were generally contracted. With the *précieuses* we can trace an increasing understanding of the dignity of women, a gradual opposition to the tyranny of men. "Since the *précieuses* can't reform marriage, they prefer to withdraw from the condition of dependence involved in sensuous love, and aspire to what they call perfect love, a love which should be free from all that is base, coarse and physical"; so said a Frenchman living at this time. People were enthusiastic about a pure friendship between man and woman—also between woman and woman—and in the salons people were fond of discussing the relation between friendship and love. The many love-speeches of Racine may be mentioned, in which the hero or heroine, even at the most exciting moments of passion could, surprisingly, give a crystal-clear picture of their passion and its consequences. All this had its origin in the discussions of the literary salons. In the middle of the century Mlle de Scudéry set the tone, both in her writings and her manner of life. Her *Astrée* marked the beginning of a renaissance of the Platonic conception of love, and the same theme is developed in many different ways in her large-scale novel *Le grand Cyrus*, published 1649–53, in which Queen Christina is one of the characters.

Le vrai amour transforme l'essence même de l'amant en la chose aimée (True love transforms the very being of the lover into the one loved). If the lady who is loved will have nothing to do with sensuous love, then the lover naturally refrains from it, and is turned into a Platonist. In her *Discours pour et contre l'amitié tendre* (1653) Mlle de Scudéry studies these questions. In *Le Grand Cyrus* Phaon gives a solemn promise to respect Sappho's wishes, "whose only desire is the possession of her heart, while she for her part promises to wish for nothing of him but his own true self". Mlle de Scudéry did her best to live in accordance with this teaching; a proof was her relationship with Pellisson, which was much admired on account of its highminded and un-sensuous character. In the evening of her life she dreamt of a love pure in heart, "so spiritual, so lofty and altogether innocent, that it in no way offended against propriety and virtue".

Christina was very well acquainted with this new trend. She took a special interest in Mlle de Scudéry, but soon made friends of Mme la Suze and Mme de Brégy also. She granted Mlle de Scudéry a pension, and presented her with a diamond worth 700 pistoles. "It is beautiful", a contemporary wrote, "to see the queen of Sweden giving Mlle de Scudéry such magnificent presents."

If the question is looked at from this point of view, the riddle is solved of Christina's love for a married woman whose husband held a high position at her court. And when we read the novels and letters of this "precious" age in France, we at once recognize their exaggerated language in the apparently passionate epistles which the queen wrote to the beautiful friend of her youth. This is literature. There are deliberate exaggerations, a fervour which is depicted as passion, but was never transmuted into reality.

Our judgment of the extravagant expressions in Queen Christina's love-letters to Ebba Sparre will be assisted if we compare them with the expressions she employs in her letters to French ladies she had never met, and with whom she could not possibly have had close relations. For example, in 1651 she wrote to Mlle de Montpensier—*la grande Mademoiselle*—a letter which ends thus: "I, whose chief aim above all else is to prize virtue, must admit that your virtue really fascinates me. I may say that I already felt a devotion to you which I hardly thought could be increased. But I was mistaken; I see that I must use loftier language; it would be a feeble expression of my feelings for you if I called it an ordinary sort of affection. It is a burning love (*un ardent amour*) which causes me to be etc." If the words *un ardent amour* appeared to the queen to be fitting in regard to such a temporary acquaintance, we must take her amorous declarations to Ebba Sparre with a grain of salt.

This does not, however, quite dispose of the question; rather does it present the problem in a different, and perhaps more serious, form. It was precisely because this fervour was so literary and was never intended to result in a union of mind or body, that it gave rise to a neurosis. Queen Christina and her circle may have thought it quite natural that she should share her bed with the most beautiful woman in the country, for whom she had expressed such enthusiasm and whose beauty she constantly extolled. Although it is probable that etiquette was observed and nothing improper took place, it is a fact that a powerful feeling developed between the two young women who were brought into such close contact with each other. In Christina's letters written after she had left Sweden there are significant references to the fact that it was she whom Ebba Sparre "loved best of all", that twelve years earlier, in 1645, Christina "enjoyed the privilege of being loved by you", and that "I belong to you in such a way that it is impossible for you ever to give me up". The "rights you have over me" are also mentioned. This is, of course, all mere writing, but they are not altogether empty words. Behind the undoubtedly strict etiquette, behind the exemplary control over all actions, a sentiment is concealed. That this sentiment could be intensified and turned into a Platonic literary cliché, made it all the more difficult to bear. Above all we must remember that Christina's nature was not conditioned in the same way as other women. She shrank with horror from marriage; the thought of bearing children was repellent to her; she did not wish, as she herself said, at any price "to be a field for a man to plough". She could not accustom herself to the idea of being dependent, least of all in a sexual manner. She did not want a fire kindled in her which she could not overcome. She could not conceive of letting her happiness and sensuous contentment depend on passion or the whims of a man. Accordingly she played her dangerous game with the lovely Ebba Sparre. It had none of the dangerous consequences which the Danish envoy, in his letters, had gossiped about in bawdy language, but it did rob the young queen of her peace of mind.

Before long she was to be caught up in a fully developed erotic neurosis, from which she could only free herself by desperate measures.

4. MAGNUS DE LA GARDIE

What makes it difficult, for anyone not familiar with the "precious" world of the seventeenth century and its code of love, to understand the queen's relations with Ebba Sparre, is the fact that at the same time Christina was entertaining an equally deep—but also Platonic—"passion" for a man. This was Count Magnus Gabriel de la Gardie, son of Ebba Brahe, whom Gustavus Adolphus had loved in his youth, and the celebrated general Jakob de la Gardie. The relationship has been much discussed over the centuries. For the most part de la Gardie has been very severely criticized. But it would seem that this whole chapter of Swedish court history should be thoroughly revised. On the one hand things seem to have, in part, developed differently from what had long been assumed; on the other hand the affair apparently had a different significance from what had been imagined. The exact truth cannot be proved, but the facts seem to a large extent to speak for themselves.

When the young Magnus de la Gardie planned to go to France in 1642, after eighteen months of study in Holland, his aged mother felt much anxiety, and wrote him a touching letter: "Now that you are going to a country and to cities where there are many occasions for frivolity and dissipation, I cannot refrain from begging and imploring you to avoid such temptations, and guard yourself against anything that would bring down on you

God's anger and punishment. Besides, you can contract serious diseases impossible to cure . . ."

She did not conceal from her son how badly things had gone with acquaintances in that dangerous country, and she concluded: "God be with you, and help you to treat the devil of frivolity with contempt."

The count paid little attention to this advice. He attracted the favour of King Louis XIII, who at once offered him a cavalry regiment to command if he would enter the French service. But this he refused. Before leaving he was able to make a formal call and pay his respects to the new king, Louis XIV. Then he went to see his family-home in Languedoc, and made, as was reported to his father, a great impression on the ladies, especially in Montpellier. When the report spread that Torstensson's army had invaded Holland, he gave up the visit to Italy which he had planned, and returned home. In the summer of 1644 he was once more in Stockholm. He was, as has been mentioned before, the only perfectly European cavalier in Sweden with an intimate knowledge of French court-etiquette.

Christina discovered him very soon. Just as she was beginning to show a certain coolness towards Karl Gustav, she started to show marked favour to de la Gardie. In 1645 he was made colonel of the Life Guards, and in March of the same year he became engaged to the queen's cousin, the Countess Palatine Marie Euphrosine. According to her he had been devoted to her since he was eighteen. In 1642 his mother wrote to him, "I hear that she prefers you to anyone else." In the summer of 1645 de la Gardie took part in the war with Denmark in Skaane. When the peace of Brömsebro was concluded in the summer he went back to Stockholm and to the court. Christina wrote to Johann Adler Salvius, supposed to be the man with the strongest will among all those she met while living in Sweden, and a man who had the greatest influence on her:

"I am quite sure of his (de la Gardie's) fidelity." She corresponded with him in a private cypher. And now began his rapid—all too rapid—career. In spite of the objections raised by Axel Oxenstierna he was sent in 1646 as envoy extraordinary to France.

Before he left, Chanut sent from Stockholm one of his detailed and masterly character-sketches. He wrote of de la Gardie:

His intelligence is decidedly above the average. Here he is considered to be very gifted. He is quick-witted, a man of firm decision in matters he understands. As, however, he is very cautious and unwilling to run the risk of failure, he is very sparing in his views and somewhat undecided in things which he has not completely mastered. He is not lacking in those qualities which at other courts would bring him friendships. He is generous and a brilliant figure, susceptible to kindness and good treatment, but these advantages do not seem to mean so much here as elsewhere. He has therefore to go to great expense with giving parties and serving wine, which he carries admirably, though it must eventually undermine his health. His present position here makes him suspicious, but this is in any case characteristic of men here. The envy with which he feels he is regarded makes him mistrustful of almost everyone. He is not yet quite at home in this position of favourite, for it was not long before he saw himself deprived of his freedom and beset with extraordinary difficulties. In his heart he loves Princess Marie, to whom he engaged himself on orders from the queen, who had not then become so devoted to him, but now he finds that he is passionately loved by the queen. Between these two feelings he has until now been clever enough to divide his duty. I think he wishes the queen's love for him was less passionate; he is afraid of the drawbacks of such as a position as he is in. What I am saying, Monseigneur, about the friendly feelings the queen has towards the count needs no further explanation, but in order to avoid misinterpretation, in case this letter should fall into the wrong hands, I feel I must tell you the truth and say that more evidence has reached us of the purity of the queen's thoughts than of her love. This love takes up a part of her heart, without in the least influencing her actions—unless perhaps there is some slackening of that attachment to the man her reason inclines her to, her cousin the Prince Palatine Karl, towards whom she behaves in such a way that he might, on reflection, think that she was just forcing herself to give these proofs of her good will towards him. So keen, however, is the Prince's intelligence that he acts as if he sees nothing, and although he and the count meet on brotherly and intimate terms, it seems to me that the count harbours some doubt and fears that the prince, in spite of the self-

1. KING GUSTAVUS ADOLPHUS AND THE CHILD CHRISTINA
Copy of an original by J. Elbfas, showing Christina as a small girl together with her father. There is probably no question of likeness yet the picture gives some idea of Christina's boyish appearance when young.

2. Christina at the Age of 15
Painting by J. Elbfas (1641) in the City Hall, Stockholm
Photo: Svenska Porträttarkivet

control he displays, might not make a counter-stroke, as soon as the marriage gives him power over the queen's heart.

This acute and accurate characterization gives us much to think about. It gives a good idea of de la Gardie's personality, as it was shown later on in Swedish politics and cultural life; here his weakness of character was foreshadowed.

In his letters to Marie Euphrosine from Paris, de la Gardie assures her of his love. He says, for example, in the French jargon typical of the time: "I assure you, my dear, that your servitor has been honoured at the court here, and enjoys approbation and favour. Be not jealous, my creature, the French ladies may possess my body, but my heart is yours."

He was apprehensive that his strong position with the Queen of Sweden might be upset during his long absence: "Many sad forebodings disturb me, in case during my long absence time, the cunning stratagems of evil men, slanders and other things may destroy my happiness."

Even at that time, as his letters show, a characteristic melancholy and feeling of insecurity already possessed the young count, who, till then, had been favoured far beyond his deserts; it is possible he himself felt his exalted position was not fully justified.

In January 1647 he returned home; the queen paid all his debts in France without checking them. In March he celebrated his marriage to Marie Euphrosine. Christina said on this occasion: "I am handing over to you my most precious possession. I am certain my cousin will always conduct herself to your satisfaction. I hope you will take this as a special favour shown to you and your family."

In May he was appointed a national councillor, at the age of only twenty-five (it may be mentioned that Axel Oxenstierna became a councillor when only twenty-three, and his son, Johann, when only twenty-eight). In September 1647 he was made assessor in the war college and the war council. Towards the end of the year he was appointed legal director for the district of Valla in East Gothland. But he was beset by a rankling sense of uneasiness. To his brother-in-law he wrote that he wanted to leave the court and relinquish everything to his "enemies and a group of mean-spirited people", whose actions he described as "tomfoolery and lies".

In 1648 he received more feudal offices and signs of favour. He was appointed one of the chief army commanders in the Thirty Years War—"he is to have command ranking immediately after our Field Marshal Karl Gustav Wrangel"—and he took part in the final stage of the great war, in Bohemia. In May 1649 he was made a Field Marshal and Governor of Livland. Gifts were showered on him. In 1651 he became master of the Queen's household and marshal of the realm. He was put at the head of the delegation appointed to negotiate peace with Poland at Lübeck. In 1652 he was appointed president of the College Chamber and senatorial president in Västergötland and Dalsland. These posts and feudal offices made him one of the richest men in the whole country. Finally he became the government treasurer.

The uneasiness the count felt during this unparalleled rapid promotion—which apparently did not at any time correspond to his real political influence—is described in Chanut's correspondence with Mazarin and his colleagues in Paris. In this he gives a detailed account of the inner tensions at the Swedish court. We may recall that Chanut, in the ample characterization he gave of the count, written before he went to Paris, described at length the queen's passion for him. When we remember the queen's fervent devotion to Ebba Sparre and recall that de la Gardie, with the express agreement of the queen, was soon to be married to her cousin, we are undoubtedly faced with a problem. Chanut's letters prove that there was a passion. He spoke of it often and was constantly worried about its possible consequences.

It came about that this extraordinarily gifted and attractive Frenchman became the most intimate friend of the queen and of de la Gardie, but at the same time gained the confidence of Karl Gustav. He was therefore in a better position than anyone else to observe how, in certain ways, de la Gardie pushed his brother-in-law aside. He recounted, too, that Karl Gustav at times spoke ill of de la Gardie, and suspected him of certain intrigues aimed at preventing his marriage to the queen. There was no justification for this. On the contrary, de la Gardie's marriage with Marie

Euphrosine was a happy one, and he sincerely wished his brother-in-law to marry the queen. He had even given him some careful advice about how he should behave if the queen showed reluctance.

But what were Christina's relations with de la Gardie? Was she serious? Was the intelligent Chanut really correct in speaking of a passion of unusual fervour?

In March 1646 Chanut wrote that the queen was so frank and confiding in speaking with him that he might almost be a minister—at that time he had not received the appointment. She was, he said, annoyed that de la Gardie's success aroused envy in certain quarters. In the same letter Chanut wrote that Axel Oxenstierna spoke of nothing but retiring, and then dying. In April Chanut gave, with emphasis, his impression that the queen was turning against the Oxenstiernas, and more and more favouring de la Gardie. On 28 April he wrote to Hugues de Lionne that in his view the queen's marriage with Karl Gustav was imminent; there was no doubt that he, "as you will see, will drive all others from the field". But he stressed the fact that all the queen's actions were guided by her reason, and her reason was always a guarantee that the queen, whatever might be her inclinations, would never fail to do "what is correct". He here mentioned for the first time the "intimate affection" the queen felt for de la Gardie. In May, so it was said, she showed her love for the count quite openly. And yet the count would be able to induce the queen to marry Karl Gustav.

Chanut's impression was therefore that the queen did truly love de la Gardie, that probably she would marry Karl Gustav on rational grounds; that she loved the count, so it was said, with such a passion as was consistent with moral purity. In his letter to Mazarin, written on 23 June 1646, Chanut made the important observation, already mentioned, that the queen was well aware of the fact that she must take a husband and produce children, but that she lacked the necessary "affection".

In July Chanut sent his detailed characterization of de la Gardie. In December he wrote that he had spoken with the queen confidentially about her growing passion for de la Gardie, and had done his best to restrain her feelings. When de la Gardie returned from his visit to France, Christina had suppressed her passion, but it was still rumoured that she wanted to take him as a husband. The count himself, however, said that in six weeks he would marry Karl Gustav's sister to whom, during his journey, he had written passionate love-letters. It may be imagined what a nervous strain this meant for the queen. A week later, on 9 February 1647, it was reported that the count's wedding would take place in five weeks' time. Chanut added, "In spite of this the queen's attraction to him seems to me to increase every day." She attempted, he said, to show unconcern; he relied on her "virtue and strength of will".

On 2 February Chanut wrote that the count had given him an account of his own position. He admitted the difficulty of the situation he was in, and asked Chanut for help in overcoming the queen's repugnance to a marriage with Karl Gustav. But Chanut had to agree that the queen's feelings for Count Magnus were just as strong as ever.

On 29 June Chanut wrote to Mazarin that things had again reached a critical point, since now Karl Gustav had become jealous of his brother-in-law. This the queen had taken badly, since she considered her feelings for the count to be pure and innocent. She could see what inconvenience her feelings might lead to, but she was not capable of banishing them entirely from her heart. Chanut had, so he said, advised her to pay more attention to the Count Palatine and at the same time refrain from showing in public and so clearly how strong her feelings were for the count. "It is extremely important that the queen should deny the rumours that she was moved by an excess of passion." There was the danger that she would fall into a serious melancholia. Yet she spurned all sympathy. Chanut ended by saying that she certainly did not open her heart to anyone as she did with him.

In September 1647, when Chanut was frequently with the queen, at Uppsala, he wrote of "her most remarkable devotion to what was good and virtuous"; he hoped this would help to moderate "the powerful feelings she had for Count Magnus". An important stage on the way to a complete cure was the fact that she regarded her friendship with the count as a feeling which she could completely control. Chanut ended: "If I may venture to tell all I was able to learn about her feelings, it would seem to me that she derived pleasure from the thought that, despite her powerful inclinations, she had never acted in the slightest way as would cause her remorse; she has not only escaped shipwreck; she has not needed to throw anything overboard so as to lighten the ship."

On 15 October 1650 Chanut assured Mazarin that the queen would "never subordinate herself to a husband".

This passion for a married man, whom Christina had no wish to conquer or with whom, apparently, she had no desire for physical relations, has been something of a mystery until now. It can be explained by that "precious" eroticism which has been described already in the account of the queen's similar passion for the beautiful Ebba Sparre. It should not be forgotten that de la Gardie was the first of the cavaliers trained in France. In the *roman à clef*, "Le grand Cyrus", de la Gardie is one of the heroes. In this novel his relations with Queen Christina are described in detail, and no mystery is made of the queen's passion for the handsome count.

At the court of Cleobuline (Christina) the nobleman Myrinthe (de la Gardie) has a distinguished place. Cleobuline loves him, but before he was made aware of her passion he fell in love with the Princess Philomène (Marie Euphrosine). Her brother, Prince Basilide (Karl Gustav), loves Cleobuline—so far all is in accord with the facts. But now imagination gets to work. The queen tries to stifle her passion, but does not succeed. In her jealousy she tries to separate Myrinthe from Philomène, and in this attempt makes use of Basilide. He cannot approve of a marriage between his sister and Myrinthe, who comes from a family of lower rank. At length the queen summons both lovers and tells them that she approves of their marriage. But now Myrinthe has become aware of the fact that the queen loves him, and he feels flattered. The queen now calls her council and announces that she will never marry; Basilide is to be her successor. The reason for the queen's refusal to marry according to the novel—and also, we may add, Paris court gossip—is her unhappy love for de la Gardie.

But this hardly fits the case. The queen's shrinking from marriage had deeper causes. It is interesting to see how this drama of the Swedish court is transmuted into an elegant, *précieux* novel of intrigue. But the question is whether, in fact, Christina's love was merely "literary". Just as with Ebba Sparre we must add that it was not a harmless literary game. Christina surrendered herself to a Platonic passion for both young people, the most handsome at her court. An astonishing warmth of sentiment pervaded her passion; the circumspect Chanut was seriously alarmed. Nevertheless the queen apparently never once thought of turning her dreams into reality. From the very beginning she never had any desire to go beyond the limits of an aristocratic passionate sentiment.

Two things should be borne in mind. On the one hand such a powerful passion must necessarily lead to a neurosis; on the other, Magnus Gabriel de la Gardie, like all the other men whose company the queen frequented, felt seriously embarrassed by the approaches of this amazon. We should not let ourselves be influenced by the fine salon-portrait Sébastien Bourdon made of the queen; it flatters her very much. No description we possess of the queen in the least resembles this enchanting picture of refined femininity. As a woman Christina was decidedly repellent; she was unkempt, and had a bad figure, a sagging chest, sloping shoulders, a mannish voice. De la Gardie must have recoiled from the approaches of this strange woman. Sooner or later, despite the politeness the court etiquette required of him, she became aware of his aversion, just as, twenty years later, she must have perceived the similar aversion the elegant Cardinal Azzolino felt for her advances.

We should remember that at that time very little was known about the subconscious mind. In their philosophy the Stoics regarded the passions as a herd of wild animals who could be tamed by reason and will-power. They could not know that those same passions could emerge in disguise. It was only with the plays of Racine and the penetrating observations of certain French moralists and students of human nature that the truth began to break through. We may assume that the queen had no suspicion that every day her condition went from bad to worse. She noted—and everyone saw it—that she was nervous, ill, irritable and feverish. It is evident that her long state of ill-health was connected with a neurosis which she had done so much to arouse, and sooner or later a severe crisis was bound to occur. It came, and its echo was heard all over Europe. One day de la Gardie, the favourite, was toppled from his high place, and was as much despised by the queen as he had been loved and admired by her.

5. THE FAVOURITE'S FALL

From about the year 1650 the queen, as has been mentioned in another connection, surrounded herself with a considerable number of foreign, chiefly French, intellectuals. They introduced an entirely new spirit into the Swedish court, and also influenced the queen's intellectual and religious opinions. The effect of the arrival of these new favourites was not at all to the liking of many Swedes, Magnus de la Gardie among them. In particular his indignation was directed against the agreeable doctor and humanist, later and abbé, Bourdelot. There were several minor clashes between them which the queen was able to settle. But de la Gardie had to resign.

In November 1653, after a session of the council at Uppsala, de la Gardie stayed behind with the queen. In the course of conversation she praised certain foreigners for their loyalty and ability. The touchy de la Gardie took this as a criticism of himself, and complained that he had lately been judged most unjustly. There were people who spread the rumour that the queen had accused him of treason and told him she no longer held him in favour. She was supposed to have said that if anyone insulted him, she would only laugh.

Rather annoyed, the queen asked, "Who said this?" De la Gardie named Steinberg, the queen's master of horse, who stood high in her favour. He was summoned, but denied he had ever said anything of the kind. But it is clear that Steinberg, whether or not he had made such a statement, was bound to give such a denial. Had he in any way confessed to having spoken in that way, he would have been instantly dismissed. For it would have been an admission that he had made invented statements about the queen.

What was de la Gardie to do? Some days later he told the queen that his chief informant was the Courland adventurer Schlippenbach, an irresponsible braggart and a member of the circle round Karl Gustav, who at this time held the high office of marshal of the court. He was said to have made the remark in question during a private conversation at Ekolsund Castle.

Schlippenbach was called, and he, too, denied having spoken. This was also quite natural. Then de la Gardie called Schlippenbach a cad and a scoundrel. The queen was unable to grasp that there were two opposing statements of equal value, and she dismissed de la Gardie from the court and forbade him to return until he had atoned for the insult. It seems she was thinking of a duel. De la Gardie turned to Karl Gustav, who advised against a duel, saying that "to decide such matters with a dagger was not becoming for a statesmen, but behaviour suitable only for young people". He then made the following characteristic remark: his brother-in-law should conduct himself like a Christian in this painful situation, for men do best in this world if they strive to gain the mastery over themselves and their passions, and look upon the vanity of this world with a *constantia animi*, a steadfastness of mind, which is pleasing to God, whether they have success or failure.

De la Gardie, however, would not yield. He wrote an appeal to the queen, which she answered in a letter which became famous and has, with little reason, been much admired. It is dated 3 December 1653, and it contains a devastating criticism of her former favourite to whom, for years, the queen had been attached, not only by friendship and regard, but also with burning passion:

> Sir, after the disgrace into which you have fallen, you wish to see me again. But I must tell you that this is entirely contrary to your interests. I am writing you this letter to explain the reasons which prevent me from accepting your suggestion. My letter is intended to convince you that the meeting you propose could only increase your discomfort. It is not for me to provide a remedy for your unhappiness; it is for you yourself to restore your honour.

What can you hope to get from me? What could I do but pity you and reprimand you? The friendship I have shown you compels me to the one as to the other. However great may be the forbearance I show you I cannot, without breaking faith with myself, pardon the wrong you have done yourself. Do not think I am vexed with you; I can assure you I am not. But in future I shall be incapable of feeling anything but pity for you. This can be of no help to you, since you yourself have robbed the kindness I showed you of all value. As you have acknowledged, you are no longer worthy of it. You have condemned yourself to exile, and I have confirmed this sentence, since I think it is just. I do not feel inclined, as people perhaps try to make you believe, to alter my decision. How can you, after all you have done, wish to appear once more before me? You make me blush with shame at the thought of all the many vile actions to which you have lowered yourself. That miserable conversation we had was devoid of the slightest nobility, greatness or generosity on your part. If I were capable of remorse, it would be because I formed a friendship with such an unprincipled character as you. Such a weakness would be unworthy of me, and as I always act in accordance with the dictates of reason, I cannot complain about the false light in which I used to view these things. I should have been in good faith all my life, had your defective judgment not compelled me to take up a stand against you. My own honour compels me to do this in public, as does a sense of justice. In all the nine years I resolutely defended you, I did too much for you. But now I no longer feel under any obligation, since it is yourself who have endangered your own interests. You have laid bare a secret which I was resolved to keep all my life, by demonstrating that you are unworthy of the success I helped you to attain. If you are prepared to listen to my criticism, then you may come to me. This is the condition I must make for my agreement to a meeting. But don't imagine that tears and humble submissiveness will cause me to feel the slightest sympathy for you. In your case I can just bring myself to remember you, but not have any discussion with you. I have resolved never to speak of this matter again, unless at the same time I condemn you. I must make you conscious of the fact that the faults you have been guilty of towards me have made you unworthy of my respect. It is the only thing I can still do for you. But be assured that you yourself must bear the blame for my displeasure, and that I have treated you justly as I shall always treat anyone.

De la Gardie made one more attempt to defend himself, but Christina, without consulting her council, deprived him of his office of government treasurer. A little later he lost his properties and feudal offices. When Christina was due to leave Sweden and there was a discussion of her expenses, she mentioned several feudal properties belonging to de la Gardie, which were promptly confiscated. The two men who had denounced de la Gardie, Schlippenbach and Steinberg, were made counts by the queen, although both of them were insignificant, not to say dubious, characters.

If the documents of this affair are examined—a task I do not propose to undertake here—the queen is shown as really antipathetic. It may be said that de la Gardie, in his bewilderment, made use of too many bombastic expressions and displayed a certain instability. But we should remember that he was dealing with a young queen whose power was unlimited. There is no proof that de la Gardie had not spoken the truth. On the contrary, it is most unlikely that such untrue statements and rumours were not put about in court circles, so full of servility and intrigue, since everyone knew that de la Gardie had been turned out of his former powerful position. And it is quite certain that no one who risked making such statements as "I have heard from Steinberg", or "Your Majesty is reported to have remarked" would have dared to confess them to the angry queen. In the absence of witnesses a denial was the only possibility for a hardened intriguer like Schlippenbach. To consider a man of his kind as more trustworthy than the treasurer is ridiculous. It is best to look at the whole thing as a discreditable affair, not for de la Gardie, but for the queen. She showed that her judgment failed her, so that she could not see through a simple piece of tittle-tattle, that she exaggerated the importance of trifles, that she gave credence to unreliable witnesses, and caused the moral ruin of one of the highest officials of the kingdom, all because he would not fight a duel with an adventurer.

But the incident has another significance which causes it to be of real interest. In the way described, Christina got rid of a man whom for years she had, unsuccessfully, pursued with her passionate admiration, or "passion", as she called it. It is probable that this haughty and in many ways infatuated young woman was not aware of the motives that had driven her to act as she did. But when we remember the intolerable situation into which the queen's almost pathological simultaneous passion for Ebba Sparre and Magnus Gabriel de la Gardie had brought her, and realize that the latter desperately resisted her and found her advances painfully embarrassing, then we can understand that Christina's reactions were determined entirely by erotic tension, her acute nervous crisis. Sooner or later she was bound to find an excuse for despising and rejecting a man who had refused her favours. A pretence, a ridiculous trifle, when a sense of honour should have prevented her from paying it any attention, was opportunely offered, and she at once made use of it. With consistent recklessness she exploited the occasion; she humiliated and insulted her former favourite, and deprived him of his position. I know of no other episode that so much shows up the great faults of her character.

Not long after de la Gardie came into power once more, and was appointed chancellor. None of his contemporaries seem to have considered him to have been in the least compromised by what had happened. He continued to show great loyalty to the queen. It would have been possible for him to abuse his position and make her financial situation, which was often desperate, even more difficult. He did not do so. He proceeded, as we shall see later, with a series of measures, some of which may appear severe, but were in reality well founded.

The episode tells us nothing of importance about de la Gardie's character. But it seems, if correctly interpreted, to show up quite mercilessly Queen Christina's erotic problems, and in particular the nervous crisis brought about by her long, *précieux* Platonic passion.

This is an important point which helps to explain why Christina was dissatisfied in Sweden and why she resolved to leave the country.

CHAPTER FIVE

Christina and Lutheranism

I. WAS SHE EVER A LUTHERAN?

In her later years Queen Christina often spoke of Lutheranism, always in a negative way, and sometimes even in mockery. In spite of her tolerant principles with regard to religion, and her horror of religious wars, no statement by her has been reported which showed the slightest sympathy with Lutheranism, the faith of her father whom she adored. Some years before her death she wrote to the Chevalier de Terlon a letter that became famous, in which she showed the utmost hostility to the cruel methods—the so-called "dragonades"—which Louis XIV was using to uproot Protestantism in his possessions. The letter came into the hands of the philosopher Pierre Bayle, who at once declared that it showed obvious traces of the queen's original Protestantism. Christina got her secretary Goldenblad to write to Bayle an anonymous letter strongly contradicting this opinion.

> You stated that you found a remnant of Protestantism in this letter. You should not have said this. You were trying to be clever; but you are mistaken; it was not clever of you, it was shameless. It is not in this way that you should speak of a queen who displays such exemplary loyalty to a religion entirely opposed to Protestantism, a queen who has sacrificed all; every one of her actions is a proof of the wrongness of your view, and shows that Her Majesty retains nothing of her former religion.

The queen also declared in many marginal notes that she had never believed in Lutheran theology, that she had never been a Lutheran. "I did not believe the religion in which I was brought up", she wrote in a fragment of autobiography. All I was told about it seemed to me unworthy of Thee (God). I saw how men caused Thee to speak in their own manner; I thought they wanted to deceive me, overawe me, make me follow them blindly. I could not bear the long Lutheran sermons, always so much alike. But I also saw that I must put up with them and be patient, and conceal my real thoughts. When I grew older I made a kind of religion for myself, and thus waited for that religion which Thou later on wouldst bestow on me and to which I felt my nature so powerfully attracted. Thou knowest how often, speaking a language the people did not know, I begged for Thy grace, I asked to be enlightened by Thee, even if this should cost me my high position and my life."

If we can rely on Christina's own statements, the situation should be clear. But then a new and more difficult problem presents itself—how was it possible for the young princess, living in the stronghold of Lutheranism and surrounded by Protestants all through her childhood, to take such a consistently anti-Lutheran attitude?

We need not dwell on the point. Christina described her youth in a very one-sided fashion, to some extent even wrongly. It is correct that with the passage of time she learnt to regard Protestantism with a critical eye. Many years went by, however, before she reached a completely clear view. There are contemporary documents that are more trustworthy than the queen's own notes, which she wrote down some years later than the events referred to. There is no doubt that the queen not only had a very intimate knowledge of Protestantism, but that at times she took an active part, and personally pursued a Protestant religious policy, in opposition to many Swedish ecclesiastics. It is true that in 1647 she said to Chanut: "Every monarch is bound to try to prevent powerful men from joining the opposition; the political situation compels me to express views on religious questions." By this remark she no doubt meant that she loyally attended to her religious duties, which were often exacting, and that she endured the long-winded utterances of her preachers without protest. She records that on one occasion, when she was a small girl, she heard a sermon on the last judgment, "in which the preacher described the cataclysm so vividly that I was filled with dread and thought that my last hour had come. I imagined that heaven and earth would collapse and bury me in their ruins. I began to weep bitterly, for I was convinced my end was near."

As Christina was leaving the church, she turned to her instructor, Bishop Johannes Matthiae, and asked: "What was the preacher talking about, Father? Why did you never tell me about this day of dread? How will it go with me when that day arrives? Will it be this evening?"

The kindly theologian merely smiled at her distress and replied: "You will go to Paradise, but in order to do this you must obey your teachers. You should pray to God and work hard."

Christina added: "This stirred up reflections in my mind that I shall never forget; for one of my age they were out of the ordinary."

Another time, a year later, she heard a sermon of the same kind, and was again frightened about the last judgment, though not quite so much as on the first occasion. Again she wept, again she asked her instructor, as they were leaving the church, when this last judgment would come, which everybody was speaking about so much?

Mathiae replied: "It is coming, it is coming. But you need not be anxious. God alone knows when it will come, but we must be ready."

Christina recorded that this reply by no means satisfied her, and that she then began to reflect, and entertain doubts. She even began to look upon her well-loved instructor with distrust.

For a third year the preacher preached on the same subject, but this time it made no impression on her. "I began to doubt everything", and one day, while she was having a lesson with her instructor, she asked him: "Tell me the truth. All those things they tell us about religion—are they just fairy-tales like that of the last judgment?"

At this the instructor was angry, and retorted that it was a dreadful sin to think in that way. He turned to Christina's aunt, and asked her to punish her with the birch.

This offended the young princess, who said: "I promise never to say anything like that again but spare me the birch, or you will bitterly regret it."

She said that she spoke these words "in such a peremptory voice that the instructor trembled before me". She was nine years old at the time.

This may all be correct, but it did not prevent Christina from taking a lively interest in religious questions and the politics of Church and State, and from pursuing the practical policy she favoured.

2. CHRISTINA OPPOSED TO ORTHODOXY

When Johannes Matthiae became Bishop of Strängnäs he published, in 1644, in place of a pastoral letter, an ecclesiastical constitution of the Bohemian Brethren adapted to Swedish conditions, under the title *Idea boni ordinis in Ecclesia Christi*. This aroused enormous interest. The superintendent at Kalmar strongly criticized Matthiae's centralizing tendency, above all his objections to baptism by the laity which, he said, could not be reconciled with orthodox Lutheranism. Matthiae replied and a sharp controversy ensued. When in 1647 the affair came to be discussed in parliament, the opposition to Matthiae was considerable. The clergy appealed to the Council to see to it that true belief should be protected in Sweden.

Axel Oxenstierna was of the opinion that it would have been better if Matthiae had never published his book. The queen answered that she saw nothing in it to criticize. But Oxenstierna insisted that the Lutheran clergy could not approve of the book, and he expressed his fear that the dispute would plunge the country into controversy. The queen was obstinate and forbade such a severe judgment. Oxenstierna was, however, not at all satisfied. He asked the queen not to shield the book with her personal authority. This was to go from the frying-pan into the fire. Christina's angry reply was that it did not need her defence; it could defend itself.

Per Brahe now attempted to intervene. Oxenstierna retorted that it was Sweden's good fortune to have only one faith, so avoiding disputes over doctrine and the troubles they could cause.

The discussion at length became so lively that Christina broke into tears. The council separated without reaching a decision. The queen formally gave way, and Johannes Matthiae produced a soothing statement. But it is certain that Christina continued to maintain her view on the question. She was so dependent on councillors with unionist ideas, that she made their ideas her own.

All this can hardly be reconciled with the later statement that she had never been a Lutheran. During this period—possibly a short one—the queen was clearly convinced that the unionist idea was the right one. This means that she was unequivocally in favour of a Protestant religious policy, even if not an orthodox one. This was confirmed by her policy during the preliminary peace discussions, when she supported unionist views.

At the same parliament of 1647 the queen showed in another way that she was decidedly opposed to Swedish orthodoxy. The orthodox party strongly urged that, in addition to the Augsburg Confession, the Concord Formula* should be adopted as a basis of belief, so as to rule out any difference and any tendency to unionist collaboration with other Protestant bodies. Johannes Matthiae made a brave attempt to prevent the adoption of the Concord Formula. He gave it as his view that such a step would mean surrendering Sweden to Germany and German theologians, which would entail an encroachment on Sweden's sovereignty. At the back of this struggle lay the differences between the two Swedish delegates to the peace-conference of Westphalia, Johann Oxenstierna and Adler Salvius. Almost all the clergy were opposed to Matthiae. Besides, there was the suspicion that the queen wanted to appoint him Archbishop of Uppsala. In this question Oxenstierna was undoubtedly on the side of orthodoxy. He and the orthodox clergy pointed out that religious unity extended beyond national boundaries, so that all were united in the same faith. Since their fellow-believers in Germany had accepted the Concord Formula as the basis of their beliefs, the Swedes should, it was said, do likewise. If Sweden took exception to the Concord

* *Book of Concord* (in Latin), first published in Dresden in 1580, a collection of Lutheran confessional documents which formed the basic book of common doctrine in the Evangelical-Lutheran States of Germany, though not everywhere.

3. Axel Oxenstierna, the young Christina's teacher
She always maintained great veneration and admiration for his genius, but quarrelled with him over and over again, and on at least two important occasions—during the peace negotiations in Münster and at the election of Karl Gustaf as the successor to the throne—fought against him and outwitted him. The experienced diplomat looked at the daughter of his king with amazement and admiration and once said that she had the makings of a true "heroina".
Drawing by D. Dumonstier (1633)

4. KARL GUSTAF

By most narrators and artists, Karl Gustaf is represented as fat and bloated, but as a young man he made a different impression. This portrait from the early 1640's gives an idea of how he looked to Christina, his enamoured playmate and cousin, up till 1645, when her personal liking for him suddenly ceased.

Formula as the authoritative interpretation of the Augsburg Confession, the Swedish church would be faced with the possibility of being considered schismatical.

Matthiae and the queen were of a completely different opinion. If, according to them, the Concord Formula was accepted by Sweden, then her freedom of movement at the peace-conference would be restricted. If Sweden should become a member of the German Empire, as was intended, it would be unwise to adhere to a creed that not only divided the Reformed church from the Lutherans, but aroused opposition in Lutheranism itself. It meant that Sweden would take sides with the Saxon Electorate as against the unionist Helmstedt theology.

In confirming the privileges of the clergy, therefore, the queen omitted the proposed paragraph giving the clergy the right to determine doctrine and the acceptance or rejection of the Concord Formula. Queen Christina "saved Sweden from the Concord Book" (Curt Weibull).

In reality Christina had inherited from her father the fear of too independent a church in Sweden. When, in the same year, 1647, she was working on a proposal the Bishops had made in 1624, for a new governing body in the Church, a "General Consistory", she inserted, in her own hand, a number of revisions in different versions. She laid it down that the consistory should include not only the clergy, but also "politicians". The archbishop was to be president, but his deputy, the chancellor, "was to have precedence over all bishops". In this general consistory Christina maintained and put into practice the principle of equal status for laity and clergy. One of the "politicians" was to be a "notary". These "politicians" were to be "well-educated men, who . . . had studied theology, philosophy and law at our academies". The bishops were no longer to be allowed to ordain clergy without some supervision.

After the queen's secretary had made a final draft of this proposal, other innovations were introduced. The queen retained the right of being present at the sessions if her presence was desirable. The sole authority superior to the consistory was to be Her Royal Majesty. In this version a stipulation was included that the consistory should keep a list of "all foreign heretics and adherents of false religions", and take good care to see that no "false doctrines were spread and no false religious practices allowed". On the other hand, religious freedom was to be safeguarded and foreigners of another faith "were not to be provoked by cunning clerics to disputes in matters of religious belief, and then persecuted and driven out of the country". Hitherto it had been forbidden to study at a Catholic university. The bishops wanted to extend this prohibition to Calvinist universities.

Once more the queen's draft was produced, and once again some fresh and radical alterations were made in it. The bishops' representations were entirely ignored. The chancellor was now to be seated on the archbishop's left, and after him were to rank all the other "politicians". In front, on the right, the Bishop of Linköping was to sit, with all the other ecclesiastics behind him. This new draft contained some notable additions made by the queen, and these clearly prove her freethinking attitude and her dependence on the unionism favoured by Johannes Matthiae. The term "pure doctrine" she changed to "correct doctrine". In the third draft she left out the adjective "evangelical" before "consistory"; she struck out the words "not to appoint a Papist or Calvinist". She did not want any private individual to be forbidden to employ a Papist or Calvinist; soon she would find it necessary to admit such persons to her own service.

But she went further. In the third version she struck out the condition that theologians "should not be allowed to study theology at Papist, Jesuit or Calvinist academies, colleges or schools". She struck out, too, expressions such as "especially the idolatry and superstition of the Papists", also the word "heretic".

Thus Christina, for the first time, revealed her new opinions—she was neutral as between the various churches. A proposal by the bishops laid it down that teachers should take an oath to encourage their pupils to adhere "to our Christian religion as it exists at present in our country and as it has been confirmed by the Council of Uppsala and other authorities". Christina struck out the words "as it exists at present in our country". She no doubt wished to protect Swedish students from "false religion and harmful opinions". But among these she did not include either Catholicism or Calvinism. She thereby showed that tolerance and neutrality which Chanut had noted and admired. She attached herself entirely to Johannes Matthiae's liberalism, and unequivocally opposed the uncompromising attitude of the Swedish church. A student of these important documents has, with justice, observed: "Christina's proposals are not a mere mechanical compilation. On the contrary they emphatically bear the stamp of the young queen's individual views on theology and politics."

The vigour with which Christina opposed Swedish orthodoxy may also be seen in the disputes which, after the parliament of 1647 and before the signature of the Peace of Westphalia, arose in connection with appointments to the university of Uppsala.

The opposing views in parliament had been settled by a prudent compromise. Axel Oxenstierna, however, continued to press for the acceptance by Sweden of the Concord Formula. Due to the appointment of Lenaeus in March 1647 as archbishop of Uppsala, a professorship in the faculty of theology was vacant. The other professor was sent as a superintendent to Riga, so that two posts were left vacant. On the orthodox side two decided anti-unionists, Klingius and Lithman, were put forward as candidates. The accepted candidate had been Terserus, who had some years before been proposed as Professor of Hebrew, but on account of Oxenstierna's opposition had been transferred to Åbo, and therefore had ceased to be taken into consideration. This was not at all to the young queen's liking. She had had a talk with him at the house of parliament and decided to try to bring this undoubted unionist to Uppsala.

Now it came to a regular tug-of-war. Axel Oxenstierna bent all his energies to get Klingius appointed. As chancellor of the university Oxenstierna had the duty of reporting on all university affairs, but Christina herself dealt with the appointment of professors of theology, without consulting him. Oxenstierna sent the queen a letter recommending Klingius; he said he would regard his appointment as an especial kindness to himself. Three days later the queen went to Uppsala, but without the chancellor of the university. After the queen returned the council met and decided against Klingius as a candidate. As usual, Johannes Matthiae was behind this; he regarded Klingius as the man who was responsible for his defeat. Christina, however, was not content with this victory; she was quite determined, despite the opposition of Oxenstierna and the orthodox professors, to have Terserus appointed as professor at Uppsala. And in this she succeeded.

CHAPTER SIX

Christina's Conflicts

I. A "HEROINE"

AXEL OXENSTIERNA paid regular visits to the castle of the Three Crowns to tutor the young queen. At an age when most girls are occupied with children's games, the fatherless young princess listened, for hours at a time, and with wide-open eyes, to the most important statesman of his generation who, from his inexhaustible store of experience, drew those descriptions of scenes, of fateful occurrences and principles which he considered useful to impart to the future ruler of the country. From other sources we know that Axel Oxenstierna was a methodical and thoughtful man, who liked to choose his words with care and take his time over decisions which might have important consequences. He was political wisdom personified; perhaps a rather dry character, certainly without any lyrical flights of thought and utterly opposed to showing any enthusiasm for anything. It was only when he spoke of the late king that there was a tremor in his voice.

Christina must have perceived quite early on that hers would be a singular fate. Under the direction of a political genius of the first order she was enabled to study the world of political developments and, like almost no one else, analyse all things from first principles. Later she frequently came into conflict with Axel Oxenstierna and in discussion with him spoke impetuously, even shed tears. She could provoke him to use some ill-considered expression on this or that topic, as occurred during the lively debate about Adler Salvius's appointment to the council. Yet she always held him in high esteem, and often gave expression to her great respect for his sense of duty and his extraordinary devotion. It accorded with her innermost convictions when, with warm words of commendation, she gave her reasons for raising him to the rank of count. In her autobiography, too, she set up a monument in honour of Oxenstierna:

> He was a very learned man who had studied a wide variety of subjects in his youth. He went on with these studies even when he was occupied with very important matters. He was remarkably efficient and possessed a thorough knowledge of international politics. He was aware of the strength and the weakness of all European countries. He was wise, with remarkable foresight and generosity of character, and possessed of unique talents. He was untiring, persevering in his work at all times with unfailing industry. In this he found satisfaction, and if a period of repose intervened he took recreation in doing something useful. In eating and drinking he was moderate, in so far as this was possible in a country and in an age when this virtue was unknown. He slept well, and used to say that nothing ever kept him from sleeping or roused him from sleep apart from two things, the news of the late king's death, and the report of the battle of Nordlingen.* I have often been told that on going to bed, he laid aside his worries with his clothes, and let them be till the next day. For the rest he was ambitious, but loyal; it was impossible to corrupt him. He was somewhat slow and phlegmatic. . . . He was one of the greatest obstacles I had to overcome when I made the resolve to give up everything for Thee (God), for I loved this great man as a second father. . . . I owe him this testimony since, although I knew almost all the greatest and most brilliant personalities of the time, I met few who could stand comparison with him.

Such was the powerful impression Axel Oxenstierna made on the young princess. He was a typical humanist of the old school, firmly attached to that combination of Christian dependence on God with stoic philosophy, which, though logically indefensible, was nevertheless very characteristic of educated people at the beginning of the seventeenth century. Christina came into contact with this stoic world in various ways. Chanut, in his remarkably accurate characterization of the queen, who was then aged

* Two great battles were fought here in the course of the Thirty Years War. Here the one of 1634 is meant, wherein the hitherto unbeaten Swedish army was defeated by the Imperialist and Spanish troops.

twenty-two, was astonished at the prominent part various virtues played in her life. It was this that led Axel Oxenstierna, in a confidential talk with a delegate from Brandenburg, to declare that the young queen was on the way to becoming a "heroine". This expression was also used about the young queen in the admiring comments of her Palatinate relations. Axel Oxenstierna wished to indicate the human ideal to which he and the other instructors of the queen felt themselves to be dedicated, and which, for a time, made a deep impression on her as well, although as she grew older it was to be replaced by a deeper understanding of Christianity.

In fact the ancient stoic ideal became, so to speak, a generally recognized aim of education among cultured classes in the late sixteenth and early seventeenth century. On all sides sensitive people were deeply impressed by the ideal of a strong personality able to rise above the anxieties and strains of existence through self-conquest, subduing passion and attaining *Apathie*, that is, a lofty indifference, the only effective safeguard for men's souls against all that was low and evil, the only guarantee of peace and quietness in which, free from all excitements, the noblest characteristics of the human soul could develop. We should not be surprised at finding this doctrine united with Catholic beliefs; after all, Catholic doctrine taught that men's good qualities were not utterly destroyed by the fall. It is more surprising to find that Stoicism struck deep roots also in Protestant countries. We might have assumed that Stoicism would be entirely contrary to Luther's teaching about man's utter helplessness. But it should be recalled that Luther's pessimistic judgment of mankind was modified at an early date.

It has been said that the young Christina's way of life could only be called stoical in a very limited sense, and that it would be more correct to describe her views as a kind of humanism tinged by classicism. This is wrong. The only correct description of Christina's attitude in her youth is summed up in the word stoic, and she herself uses this word to describe her original opinions. "Stoicism", she wrote once, "was my philosophy for a long time past, but it did not bring me happiness." On another occasion, in one of her maxims, she dealt with the contrast between the two ways of life which she had tried; she called the first Stoicism, the second mysticism. Her contemporaries also spoke of Stoicism; Justus Lipsius published instructions on the stoic way of living; French scholars were able to show that literally all the writers of the century, Christian and non-Christian alike, were influenced by the stoic virtues; and a profound French student of the period, studying the human ideal of the early seventeenth century, came to the conclusion that it should, in accordance with the terminology of the time, be described as "Neo-Stoicism".

It is therefore quite right and proper to describe Christina's attitude in her youth as stoical, though as a young girl she had no idea there was any conflict of principle between Stoicism and Christianity. She only came to understand this when life had shaken her proud belief in mankind and taught her that it is by no means certain that man can master his passions by his own strength, and that to a true Christian a quite different path to peace and happiness is revealed.

Christina thought of herself as a "heroine". She was remarkably self-conscious in her attitude. The detailed notes she wrote down later about the years she spent in Sweden, show that she was convinced of the greatness of her achievement. It was by her own merit that Sweden had become greater than ever, so she imagined, and she was never willing to admit that during her reign, her country had been caught up in extraordinary difficulties both political and economic. She often spoke of having devoted her whole life to her country and her subjects; it is, however, hard to see what specific actions of hers she could be thinking of. She also said that in her reign the Swedish armies had always been victorious. She considered the Peace of Westphalia her own work, her personal achievement.

With rapt attention the young princess read the lives of the great heroes of ancient times, Cyrus, Alexander, Caesar, Scipio; surprisingly often she used to declare that she held them in even higher honour than her celebrated father. She also told how she, as a young girl, achieved self-control. She entitled one of the chapters of a draft for her autobiography: "The power I have over myself and my passions". Indeed she practised these exercises so much that she became an expert at dissembling. This was fully in accord with the code of behaviour of the time, which determined that a prince must at all cost conceal his inmost feelings and at the same time try to get other men to reveal theirs. With Christina this often led to duplicity and deceit. Another chapter of the autobiography she planned to write was to deal with "the resolutions I have formed to show myself, by my industry and hard work, worthy of my birth and high position".

Christina's sense of duty, her deliberate cult of rectitude, and her exalted sense of morality filled all those who knew her with astonishment. An Italian Jesuit called Malines was as enthusiastic as Chanut about these features of Christina's character. He was impressed by "a complete absence of vanity, combined with human greatness and a thorough and correct appreciation of all human conditions, as if she was born in possession of the quintessence of moral philosophy". It was Christina's highest aim never to do anything which could cause her to blush with shame and at all costs to subordinate her own happiness to her duty. . . . It is, of course, another question to what extent she could distinguish between her duty and her personal interests.

At an early age she thought that everyone admired her and considered her someone unique, a kind of faultless masterpiece of creation. She herself recounts how she listened with pleasure to the most servile flattery that was constantly bestowed on her, and how she was "exceedingly self-satisfied". As one of her councillors said, the young princess possessed an "extraordinary ingenium".

She was very conscious of it when she showed such brilliance in foreign languages as a young girl, when she astounded the learned Comenius with her mastery of Latin, when she buried herself in learned studies and thought it would not be possible to find anyone sufficiently skilled to teach her. Later, however, she came to realize that the demon of pride had long held her in its power, and she regarded this pride of hers as the gravest of her faults; in later life she constantly strove to overcome her exaggerated and unrealistic self-complacency.

In her early years her pride was prompted by a theory that gave support and justification to her stoic faith—that is to say, the idea, current at that time, of the utterly exceptional place occupied by an anointed monarch. Christina held this view in absolute earnest. She often spoke of her own greatness. She was of the opinion that God had given her a heart which nothing could satisfy, and she called her own character noble and good. Without apparent embarrassment she compared herself with the greatest characters of history, and thought she had a likeness to Alexander. Like Louis XIV and the Stuart King James I, she thought of herself as a representative of God and always emphasized that she was not accountable to any man. When she became a Catholic, she was bound to find it hard to accommodate herself to the practice of confession. As a young queen she believed God had called her to undertake a unique task. She was the leader of what she thought to be the strongest military power in Europe, and responsible for its fate only to God. She strove honourably to school herself for a complete fulfilment of her duty, and she became a skilful and successful expert in political affairs. She was, however, unable to distinguish between the greatness of her calling and her own human destiny. She was on every side admired for her genius, her greatness and her honour, and the homage she received never made her feel uncomfortable. She thought it was justified and accepted it as her due. She was convinced that she was unique among her contemporaries.

In all this, her tendency to exaggerate touched on the eccentric. In many respects Christina made a deep impression, but her talents were over-rated by herself and her contemporaries. By no means can she be classed with the great figures of history; she had not inherited many of the noble human qualities of her father. But from two such important princely families as the Hohenzollerns and the Vasas, she certainly did inherit some exceptional qualities: courage and a strong will above all. It is hardly possible to consider her as highly intellectual. It is true that she is often described as having first-class intellectual gifts, as one who could correspond on equal terms with the scholars of her time in various branches of learning. When we read her letters to these scholars, however, we find that she never put forward really interesting and original points of view. She was content with agreeable phrases, but these were in most cases polished up by her elegant French secretary. She entered into correspondence with such gifted men as Pascal, Gassendi and Descartes, but none of them could have found her letters particularly stimulating. The only one of these whom she came to know well, Descartes, was decidedly disappointed with her and declared she had no understanding of philosophy. On the other hand, she took an interest in books and manuscripts, was a considerable collector, enjoyed being in a scholarly atmosphere, had a sense for beauty and a love of art and music. All this would seem to fit the notion of a gifted student rather than that of a genius.

We should remember that there were other important women at the time who felt themselves to be as independent as Christina, and were marked by the same unbelievable pride. Two ladies of the French nobility, with whom Christina corresponded and whom she greatly admired, are particularly striking examples of this; the first was "la Grande Mademoiselle", the Duchess of Montpensier, daughter of Gaston of Orléans, the second, Madame de Longueville, sister of the Prince de Condé.

During the Fronde, Mademoiselle de Montpensier rode side by side with Condé at the head of his troops, "wearing pearls and ostrich-feathers, with corkscrew curls and caparisoned like a cavalry officer; a veritable goddess of victory of the age of the *précieuses* blue-stockings and the bombastic metaphor". She allowed herself to be portrayed as Pallas Athene, and she fired cannon against the foe when necessary. She was not concerned with the blood of an inferior class that flowed in her veins, but held herself to be of divine descent until, at length, she fell in love with a repulsive creature called Lauzun, and thus came to a miserable and humiliating end. This grotesque though important woman shows that the Swedish queen was not the only woman of her day and age to be proud, to despise men and to be full of self-admiration. Both women were to succumb in the same humiliating way to the passion, which they imagined they had mastered.

Mme de Longueville differed, both mentally and intellectually, from "la Grande Mademoiselle". But with her we find qualities which we are tempted to describe as unwomanly. Once, for example, with her blue eyes and fair hair, she stood hidden behind a curtain and coldbloodedly looked on while Coligny fought a duel with the Duc de Guise on the Place Royale. During the siege of Paris in 1648 she deserted her brother, the Prince de Condé, and followed La Rochefoucauld like a slave. When the Prince was taken prisoner, she fled from Normandy to Holland, amid unheard-of hardships and dangers. She took it on herself to start negotiations with the Spaniards, which was bound to annoy the great soldier Turenne. But Mme de Longueville was not without feeling for people in distress; she went to the Cistercian nuns at Port Royal, withdrew into a convent and wrote a general confession, which still exists and wherein she frankly and without any attempt at justification admitted that pride had ruled her life with such terrible rigour.

It would be possible to name other noble ladies of the time, warring, intriguing, unbearable in their pride, who finally collapsed, either through a humiliating passion, or by coming to realize that they might devote their lives to more serious tasks. At the papal court there were such mannish women, who proudly modelled themselves on the heroes of antiquity, defied the man's world and tried to win honours usually reserved to men. Christina thought herself unique; but there were more women of her kind than she imagined.

2. "LUTHERANISM CANNOT BE THE TRUTH"

Before long Christina felt the earth quake beneath her feet, in ecclesiastical and religious affairs. She looked at religion with the eye of reason; she wanted to know just how things happened. She was familiar with the latest scientific knowledge and she wanted to find out how the church's doctrine could accommodate itself to these remarkable discoveries. Was it really true that the earth was no longer the centre of the universe? Or that there were other, far larger, worlds than this? Or that man lived merely in an insignificant corner of the universe, and was wrong in imagining himself to be the centre of it? To get an answer to these questions, which her Swedish theologians were obviously in no position to discuss, she called on important men abroad, Descartes for example, and summoned them to her court. Her attempts to get Catholic priests to come to Stockholm were always made with emphasis on one requisite—they must be "mathematicians", men well acquainted with the contemporary sciences.

She was the only person in Sweden who drew a logical conclusion from the never-ending disputes of the Protestant theologians. Whatever one might say of the other religions, Lutheran Protestantism could not possibly be the true church. The reason it could not be true was that it lacked stability and unity, that Protestants could not live side by side with one another without splitting into sects, while everyone declared his interpretation was the right one. At the beginning Christina knew nothing of Catholicism. She acquired some knowledge from her long talks with Chanut, and got the notion that most of what she had been taught was wrong. The picture Protestants gave of Rome must, she thought, be a malicious caricature. Above all she found that Catholic doctrine had unity and consistency, whereas Protestants were divided into sects, each of which claimed that its interpretation of the Scriptures was the right one. She made the same discovery as John Henry Newman much later, namely, that though there might be human corruption and depravity in the Roman Church, doctrine was uncorrupted and uniform, a logical continuation of the teaching of Christ.

Her gradual realization of the truth seemed to exacerbate her neurosis. With loyal obedience she listened to the interminable sermons of the court chaplains, among them the dangerous Erik Emporagrius, whom she detested. She went to the Lutheran Holy Communion. In the course of fulfilling this meaningless duty she was tormented by persistent uneasiness, by the thought that this cannot be true, cannot be right. Sooner or later, she felt, she would have to break with it.

Quietly the young queen, who was admired but naturally very isolated, struggled through a crisis, whose nature we can to some extent understand from her own account and from her talks with the Italian Jesuits who had come from Rome. This period, full of perplexity and unrest, lasted some five years, from 1643 to 1648. This period may be described as a crisis of belief, but it seems to have been entirely intellectual; it was an unsatisfied longing for a clear revelation of the truth. Christina tested the various religions and compared them with one another. She began to suspect that articles of faith were perhaps mere political inventions intended to deceive simple people. For a time she thought that no historical religion could be truer than another. She herself admitted that she had doubted the highest mysteries of Christianity. She had, of course, believed in a Supreme Being, but had doubts about particular Christian dogmas, especially the Incarnation, Redemption, the Resurrection, and miracles. It is noteworthy that her critical attitude persisted long after her conversion. Christina herself described it later: "I thought nothing of the religion in which I was brought up. . . . As soon as I was grown up I made up a religion for myself, and waited for the religion which you (God) would bestow on me, for which I had such an intense longing. You know how often, in words that meant nothing to the crowd, I prayed to you to enlighten me, and promised to be obedient even if it should cost my happiness, even my life."

If she expressed herself in a rather affected way, it was because this was how the queen wanted to be remembered by future generations. But her account tallies with the statements of her contemporaries. Christina's point of view, in the years before she made the acquaintance of the French freethinkers and the Italian Jesuits, may be summed up as follows:

She believed in the existence of a personal, all-powerful God, to whom she turned using language that was meaningless to those surrounding her. With regard to certain dogmatic details, such as the "highest mysteries", she had a critical attitude, though she did not deny them. The great respect for the truth of the Gospels which, according to Chanut, she showed at first, seems to have disappeared gradually in the course of this critical period. Her new religion could not logically be linked with Protestantism, and evidently it corresponded even less to Catholicism. She recognized strict principles of morality, and found in reason the key to the rectitude of men's actions. She seems to have been without any idea of Christ as Redeemer. Her very awareness that she was alone in harbouring such free, heretical views must have been profoundly disturbing to her.

3. THE NEUROSIS INCREASES

Various circumstances contributed to increase Christina's discomfort. Again and again she must have asked herself, What am I really? She was not like other people. But did this mean that she was superior to all other women, or that in some puzzling way she had turned out a failure? From her autobiography we can see how these questions tormented her. She thanked God that she was not like other women, that she was free from the weakness of her sex, and had a truly manly character. There is no doubt that she held femininity in contempt, despised those creatures who were content to take second place to men, who subordinated themselves, who obeyed and were excluded from the only really worthy human activities—politics, science and art.

She may, however, have become aware of something quite different: that she was a woman whom no man looked upon with favour, or wished to be intimate with. Yes, she was certainly different from other women, but perhaps this was not altogether due to a superiority of intellect or will-power; might it not signify an inferiority, an abnormality? She was very conscious of being a woman, and often defended herself violently against suggestions that she was a hermaphrodite. She knew her body was capable of bearing children. But she could not fail to notice that all the distinguished men whom she approached drew back in something like terror, though etiquette obliged them to observe a decorous servility. Beautiful women attracted her, and she must often have made a comparison between herself and her friend of the same age, Ebba Sparre, whose beauty inflamed men's senses and exercised a powerful attraction on her also.

It is evident that Christina was soon in the grip of a serious neurosis. Signs of this we have already observed in her foolish altercation with Magnus Gabriel de la Gardie, when she was more inclined to trust a notorious adventurer and liar like Schlippenbach than a trusted friend, and was hardly conscious of the fact that this was entirely due to her wish to find a means of discarding her former favourite. Subsequently she took up with other men, such as the handsome duellist and adventurer Claes Tott, only to forget them as quickly. She burrowed into the medicine of the time, and studied all the books she could procure on the subject of unusual pregnancies, defective children, "hot and dry" women who were incapable of bearing children, and manlike women. All this time she lived in absolute sexual continence. Neither during her time in Sweden, nor when she was in Italy, was there the slightest indication that she had sexual relations with a man, all statements to the contrary come from the most dubious sources. It must be said, however, that this was in no way due to any lack of interest in sex on Christina's part. On the contrary, her impulses were strong and she spoke openly about her temptations. She said that her impulses were as powerful as her pride, and that she had often been near the abyss—that is, sexual surrender—and then had been saved at the last moment. She said that if she had been born a man, she would probably have wrecked her life in adventures with women. Undoubtedly she had a normal desire for men.

We have seen how this desire lay concealed behind a platonic passion in the style of the *précieuses*. We have also shown what a neurosis this was bound to produce. The strain on her nerves grew stronger, during the time she governed in Sweden she was almost continuously ill. When she found a doctor at last who understood her condition—the French doctor Bourdelot—he diagnosed, in some trepidation, the parlous condition in which the queen found herself and succeeded in curing her by deflating her superiority complex, cutting down her hours of work, inducing her to adopt a better diet, to take more sleep and occupy herself with something more diverting and more digestible than old folios and tiring council-sessions. From the learned medical terms Bourdelot uses, it is clear he had diagnosed her neurosis: her condition was caused by the irrational way she lived, and the remedy was to persuade her to relax, take more rest, occupy herself with pleasant and harmless amusements, and give up trying to act the part of a disciplined superman who trusted nobody and taxed her nerves and will-power to an excessive degree.

The most important thing was that Christina had undoubtedly become conscious of the irrevocable contradiction between her duty as Queen of Sweden and her physical condition. Had she been a man—and to be this was her life's ambition—the problem would have been easier to solve. But she was, unfortunately, a woman, and even more, an abnormal woman in certain respects. She had no wish to play the part of wife and mother, and felt a contempt for all specifically womanly qualities. This was her nature, and she neither would nor could change it. She was repelled by the idea of being a wife. Though throughout her reign she was exhorted on all sides to marry, she always evaded an answer. She knew very well that it was her highest duty to give an heir to the throne, she ought not to shirk this duty, she was very well aware of the dangerous consequences of her dying without leaving an heir; but how could she surrender to a man? Probably as a consequence of her mother's fate, she shrank from child-bearing, or rather had a perfect horror of it. That is a proven fact. We may, however, surmise that this aversion concealed the disturbing, unexpressed reflection that perhaps, however distasteful it might be, she would give birth, but that her children might turn out to be unfit or abnormal—"a Nero quite as likely as an Augustus". The medical authorities had declared that she was a "hot and dry" type of woman, and that children of such a mother were often deformed, or the woman was unable to have any children at all.

After many years of brooding over the problem, Christina hit on the solution. She could no longer remain Queen of Sweden unless she married and gave the country a successor to the throne. But as she would not marry, she must abdicate. Before doing this, however, she must see to it that there should be a successor who was really suitable and fulfilled her high ideals of what a King of Sweden should be.

She now set to work with energy, used all her cunning, her dissimulation and eloquence to implement her decision. She had literally all the leading men of the country against her. She was still in her early twenties. Axel Oxenstierna and the council, composed of strong-willed, experienced and able men, condemned the plan with all their strength as completely impracticable. But Christina was to carry it through.

4. THE CATHOLIC IDEAL OF VIRGINITY

Here we must refer to another motive which Christina has mentioned herself. It is hard to be definite about it, and it must be discussed with some reservation, since it appears only in a late source; but it cannot be passed over entirely.

The draft of Christina's autobiography, which is written in the third person by her secretary, but revised and corrected by Christina, has two passages about the queen's leaning to Catholicism. It is true that Christina crossed out the original text and began with a revised version, but the following can be read quite clearly:

> The first occasion on which she paid any attention to the Catholic religion was when people told her that the Catholic Church would not allow layfolk to read the Bible, that it held celibacy in respect, and believed in the fires of purgatory. One day, when she was taking a rest in the company of her tutor, she called out: "How beautiful this religion is. I should like to belong to it." It was proposed to give her a beating for speaking like this, but her aunt, who would have had to administer the punishment, thought better of it. The queen, she said, is only nine years old and such a punishment would not be proper.

It will be seen that there were three aspects of Catholicism that had aroused the queen's interest. Above all it was celibacy, the ideal of virginity, that fascinated this precocious, nine-year-old girl, the notion that it was not an unseemly defect, but rather a great virtue, to live a celibate life. Catholicism, she went on to consider, gave an especially high place to innocent virgins, and treated them with great respect. Protestantism, on the contrary, regarded virginity for religious reasons as of no value.

In a later passage of the manuscript we can see quite clearly the following: "It was her attraction to celibacy that gave the first impulse to the queen's honourable change of religion."

In an alternative reading there is a note which shows even more clearly the connection between her early leaning to celibacy and her later resolve "never to marry".

Thus Christina admitted that the Catholic ideal of virginity impressed her in her early years. How much her physical constitution and her upbringing contributed to this enthusiasm we have seen already. It is not perhaps rare to find similar physiological causes in women mystics and virgin saints; to a non-religious observer this fervour may appear childish and meaningless. Here we might perhaps look for the solution to one of the secrets in Christina's life, not an unlikely one at that, if we bear in mind that other great women felt drawn to the same pure life of a virgin at a tender age and found in it the same sense of freedom. We must examine the conditions that gave it all a concrete significance for Christina.

At an early age she must have perceived that she was not constituted quite like other people, and now a remarkable world opened up before her, in which it was not considered shameful to lead a life of virginity, but on the contrary was regarded as worthy and honourable. We know from the biographies of Joan of Arc and Catherine of Siena, to mention only these two examples, that in their childhood they were irrestistibly attracted to the ideal of virgin purity; the literature of Catholicism has many examples of young girls promising God perpetual chastity—long before they were sexually awakened and liable to feel restless or anxious about this way of life.

Something like this may well have taken place with the lonely little princess in the castle in Stockholm. Matured at an early age, she began to look into medical writings, reflect on her mother's tragedy and become aware of her own bodily constitution. It may well be that her vague feeling that an uncommon destiny awaited her gathered strength. In the depths of her soul, buried beneath the masculine ideals of character and education that had been impressed on her, her desire for a life of perpetual purity, for perpetual virginity, may have quietly ripened within her. This desire was stimulated yet further when she became conscious of the apparently insoluble contradiction in which she lived; between her duty to marry and give her country an heir, and the possibility that she would be unable to bear normal children. But if the succession to the throne could be assured by her making Karl Gustav her heir, her duty to her country would be fulfilled. Otherwise she was condemned to go on living as a celibate, a way of life that was unusual in Sweden, indeed was regarded with contempt; yet outside Protestantism there was a society in which this difficulty was no problem, a society in which chaste young women were honoured and respected: according to her own testimony, this was the earliest motive for her decision to embrace the Catholic faith.

When Christina grew up, she was possessed by a powerful longing for love, a desire which she openly acknowledged. But it was obvious that in her case this desire could not be satisfied. As she realized this, her dream-wish revived; it grew stronger and stronger, and led to the conclusion that a great love could find no human fulfilment. From this point, her path was to lead on to the mysticism that filled her life in her closing years.

5. A PORTRAIT OF CHRISTINA

It may be useful to pause here a moment and consider the portrait of Christina that adorns the cover of this book. It was painted by Sebastian Bourdon, a French salon-painter who had done innumerable portraits of the queen. He painted also the well-known picture of Christina on horseback, which she presented to the King of Spain and which attracts attention in our day as it is displayed in the Prado. The famous picture of Christina now in the National Museum in Stockholm—a copy of it is kept in the castle of Häringe—was also painted by Bourdon in 1653. The previous year, immediately after his arrival in Sweden, Bourdon made the remarkable portrait which is at Bystra, the one reproduced on the cover of this book. A close resemblance can be seen between the two portraits. That of 1653 is, like the picture of Christina on horseback, a drawing-room portrait, obviously flattering but also, we might say, banal. The Bystra portrait, with its flowing, almost untidy, hair, is distinguished from the picture in the National Museum especially by the fact that it betrays a lack of harmony, does not even omit an indication of the neurosis to which the queen was subject. Her face, in spite of the fact that the artist has enlarged and improved the look of her eyes, reveals great sensitiveness and an obvious restlessness. Masculine characteristics are, in this picture of Christina, not yet so emphatically depicted, but who could help being impressed by the fact that this is a representation of a very remarkable woman? Earlier Christina had been painted a number of times by David Beck. He did not flatter her like Bourdon; he never tried to produce drawing-room portraits. He may thus have come closer to giving a true picture of her external appearance. But he had no understanding for the secret of her psychology. He painted a self-confident, vigorous, peasant-like matron with a splendid bosom and an appearance of calm. The Frenchman Bourdon, however, at once discerned the fluttering restlessness and mysterious tension that went to make up the soul of this singular woman.

The eyes in the Bystra portrait speak plainly; in their flickering they reveal a fearful anxiety.

CHAPTER SEVEN

The Great Intrigue

I. A SEMI-VICTORY

So Queen Christina was firmly resolved never to marry, and in spite of the fact that for years her entourage kept pressing her to choose a husband and provide the kingdom with an heir, she always refused. Sometimes she promised she would consider the matter, at other times she said the only possible choice would be Karl Gustav, Count Palatine; but then she declared again that there could be no question of marriage for her: "I am unable to marry. That is how it is. I need not give my reasons. I have no inclination to marry. I have earnestly prayed God to let me change my attitude, but I have not been able to do so." If this was an indication of her Catholic leanings, the words "I am unable to marry" would not make much sense, for even as a Catholic she could of course have married. It was also said that "Her Majesty could not commit herself to marrying and had good grounds for it; though she preferred not to say what they were, she hoped not to have to be ashamed of them in God's sight". Probably a whole complex of conscious and unconscious motives prompted her attitude, and it would be too hazardous to make out that one motive was more decisive than another.

Christina was by no means the irresponsible woman she is often made out to be. She had her faults, sometimes her pride broke through, her behaviour was certainly not always endearing. But when she was faced with important decisions, she never acted thoughtlessly or on the spur of the moment. We know that she was possessed of a proud strong moral sense, always wanting to do what was right and eager to carry out her duty. Her most pressing duty as Queen of Sweden was, however, to see that the future of the kingdom was assured, and most important of all, the *sine qua non*, was to provide an heir to the throne; failing this there was danger of internal conflict, perhaps a rising of the nobles, and a strong risk of an elective kingdom being established with all its uncertainties, or claims to the throne from her Vasa kinsfolk in Poland. Christina bore all this in mind, but after much thought she was still firmly resolved not to marry on any account. So another way had to be found to safegaurd the interests of the kingdom; she would have to persuade the country to choose an heir, and it would have to be someone with the necessary qualifications: where was such a man to be found?

There was only one man whom Christina could possibly think of, her cousin Duke Karl Gustav, son of Katharina, her father's stepsister, and Johann Kasimir, Count Palatine. She had often expressed admiration for his qualities and said she had confidence in him. On the other hand she had rather insultingly rejected him as her suitor. To present him with the throne without giving him her hand, in itself constituted a delicate situation. Moreover the Counts Palatine, though related to the royal house of Sweden, enjoyed no great popularity there. Many people looked askance at Johann Kasimir, though Gustavus Adolphus had always shown great confidence in his brother-in-law and they were on friendly terms. But a political group had formed around the Counts Palatine of which an important member was Carl Carlsson Gyllenhielm, Gustavus Adolphus' stepbrother. Naturally there was a certain amount of hostility between this group and the Oxenstiernas when it became evident that the Counts Palatine coveted the Swedish throne for Karl Gustav. When, for reasons that have still not been clarified, Christina put an end to their friendship, but without losing her respect for him, the rejected suitor found himself in a very awkward position. Later, as king, he was to show himself possessed of exceptional powers of decision, and his amazing intrepidity was to carry him from one victory to another, but he proved quite helpless and anxiety-ridden when it came to wooing the woman he loved. Not that he scorned women—in fact over the years he fathered a considerable number of illegitimate children. But towards Christina he always felt disconcerted and unsure of himself.

Of course she held all the trump cards, his fate was wholly in her hands.

Historical research has disclosed that Carl Carlsson Gyllenhielm was the first to provide a solution. As early as 1646—that is, immediately after the queen had rejected Karl Gustav—he suggested that there was perhaps a way out, apart from this marriage: the queen could arrange that in due course the succession went to a certain family, say that of the Counts Palatine. Gyllenhielm, who was fully aware of the risks involved, considered it inadvisable to give the heir to the throne a dukedom of his own, and he and the Palatinate recalled that Gustavus Adolphus himself had mentioned Karl Gustav as a possible candidate for the throne after his death.

At first the plan seemed to have little prospect of success. How indeed were Council and Estates to be convinced of the need to nominate a foreigner as heir to the throne while the queen still reigned? The question of marriage came up at the 1647 Diet. The queen sent a message to the Estates that she needed more time to consider the matter. "Her Royal Majesty wanted to reflect whether, apart from this solution, other ways could not be found to safeguard the country." She hoped the Estates would think over these possibilities and determine upon a "sure succession" for the realm. But Karl Gustav's name was not mentioned on that occasion, and he still lived in hope of winning her hand one day. Then the queen told him frankly she would never marry him for love. However, most people knew nothing of this, and it was generally assumed that the queen would eventually give in. It was time Karl Gustav was given a wider field of activities: the queen decided to appoint him commander-in-chief of the Swedish army in Germany. But the Diet did not like the idea: how could the army be entrusted to the Count Palatine before he married the queen? Not till he was her husband should his appointment as commander-in-chief be considered. Curiously enough, Christina found herself compelled to accept this condition: she promised to marry him; whereupon, in February 1648, he was appointed commander-in-chief. But Christina let him know at once that her promise of marriage was a pure subterfuge on her part, simply to ensure his appointment. For the first time Christina was indulging in machiavellian political intrigue, and Karl Gustav had to promise to play his part as apparent husband-elect. She had a long interview with him before he left for Germany, at which Magnus Gabriel de la Gardie and Johannes Matthiae were also present. She said she wanted neither to end all hope of a marriage nor to put it to him as a certainty, but promised that should she ever marry, he would be her husband; there could be no question of any other man. But she wanted to see if she could not get him elected as heir to the throne without necessarily marrying him at all, though if the Estates were against it she would have to swallow the bitter pill and marry after all.

At the 1649 Diet the Estates approached the queen and begged her to keep her promise. But she retorted with her own proposal: Karl Gustav should be proclaimed heir to the throne now, before the wedding, or the realm would otherwise be without a successor if she were to die suddenly. Of the many who rose to speak in the Council chamber, all were against the plan. Jakob de la Gardie was concerned, as an army general, lest Karl Gustav might grow desperate at the uncertainty, and he too might then remain single; and what good would that be? And supposing Christina took a fancy to someone else, what would become of the duke? If he were to have children, "one set of heirs would have to give way to the other". Moreover, Karl Gustav might force someone else on the kingdom, his brother, or other of his kith and kin, and this would mean there would be other hereditary princes to provide with dukedoms. Jealousy would arise between the queen and the hereditary princes, locking them in bitter rivalry.

Christina had her own views about this opposition. She kept an eye on what was happening in Europe and had a shrewd suspicion that certain intrigues were on foot, for the nobility had leanings towards an elective state. The Councillors openly favoured the elective system "as is current in Poland", and "the Privy Council want an elective state again"; such was her summary of the situation. "If anything happened to me, I wager that Duke Karl would not come to the throne."

As the opposition showed no signs of relenting, Christina had to play her trump card. Having once declared, "I am unable to marry . . .", she now made a new suggestion: Karl Gustav should be recognized as her heir in any case.

The queen herself conducted the debate at the Estates' committee meeting on 28 February; something had to be done in good time, she said, or the kingdom would decline as it had done formerly when it was an elective state. In her best Machiavellian manner she declared that the choice of an heir would be no impediment to her marriage with Karl Gustav; on the contrary (but she knew this was not true). "However, no one can *compel* me to marry, neither heaven nor earth." She was against postponing the choice of an heir, for she had no right to consider "what is best for me, or what is to the advantage of Duke Karl, but solely *securitas patriae*, the country's security, should be our criterion". This she honestly meant. She went on: "See to it that your decision, here and now, is such that you will not lose face; decide categorically, on grounds for which you can answer before God and posterity, uninfluenced by side-issues such as this marriage question; on that point you shall hear my final decision when the coronation takes place."

The nobility, however, did not yield a hair's breadth.

So Christina had to think of something else. And now for the first time this girl of twenty-two revealed her political talent; she managed to bring the clergy and the middle classes round to support her by warning them of what the nobility were up to; if the middle classes turned down her proposals, they would find after her death that they would have as many kings in the land as there were privy councillors and stadholders—at least that is what she is said to have told them.

The nobility too was disunited—the lesser nobility against the greater lords. Finally the Council gave in. The queen sent Nils Tungel, court chancellor, to Axel Oxenstierna, to obtain his signature to the decree proclaiming the succession rights of Karl Gustav. "When His Excellency heard what my mission was, he looked annoyed and said: "That is something of which I prefer to know little; I wanted to be so far away that I should not hear another word of it." Later, he is said to have declared: "If at this moment I stood by my open grave and had the choice, either to lie down in it or sign the succession decree, the devil take me—I mean it seriously—if I had not rather lain down in my grave than signed."

As Chanut reported to Cardinal Mazarin: "In my view, three things account for the queen's decision—the fact that she herself shrinks from marriage as such, though she likes the prince and respects him; an iron determination not to let her own interests count when the welfare of the country is at stake, and a stubbornness which closes her mind to views for which, taken all in all, there is a lot to be said."

Finally, Karl Gustav was accepted as heir to the throne. The queen had defeated the greatest politician of her time, Axel Oxenstierna, and his whole set of advisers. In Karl Gustav's entourage, Schlippenbach soon started canvassing dangerous ideas; the duke should try to get command of the whole army, then power would have to be divided between him and the queen; whether with the queen's support or against her will, he should seize the crown. So Axel Oxenstierna and Jakob de la Gardie had good cause for concern. But Christina did not take it too seriously:

"It may be true", she told the Council, "that I shall sometimes find myself in tiresome rivalry with the duke, but I hope God will guide me and not let me attempt anything for my private advantage, but always make me keep in sight what is best for the realm. Perhaps another could govern better, but I shall never be second to anyone in my passionate desire to promote the welfare of the realm."

2. THE INTRIGUE SUCCEEDS

That was only half the battle. Karl Gustav was her acknowledged heir—but he was only to come to the throne if she died without children. He was not wholly satisfied, indeed what had he gained? Christina was particularly disappointed because this solution did not bolster the conception of a hereditary monarchy. Then she had a bright idea which altered the whole situation.

All over the country, dissatisfaction with the rule of the

nobility and their abuse of power, was steadily growing. The peasants sought by all possible means to safeguard their freedom. The clergy and middle classes supported them, and the nobility were threatened with isolation. At the 1649 Diet, the queen sought support from the three non-noble estates for the first time and sided with the oppressed peasantry. Axel Oxenstierna was filled with consternation, he was appalled at the new hostile alignments and expected civil war.

Then there was an exceptionally bad harvest, which did not improve matters. When the Diet met in 1650, dark clouds hung over the land. The queen alone was full of hope. The economic issues were beyond her comprehension, but as a born political realist she immediately saw where her opportunity lay; she could break the nobility's opposition to the decree of succession by playing off the other three estates; this meant making approaches to the nobility's enemies by sowing hopes in their minds; the nobles' privileges, said the queen, must be somewhat curtailed. Everything would be put right at the coronation, and that would be the time to solve this delicate question too: "Now or never!"

So the queen made handsome promises that in fact did not commit her to anything concrete, and thus gained the support of the three other estates, all of which energetically set upon the nobility. It was mooted that the only proper solution was a "reduction"—a whole lot of farmsteads and properties had been given away unnecessarily and they should now return to State ownership. It was Christina who was responsible for this, but the barb was meant not for her but Axel Oxenstierna; the queen, they said, had been taken in and not realized what was going on.

Axel Oxenstierna would not hear of a "reduction". Sweden, he said, was wealthier than ever before, the population was much better off, the crown had much larger resources at its disposal than it did at the time it possessed the properties in question; and the gifts had been made in legally binding form. Against this view the estates contested that the bestowal of State property was against the law of the land. They easily exploded Oxenstierna's individual economic views, for customs and excise duties were obviously unreliable forms of income, and security only existed when the old State domains were the backbone of State revenue. Nor was it true that revenue from customs was rising and properties were better run when owned by the nobility; on the contrary, the nobles neglected many of the large farms and drove the peasants off their homesteads and holdings.

Oxenstierna turned a deaf ear to all such pleading and retorted that they were due to nothing but prejudice prompted by envy and egoism; the damage to the said properties would be far greater if they were reclaimed by the State than if left to the nobility; the plans of the other estates could only lead to the collapse of the country, and they were nothing but criminals. "The sword!"—this was the only piece of advice Oxenstierna could give the queen, as the one means of quelling the middle-class opposition.

In reality, Christina by no means shared the attitude of the non-noble estates with regard to the economic situation. In so far as she considered the question at all, she was bound to agree with Oxenstierna. But in this particular case she was not concerned with the country's welfare but only in breaking the nobility's resistance to her plans for the succession.

There were risings here and there due to famine. The non-noble estates were working out their plan for the reduction, culminating in a petition to the queen couched in no uncertain terms; it demanded the return of the properties to the State. To their boundless consternation the queen rejected their proposals. Simultaneously she asked the bishops to see that caution was exercised in sermons and reference to the situation avoided. A week later the queen summoned a committee drawn from the three non-noble estates, and without quite withdrawing her promises, said that *for the present* a reduction was out of the question, because the nobility would rebel. She produced a new set of promises.

The estates were utterly taken aback. At that time the queen had at her elbow a man of exceptional energy and immense cynicism, John Adler Salvius. He won her confidence as no other Swedish politician was to do. He took a certain amount of interest in the reduction plan, but first and foremost his intention was to break the resistance of his mortal enemies among the higher aristocracy. It was Adler Salvius who invisibly guided the queen's hand, it was he who put into her head the idea of posing as the saviour of the nobility, who would of course be expected to show their gratitude in various ways, including, needless to say, a willingness to comply with her wishes in the matter of the succession.

The great intrigue succeeded. By standing out for reduction, Salvius made the nobility compliant. And by letting the other estates be pushed into the background again, the queen gained the gratitude of the nobility: its very survival depended on the queen. Now she could dictate her terms.

Without further difficulties Karl Gustav, and his future male progeny, were appointed hereditary heirs to the Swedish throne.

In all this Karl Gustav's role was an unenviable one. He was practically never asked for his views, being treated as a pawn for Adler Salvius to use as he chose. "Your Eminence cannot imagine how subdued and shy the duke is in the queen's presence," wrote Chanut to Mazarin. Without any effort on his own part, merely grumbling and lamenting, and drinking hard at times, Karl Gustav became hereditary prince of Sweden. One of the great surprises of history is that this poor fellow was to display unique powers of leadership once he was on the throne, with courage, determination and strength of will. On his early death he left a kingdom expanded to its fullest extent, for he led it on from victory to victory.

So the man who stood trembling so pitifully in Queen Christina's presence eventually became an invincible warrior.

CHAPTER EIGHT

Christina and Descartes

I. THE PROBLEM

It is commonly held that Queen Christina's real reason for turning to the Catholic Church was the barbaric, primitive and positively aggressive manner in which her father's Lutheran faith was presented to her, while she met Catholic doctrine through two superior, distinguished and cultivated personalities—Chanut, the French ambassador, and Descartes, the French philosopher and mathematician: it was her aesthetic sense and high intellectual standards that prompted her to choose the aristocratic religion and reject the plebeian one.

Some such motives may well have played their part, but they were by no means decisive. Descartes was important, but for quite different reasons; he did not make a Catholic of the queen. Long after his death in Stockholm (1650), the queen paid tribute to his scepticism as constituting a third point of view, beyond the two conflicting Churches. Her conversion had other, not properly religious, grounds, and Descartes had practically nothing to do with it.

However, the question is a fairly complicated one. In Hamburg, in 1667, the queen complied with a request to draw up a statement that she had sought guidance from Descartes in mathematics (i.e. natural science) and philosophy, and for a time taken lessons from him. He also "contributed to a high degree to our glorious conversion: God's providence made use of him, and of his renowned friend Chanut, to give us the first inklings of it". This she wrote later on, when Descartes' reputation was in jeopardy. In an unpublished letter, she again attempted to make out that Descartes had died a good Catholic.

But much earlier, the queen had expressed entirely different views. In a letter from the queen's doctor, Wullenius, who loathed Descartes and his theories, we find a most damaging condemnation of him: no keen thinker could possibly see anything sensible in his philosophy, to say the least it was extremely doubtful whether he went to heaven, and posterity was bound to reject him utterly. This might well have been no more than the personal view of the writer, but in a postscript Wullenius added that the letter had been seen by the queen before it was posted.

So what are we to believe?

2. THE CORRESPONDENCE

Descartes and Chanut were old friends. Once, in Chanut's presence, the queen raised one of those debating points that were so fashionable at the time: Which is worse, the abuse of love, or of hate? Chanut passed the question on to the philosopher in a letter, together with several others: What actually is love? Is natural enlightenment sufficient for us to love God?

Here we see the young queen completely in her element. The two questions were as vital to her as life and death (we recall her relationship with Ebba Sparre and with de la Gardie, and her strong liking for the proud path of virtue). Again, what connection is there between our natural reason and religious revelation? These questions recur in the reports the Italian Jesuits wrote of their discussions with the queen, as we shall see later.

To the second question Descartes replied that of course he believed we could love God with the help of our natural gifts. But to forestall possible theological issues he added prudently, he would not contest that God's grace was necessary: we have to remember God is a spirit, a thinking Being; as our own capacity for knowing made us somehow like him, we should regard our souls as an emanation of his superior intelligence.

In May 1647 Chanut reported to Descartes that his answer had greatly interested the queen; in fact she declared Descartes must be a very happy man and she envied him his renown. As to what he said about passion (we have not given his whole answer), she could not rightly judge as she had no experience of it. (Though both Ebba Sparre and de la Gardie described the queen's feelings for them as passionate, she did not do so). She also made a significant critical allusion, instructive as to her range of interests: she did not agree with Descartes in holding that the universe was infinite, she doubted whether the hypothesis of an infinite universe was tenable without coming into collision with Christian doctrine.

So we see what was occupying the queen's mind. She too believed God could be fully and wholly loved apart from revelation, Church and sacraments. But she was certainly not a freethinker or an atheist, she had no desire to break away from basic Christianity. Therefore the universe must be finite. On that account she found the new conceptions of Copernicus and Galileo disturbing.

In this same letter of Chanut's another question was raised—surely at the queen's request: What is the inward secret impulse that makes us one man's friend but not another's, even before we know his qualities? This led to a second question: In choosing his friends can a man of integrity follow the secret pull of his heart, though is it obviously quite unaccountable? And is it wrong to enter into a close friendship without taking ethical or other considerations into account?

Then Chanut comes to an even more important point—the queen's attitude to the Church and her views on it. Christina be lieved that man is evidently the goal of creation and its finest product, on whose behalf all else was created, thus proving God's covenant with man in the Word that became flesh. Hence the inadmissibility of regarding the universe as infinite: man could not maintain the rank assigned to him if he began to feel that he—and his whole world—were but an insignificant speck of dust in the mighty cosmos.

Here emerge the real problems that occupied her mind: not those conducive to remorse and self-accusations, but rather intellectual ones, on how the Christian faith was to be reconciled with modern science. These more philosophical ponderings, rather than any religious experience or crisis, rather than a "conversion" in fact, were what induced her to draw gradually closer to the Catholic Church.

Descartes's reply of 6 June 1647 is interesting. After a cautious preliminary reference to the "Cardinal of Cusa" (Nicholas of Cues) and other doctors of the Church, who held the universe to be infinite without giving the Church cause to intervene, he made a distinction: he had not meant to say the universe was infinite, but only that it was indefinable.

With the obvious intention of asserting his Christian orthodoxy, being at the time under heavy fire from the orthodox Dutch, who even wanted to have him branded an infamous liar, he explained it like this: "Infinite" was an expression which rightly belonged only to God the Father, but it was defensible to declare the universe "indefinable" if there was no proof to the contrary. To his mind, there really were no reasons for supposing that the matter of which the universe was composed had any limits. This is important: Descartes accepted the new scientific views and adhered to them firmly. But this was no reason for breaking with the Church. Perhaps for the first time in her life, Christina was encountering a thinker who had no qualms in holding that the teaching of the natural sciences and the doctrine of the Church might agree. This was the great theory for which she was to be grateful to Descartes later, after his death: it may have saved her from rebellion, or sheer rejection. Descartes was of the opinion that the objections to modern science came from insufficiently educated theologians. True Christianity, intelligently and comprehensibly explained, had nothing to fear from science.

There were further questions: Christina asked Descartes to tell her what was the highest good. We are familiar with the proud, stoic faith of her young days: she had the feeling that the stoic virtues of self-control, detachment, and so on, scarcely differed from the basic Christian virtues. Lutheran theologians would doubtless have replied that the highest good was a sense of peace in our soul, to love the Son of God and be guided by his spirit. Descartes' reply came in the first letter he addressed to her directly, on 20 November 1647, and laid the foundation-stone of the new cultural outlook she was in process of making her own.

Starting from the statement that God must be the highest good, being incomparably more perfect than anything created, he said the old philosophers, ignorant of "supernatural bliss", remote from the "light of faith", reckoned solely with the values we can possess in our earthly life. For them, man's highest good was therefore his honest desire to do what is right, and the peace this resolve could bring. He quoted Zeno and Epicurus: Zeno held virtue and honour to be the highest good, while Epicurus rated gratification and pleasure higher. Descartes believed he could resolve the apparent dilemma: gratification implied the right use free will and "free will is in itself the noblest thing we can possess, above all because it makes us like God to some extent, and appears to free us from being objects of his creation."

We must analyse this reply. First we have a few cautious remarks about God, then a concluding sentence containing no reference to Christianity at all. Here as elsewhere, Descartes assumes he is a good Catholic, but he leaves out original sin and overlooks the need for quiet submission to a higher will. His view of man is so far from Christian humility that he makes out that man's free will sets him up almost as God's equal, hardly subordinate to Him at all.

This must have appealed greatly to the young queen, for it went counter to Lutheran doctrine and the condemnation of self-glorification, with its stress on the creature's lack of freedom; as a stoic, Christina could never become reconciled to the consequential pessimism of the Lutherans, and she heartily detested the even stricter views of Calvinism. Just as she was coming to terms with these problems, she became acquainted through Descartes with the concepts of Catholic doctrine which concede a measure of freedom to humans, and fell upon them avidly.

Without realizing it, however, Descartes had overstepped the bounds of Christianity in his disregard of sin and redemption.

Meanwhile Descartes sent the queen his work on the passions, later to become so famous, and told Chanut he would let her have a selection of his letters to Princess Elizabeth Palatine, with a somewhat contrived attempt at reconciling his classic concept of virtue—peace of soul and beatitude being its highest object—with basic Christian belief, but without a single mention of Christ or his works. This was the first time Christina came across an outstanding philosopher who, though he claimed to be a Christian, and to adhere to the Christian conception of God, yet disregarded the redemption. His moral teaching was humanistic rather than Christian. She was patently delighted with his philosophy, for it seemed to provide the answer to a whole series of spiritual problems that had been distressing her. In September 1649, at the queen's invitation, Descartes came to Stockholm; his intention in doing so was two-fold: to gain a powerful patroness as a safeguard in his dealings with his orthodox opponents, and to put in a good word for his zealous correspondent, Elizabeth of the Palatinate, at her special request.

3. DESCARTES IN STOCKHOLM

There has been much discussion as to what went on in Stockholm. The truth is that the young queen made a great impression on Descartes, and even if we discount the servile terms in which it was customary to address royalty, it still cannot be denied that the most profound thinker of the times gave a very flattering picture of the Swedish queen. He began by deploring the cold: "Here a man's mind seems to freeze in winter, just as the water freezes."—"In spite of the graciousness and majesty apparent in all the queen does, her friendliness and kindness are also evident, so that all who love virtue and have the honour of approaching her, feel bound to devote themselves utterly to her service."

Curiously enough, up to the end of 1650 there was hardly a single opportunity for personal contact. The queen recommended that Descartes should spend the first four to six months in making himself familiar with the new conditions, and during that time there was not one real conversation between them, though she encouraged him to write the libretto for a ballet, *La naissance de la paix*, performed on 9 December. According to other reports, Descartes wrote a play too. Further, he drew up the statutes for the queen's academy and made barometrical notes for Pascal.

It was not till the new year that the queen had a talk with Descartes. In January 1650 he reported that since December he had had five or six conversations with her in her library, but the official historian, Freinshemius, was also present. On that account alone,

Catholic questions will not have been mooted. Descartes himself was thoroughly disappointed—he found no philosophical insight, no real interest, in his royal pupil:

"She is entirely engrossed in her literary studies, I still do not even know if she ever concerned herself with philosophy at all, and can therefore say nothing about her philosophical interests nor can I tell whether she will have time for any. Consequently I still do not know whether I shall give her satisfaction in this respect, or be of any use to her. She is passionately interested in literature and is learning Greek and collecting numbers of ancient books; perhaps this will change. . . . In spite of all, and though I have a specially high regard for Her Majesty I do not believe that anything will keep me here beyond next summer . . . "

Then on 22 January, Descartes fell ill. Ten days later he died: this event has maliciously been termed Sweden's one contribution to the history of international philosophy.

In the course of their last meetings, the questions they discussed were not religious but philosophical. Later, the queen told how they had chiefly talked about Descartes's *Principia*, which she had tried to study with Freinshemius's assistance. She also said how much she appreciated his *Meditations*, and wished that the method by which he proved the existence of God and the difference between soul and body, the geometrical method, could be adopted in all the sciences.

Should it thus be assumed that Descartes was of no significance to Christina on her road towards the Catholic Church? In 1667 Christina admitted she had hoped Descartes would give her "quelques teintures de la philosophie et des mathématiques" (some smatterings of philosophy and mathematics), and had taken lessons with him. But they did not discuss the Catholic faith. On the other hand, she said that the ease with which she was, later on, to overcome certain difficulties which separated her from the Catholic Church, could be traced back to "what she heard Descartes say". So Descartes helped her to clear up certain intellectual difficulties.

At no time did Christina show any interest in him apart from that. She even taunted him for spending his latter years studying the question of how to lengthen life (we know, from other sources, of Descartes' remarkably lively interest in the problems of old age). She also said he wished to de-throne Aristotle.

Clearly neither Christina nor Descartes experienced any deepening of their Christian faith through their meeting. For both, any interest in Christianity was confined to intellectual questions and the more external ecclesiastical ones.

There seems to be practically no evidence for the view that Descartes was instrumental in bringing about Christina's conversion.

CHAPTER NINE

French Invasion

I. FRENCH LIBERTINISM

SINCE the beginning of the eighteenth century, the word libertine has meant a man given to loose living and cynicism. In the seventeenth century it had a different meaning: by no means was a libertine necessarily immoral; on the contrary, in their private lives and socially many libertines were very respectable, upright men. But they were free-thinking, even though, externally at least, they remained within the framework of the Church. Only very few dared to flaunt the authority of the Church; it might have had serious consequences. But with regard to certain assumptions, appearances and dogmas they gave free play to their critical faculty, often staying within the Church's fold solely from prudence or cowardice.

Queen Christina was greatly influenced by libertine ideas, and it is impossible to understand her attitude to current problems if this is disregarded.

There were two main factors that left their mark on what would today be called cultural debates, in France and other countries: first, the wars of religion and their negative effect, the revulsion and even despair, they aroused in so many thoughtful men. Inevitably, the sight of Christians continually at loggerheads was bound to awaken general scepticism towards any theory connected with dogma or the Church itself.

Then there was the new science, giving educated people an entirely new conception of the universe, overthrowing the old view of the cosmos and causing an apparently considerable portion of the Church's structure to totter. Sixteenth-century culture was mainly humanistic. In her early years, Christina had enthusiastically identified herself with it. The seventeenth century produced another kind of scholar: they were no longer literary men and moralists, but scientists. Copernicus, Tycho Brahe, Kepler and Galileo were the great men of their time. The initially discouraging attitude of the Church could not prevent the new knowledge from spreading all over Europe north of the Alps, largely by means of the printing presses of Holland.

Besides these two events—wars of religion and the rise of modern science—we must also reckon with the appalling decadence of the Church in France. It all helped to pave the way for new attitudes to life. Positively revolutionary ideas had come up out of Italy: Giordano Bruno taught in France from time to time; Campanella had many disciples in France long before he had to take refuge there himself. Lamentations over the ubiquitous libertines grew more and more frequent in ecclesiastical circles, and tracts were issued attacking this insidious newfangled movement. In 1623 Mersenne gave the number of libertine freethinkers in Paris alone as 50,000—a highly unreliable figure. But certainly there were numbers of dangerous books in circulation. The best known is *Les trois imposteurs*, the three impostors being Moses, Christ and Mohammed. The author did not deny there was a God, but why should we suppose him to be as the Churches represent him? How were we to decide for one rather than the other: Christ, who wrote nothing himself, Moses, who was a magician, or Mohammed with his Koran? Surely the only rational thing was to keep to natural religion: for a God that created evil as well as good was hardly lovable; in the Old Testament he showed himself blood-thirsty and wicked, leading men into temptation, permitting their fall, and finally sacrificing his own son.

There were several books of the same kind enjoying wide currency, though not all went as far as *Les trois imposteurs*. Libertines could be encountered in all the *salons*—men who remained in the Church and were in some cases priests, but who regarded certain doctrines with the greatest scepticism. The philosopher Gassendi was typical of these: he was a great relativist and epicurean, but also a parish priest, and legends were woven around his holy death. Perhaps, though with reservations, seventeenth-century libertinism can be regarded as a free-thinking fringe on the outer edge of the Church.

One of the Italian Jesuits whom Christina called to Sweden noted in his report that she invited scholars to come and expound their religious views. It has also been said that in the last years of her reign, Christina was strongly under the influence of French Catholic scholars; in reality it was not so much the piety of these men as perhaps their unbelief that affected Christina. She admitted to the Italian Jesuits that she had discovered Lutheranism to be incapable of satisfying her intellectually—or, we may assume, emotionally either. So, she said, she had begun an intensive study of the various creeds and the conflicts between them. This phase of intellectual and spiritual insecurity and questing lasted for five years, during which she approached all such questions from a purely rationalistic standpoint, in the belief that many articles of faith were simply political inventions intended to keep the people down. She herself set to work comparing Moses and Mohammed, and gradually came to the conclusion that no religion could be true; she deplored that during this period she doubted the truth of the highest Christian mysteries—by which she presumably meant the Incarnation, miracles and Resurrection. Consequently she decided that her best plan was to do what convention required of her, while maintaining her doubts: it was all so unimportant, it mattered so little which Church or sect you belonged to; the only things that carried weight were, never to act against the precepts of reason, and to do nothing of which to be ashamed. She had been encouraged in this view, she said, by certain learned and able men whom she had called to her from abroad: they were not Catholics and from childhood they had rejected Catholic doctrine.

These were obviously her new teachers. In fact what attracted her to the French scholars was not so much their supposed faith and apparent dependence on the Church, but the opposite—their rejection of spiritual things. It is strange how Christina remained quite out of touch with the great Christians who were so influential in France at that time. There is no sign that she appreciated Pascal, to whom she appealed for light on scientific matters, or Port-Royal, or François de Sales, the French Carmelites, Bérulle,

Vincent de Paul or Madame Acarie; whereas she was familiar with the works of the libertines and collected around her a host of clever, subtle, challenging French intellectuals, some of whom were thoroughly heretical men.

2. CHRISTINA AND THE FRENCH LIBERTINES IN STOCKHOLM

The most famous of the French intellectuals at Queen Christina's court was Pierre Bourdelot, a medical doctor, who came to Stockholm early in 1652 and remained for a year and a half. Conservative circles, including her former favourite, Magnus Gabriel de la Gardie, regarded him as her evil genius personified. He was said to engage in political intrigue and during the last years before her abdication it was he, among other foreign advisers, who directed the queen's foreign policy—or so it was believed. That is pure fancy. Bourdelot played no part in politics and was no demon. But it is true that he had a strong influence on the queen, on her health and her intellectual interests.

The reason he was in Sweden at all was that Christina was dissatisfied with her doctor and wanted a new one. Bourdelot had won fame as doctor to the Prince de Condé, whom the queen much admired; and on hearing of the queen's constant ill-health, the Duchesse de Longueville recommended Bourdelot who was her own doctor at the time.

Bourdelot had studied medicine in Paris and then accompanied de Noailles to Rome when he went there as French envoy. There he adopted the *soutane* "to comply with local custom". He made many friends and was for a time intimate with Cardinal Barberini.

In 1638 he returned to Paris and became a member of the Condé household. According to his own account he won undying fame in one of Condé's campaigns against the Spaniards. When his uncle Jean died he inherited a large library, including some valuable manuscripts. As a doctor he had modern views and was in some respects exceptionally far-sighted. In a debate he defended the soul and disapproved of a scientific enquiry into certain phenomena of diabolical possession at Loudon.* Saint-Simon cites a curious occasion on which, with Condé and possibly Anne de Ginzague, he had tried to burn a piece of the True Cross, of which the wood was traditionally held to be incombustible. When the Fronde troubles made life too uncomfortable, he fled northwards "so as to enter the service of the Queen of Sweden as her private physician".

Bourdelot soon discovered how overwrought the queen was and how poor her health. Her former doctor had treated her *à la suédoise*, making her eat heavy meals and drink a daily half-glass of brandy with pepper in it. Bourdelot accomplished almost a miracle, for which the queen remained grateful for the rest of her life. He it was who diagnosed her as "a hot, dry woman" and ordered chicken broth and veal, told her to take a daily bath, and "gradually cooled her down". A month later she had recovered, her feverishness left her, never to return.

During this period, Christina turned her back on the group of older humanists and scholars at the court, who retaliated by insinuating that Bourdelot forbade her to read and encouraged her to be frivolous. That is hardly fair. It may have been on his advice that the queen gave up brooding over old manuscripts, but the collection of manuscripts which Bourdelot himself brought the queen contained no fewer than three hundred and seventy items, some of inestimable value. So he was not at all adverse to culture, but advocated a different kind from that adhered to by the queen's sternly humanistic friends. He was a typical libertine; he had true Parisian *galanterie* and composed odes, sonnets and occasional verses, organized ballets on royal holidays and introduced artists to the queen. He sang to his own guitar, was a connoisseur in perfumes and had admirable insight into the mysteries of French cooking. In Stockholm he shocked people with his cheerful, bustling ways and impudent manners. But he was sent all the best dishes from the royal table and drew a high stipend, as everyone knew.

Magnus Gabriel de la Gardie could not stand the sight of the new favourite and tried hard to get rid of him. Once, in most

* See Aldous Huxley's *Devils of Loudon* (1952).

haughty tones, Bourdelot happened to mention his perquisites, whereupon de la Gardie stormed off to complain to the queen, but Christina stood up for her Frenchman, lauding him to the skies. Then de la Gardie tried a different line, minimizing the episode, and he just managed to get away with it. But he continued to make Bourdelot's life as unbearable as he could, till finally he had had enough and decided to return to France. The queen did all she could to keep him.

When he finally departed—not till he had heard from the queen her secret resolve to change her religion and leave the country—Christina was instrumental in obtaining for him the benefice of a prosperous abbey which brought him an income of five thousand pounds. But before long he was in difficulties with his monks; they accused him of cutting too much wood in the monastery forests, setting the Fathers at loggerheads with one another, and similar misdeeds. Not in the least put out, he retorted that monks were dissolute fellows, and in one case things came to a head in a lawsuit lasting the whole of four years.

Back in Paris, he once more basked in fame and honours. Some highly-placed personalities attended his academy. Someone with inside information wrote a lively description of him, standing with a letter in his hand from Queen Christina or Madame de Sévigné, playing with Condé's children, bustling about and behaving very childishly, but with disarming artlessness; he believed in nothing but considered himself a good Christian, and was inordinately proud of his title as abbot.

Such was the man who for eighteen months ruled the Stockholm court, revolutionized the queen's way of life, snapped his fingers at the bewigged old fogeys of the court, circulated an atheistic catechism among higher ecclesiastical circles in Stockholm, and came out with the most daring libertine views in the queen's academy.

But there were other sceptics and free-thinkers in Christina's entourage: for instance Mazarin's learned librarian, Gabriel Naudé, who had studied in Padua and was imbued with the free-thinking ideas of that university. In his letters he described its scholastic freedom, its enlightened scholars and above all, its enchanting

Italian women in glowing terms. Italy was full of libertines and atheists, he noted with satisfaction. Once back in Paris, he and Diodati, Gassendi and La Mothe le Vayer formed a society, *La Tétrade*; though they did not break with the Church—Gassendi and La Mothe le Vayer were priests—all four were sceptics and free-thinkers. They combated superstition and denied the miracles of the Bible.

Naudé, an extremely gifted man, came to Sweden in 1652 on Bourdelot's recommendation. He has left us an enthusiastic description of the queen. His opinions on her intelligence and education are valuable, for he was a highly cultured man with a keen critical sense; he declared that even in Italy he had never come across collections as interesting as Christina's. He attended academy meetings and knew the queen personally. It is important to realize that in those critical years, Christina had at her side one of the greatest free-thinking scholars of the day, a friend of Gassendi and La Mothe le Vayer. Doubtless she was thinking of him when she told the Jesuit, Paolo Casati, of the scholars at her court who had lost their faith and encouraged her in her scepticism.

An occasional visitor to the court was the good-natured poet and lusty drinker, Saint-Amant, who later wrote a blasphemous poem. Another French poet, Hercule de Lacguer, seigneur de Massaquiez, was also received at court and gained the title of *secrétaire des commandements et inspecteur des galères de la Reine*.

The list could be continued. What is remarkable is that Christina did not invite a single Christian of any standing to her court, but solely men who held opinions extremely critical of Christian dogma, or indifferent to it, even if they never reached the point of breaking with the Church. She even tried to get Gassendi to come to Stockholm, but he did not do so.

This whole cultural current was bound to have a strong influence on the queen's mind; it is evident even in a very light-hearted letter she wrote to the notoriously frivolous Countess de Brégy, whom she wanted to keep in Sweden, making her generous offers. But it is mainly to be deduced from the choice of books she sent for; she was a zealous collector of the most outrageous libertine literature.

Soon after Descartes' death, the queen read Gassendi's work on Epicurus, and she wanted at any price to procure Jean Bodin's *Heptaplomeres*, one of the most scandalous books of the time. In 1650, Vossius searched Paris for it on the queen's behalf, and when the first volume reached Stockholm she was greatly disappointed and wondered if it was the right book; it did not seem to her at all shocking. And yet it is an extremely daring book, known as the *Summa* of libertinism, and containing a series of discussions among scholars, each representing a given viewpoint, Catholic, Protestant, Mohammedan and rationalistic. Curiously enough, all of them believed in God and acknowledged the truth of the Old Testament, but were critical in their attitude to the New Testament. The queen received the work just as she was about to receive the sacraments of the Catholic faith from Father Guemes. It shows how little she realized the difference between her friends' free-thinking ideas and real Catholicism. In fact she became a Catholic with the aim of obtaining more scope for her free-thinking attitudes.

Pierre Garasse's famous work, *La doctrine curieuse*, was one of the books which the queen tried to obtain in 1652, and when she read the manuscript of Peyrère's controversial *Praeadamitae*, with its corroding attack on Moses, she persuaded the author to have it printed in Holland without delay. But what interested her most of all was that malicious work, *Les trois imposteurs*, already mentioned. Johann Adler Salvius himself possessed a copy of it, and he had an exceptional knowledge of contemporary French thought. On his death in 1662, before the body was cold, Christina sent Bourdelot to his widow to get hold of the book, but he was told that shortly before his death Salvius was seized with remorse and had it thrown into the fire; which shows he had taken the book seriously and grasped its significance. The queen went on trying to get hold of a copy nevertheless.

René Pintard, a French writer well-versed in libertine literature, whether printed or not, has written conclusively:

"This young lady was interested in the whole of the literature, published or clandestine, in which seventeenth-century people could read about those non-believers and rebels and know all about them, their numbers and the subjects of their discussions; and all that was read by a Naudé, a La Mothe le Vayer or a Guy Patin, filling them with amazement, doubt and eventually with enthusiasm; the books tucked away on the remote shelves of their libraries; books that made pious folk shudder and which decent men mentioned only in whispers."

3. A CLOSE-UP OF THE QUEEN

Queen Christina was thus on friendly, lively terms with intellectual French writers of the Enlightenment, and was a zealous reader of the main libertine publications. What is harder to demonstrate is that she believed all they said. We quoted a remark of hers showing how these foreigners, apostates, more or less, from the Catholic faith, strengthened her theory that one religion could not be truer than another. Eyewitnesses who recorded her attitude and observations during her last years in Sweden, gave a description of her that was in complete contrast to Chanut's portrait in 1648 of a serious and virtuous person who permitted no scepticism where the historical truth of the Gospels was concerned.

A French nobleman named Philippe Bourdon de la Salle, serving at the queen's court in 1653, left an account of his impressions which can be considered reliable. Compare his remarks with Descartes's or Naudé's, for instance, and a certain difference does emerge; he believed she had no feeling for religious matters, and produced evidence of her frivolous, cynical way of talking; she was fond of declaring that the popes were the most skilful politicians in the world because they managed to establish a monarchy supported by the very men who should by rights strive to shake off their domination.

There were other similar comments from French sources. A Calvinist named Saint-Maurice turned up in Stockholm, where he was at first a steward to the court. After the queen's abdication he composed a slanderous pamphlet, and perhaps two, which had wide circulation. Libels are not as a rule trustworthy evidence, but in this case the remarkable fact is that they are not directed against the queen at all, for the author felt sorry for her, lamenting her fate, as a Calvinist, opposed on principle to everything

Catholic, was bound to do. The man he abominated was Bourdelot, the real object of his libel. Then there were the Spaniards: all Calvinists hated them above all, and he was horrified that the queen should have betrayed the Protestant cause and got involved with that despicable race, for all of which he blamed Bourdelot. If we compare his description with other reliable letters from Stockholm, we have to take him at his word. He shows how the queen conveyed her discontent at long sermons by tapping her seat with her fan or playing with her dogs; how she sat on a chair upholstered with satin, propping her head and arms against another chair. If he had intended to malign her, he would have produced more damning evidence. The queen, he said, liked naked statues regardless of the protests of puritanical ecclesiastics (she was to have the same trouble in Rome, when she protested that Adam and Eve were stark naked according to Scripture). He was inclined to think Christina made shocking remarks rather to display her brilliant intellectual powers and show off her knowledge, than with the intent of expounding a coherent and well-thought-out libertine philosophy.

Anyone at all acquainted with the letters of the period will agree that these extracts from the first of the two libellous writings are convincing.

The other one is very kind to Christina, stressing her great generosity, and it contains a few remarks on her theological views; for instance that she doubted the truth of the Incarnation—which is significant, for throughout the process of her spiritual development she tended to omit Christ and confine her interest to God alone. The cynical remark that the "fable of Christ is of great use to the Roman Church" is attributed to her; she was also supposed to have said that she knew no fear of God and could feel no remorse for what she had done, and to have made other similar remarks at different times. She is said to have declared religion to be an illusion, to have regarded Plato's world-soul as the only admissible form of immortality, and to have been convinced that Moses was a fraud.

We are not compelled to believe she said these things, though there is a family likeness between them and other authentic remarks of hers. From other sources we know she read books in which Moses was treated as a fraud; she was familiar with Plato and the Neo-Platonists, and toyed with the idea that religion might be nothing but an illusion; all this is plausible enough if we remember her libertine proclivities during her last years in Stockholm, and her comments to the Italian Jesuits.

4. CHANUTS REPORTS

Perhaps our best source is the collection of Chanut's letters, not only his correspondence with the queen but even more so his letters to his colleague, the diplomat de la Barde, and the latter's replies. The two men discussed the queen's conversion to the Catholic Church at great length.

The old idea that she experienced a religious crisis after coming under the influence of noble and devout Catholics, emerging as a convinced Catholic herself, is no longer tenable. There is no evidence that she was even capable of such a crisis at the time. She felt drawn to Catholicism because she believed, mistakenly, as she was to find out, that unlike Lutheranism it left her free to indulge in a good deal of intellectual scepticism. When Christina took her decisive step, de la Barde wrote in some concern enquiring—with every justification—whether the queen's Catholic convictions were at all sound. On 13 October 1654, Chanut compiled a full reply: this letter is of great value in any attempt to estimate the queen's religious convictions, and also those of Chanut. He concluded: ". . . I will now return to the cause of our exchange of views. I am of the opinion that without at all demolishing the whole structure of ideas erected on the foundation of natural reason, the Queen of Sweden could easily correct those views which—as you so rightly point out—do not wholly agree with our doctrine. And I hope that by the grace of God she will do so. . . ."

This may well be the most important document available on Christina's religious views at the time of her conversion. De la Barde was a devout Catholic who had his information from a close friend of Christina's, and he discovered that her faith lacked one essential element: apparently she hesitated to abandon her proud humanism, she had too much faith in her reason and went her own way regardless. He wished she would admit outright that her former views were sinful. Chanut replied that he did not consider it necessary. He too recognized the lack, but hoped grace would supplement what nature had begun, and that Christina would gradually acknowledge the truth in its entirety. De la Barde considered that Christina's main defect was a complete lack of belief in Christ; she had wrong ideas about the Incarnation and though she formally accepted the whole of Catholic doctrine she regarded the Incarnation as an invention unworthy of credence. In other words, like her libertine friends, she reserved the right to explain certain dogmas of the Church along her own lines—or reject them altogether.

This is much stronger evidence than the rumours about the queen's immoral life that were circulated by the reports of certain other diplomats in Stockholm, above all the Frenchman, Picques, and the Dane, Juel. Early in 1653 the most inconceivable and shameful rumours were being passed around: that she was leading an "abominable" and frivolous life, blaspheming God in public and that she had even made some gentlemen undress to their shirts and underpants at a masked ball. Her relations with young people were a disgrace, especially her behaviour with the handsome Count Tott; it was also said she was having an affair with the Spanish general Pimentel. She even got drunk, they said, though we know she never drank wine. Further, she was accused of having an illicit relationship with her pretty friend Ebba Sparre.

This is merely irresponsible chatter on the part of a rank outsider; he had none but the most superficial knowledge of what was going on and he hated the queen as any good Dane of that time was bound to do.

If Christina was drawn to Catholicism, it was not at all because she considered it to be a source of moral strength and sought in it a depth of devotion, but because she believed she found in it more intellectual and spiritual toleration than in Lutheranism.

CHAPTER TEN

The Catholic Mission in Stockholm

I. CHANUT'S EMBASSY CHAPLAIN

SHORTLY after his arrival in Sweden, Pierre Chanut, the French diplomat, sought a chaplain for his embassy. On 7 July 1646 he could thankfully confirm the appointment as embassy chaplain of Father François Viogué.

He was an Augustinian hermit monk, appointed by the Propaganda Congregation in Rome. It was his mission to entertain as friendly relations as possible with the Swedish queen and influence her; the keen interest taken by the Congregation in this mission is betrayed by the fact that in August of the same year a Dominican in disguise was to be sent to Sweden under French protection. Chanut was on tenterhooks about this, writing to the French foreign minister that it was out of the question, that such a course was pointless at the time and might well harm French interests. On the same day he wrote to Rome that he would be grateful if this hazardous project were abandoned.

The embassy chaplaincy came under the heading of "apostolic mission to the northern lands". Chanut wrote offering to supply addresses, in order to "penetrate as far as possible into the clandestine religious zones, for I do not believe that religion is quite extinct in Sweden"; he added he would himself do all he could to further this work once he came into contact with leading families of the realm, and he would see to it that Father Viogué kept the Propaganda Congregation informed regularly.

So we see how far Rome was prepared to go in an effort to establish relations with Queen Christina and to win her over to the Catholic faith, long before she herself, as far as we know, had the slightest thought of making the change. Chanut was full of hopes, he was more or less convinced that the Swedes held on to Lutheranism for reasons of state alone.

In February 1648 he wrote that for the first time he had had a long discussion with the queen on matters of religion. On that occasion the main topic was the Jewish religion: she looked at things very objectively and would easily be persuaded of the truth, once she had met the Catholic religion in all its purity. Calvinism alone she abhorred; but her favourite authors to read on a journey were still Epictetus, Tacitus and Virgil.

One school of thought maintains that France cannot have been eager to see the queen converted to the Catholic faith, for she would inevitably have to leave the country and so France would lose a valuable political ally. But the fact remains that up to the last moment Christina reckoned she would be a secret Catholic, and the official missionary at Chanut's side put all his efforts into obtaining this very thing. His reports in Latin to the Propaganda Congregation reveal how seriously he took his task. If religious freedom were the order of the day, he wrote, many Swedes would very soon be Catholics. Even now quite a few spoke openly of their sympathy for Catholicism. But Swedish ecclesiastics hated Catholic doctrine, though they hated the Calvinists still more: even the queen expressed her distaste for the Calvinists' religion, saying that those who had been sent to her had no religion at all, no services and no God.

Viogué has also written a description of the queen which makes us suspect that he did meet her after all. The twenty-two-year-old queen of the Swedes, he wrote, was without doubt a natural phenomenon, if natural gifts were to be considered as signs of God's favour, God being the source of both nature and grace. She had an extremely sharp mind and good critical ability, she knew Italian, French, Latin, Greek and German, spent her time in philosophical studies, was fond of discussing the virtues and hearing about them, and was often involved in conversations on religion with Chanut, a profoundly religious man who greatly appealed to the queen on account of his culture and high personal integrity. Viogué said he believed that one day, through Chanut's influence, God would perform the great miracle that was expected. The queen did not abhor the Catholic religion, he added: if she were to change her faith, she would certainly choose no other. This report was dated 5 June 1648.

In other words, it is evident that alongside the Jesuits there was another mission at work in Stockholm, directly responsible to Propaganda, to obtain the Swedish queen's conversion.

2. A DELEGATION FROM PORTUGAL

In July 1648, a Portuguese mission arrived in Stockholm whose immediate object was to pay its respects to the Swedish queen on the occasion of her forthcoming coronation; its secondary purpose was to engage in trade talks. The head of the mission was José Pinto Pereira, formerly King John's financial representative in the East Indies. The negotiations were of no great interest to Sweden and they made slow progress. In March and April of the following year, however, Christina received the Portuguese on several occasions. The envoy was always accompanied by the legation secretary, Gomez de Serpa, who acted as interpreter, for he said he unfortunately knew only his mother tongue and could not converse with the queen in Latin. But one day de Serpa fell ill and Antonio Macedo, another member of the mission, took his place. Whether de Serpa's illness was a blind or not, Chanut let it be known that his Latin was "grotesque and ridiculous".

There was another member of the Portuguese mission, Giovanni Andrada. Not a single Swede knew that the three Portuguese, or at least two of them, Antonio Macedo and Giovanni Andrada, were Jesuits in disguise. Nor do the Swedes seem to have seen through the envoy's stratagem, yet it was extremely unlikely that he knew only Portuguese and no Latin, for he had spent years in Paris and was a cultured man. In fact it was a clear case of Jesuit intrigue. The envoy spoke deprecatingly of his linguistic abilities so as to give one of his Jesuits a chance to come forward, and the plan succeeded.

Thus Queen Christina had an opportunity to speak to the Jesuit in the envoy's presence. Their discussions strayed far from the topics under consideration, which seemed to annoy him. Macedo apologized to his superior saying that the queen was fond of bringing up literary and scientific questions which courtesy forbade him to leave unanswered. Then she discovered he was a Jesuit. It would have been a simple matter to show him up and have him thrown out; she did nothing of the sort; on the contrary she maintained long and intensive conversations with him on subjects concerning the faith. To his astonishment Macedo discovered that the queen was not at all hostile to it, he answered her questions readily and zealously, and observed that she listened to him with pleasure. We know from his report to Rome that above all Christina liked to discuss scientific questions. She enquired for instance about the attitude of Catholicism to the new conception of the universe, and to Galileo's teaching, which had recently been condemned by the Church. Macedo's point was that the queen wanted to know how the new scientific views could be reconciled with the Catholic faith.

As it happened, he was not an expert in this field, and he advised the queen to get in touch with Catholic priests who had had a scientific education. He himself could not remain much longer without rousing suspicions, and Pereira, the envoy, pretended to be getting restless at the delays and tired of all those private conversations from which he was excluded. On 2 August 1651 the queen told Father Macedo that she was thinking of leaving the Lutheran Church and returning to the Catholic Church. Moreover, she told him that as soon as he returned to Rome he should kindly ask the Jesuit General to send two specialists with scientific training to Sweden. At considerable risk to herself she also wrote him a letter in her own hand:

> Father, the respect which I so rightly entertain for the renowned Society of which you have the honour to be General, has for many years made me wish to make your acquaintance in order to impart to you the feelings of veneration which are prompting me to seek your friendship. Now chance has come to my aid and I have made the acquaintance of Father Macedo. I should consider any further hesitation on my part to benefit from your acquaintance to be shameful. I therefore beseech you, Father, to heed the proposals he will put to you, in my name, and to grant them your full confidence. Please be assured that I shall count myself very fortunate if, through

some Italians of your Order, I may receive an assurance that—unbeknown to you though I be—you would deign to consider me worthy of your friendship and correspondence. I have begged Father Macedo to obtain this consideration for me, and to tell you the reasons why I desire it. I pray you to let me know as soon as possible what I may hope from you, and whether you agree to the proposals the said Father will make known to you. I shall be eternally grateful if you fulfil my request. I shall endeavour, as occasion arises, to give you proof of my sincere gratitude.

This is obviously a very surprising letter for the ruler of the most powerful Protestant nation of Europe to write to the General of an Order that was putting all its efforts into undoing the Reformation. We have to remember, however, that the letter expressed no sense of obligation, there was no mention of a conversion to the Catholic Church. Christina, as is clear from Father Macedo's report, merely wanted an opportunity for an exhaustive discussion with two truly representative Catholic theologians possessing a thorough grounding in philosophy and science.

By word of mouth, Father Macedo declared the queen "wished to get to know the Catholic faith through and through, and to perform a great deed in God's service were she inwardly convinced of the truth".

Then what did Father Macedo do? In August 1651, he carefully arranged his departure to look like flight. If he had simply slipped away, the Swedish authorities might have wondered why a man in whom the queen was so greatly interested should suddenly disappear. The Portuguese envoy, who must have known what was going on, expressed dismay. To keep up appearances the queen instigated a search for him, which unfortunately tracked him down to Hamburg, where the queen had had him sent. There he was taken in custody. Oxenstierna knew he was a Jesuit, Chanut too knew that he had held religious discussions with the queen; the rumour spread that he had disappeared taking important documents with him which belonged to the Portuguese mission, and was on his way to Spain, the possessor of mighty secrets.

But Macedo showed the queen's passport and was immediately

released. It remains a mystery how Christina was able to explain the fact that behind the back of the Portuguese envoy she had given an official in his employment a passport, three hundred ducats for travel expenses and a costly gold chain. This alone is sufficient to show that the envoy was playing a preconceived part: he must have been in the secret all along.

CHAPTER ELEVEN

Why did Christina wish to leave Sweden?

I. THE STOIC SUPERWOMAN AND HER SACRIFICE

BEFORE we go any further, we must look at the important question of *why* Queen Christina wanted to leave Sweden.

Until quite recently, there was no agreement on this point. Curt Weibull made an ardent plea for the view that it was all quite simple: it was due to Christina's secret conversion to the Catholic faith through Chanut and Descartes: she admitted this to Macedo on 2 August 1651, and five days later she informed the Council that she was thinking of abdicating; the matter was self-evident.

But as we have seen, it was not so simple. We must begin by rejecting Curt Weibull's suggestion of a conversion brought about by Chanut and Descartes. There is nothing to indicate that a compelling religious crisis occurred, and the motive for the queen's decision was quite different: she wanted to be rid of the strict orthodox Protestantism which so cramped her modern free-thinking tendencies, and to live in a Catholic atmosphere more congenial, she believed, because it was more liberal.

Again, Curt Weibull's assumption that a close connection existed between conversion and abdication, is untenable. Between them, Nils Ahnlund and Sven Ingvar Olofsson have proved that Weibull's view is groundless, for he overlooked the fact that Christina had spoken long ago of her intention to abdicate. In 1651 she told the lords of the Council that she had been thinking of it for five or six years, which takes us back to 1646. Somewhat later, in 1654, she said to Chanut, "You know I began contemplating this move a long time ago, but I only decided eight years later to put it into effect", and this too points to the year 1646. In 1649 it was recorded in the Council that she had "deliberated over it for three years, and not a day passed without Her Majesty considering it". It is hardly likely that Christina would have repeated the statement so often if it was not true.

And as early as 1648, the queen offered Karl Gustav the position of heir to the throne.

Clearly the idea of abdicating was connected with her personal problem as a woman, her thoughts on the place of woman in society, and her plan to make Karl Gustav her successor. Catholicism had nothing to do with it.

When we realize that Christina underwent no grave religious crisis, fresh problems emerge. Why should she not have remained in Sweden as a single woman, a humanist, perhaps secretly a Catholic—and possibly travelling frequently abroad? Surely the mere existence of a recognized heir was no reason for laying down the crown and leaving the country?

Other circumstances came into play; there is good evidence that Queen Christina was much impressed by French culture as she had observed it at her Court; she found it considerably more stimulating than her official duties. And she longed to visit Italy. She thought of inviting an Italian philosopher to Sweden, she wrote a pathetic letter to the Duke of Bracciano, Paolo Giordano II, full of her longing to see Italy and its art treasures. We saw how ambitious she was to do something positive for peace in Europe—towards the end of her time in Sweden she even tried to mediate between France and Spain, a task that was to occupy her mind for nine years after she went to Rome.

It does not seem likely that the economic problems of the realm worried her at all: she never showed any real interest in such matters. In Rome, her own financial difficulties were for a time exceedingly trying. But she considered herself to be perfect and answerable to no one, and it is inconceivable that she should have felt responsible, even partially, for the existing state of Swedish finances.

But something else is involved, a point expressly and repeatedly made by the queen on later occasions: all her life she had striven to be a stoic superwoman, with sovereign control over her passions, unmoved by transient events, called by God, god-like in the literal meaning of the word. She once wrote that in making Karl Gustav king she was acting "just like God creating the first man". She often toyed with the idea that man, to be like God, need but hold to the truth and do what is right. For a long time she rejected purgatory and her own need for a Redeemer. During her final period in Sweden, when half Europe was honouring her as Queen of Peace, the Pallas Athene of the North, a Diana of pure virtue, she believed every word of it and seriously imagined herself to be someone very special and unique in history. Only the great heroes of antiquity, Cyrus, Alexander, were her equals. She liked to rank these heroes high above her father, Gustavus Adolphus, but believed she surpassed them in one respect; one sacrifice they never made, the greatest of all: the sacrifice of themselves. Now Christina did not use the term in a Christian sense, it was not for love of God or man that she wanted to sacrifice herself, but for love of virtue: she wanted to do something unutterably noble and be the greatest figure in history. Her special sacrifice would be to offer her privileged state, her crown, her country: she alone was in a position to do this. She believed—and did not mind saying—that she was among the most favoured of all created beings. She had settled the problem of love, and the conduct of her private life, in what she considered a noble way, never giving way to a lower instinct or a selfish urge. The ultimate proof was, however, still lacking, but born to be "queen with absolute power of the most famous nation in the world", she would accomplish what no one else had ever done before, she would eschew human greatnesses in order to achieve a unique inner greatness. In one of her latter-day maxims she noted: "Not many have renounced their kingdom. I can only think of Diocletian, Almansor, Charles V and Christina." If she could carry out her resolve—and it had to be done in the face of stark opposition, for no one supported her—she would be acting on the precept of the ancient philosophers better than anyone: vanquishing not only her own enemies and those of her realm but even more dangerous foes, to which most people are wont to submit, her own passions and her own refractory self. Thus she would raise herself above all the restrictions of her temporal existence, and create her own proud, godlike destiny.

These motives were certainly accompanied by other, more subconscious ones. How they conspired to bring the queen to her ultimate decision it is impossible to tell. Religious, or rather confessional, promptings were also involved, but before pursuing this line of thought, we must pause for a moment.

Had Queen Christina really experienced a religious crisis, and been filled with Christ's spirit and overwhelmingly convinced that the Roman Church was His Church, it might have accounted not for her abdication, which was already decided—but for her flight from Sweden. But no such crisis ever took place; of that we are sure. We have now reduced the question to its bare terms: Did Queen Christina leave Sweden because she had become a Catholic, or did she possibly adopt a semblance of Catholicism because she had other reasons for wanting to leave Sweden?

That is the problem before us. Not under any circumstances could Queen Christina settle in one of the German Protestant lands, for if she did she would soon be forgotten. But in January 1654 she proposed to the English ambassador in all seriousness to let the English fleet occupy Zealand: if Cromwell "would agree to give me that land to live in, I should lay down the crown and settle there". So we see that for Christina the main object was to get away from Sweden and find a new home. To the ambassador, Whitelocke, she spoke at length, giving the reasons for her plan and stressing the point that a woman should not rule if she could not fulfil the obligations of a ruler, and insisting on her need for peace and quiet. We can make what we like of that. Understandably, she would not want to tell an English Puritan of her Catholic leanings, especially as she was extremely critical of the Puritans' lack of toleration to people of other faiths. That she toyed with the idea of settling in Zealand (as ruler, of course) and not in a Catholic country, gives food for thought. From every point of view it is clear that she wanted above all to get away from Sweden; where she settled next was less important, at the moment. She was a victim of her severe neurosis, as we saw earlier; she put out feelers in various directions, for she needed a guarantee that she would, in the future as in the past, live in splendour and majesty. At first she spoke of residing in Spa; she mentioned France, and in conversation with Whitelocke, Spain; she dreamt of Italy, but the thought of living in Protestant Denmark was not unacceptable. During these years she sometimes hinted in letters that a conversion was a difficult and risky undertaking: she regarded her own views as a third neutral standpoint over and above religious rivalries.

None of this makes it likely that in the year 1650 or so she became an absolutely convinced Catholic, and for that reason decided to lay down the crown and to leave the country, since no Swede was allowed to be a Catholic. It seems nearer the mark to believe that wanting to leave Sweden at any price, she still considered it impossible to do so without first obtaining sufficient guarantees for her future life in the country of her choice. For a number of reasons she would prefer a Catholic land, but as a Protestant she would have difficulties, and be a permanent object of mistrust. So she toyed with the idea of changing her religion, a course all the easier for her since she believed she found in Catholicism an open-mindedness and toleration offering wider scope and opportunity for free development. That nothing like conversion was present is clear from her own undecided mind, as when she talked to Whitelocke about the Zealand project, or later in Flanders, in conversation with Father Guemes, her future confessor. In Rome the complex situation was appreciated and a relapse was half-expected. The Jesuit General discussed it with Father Annat, his French assistant, whom the Queen may have met later on in France. He was sceptical, and it is easy to see why. He was a close friend of de la Barde, the French diplomatist, who had received disquieting news from Chanut of how unreliable the queen's Catholic convictions really were, and how libertine and humanistic her views still remained, even after her departure from Sweden. We saw Chanut's attempt to reassure his colleague, who was really alarmed.

2. THE QUEEN'S OWN ACCOUNT OF THE SITUATION

How the queen herself envisaged her renunciation of the crown and her departure from Sweden, emerges from a letter to Chanut in 1654, replying to an anxious enquiry. She wrote,

> I am not keen on applause. I know that the part I have played cannot be governed by ordinary stage rules. It is regrettable when something strong, virile and powerful makes no impression. I leave everyone to form his own opinion as he sees fit: I can deny nobody that, and even if I could I should not wish to. I know that a minority will judge me favourably, and I am sure you are one of the few. Others know nothing of my motives and little or nothing of my character and way of life, for I let no one look inside me—except you and another friend, whose soul is great and noble enough to think as you do. *Sufficit unus* (one is enough). The rest I despise. In the great tranquillity I wish to create for myself, I shall never be so unoccupied that I need waste a single thought on these people. I shall spend my leisure time reviewing my former life and ridding myself of my faults, but without remorse. How greatly shall I rejoice in the thought that I cheerfully showed kindness to some people and pitilessly punished those who deserved it. I shall retain the pleasant consolation of never having treated anyone as guilty who was innocent, and indeed of having spared some who were guilty. I reckoned the good of the State above all else. I gladly sacrificed everything to it, I have no cause to repent of any government measures. Without being arrogant or vainglorious, I exerted my power, and I lay it down painlessly and with ease. No need to feel concern on my behalf. My condition is secure. My well-being is not exposed to the vagaries of fortune. Whatever I may set myself to do—I am happy and shall remain so. . . . Indeed I am happier than any other and shall continue to be so. I have no fear of the Providence of which you speak. *Omnia sunt propitia*. If Providence is to determine my destiny, I subject myself blindly to its will. If the choice is left to me, I will muster the powers with which my soul has been endowed and thus achieve happiness. Happy I shall be as long as I am assured I have nothing to fear from man or God. I shall spend the rest of my life in familiarizing myself with these ideas, strengthening my soul and from my haven watching the stormy passage of my fellow-men, whose lives are at the mercy of

the waves because they failed to give their minds to such thoughts. Am I not enviable? If my state of mind were generally known, too many envious men would grudge me my happiness. You yourself certainly have a sufficiently high opinion of me not to envy me, and I deserve this from you, for I readily admit to owing some of my views to you. You made me familiar with these views in our talks together, and I hope to be able to discuss them with you again one day, at leisure. I am sure you will keep your promise and remain my friend, in spite of these changes. I am indeed renouncing nothing worthy of your consideration. . . .

This letter deserves a closer scrutiny. That it contains no mention of Catholicism is perhaps explicable, the change was presumably not yet common knowledge; Christina had first to obtain guarantees for her future life. On the other hand, the letter provides us with quite a sincere outline of her motives. She writes as a stoic, not as a Christian. Happiness is her main aim in life and the great tranquillity of a mind aloof from criticism and other people's opinions—the Stoics' *apathie*. She planned to devote her time to self-improvement, practising high virtue and striving for stoical perfection. Her fellow men are referred to as objects of scorn; no word of love for her neighbours. She writes she has nothing to fear from God, thus revealing the full extent of her illusions: she has no trace of awareness of sin, nor even of her own imperfections and shortcomings, declaring outright that she has nothing to repent of.

The letter is admirably written but striking in its immaturity; it gives a clear impression of Christina's state of mind at the moment of her abdication. She enumerates her motives, the chief of which is to let her personality unfold in an atmosphere of calm to ever greater perfection. No mention of a religious crisis or conversion; in its boundless egoism and aloofness, her approach is totally unchristian. This serves to endorse our suspicion that Catholicism was merely a cloak under which Christina could the more easily effect a transformation in her life which she wished to do for quite different reasons.

3. THE ATTRACTION OF ITALY

There were many reasons why Christina chose Italy. The most important was no doubt that in any other country she would have had to subordinate herself to another king or prince. Naturally the Pope came first in Rome, but apart from him, no one could take precedence of the Swedish queen.

Christina had fallen in love with Italy at an early age, a fact that has often been overlooked. She invited a whole Italian opera company to Stockholm, and an Italian musician set the Lord's Prayer for the abdication ceremony. She often said how she wanted to have a great many Italian scholars—philosophers and scientists—at her Court; and we know that long before her departure from Sweden she was fully versed in Italian art and music.

Her longing to be in Italy can also be deduced from her correspondence with Paolo Giordano II, Duke of Bracciano. She sent him a miniature portrait of herself, with the remark that she would never have sent a likeness of the not-at-all beautiful original had he not expressly asked for it. She added how much she would like to be in the portrait's place—on the way to Italy. The duke answered with lively interest and sent her his poems. In the course of their correspondence the queen enquired about Italian artists and asked which of them were held in highest esteem in Rome at that time and whether Bernini had finished his fountain on the Piazza Navona? Was he planning something new? Were any of the new composers greater than Carissimi? What was the reputation of the poet Guarini, and of Graziani's poem, *Conquisto di Granata*. The duke replied that Guarini's pastoral, *Il pastor fido*, enjoyed considerable popular success but that the connoisseurs thought little of it. As to Bernini, he had just finished Cardinal Cornaro's chapel in Santa Maria della Vittoria.

What was the origin of Christina's keen interest in Italy and her ardent longing to go there? No other country so much attracted her, not even France, in spite of the strong impression French culture had made on her mind.

We mentioned an opera company she invited to Stockholm:

from the moment she arrived in Rome her interest in Italian music showed how much it meant to her; she soon had her own orchestra and gave highly-thought-of musical soirées at her various residences. It opened a whole new world to keep her entertained and spellbound. Then a great number of Italian works of art were brought from Prague as war-booty; they soon won her special affection. She had no use for German art, not even for an artist like Dürer, but she passionately admired a number of Italian artists, specially Correggio.

It was alleged that pictures of Correggio's were used to block the windows of the palace stables in Stockholm, but this is wholly untrue. On the contrary, Christina had Correggios with her all her life long, they hung in the Stockholm palace and she took them to Rome with her, giving them a place of honour in her new gallery in the palazzo Riario. Christina possessed Correggio's masterpiece, *Danae and the golden rain*, his *Leda* too, and *Jupiter and Io*. It is curious how many strongly sensuous pictures hung in Christina's collection: Andrea del Sarto's *Leda*, Titian's *Venus and Adonis*, *Venus and the Shell*, *Reclining Venus*, *Venus and the Glass*, Andrea Carracci's *Danaë*, Francesco Salviati's *Rape of the Sabines*, Giulio Romano's *Jupiter's Galantries*, Paolo Veronese's *Venus and Adonis* and his striking (though almost pornographic) *Le Respect*, also Guido Reni's *Susanna and the Judges* and Guido Cagnacci's *Women Martyrs*.

Her collections also contained numerous religious pictures, many of little interest; there were Raphael's *Madonna del Passeggio*, Correggio's mysterious picture of Christ entitled *Noli me tangere*, Tintoretto's not much more attractive *Christ and doubting Thomas*, and many another. But the most remarkable pictures of the collection were daring studies from the nude, a great challenge to contemporary Swedish taste, and a source of considerable vexation to the older members of the Swedish court.

After all we observe of the suppressed eroticism in the young queen's character, it is particularly noteworthy that her image of Italy, her dream-land, was determined, first by Italian operatic music, so ravishing to inexperienced Swedish ears, and secondly by sensuously exciting Italian nude paintings, regarded as outrageous in those northern latitudes. We know that even before leaving Sweden the queen zealously defended those nudes of hers against all puritanical attacks, and upon her arrival in Rome she immediately ordered the veiling to be removed, which the prudent Pope had caused to be swathed about the loins and hips of the statues in the queen's palace.

Queen Christina was a complex personality. It is impossible to account for her departure from Sweden by ascribing it to a single motive, it was due to an interplay of a whole series of more or less conscious motives; alongside political day-dreaming, the intellectual pleasures of discovery, the hope to make a decisive contribution to a future European peace, there was a leaning, sincere in some aspects, towards Catholic thought and towards the Church as unassailable authority, together with a secret dream-wish concerning Catholic virginity, heightened by her own incapacity to love a man as a husband and unite with him; and in this connection the potent effect on her of Italian nude painting must not be disregarded. Here we are not restricted to hypotheses, for we know from her own often very explicit statements that she took great pleasure in contemplating the splendid female nudes in the works of Correggio, Titian and Paolo Veronese which her uncouth generals obediently brought to Stockholm for her, back from their campaigns. She always liked to have them around her.

CHAPTER TWELVE

Abdication

1. FIRST ATTEMPT IN 1651

On 7 August 1651, the queen informed the Royal Council that she wished to abdicate in favour of the heir to the throne. Rumours had preceded this announcement, and Christina's plans had been known to a chosen few for some time. None the less the Council were utterly aghast. Christina gave three main motives: the welfare of the nation required she should relinquish the throne; so did the position of Karl Gustav; and, finally, she yearned for tranquillity. The nation needed a good commander-in-chief who could lead the army—and perhaps this was the decisive factor. The queen added that she had been considering the matter for years and her decision was now irrevocable. She did not desire the Council to express an opinion or to give "counsel", but simply to consent.

Axel Oxenstierna declared the matter to be too serious to settle in a hurry. As usual he begged for time to consider it. Christina retorted that she saw no reason for delay, since Karl Gustav had already been recognized as hereditary prince and had thus been accepted in principle as fit to rule the country.

Whereupon she left the council chamber.

The councillors were faced with a dilemma. Apart from anything else, the nobility needed the queen to defend them, for plans were brewing which threatened to curtail their power. Though she had once taken sides with the non-noble estates against the nobility, she soon reverted to them.

There were many conjectures about the causes of her surprising decisions. Of the Catholic inclinations of the queen, as good as nothing was known. Though someone or other might suggest this as a possible motive, no one really imagined that the daughter of Gustavus Adolphus would dream of a conversion. Finally, it was agreed to draw up a petition. Axel Oxenstierna composed it, and on 12 August it was signed by thirteen councillors.

Oxenstierna's line of thought was rather touching. He referred to the queen's solemn promise before God to be Queen of Sweden and rule the land according to His laws. A bond so firm and so often reaffirmed could not be undone one-sidedly without errors and misunderstandings creeping in, though no one doubted Karl Gustav's qualities and suitability. But Christina was *de facto* queen of the realm, she loved her country and her subjects, she possessed understanding, experience and renown, and she had an exceptionally happy flair for foreign and home affairs. That the queen would obtain peace of mind by renouncing the throne was doubtful, and the question arose whether such self-engrossed leisure was to be reconciled with the duties of a sovereign. "All men are from birth subject to trials and tribulations, especially kings and rulers, whose duty it is to find satisfaction and pleasure in their work and to flee from solitude and tranquillity as things incompatible with a sovereign's obligations." Of course weariness might occur, especially weariness of the many complaints, the tears and lamentations of one's subjects, and the frequent and often so absurdly motivated intractability with which they plague and torment their betters. But the queen could be relieved of this plague.

Per Brahe only reached Stockholm on 21 September, but he immediately set to work on a new petition which was handed to the queen nine days later in the presence of all the councillors.

An entry from his diary is relevant:

"Her royal Majesty discussed her abdication with the councillors, but they objected, both in writing and by word of mouth."

Much later, in 1668, Magnus Gabriel de la Gardie gave an account of this audience with the queen. Everyone drew back, no one wanted to be spokesman, till finally de la Gardie himself had come forward. Three councillors, selected perforce by himself, were to follow him, including Schering Rosenhane, who faltered several times on his way up and tried to turn back. When the four entered the hall where many people had gathered, the queen gazed at them and asked what their business was. They desired to be allowed to enter for a private interview, and then they handed her their petition. "Her Majesty read it through, broke into tears and answered very graciously that she would think over the sincere and well-intentioned counsels given her, and thanked us for them very warmly."

Then the four councillors went back into the council chamber. "The other members of Council were very anxious," de la Gardie reports, "some of them came to meet us on the stairs and could, not suppose but that we had been dismissed with harsh words. When they heard the message we received from Her Majesty, they were extremely pleased, especially Erik Ryning, who wept for joy".

We also have Per Brahe's account of this audience. The queen told the four councillors, he said, that she wanted to bear the responsibility for her decision herself and not burden the Council with it. She had also asked that the Council should meet again to consider the matter and advise "how it could best be dealt with". For it was her wish that the Council should agree to her plan and give it their support.

In reality Christina did let herself be influenced. After a number of further negotiations, a decision was reached in November. Christina withdrew her intention and promised to remain ruler of Sweden.

We may wonder what produced this change of heart. It seems likely that Christina deemed that the ground had been insufficiently prepared. The lamentations of the counts Palatine—Johann Kasimir took the whole affair as an attack on his son, who was obviously in for a bad time!—worried her not at all, she regarded her relations as so many pawns on the chessboard. Her real adviser, however, Adler Salvius, suggested that a decision might in certain circumstances have very disagreeable repercussions in foreign affairs, and this struck the queen as being relevant. Undoubtedly another factor came into play too: so far she had made absolutely no preparations for her future life. She was in contact with several powers, she had sent a messenger to the Jesuit General, and she endeavoured to establish contact with England and Spain. Much remained to be done before she could put her plans into effect. How undecided the queen was is revealed by the fact that after this first attempt she wrote no fewer than three letters which hint at something like a retreat from Catholicism and from conversion in particular. Possibly these letters were meant to conceal her true objective, but they may have been sincere, in which case they reveal a fresh disquiet, a kind of relapse, though it remains unknown whether due to religious doubts or political considerations. Probably the whole project was simply not sufficiently mature at the time.

In her old age, Christina noted in the margin of a history book that her reason for delay was, that so far she had left much undone that would be to the benefit of the Swedish State. We are perhaps entitled to believe her.

2. CATHOLIC PRIESTS AT WORK

We now come back to the Portuguese Jesuit, Macedo.

He travelled as fast as he could and reached Rome on 18 October, where he delivered the letter not to the General of the Order but to his second in command. It has always been currently held that the letter struck Rome like a thunderbolt. That is to underestimate the Jesuits. They had seen many sovereigns change their views, they were moreover too experienced to believe that anything had happened as yet.

After discussion with the papal secretary of State, Fabio Chigi, later known as Pope Alexander VII, and having sought extensive counsel from Father Annat, his assistant for French affairs (the queen's letter was written in French, and her French leanings were suspected; in fact the French intellectuals of her Stockholm circle may well have been under observation), the Jesuit General selected two men, Francesco Malines, professor of theology in Turin, and Paolo Casati, professor of mathematics (i.e. science) and theology at the Collegio Romano in Rome.

Why were precisely these two men chosen, and to what extent were they specially qualified for their important mission?

Paolo Casati was born in Piacenzo in 1617 and became a Jesuit in 1634 (he lived till 1701). He was, as we said, professor of mathematics at the Collegio Romano, and at the age of thirty he had been appointed rector of Parma University. He was a typical Renaissance scholar, interested in meteorology, astrology, physics, geometry, mechanics and hydrostatics; he wrote on the subject of volcanoes, and devised a compass. In 1649 he produced a book, *Vacuum proscriptum*, and in 1655 a work that was to make him famous, *De terra machinis mota ejusque gravitas et dimensio*. Then came a series of other learned works, all, with one exception, on scientific subjects. After the great scandal over Galileo, he was one of the first Jesuits who gradually paved the way for the acceptance of a new conception of the universe.

The other Jesuit, Francesco Malines, was less well known. His name does not appear in the Jesuit encyclopaedia, nor were his accomplishments of particular note. But he possessed other qualities which made him a good choice for this particular mission. He was an aristocrat, the elder son of Count Giovanni de Malines, Signore di Bruino, chamberlain of Savoie. Born in 1613, he was first, page to the duke, then made way for a younger brother, and became a Jesuit. As a theologian he was unknown. His only proven merit in this connection was his aristocratic birth, education and familiarity with Court life. But he did also teach scientific subjects.

As we remember, in her talks with Father Macedo the queen expressed the wish to call to Stockholm "two members of your Order well versed in the natural sciences" (*esperti in ogni scienza*). The Jesuit General did exactly what the queen requested. It is important to realize this, for it gives us a rare opportunity to penetrate more deeply into the problems that beset her mind. They were not in the first place religious or moral problems at all, and naturally it never occurred to the queen to discuss her personal difficulties. After her talks with Descartes she was specially anxious to know whether the audacious ideas that had been introduced into her Court by a set of French free-thinking libertines could really be countered by the Church's best brains, or whether the Catholic religion was sufficiently broad-minded to tolerate new ideas, for, as she knew very well, they would never prove acceptable to Swedish Lutheranism.

The Jesuits selected for this mission were now preparing for their journey. They did of course have to travel under assumed names and with false passports: they came as D. Lucio Bonnani and D. Bonifacio Ponginibbio. Both received a letter to the queen from the Jesuit General. Their journey was kept secret; only very few knew of it.

In their instructions the purpose of their journey was given as the spread of the Catholic religion and above all the conversion of the person who had invited them; in future correspondence this person would be named Signor Teofilo. It was firmly impressed on both of them that they were on no account to meddle in worldly matters, in politics for instance. Their task was to be a purely spiritual one, the winning of a soul. They were informed that the queen had a special interest in Greek literature and ancient philosophy. Like everyone else, Father Macedo had been impressed by her cult of the stoic virtues, and the two Jesuits were advised to rub up their knowledge of the classics so as to be armed to meet the queen on her own ground, should occasion arise. They were also to be familiar with the more important contemporary stresses and strains. Now this certainly did not refer solely to points over which Catholics and Protestants could not agree, but was to include epistemological problems in which the queen was particularly interested, for instance the tension between science and the Christian faith.

By good fortune we have fairly accurate information regarding the line of thought followed by the two Jesuits during their stay in Stockholm. For after meeting the queen they wrote to Rome asking to have a book sent them without delay, *L'Uomo di lettere*: forgotten today, it was famous in its time. The author was a Jesuit, Daniello Bartoli (1608–85), with whom the queen was to come into contact during the great Quietist debate. He was one of Italy's great seventeenth-century writers, belonging to the same generation of humanists as Casati, whose intimate friend he was. Bartoli set to work to find a *modus vivendi* between the ancient philosophers and Christianity, or more precisely, between the speculative scholastic method and Galileo's experimental approach. He discussed modern science with amazing tolerance. He respected both Galileo's opponent, the Jesuit Father Scheiner, and Galileo himself even after his condemnation—perhaps because he had invented the telescope. He warned against two great errors: seeking God's truths with a philosopher's curiosity, and seeking the truths of philosophy with the assurance of faith.

This benevolent attitude towards modern science, this Christian moralism, was eager to take over from the Stoics all that was of value in their philosophy, but without making any concessions on the side of Christianity, and it appeared important to the two Jesuits to make this clear to the Swedish queen. Thus we are given an insight into the nature of the arguments Christina brought up for discussion with them and the problems with which she was concerned.

But to return to their journey: they arrived in Stockholm in March 1652, travelling across Denmark in the company of the Councillor Schering Rosenhane. They reached Stockholm in exalted company too, that of the master of the royal horse, General Wachtmeister. By chance Christina heard of the arrival of two foreigners, Italians, and wondered if they were musicians. No, said Wachtmeister, they were two noblemen who wanted to visit Sweden. Christina saw through the coincidence and desired to make their acquaintance. On the following day they were called to the palace and were welcomed in the presence of the Court. Only conventional courtesies were exchanged at this stage. But at a moment when no one could overhear, the queen asked Casati in a low voice, "Perhaps you have a letter for me?"

The learned Jesuit had also learnt to be prudent, and without turning round he answered, in equally low tones, "Yes."

The then queen sent her chamberlain, Johann Holm, to fetch the letter. On the very next day she received the two Jesuits in the palace, arranging to remain alone with them; and to achieve this she put on a little act, turning to Schering Rosenhane with mock gravity and declaring she did not know what to make of the two gentlemen. The gullible Rosenhane replied that they were two irreproachable gentlemen and there was not the slightest cause for distrust.

On the important talks that followed we are well informed through the reports drawn up later by the two Jesuits, Casati and Malines. The more interesting of these two documents appeared—when the so-called Albano collection in the Vatican was sold to Prussia in 1857, the ship conveying it sank in the Tyrrhenian Sea—but fortunately Leopold von Ranke, the German historian who later became so famous, had already been in Rome and copied the document. So we know that the two Jesuits were deeply impressed. "We were amazed", wrote Malines, "when we found a five-and-twenty-year-old princess so lacking in all the vanities that usually beset the great of this world, and with so sure a judgment of the true worth of things that it seemed she must have come into the world with the quintessence of moral theology born in her." So, like Chanut and others, they were startled to see how seriously Christina took the stoic ethic, and we understand why they sent for Bartoli's book, for among other topics it dealt precisely with the proper connection between ancient ethics and Christian views. In it we read: "Jesus is our whole philosophy", and the Stoa is more like a sculptor's workshop than a learned school for the training of philosophers. The stoic method is to wrap the soul in a coat of mail, till it is inaccessible to spontaneous reactions like love and hate. But when Christ, who is himself the truth, shows the way, then every philosophy falls silent.

Naturally, no personal religious difficulties were ever mentioned, the only aim pursued was intellectual clarity. The queen posited epistemological problems: was there really a difference between Good and Evil or should an action be judged according to the harm or benefit it brought about? What was the truth about immortality? Did the Church in fact seriously contend that the human soul lives on with God for all eternity? And she brought up her old favourite, too: When all religions were at loggerheads with one another—how was one to be sure? Was it not wiser, as a matter of form, to follow the conventions and religious customs of one's country, but otherwise be ruled by one's reason? And what was one to make of the habit Catholics have of praying before saints, relics and holy pictures? However, the main problem was: How could it be proved that the Catholic religion in particular was the true one? What constituted its criterion? The scientific conception of the universe was also discussed: Christina wanted to be told how it could be reconciled with the world as portrayed in the Bible. To what extent were the Bible stories to be taken symbolically?

After all, Christina was engaged in conversations with two missionaries with scientific qualifications, who were expressly charged to do their best to win her over. The queen's epistemological queries were easily dealt with: the doctrine of the Catholic Church might in a certain sense be said to stand *above* reason, but never in contradiction to it, for it was merely incapable of explaining all the mysteries with which man is surrounded. They were surprised at the speed with which the queen grasped and followed their line of thought. As Jesuits, they had a more exalted idea than the Lutherans of man's capacity to determine his own fate, and could thus elucidate what had appeared to the queen as a knotty problem of opposition between the views of the ancients and the Christian doctrine of man's dependence. While Luther taught that even in his best moments man is subject to sin and incapable of achieving his own salvation, the Jesuits declared that God's grace accompanied man and made it possible for him to fight and conquer sin—a doctrine that the queen was bound to find encouraging in every respect.

Thus what Christina learnt from the two Jesuits was a modern, rational form of Catholic doctrine, certain aspects of which were hardly to be distinguished from the free-thinking trend within the Church with which she had become acquainted through the French intellectuals she had invited to her Court. She concluded that evidently she was not far wrong in retaining her scepticism in given respects, for she recognized that in the Catholic Church many things remained open. On the other hand there could be but *one* truth. None of the conflicting sects could claim to be the true Church of God, whereas Catholicism with its history, its unbroken link with Christ, its saints, its constantly reiterated miracles and its rational philosophy, really had the right to make this claim. She joined in the discussions and listened, but finally was honest enough to tell the two Jesuits that though she had indeed understood all they said, she could not be a heartfelt Catholic. She must have meant that though impressed by Catholicism, and even able to assent to it on account of its clear appeal to the intelligence and its toleration, she knew she had never experienced a deep-seated personal conversion. This caused some disappointment to the Jesuits, but then she added that she was nearer to Catholicism than they might suppose. And at that they realized they had achieved their purpose.

3. WAITING

Before we pursue the further unfolding of this drama, there is more to be said of the other Catholic contacts Christina had taken up.

As we saw, Father Macedo left Stockholm in 1651 to return to Rome. But a year earlier, on his homeward journey from Stockholm through Copenhagen, the Dutch scholar Salmasius spoke to Bernardino de Rebolledo, the Spanish king's minister, and told him of the Swedish queen's remarkable ideas. Salmasius was himself a Protestant with no sympathy at all for Rome; but neither had he any cause to conceal his impression that Christina showed strong sympathies for Catholicism. The Spanish diplomatist, a devout man with literary leanings, had a priest attached to his embassy, a Jesuit, Godfried Francken, good-natured rather than sharp-witted, belonging to an older school of theology and science than the two gifted and experienced Italian Jesuits (this was before they came to Stockholm). He was all agog to convert the queen and begged to be sent to Sweden. He obtained access to the queen, in disguise of course, and found occasion to speak to her on religious matters. To Christina he appeared full of good will but incapable of satisfying her intellectual demands. Nevertheless she persuaded him to stay in Stockholm, though he himself wanted to go back to Copenhagen and seek advice from the Spanish ambassador. In that same year, in Copenhagen, Francken had held a public discussion with the professor of philosophy Johannes Zoega, on the immortality of the soul. He sent the queen a paper on this topic, or he may have brought it with him, but apparently it did not make a great impression on her. He visited Stockholm no fewer than three times in one year, posing as a teacher of mathematics. Finally Christina let him know that she was in contact with Rome and had sent Macedo to the Jesuit General. Slightly hurt in his feelings, this devout but obviously somewhat naive man suggested that it was hardly necessary as there were theologians enough in the Spanish Netherlands who could be invited to come to her. So the queen begged him to send her a colleague of his, one versed in mathematics. It is clear that Francken had not been able to remove her doubts, and also that the queen was more interested in questions of faith than in the ethical problems she discussed with Francken. He wrote at once to the superiors of his Order in Brussels.

The Order's provincial, Engelgrave, immediately took the matter up and contacted Rome. His choice fell on a Jesuit named Nutius who possessed scientific qualifications. He left for Sweden in February, but did not arrive in Stockholm till 1 April, by which time the two Jesuits from Rome were already there.

But Francken had been entrusted with another important mission by the queen: she sent him to the Spanish envoy in the Hague, to inform him and the Spanish government of her Catholic views. In addition she expressed the wish for an opportunity to discuss the matter with a representative of Archduke Leopold William, the Spanish king's highest representative in Brussels. But the letter Francken delivered was on a totally different topic, namely the possibility of increasing trade with Sweden by opening the Schelde. So the Queen of Sweden was negotiating with a foreign power behind the backs of her councillors, using a Catholic priest as a go-between! One can imagine how the Spaniards disliked it. But Francken, simple fellow that he was, does not quite seem to have grasped the situation. He gave out that the queen "was very taken with the Catholic religion" and sought contact with Antwerp as it was a Catholic city, and that by this means much could be done for winning Sweden back to the Catholic faith. The queen herself can hardly have entertained so naive an idea as that Catholic tradesmen and seamen could influence Sweden. Her purpose was a totally different one: by means of a satisfactory trade agreement she wished to establish contact with the greatest Catholic power in the world—she still was feeling her way as regards Rome. As she already knew, she would need influential friends once she left Sweden, and the Spanish king could be one of them, perhaps the most important of all.

In May, Francken was back in Stockholm and found it positively swarming with Jesuits. He brought with him another, Hubert Langlois, who under the name of M. de Saint-Hubert turned up as a layman attached to the French embassy. But evidently the queen had not much use for the two Flemish Jesuits, probably because she found them old-fashioned and unable to tackle her intellectual difficulties. In any case Nutius was soon discovered. In April, news came from abroad that he was in Stockholm, with a suggestion that he was not there merely "to catch fleas". In other words, it was suspected he was a Catholic missionary. Though convinced that his mission had failed, he remained in Stockholm till 8 May. He had no idea what the queen was telling his Italian brethren, of whom she spoke to him in terms calculated to confuse. One day she even asked that they should be prevented from coming—pretending therefore that they had still not arrived.

The Jesuit General directing this delicate affair soon realized it was inexpedient to have two parallel missions in Stockholm, and that Casati and Malines were better suited to cope with the situation than the fussy Flemings. But for a long time afterwards the question of which of these two groups had had the honour of first influencing the Swedish queen was a source of disputes between them.

Right up to the last moment, the queen went on studying the possibilities of a compromise. For instance she asked the two Italians if she might receive communion according to the Lutheran rite once a year. She seemed to imagine she might simply become a secret Catholic, while remaining in Sweden and keeping up appearances as a good Lutheran. Naturally the Jesuits explained that this was out of the question. They made the position perfectly clear: she would have to abdicate and leave the country. She decided to send one of the Jesuits back to Rome to obtain further instructions. In May, Casati set off with a letter from the queen to the Jesuit General. He reached Rome on 6 September, while Malines remained in Stockholm. After dreaming of converting the whole of Sweden, that good soul Francken retired crestfallen; later he died a martyr's death in Guinea.

4. THE FINAL PREPARATIONS

For the time being Christina had given up her plan to abdicate; at least that is how it appeared to the outside world. In the following years she had a lot to do. The economic crisis got worse and a first attempt was made to clean up the nation's finances. That was when the queen got rid of Magnus Gabriel de la Gardie. Court life and the theatre flourished, but the queen appeared more tired and nervous than ever. She declared forcibly that she was weary of the business of ruling, but she loyally carried out all her duties with her usual application. Her relations with the Oxenstiernas improved, and in many respects the situation seemed less tense.

And yet it was precisely during this period that her ultimate decision matured. An unexpected event was to come to her assistance.

On 12 August 1652, the Spanish general, Don Antonio Pimentel de Prado, came to Sweden. Before he left Spanish Flanders, the Jesuit Godfried Francken turned up there with that remarkable letter from Christina to the city of Antwerp. Francken brought the news of the queen's strong sympathies for Catholicism, and this was regarded as so important as to demand great discretion. Presumably, Pimentel was not told. During his first conversation with the queen he did not refer to it, nor was there any mention of the Schelde proposals. But Christina immediately appreciated that an opportunity was there for the seizing. To be a Catholic, it was not spiritual support that she lacked, for as a converted queen she could count on the most forthcoming reception anywhere in the Catholic world, but she was shrewd enough to realize the necessity of political and economic support. We do not really know what hopes she had of Spain, but she would have to decide for one country rather than another, where she could stay initially. She had as we know a choice of several countries. In the long run it was Spanish Flanders that attracted her most.

Pimentel soon became a constant guest at court festivities and banquets, and he was much impressed by the queen's diplomatic talents, mentioning her "sly inventiveness"; he had more than an inkling of the double game she was playing. As an envoy he possessed limited powers, functioning rather as observer and reporter.

We know that after a month in Rome Casati came back to Stockholm with a welcoming letter to Christina from the Jesuit General. A letter he wrote to Malines was seized, and the queen asked him to remain in Hamburg for the time being and find some secret means of getting the Jesuit General's letter sent to Malines in Stockholm. It probably reached Stockholm in November. Now at last—though possibly much earlier too—Christina knew that there was no obstacle at all to her conversion in Rome.

Christina then undertook a daring political move on her own account. She made the offer of an alliance to Spain—Spain, still the leading Catholic country in Europe. This was not compatible with traditional Swedish foreign policy, as Axel Oxenstierna pointed out, founded as it was on co-operation with France, Spain's deadly enemy. Oxenstierna did not want Sweden to become involved in the great maritime struggle. But Christina had the notion that Sweden ought to belong to a Spanish-English bloc directed against the economic superiority of the Netherlands. She also wanted more or less to wind up Swedish policy in Germany and, under certain conditions, relinquish bastions in Germany in favour of the Habsburgs—a very surprising measure. But is it likely that a ruler on the point of leaving her country would engage in such hazardous policies? It seems more probable that even at this point Christina still wanted to keep the door open for effecting a complete change-over of Swedish policy—perhaps, as a secret Catholic, weakening the all-Protestant line and instead, bringing Sweden closer to arch-Catholic Spain. It was a programme Christina could not of course broach with leading Swedish politicians. But it also met with opposition from the Spanish king.

All this time Christina maintained the best possible relations with France. She was thus pursuing a cynical, clever double policy that fills us with amazement. Sooner or later it was bound to lead to a crisis.

Perhaps these adventurous sallies were in part a result of the death, in August 1652, of Christina's reliable counsellor, Adler Salvius. She could find no substitute for him. In the years before the abdication, she had at her side a set of nobles of very slight political capacity: Tott, Steinberg, Dohna, and two foreign adventurers, the Dane Corfitz Ulfeld and the Pole Radziejovskij.

It must have been in March 1653 that Christina first confided her secret plans to Pimentel: that she was thinking of relinquishing the crown (surely no great sensation after her attempt at abdication in 1651), and intended to leave the country. Yet another Catholic priest was then at Pimentel's side, Karl Alexander Manderscheydt, an official member of his embassy staff. In April Christina took a somewhat striking measure, she endorsed a recommendation to the Regensburg Diet to elect the King of Hungary (son of the Habsburg emperor Leopold III) as Roman Emperor, thus giving the support of Sweden to the House of Hapsburg in this important matter. It is to S. I. Olofsson, the historian of Pimentel's stay in Sweden and his usefulness to Christina, that we owe these particulars:

"Thus for the sake of her own private plans, Christina undermined one of the main pillars of Sweden's claim to be a great power. The country's symbolic position as leading Protestant power in Germany and promoter of peace in central Europe was lost in consequence. The causes of the resulting withdrawal of Sweden from great-power status can partly be traced to this fateful decision of Christina's."

It is doubtful whether the matter was really so serious, and it was perhaps not so very revolutionary of Sweden to support yet another Hapsburg as German Roman Emperor: what other candidate deserved her support? But Pimentel was quite right to regard this step of Christina's as a major success for Spain.

In that same month of April, Chanut came back to Sweden. With great ease he renewed his contacts with Christina as her close and loyal friend, and was soon in a position to tell his government that Sweden's relations with France were really in no danger. True, he did not yet know of the intensive talks that were taking place at that very time between Christina, Pimentel and the two

Catholic priests, Malines and Manderscheydt, about the way in which the queen's conversion was to be arranged. We do know that Pimentel urged the queen to rely completely on the Spanish king in this important matter. It was agreed that the Jesuit Malines should travel to Rome via Madrid, so that he might personally give the Spanish king all the necessary explanations. Malines left Sweden at the beginning of May.

Chanut seems to have summed up the situation correctly. There was no subsequent Swedish-Spanish alliance. Sweden continued her traditional policy of friendship with France. Christina kept her true plans secret from her good friend Chanut and assured him with the utmost sangfroid that Pimentel had only been assisting in reorganizing her court, and neither had, nor would have, the slightest political importance.

But it was not long before Christina gave away her other plans, both to Chanut and to the French doctor, Bourdelot. She informed them that she needed France's financial support and proposed it should take the form of a guaranteed French annuity. As security she suggested, first, a settlement of the old Swedish subsidy-claims from the last phase of the German war, amounting to a hundred thousand imperial *taler*, second, a very odd plan for selling Swedish warships to France at not less than three thousand imperial *taler*. So Swedish State property was to be turned into a private annuity for the queen! Chanut and Bourdelot did what they could, but nothing came of it.

It was soon apparent that Christina was not negotiating exclusively with Spain: in due course she began to load her valuables on to the ship *Fortuna* which was to sail to a French port. Under the supervision of the French art connoisseur Raphael Trichet du Fresne, the finest Gobelins from her palace and the most valuable manuscripts from her library were assembled on this ship, especially Mazarin's, which she wanted to return to him. The Jesuit General in Rome undertook to have these treasures, valued at five hundred thousand pounds, transported from France to Rome, which was evidently Christina's chosen destination.

At this point yet another Catholic priest turned up in Sweden, a Dominican, Juan Baptista Guemes, attached to the Spanish envoy de Rebolledo. He came to Sweden by chance, after a shipwreck, but remained, and in Stockholm he was in contact with the queen. Later on it was he who was to receive her into the Catholic Church and become her first confessor. This priest played a significant part in Christina's life. His first mission on her behalf was to go to Spain and inform King Philip of Christina's ultimate intentions. He departed in September.

In November 1653, Christina took a further preparatory step: she appointed Pimentel's friend Don Garcia de Yllan as her private representative in Spanish Flanders. Officially he was on a trade mission, in reality, however, he was to be there to make the financial arrangements for her arrival.

By the beginning of 1654, Christina deemed her preparations to be sufficiently advanced for the question of her abdication to be brought up once more. On 11 February, she announced categorically that it was her intention to renounce the throne at an early date and make Karl Gustav king of Sweden. By now Axel Oxenstierna could no longer prolong his opposition. Perhaps he had observed that Christina's interest in State business was dwindling, or perhaps he had gained a higher opinion of the capacities of her heir. But just as in 1651, a petition was drawn up and delivered to the queen on 13 February, the author being, once more, Axel Oxenstierna. It was signed by twenty-five gentlemen of the Council and contained the proposal that the queen's burden of government should be lightened by allowing Karl Gustav to share it. Christina declined emphatically; she had her private motives which she could not yet name. Per Brahe intervened with determination and spoke to the queen in severe, reprimanding tones—a thing hardly anyone else would have dared to do—saying that whoever had ventured to advise the queen to take such a step was "a scoundrel and no honourable man". Christina gave tit for tat, and retorted: "Supposing it was the archbishop who recommended my abdication?"

All through the spring, Christina's future maintenance was under discussion. She wanted an annual income of something like two hundred thousand inperial *taler*. This sum was to be provided from portions of the national properties now to be retrieved from their former feudal lords by the process of "reduction" (confiscation). Thus the cost of her maintenance would involve no large extra national expenditure. As a last gesture of friendship for Spain, Christina declared the representative in Stockholm of the "Duke of Braganza" to be *persona non grata*, without consulting the Council. Thus, to please Spain, she broke off relations with Spain's enemy, Portugal.

Now all that remained was the abdication itself.

5. THE ACT OF ABDICATION

Early in the morning of 6 June, Karl Gustav and the councillors of the realm met in the queen's chambers at the palace of Uppsala. Fair copies of the queen's declaration of abdication, Karl Gustav's guarantee of her future maintenance, and other documents were distributed and duly signed and sealed. Everyone was in gala dress, all but Karl Gustav who appeared discreetly in black, while the queen wore a snow-white taffeta dress. The symbols of the nation's highest honours were once more placed upon her, the coronation mantle of blue satin was laid on her shoulders, lined with ermine and adorned with the three crowns of the Swedish coat-of-arms in gold. The holders of the five highest offices in the realm in turn handed her the symbols of power. The Sword and the Key were too heavy, so the Sword was borne by Lars Kagg, representing Gustav Horn who was absent, and the Key by Hermann Fleming in the place of Magnus de la Gardie, who naturally could not be there. Oxenstierna, now grown old, handed her the Orb, and the admiral of the realm, Gabriel Oxenstierna, the Sceptre. Finally, an old friend of Gustavus Adolphus', the *Reichsdrost* Per Brahe, came forward and placed the Swedish royal crown on her head, a crown which she was ready to renounce for ever. "It is the second time I do this," he said, adding that he would refuse to take it from the queen's head in the Royal Hall, for he desired everyone to know how little he was prepared to participate in a ceremony that was to him a deeply tragic one. For the same reason, Axel Oxenstierna had begged not to have to preside over the act of abdication and Schering Rosenhane did so in his place. When all the preparations were over, Queen Christina entered the Royal Hall soon after nine o'clock in the morning, followed by noblemen and councillors; the non-noble Estates and many onlookers had been waiting for some considerable time.

The lower part of the hall was reserved for the Estates, the onlookers crowded along the sides and above. Right in front, a platform had been erected with steps leading up to it; there stood the silver throne which Magnus Gabriel de la Gardie had presented to the queen for her coronation. To the right, below the throne, was a chair for Karl Gustav, to the left a table with cushions for the royal symbols to be laid upon. The men holding offices of State—Per Brahe, Axel Oxenstierna and their colleagues—stood with sombre faces at some distance from the throne. Nearest to the queen, evidently at her own express wish, stood on this occasion her new favourites: Claes Tott, Steinberg and Schlippenbach. Not one of them was really a representative of the nation from which Christina was about to take her leave.

Last of all came Schering Rosenhane to read the declaration in which the queen released her subjects from their oath of allegiance to her; with certain conditions, duly enumerated, power to rule was transferred to Karl Gustav. After the reading, Rosenhane handed him the document and received from him another, which he also read out. It contained the prince's pledge to carry out the aforesaid conditions conscientiously. At the end of the reading Rosenhane gave the document back to the prince, who advanced to the throne bowing deeply and handed it to the queen.

Then the queen made a sign to the five highest officers of the realm to come forward and remove the national symbols: Sword and Key were laid on the table, and on a signal from the marshal of the realm, first Axel then Gabriel Oxenstierna stepped forward to receive the Orb and Sceptre; these too were laid on the table.

Next the *Reichsdrost* was expected to come forward. The marshall of the realm kept making signs to him, but Per Brahe, honourable man that he was, stood motionless. The queen, too, waved to him several times, but he did not stir. Then the queen took the crown from her head herself, upon which Per Brahe came forward and took it from her hands. Finally, her two chamberlains removed the mantle which was also laid on the table.

The tale has often been told of the powerful impression made by the queen as she stood there in her simple white dress with only a fan in her hand. She quietly went to the edge of the platform and slowly descended the steps. She stopped on the bottom step. The marshal of the realm made a sign and Christina began to speak: "I thank God the Almighty", she said, "who let me be born of royal blood and made me queen of this great and mighty realm; I also thank Him for having endowed me with exceptional success and favours. I wish to thank also the men who carried on the government of the nation before I came of age, and the royal council and the Estates for the loyalty and devotion they have always shown me."

Christina then reported on what had been accomplished during her ten-year reign, and continued: "While I was thus carrying out my obligations, I never did anything with which my conscience would have to find fault. As far as in me lay, I sacrificed my tranquillity to promote yours and to obtain for you the advantages that you now enjoy. My conscience confers its positive and sincere approval on the whole of my reign."

After these words, so characteristic of her, she recalled the great merits of her dead father: "In this prince (turning to Karl Gustav), I give you a king who possesses such great qualities that he will diligently follow in the footsteps of my father and bring you prosperity. To ensure this prosperity of yours was my sole motive in contemplating the step I am taking today; I swear by my honour to promote the welfare of Sweden and her people in the future too."

Christina's speech lasted about half a hour, it was delivered with extraordinary ease, though with clear evidence of emotion —at moments her voice faltered and her eyes filled with tears. Naturally she made a strong impression on those present.

Per Brahe wrote: "Her Majesty spoke so well and so fluently, though at times sobs broke in her throat. Her Majesty moved many honourable men to tears, and everyone lamented that with her the royal line came to an end far sooner than God had appointed. She stood there like a lovely angel."

Schering Rosenhane replied to the queen's speech on behalf of the Estates. He spoke of the deep distress the Estates experienced at the queen's decision, one to which they must consent, though against their will. He thanked her for the good choice of a successor and for all the care she had taken of them as their sovereign. Finally, he begged the queen's pardon if any of them had ever been so unfortunate as to act against her in any way. After this speech, first Rosenhane, then the representatives of the four Estates, kissed the queen's hand.

Then the queen moved from the bottom step—the whole ceremony was, as we have seen, extremely well staged—and turned to Karl Gustav, who advanced towards her. She addressed him too, reminding him of the many and great kings who had sat on the throne of Sweden, and charging him to follow their example. She well knew the admirable qualities he possessed, and it was on their account, and not because they were kin, that she selected him as her heir. The sole thanks she would ask of him were, to see her mother was well cared for, and to look after the friends and servants whom she had to leave behind.

Then Christina took him by the hand and led him to the throne, pointed to the royal symbols in the table and begged him to place them upon himself. However, Karl Gustav's next step was to entreat her to resume her royal state and take up the throne again; she demurred, and there ensued a rather long interlude, with many flourishes and fine phrases after the fashion of the day, each intent on yielding first place to the other. In the end, they both stood once more at the bottom of the platform.

Now Karl Gustav spoke, gave thanks, turned to the Council and Estates, vowed to rule according to God's Word and the laws of Sweden, and finally prayed that the God of peace would bless his reign (a prayer that was not fulfilled) and that this great change would have no adverse effect upon the country and its inhabitants. Karl Gustav spoke with confidence and vigour, making a very favourable impression. Schering Rosenhane replied on behalf of the Estates and took the oath of loyalty and obedience, then the spokesmen of the four Estates came forward once more and kissed the new king's hand.

And so it ended. A contest over precedence now arose between Christina and Karl Gustav; each wished to walk on the left and accompany the other home. Finally the martial prince won the day.

Immediately afterwards the entire council, led by Axel Oxenstierna, appeared at the queen's residence and paid their last formal call on her. After them came, first, the representatives of the court and then the nobles. The queen shook hands with each of them.

Four hours later, Karl Gustav was crowned in the cathedral. Christina did not wish to be a witness of this ceremony, and spent the time taking a walk outside the city.

Later still, Christina wrote the following icy letter to her mother:

> As fate compels me to depart for ever from this city in which I was born, I shall thus be deprived of the honour of conveying my submission and reverence to Your Majesty. I consider it appropriate to take my leave of Your Majesty and beg you to give your consent to my decision, which will part me from you for ever. I know, Madam, that my conduct has not always enjoyed the honour of your approval, and that my final resolve will not please you, But the destiny that has elected to make me the happiest of all mankind requires that I accept my happiness at the cost of your disapproval. Do not think, Madam, that on this occasion I experience no distress at being deprived of the favour of seeing you once more. But as I know that I can be of no further use to you, I feel far less compunction about it; I know indeed that I am the only one who really suffers from this omission. Therefore I take leave of Your Majesty and thank you with all the submission and reverence I owe you, for the favours and the grace which I received from you at the time I had the honour to lie at your feet. In the position in which I now find myself, I can wish for nothing more fervently than to die after kissing your feet. But as fate considers me unworthy of this honour, I will renounce it without complaint, and will never cease, from wherever I may be, to accord Your Majesty such honour and reverence as are due to you. I humbly beg your forgiveness if I have

fallen short in the reverence I owe Your Majesty. God is my witness, that in accordance with my duty I have constantly been aware of this duty of reverence, and should I have been so unhappy as to have failed in my duty Your Majesty, I shall henceforth make it impossible to do so by expelling myself from the land, so that in future I shall be deprived of the honour of meeting you. Pray be satisfied with this reparation for my faults and spare me the distastefulness of your censure. Whatever Your Majesty may elect to do, I shall always bear in mind what I owe to you. I shall never indulge in any feeling that might cause Your Majesty to regret having given birth to me. In conclusion, Madam, I venture to assure you that I shall never commit any act unworthy of the daughter of the great Gustavus. I am and shall always remain, wherever I am, Your Majesty's very humble and obedient daughter and servant,

Christina.

Book II

CHRISTINA IN ROME

CHAPTER ONE

From Uppsala to Rome

I. EUROPEAN EXPERIENCES

AFTER the solemn abdication ceremony in the palace of Uppsala, in June 1654, the queen was eager to leave the country as soon as possible. Everything had been prepared beforehand.

The clergy wanted to include in the abdication decree, which guaranteed her a yearly income, a clause by which she in return for this guarantee would undertake not to give up the Protestant faith. It was quite unnecessary, she replied, and might even look as though there were some reason to doubt her adherence to the Lutheran doctrine in which she was born and reared, and to which she intended always to remain loyal. This was frankly dishonest and the fact that she stopped for a day in Stockholm and took the opportunity to go to the Palace church with some ostentation and take communion there, precisely to stifle rumours about her impending conversion, was quite in keeping with her cynical policy in general.

After a few more days in the capital, Christina gave out that she was travelling to Kalmar where Swedish ships were awaiting her, for she had expressed the wish to take the waters at Spa. In fact she never intended to travel via Kalmar, but set off direct and non-stop for Norrköping. However, even this was a ruse. She wrote blandly to King Karl Gustav that illness and adverse winds had made it impossible for her to embark at Kalmar and that she was now thinking of travelling through Denmark. She moved rapidly to Halmstadt, evidently in a very carefree and sardonic mood. From there she wrote to the French Epicurean philosopher Gassendi. She crossed the Swedish frontier, near Båstad, whereupon, it is said, she gave full rein to her joy.

The rest of the journey was decidedly romantic. Disguised as a knight, Christina called herself Count Dohna; she wore a sword at her side and carried a gun on her shoulder, put on high boots and rode astride on a man's saddle. Some doubt has been cast on the story that she met the Danish royal couple; the report runs that in an inn she recognized the Danish queen, supposedly disguised as a maid, and could not resist the temptation to mimic the Danish king, remarking afterwards that "curiosity killed the pussy-cat", or words to that effect. The story sounds too good to be true, but surprisingly enough it may well be true.

Otherwise the journey went forward without a hitch; the queen was in good physical training and covered the trek to Hamburg in six days, arriving there on 3 July. She stayed for a few weeks, took part in the festivities organized in her honour, visited the scholars and humanists of the city and condescended to receive the homage of a number of princes who had hurried over to pay their respects to her. From Hamburg comes a story which other sources declare to have occurred in other towns: Christina was seen in church apparently deeply engrossed in a prayer-book; one day she left it behind, and it was found to be a Virgil.

On 17 July, Christina set off again, once more in men's clothing. On her way to Holland she paid a visit to the Jesuits in Münster. Immediately upon her arrival in Deventer—late in the evening—she sought out the famous scholar Frederik Grovonius, and his equally renowned son, Jakob; she wanted to discuss learned topics with them and visit their library. In Holland she travelled incognito, but in Amersfoort visited a famous lady, Miss Schurman, for she knew her books and admired her miniatures, glass engravings and other works of art.

On 5 August, and still in men's clothing, Christina arrived in Antwerp where she moved into a splendid house which Don Garcia d'Yllan, an extremely wealthy Portuguese Jew, had placed at her disposal; this was all arranged beforehand. A Swedish report gives an accurate account of all her actions in this country, which was then under the Spanish crown. Christina was immediately surrounded by noblemen who rode up from all parts of Spanish Flanders. The idol of her youth, the Prince de Condé, hastened to write her a letter accounting for the defeat of the Spanish army at Arras, with apologies; at that time he was fighting against his own country, but that does not seem to have caused any concern to Christina. On 17 August she went on to Brussels to look at the churches and works of art, above all the large collections in the palace, consisting of treasures brought back from America; she also visited the Jesuits and the Carmelite monastery. Don Garcia d'Yllan had a palace there too, named Bornival; on 22 August she paid a call on him.

For September, we have a letter from Antwerp in which the famous general Montecucolli, who was to be a close friend later on, described her way of life: "Excursions, music, visits to the theatre . . ." The entertainments put on in Christina's honour made Antwerp look to him like "one of those happy islands that breathe peace and quiet in the midst of the tumultuous ocean, or one of those giant mountains soaring above mists and clouds which cannot disturb their tranquil majesty".

It became apparent that Christina spoke French extremely well, except that on the slightest pretext she broke into rather offensive expletives, "Pardieu. . . . Dieu me damne. . . . Mordieu. . . . Ma foy. . . ."; no doubt she had picked them up from the happy-go-lucky libertines who frequented her palace in Stockholm.

One day, Don Garcia d'Yllan invited the queen to his country house at Contich, near Antwerp. The festivities began with a ride, and after it the tables were groaning under the load they bore. As Christina rose from table, a terrible din broke out; the ladies who had stood demurely waiting now threw themselves on the dishes—"les mains y allaient de furie"—and the Flemish guests improvised a sort of *kermesse* which developed into a regular riot, with shouting, singing, music and thundering canon. When Christina came back to Antwerp the citizens fired a salute and a torchlight escort accompanied her home. The next day Christina was observed to be in some discomfort at the theatre—"fut mal à son aise—se remuant beaucoup sur la chaise", as a contemporary rhyme put it.

Then Archduke Leopold came to Antwerp to pay his respects

to the queen, after a delay due to the siege of Arras. During his visit she resided in the Saint-Michel convent and expressed the desire to be present at church services unobserved. Hitherto she had not shown the slightest sign of any intention to become a Catholic. The archduke suggested she should live in the Brussels palace, but she refused; she did not want to become too dependent on the Spaniards, but wanted to keep a free hand to negotiate. She told the archduke she had met the Spaniards half-way before leaving Sweden, in sending the envoy of rebellious Portugal home, but had been unable to prevent Karl Gustav from taking him back into favour. In the Saint-Michel convent Joost van Egmont, a painter of the Rubens School, painted some portraits of her, including the one in which she wears a Roman helmet, with a flower in her hand and a dog at her side. We know that on that occasion the queen expressed the wish to stay in the convent. It might be concluded she wanted to prepare for admission to the Catholic Church, but nothing came of it.

Christina had already written to the Prince de Condé when she was planning to abdicate. Shortly before she left Sweden, she wrote again, saying she must find "peace and quiet"; the price she had to pay for it was high, she said, but she would never be so cowardly as to regret her decision. Not a single word as to religious motives! In fact, the way Christina put it made it appear that she would never have left Sweden and her exalted position there, had she not believed it was necessary to her happiness ("je n'aurais pas quitté l'avantage que la fortune m'a donné, si je ne l'eusse cru nécessaire à ma félicité")—truly a surprising line of thought. No mention of a conflict with her duties nor of any nobler motive; the criterion of her actions was exclusively the degree of happiness to be gained! Haughtily she added, it would doubtless be much more attractive to "réussir ou mourir dans une si haute entreprise que celle du grand prince de Condé"—i.e. in betraying his country!

Equally curious is the fact that a formal meeting with the idolized hero was baulked by a question of étiquette; Condé requested to be received with the same ceremonial as Archduke Leopold, son of the Emperor—and Christina could but refuse.

During the first part of her stay in Spanish Flanders, she

5. EBBA SPARRE
Painting by Sébastien Bourdon (1653), in the National Gallery of Art, Washington
Photo: Svenska Porträttarkivet

6. MAGNUS GABRIEL DE LA GARDIE
Painting by Matthias Merian (1649), in Castle Skokloster
Photo: Svenska Porträttarkivet

maintained close relations with Spain; indirectly she had requested the Spanish king to approach the Pope in Rome in order to prepare her admission into the Church and her residence in Rome. All this was taking time—the Spaniards are slow-moving, wrote Christina's biographer, Sforza Pallavicino. During her wait, various matters arose showing how much caution was advisable. The Swedish State had formally undertaken to provide for her maintenance, but it soon appeared no very simple matter to obtain payment; for decades on end the queen's life was to be embittered by financial difficulties partly connected with the fact that Sweden was at war. Now she tried to arrange for one payment of a lump sum instead of a pension. Obviously she wanted the matter settled once for all before formally adopting Catholicism, for while still in Sweden she had foreseen that the pension might be withdrawn if she gave up her Lutheran faith. In Brussels gossip was rife and there was some misgiving as to the nature of her relations with Spain. There were tales of how, in the last days in Stockholm, there had been nocturnal visits to the palace by the Spanish general Pimentel: it was said he had repeatedly stayed as late as five o'clock in the morning. This may well have been true. But no special grounds need be adduced; Christina naturally wanted not to be disturbed while discussing the many complicated problems involved in her impending adoption of the Catholic faith. Pimentel now appeared in Brussels. Whereupon Christina's old friend Chanut called on the French envoy in Stockholm to discover whether she was really in process of establishing such close relations with Spain that French interests might suffer. Chanut was soon reassured.

2. THE RELIGIOUS QUESTION

Soon after her arrival in Flanders, Christina wrote to Countess Ebba Sparre, her intimate friend. She said her happiness would doubtless be complete if only Ebba were there to share it. We mentioned this letter earlier (p. 60) but it has a remarkable postscript:

> Please give my kind regards to all my friends, male and female, including those who are not interested. The latter I forgive whole-

> heartedly, for I do not feel hurt at all. I forget to tell you that I am getting on extremely well, I am garnering lots of tokens of respect, and am on good terms with everybody except the Prince de Condé, whom I only see in the theatre or at Court. I eat well, sleep well, read a little, chatter, laugh, go to plays, French, Italian or Spanish ones, and pass the time in the most agreeable way possible. In a word—I hear no more sermons, and as Solomon advised, I keep clear of all preachers. For one should live in contentment, eating, drinking and making merry.

What an astonishing statement! Christina was said to be eating well, though many eyewitnesses affirm she never cared for good food; she was sleeping well, though we know she despised people who took more than a few hours' sleep; she said with Solomon that one should eat, drink and be merry, whereas we know that all her life long, both before and after her stay in Flanders, she absolutely refused to drink wine, believing it was bad for her. But the next point, expressing her scorn for preachers and sermons, might give ground to the belief that this letter belongs to a whole series of forgeries: it seems to contradict all we know of her from other sources.

But judging by other criteria, it may still be genuine: let this be a warning to us. When a historic personality suddenly appears to adopt a mode of expression out of tune with earlier statements, it *may* be due to the impossibility of speaking frankly on the earlier occasion, or during a long period when a mask was worn of necessity. Christina wore her masks cleverly, her self-discipline was so impeccable that even someone long accustomed to her ways might doubt if it was really she who was speaking here. But then we find that the tone of the letter and its line of thought do agree with what other contemporary sources reveal of her behaviour during this interlude. We have no reason to doubt Christina's sincerity in giving up her Protestant faith, nor in adopting Catholicism. But we have to admit that two quite different reasons drew her to the Catholic Church: first, it was not split into numbers of mutually conflicting sects; and then, in certain matters, which she considered to be of less importance, it was tolerant. Her intentions in adopting the Catholic faith were sincere, but the brand of Catholicism she chose, with a great sense of deliverance, was that of the libertines, the "free-thinkers". If we did not know this, Christina's behaviour and talk in Flanders would be incomprehensible. When earlier historians, who assumed her to have been a strictly dogmatic Catholic, were confronted with her many cynical, frivolous, semi-blasphemous remarks they were bound to take refuge in a most improbable hypothesis, concluding she must be playing a deliberate part. Catholic writers in particular are all too eagerly apologetic in describing their impressions of what went on in Flanders. Sforza Pallavicino, later a cardinal, gave a very distressed account of her journey on to Rome:

> Outwardly she concealed most carefully the fact that she was a Catholic. All she was concerned about was conforming to the demands of conscience, so as not to perform some act that would lay her open to the charge of heresy. Hence the unreliable and ill-intentioned rumours that she had no religion at all; formerly a Lutheran, now an atheist, she was neither true to her former sect nor had taken up any new doctrine. The queen's freedom of speech certainly supported this view. She was neither devout nor prudent, but doubtless it was a clever trick to conceal her true beliefs. Her mannishness was all part of it: she was not at all prepared to put up with the usual restrictions on the female sex, and her royal blood had accustomed her to be a law unto herself and not accept dictation from her subjects.

Like many a later historian, Sforza Pallavicino held the view that Christina was playing a part because she was worried about her subsidies from Sweden; she was endeavouring to get the promised annuity exchanged for a once-for-all lump payment, and only when that was settled would she come into the open as a Catholic.

This might explain why she postponed her public conversion, though when it finally took place no settlement had been reached—but it can hardly explain her cynical, blasphemous talk and outrageous behaviour. There are many descriptions of Christina in Flanders, and all to the same effect: the great Condé himself wrote to the Comte de Fiesque about Christina's efforts to reconcile him with the French king:

> Ordinary people, and particularly priests, have begun to spread rumours about this peace proposal. They say Christina acknowledges no God, has not a single priest at her court, preaches atheism openly, cannot open her mouth without libertine expletives peppering her talk, and goes so far as to publicly defend the vices of all nations and both sexes, not finishing a single sentence without blaspheming.

Condé went on to say how distressed he was at the bad reputation the queen was rapidly acquiring in Flanders—though he would not like to be considered a prude, for he was her friend and respected her.

This is mere rumour: Christina hardly met the prince at all, for reasons of etiquette, even though for years he had been her great hero and they had carried on a friendly correspondence. But Condé was not alone in his views.

From Brussels, in 1655, Christina wrote once more to the French philosopher Gassendi, thanking him for still holding her in honour in spite of her surprising step. "Your respect will rehabilitate me in the eyes of those who have a bad opinion of my actions, and your reassurance will sufficiently endorse my own conviction that I have acted rightly." That does not sound very self-confident. We must, however, remember to whom the letter was addressed: Pierre Gassendi was the foremost neo-Epicurean of the century. The very fact that Christina turned to him in particular, counting on his approval of her actions, is significant. The letter was written in January 1655; by then Christina had already renounced her Protestant faith. How far Gassendi was aware of this is not known; perhaps Christina was merely referring to her abdication. In any case it is remarkable that at such a point she did not confide in one of the more prominent French bishops; but no, the man whose approbation she wanted to be sure of was the greatest and most famous of the Epicureans.

Somewhat earlier, Christina had visited the Jesuits at Louvain. One of the Fathers remarked that the queen would surely be the equal of St Bridget, still the only saint of Sweden—and indeed of the entire North of Europe. Christina is said to have retorted that she would rather be counted among scholars than among saints.

Here we come to what constitutes the main proof of what Christina's views really were. The story occurs in 1656, not long after her solemn reception into the Catholic Church. At the time she was travelling in France—we will come back to that journey later on. In Dijon she had a meeting with a French scholar, Claude-Barthelemy Morisot. The queen asked him what religion he belonged to. In some surprise the learned man replied that he belonged to the Catholic religion, but had he been brought up in another, he would still have adhered to the Catholic faith, in order to follow so great a princess in doing so. Christina then enquired what religion she herself held, in his view. Morisot naturally answered, it was generally known she had renounced the superstitions of her country in favour of the one true Catholic religion. "You are mistaken", said Christina, "Illa Morisotum ignorantiae accusavit, seque Philosophorum, religionem (verba Christinae sunt) omnibus aliis praeferre, testata est" (i.e. she said that Morisot was not well-informed, since (and these are her own words) she prized the religion of the philosophers above all others). By which she meant Morisot had no idea of her real position. By philosophers she meant those of antiquity, specially the Stoics. Morisot must have been somewhat taken aback; he replied that he considered the religion of those philosophers to be rather too generalized. Christina said the philosophers' religion was splendidly and unequivocally set out by Lucretius in his *De rerum natura*. This was the only religion she had adopted. And finally she gave the scholar a piece of advice: to write a commentary on Lucretius.

Thus in a confidential and well-authenticated conversation with a leading French intellectual, a bare year after her reception into the Catholic Church, Christina admitted that she was in complete sympathy with the profoundly pessimistic Roman philosopher and poet who stood for the most pitiless form of materialism.

There are many other instances of the same kind that could be cited, while there is no evidence at all to suggest the contrary, no instance of a devout or humble attitude or a strict dogmatic viewpoint in Christina. The witnesses are unanimous: Christina appeared consistently as a libertine, hated piety and churchiness and even immediately before her reception into the Church made no attempt to conceal these innermost convictions of hers. If anyone still wants to interpret her conduct during that important year in Flanders as a mere blind and subterfuge, the probability is further undermined by her behaviour during the first years in Rome.

It seems more likely that to the last minute the queen wavered. She had several reasons, as we have seen, for regarding conversion to Catholicism as the most practical solution, but she hesitated for a long time. We know it from a priest, the Dominican, Father Guemes, who was in touch with her in Flanders and for the first years in Rome. Until she actually abjured the Protestant faith at his hands, he greatly feared she might simply change her mind and remain a pure libertine.

We find the same concern in correspondence between her friend Chanut and his devout colleague, the French diplomatist de la Barde, whom we met earlier (p. 133). De la Barde was deeply disturbed; either one is for the Church or one is against it: "I belong to those who hold that you have to decide either for what is good or for what is evil; in this matter there can be no half measures." In the queen's letters to Chanut—which were immediately copied and distributed (perhaps at her own suggestion), he detected rather "the ideal of the pagans and philosophers". He also wrote—and he may have been quite right: "She has got no further than those who learn to know God through the visible things He has created, that is, through philosophy which confronts us with the necessity of acknowledging the principle lying behind all visible things", adding, she needed now "what God alone can give her, and in addition spiritual guides untainted with the philosophy of the pagans and their morality, to which she conforms all too thoroughly". So de la Barde regretted her libertinism; he also regretted her coming to Antwerp dressed as a man: "I should be in favour of her rising above her sex through spiritual rather than corporal exercises, should she want to emulate manly qualities in the future." Finally he said how much he regretted not finding in this royal lady's letters what he had sought there: "I was under the illusion she would name the motives that had urged her to renounce her crown."

Chanut, who knew Christina better than most, came to her defence when de la Barde refused to admit that she was a sincere Catholic—but he had to agree she had a long way to go before she would be ready to abandon her present humanistic standpoint in favour of the pure doctrine of the Church. He pinned his hopes on the future.

A correspondence between two Swedish clergymen, Pastor J. G. Gezelius and Provost J. Guthraeus, in the early part of 1655, throws a good deal of light on the queen's attitude. Apparently she had written fierce letters to people who declared she had submitted to Catholicism. An abbess was said to have congratulated her because she hesitated to marry and forsook worldly power; asked if she was attracted by the quiet life of a nun in a convent, Christina is supposed to have replied that the first points were correct, but she would still rather marry than be a nun. On the subject of monks, she is said to have declared: "Nowhere have I ever seen so many idiots together." This story must be pure invention: there is much evidence that Christina treated the monks she met with great respect and reverence.

In fact the queen regularly visited monasteries, discussed learned and theological questions with the Religious and expressed her intention to spend some time in a religious house. Every now and then she secretly went to Mass. From these facts, as from the equally credible accounts of her cynical and sceptical remarks, there is only one conclusion to be drawn—she clung stubbornly to the line she had adopted: it led her to Catholicism, in principle she acknowledged its authority, but she wanted to become a Catholic in her own way; she also wanted not to forgo the right to criticism in matters that seemed to her of minor importance. These were the problems she raised in Flanders—the same ones as she had discussed with the French free-thinkers she gathered around her in the palace of Stockholm.

After a time her entourage noticed that Christina's original high spirits had given way to melancholy and absent-mindedness.

This was thought to be due to her mother's death—for no one in Flanders had any idea how little mother and daughter had ever had in common. The truth was, the time was drawing near when she would have to come to a decision, either to take the definite step of becoming a Catholic officially, or to find another way out. Presumably she would have preferred to wait, for her future material sustenance still seemed quite insecure. But she had started the landslide herself and could no longer hold it back. Towards the end of the year 1654, she realized that something must happen. She chose, however—as so often in her life—a cunningly contrived middle course. She still did not come out into the open as a Catholic, but consented, under strong pressure from the Dominican Father Guemes, to take one step forward. On Christmas Eve, in the private chapel of the archduke in Brussels (of course not in his bedroom, as has been said), a secret ceremony took place at which she abjured her Lutheran faith.

It is further known that she frequently visited the Jesuits in Antwerp, at their house in the rue Ruysbroeck, and discussed religious problems with them. She also paid a visit to the learned Jesuit Bollandus. How much she was committed to silence and how well she was able to keep her secret is apparent from the fact that the Jesuits taking part in these discussions had no idea that she had already abjured her Lutheran faith.

Christina had the intention of leaving matters at that for the time being, though she still planned to travel on to Rome. But she received some news that meant one thing only: the Pope did not think he would be able to prepare a reception worthy of the queen before she had been officially received into the Catholic Church. Now it was too late to retreat, and as she could no longer procrastinate she decided to inform the world of her reception into the Catholic Church on her way to Rome; very few people were in the secret or knew when or where it was to take place.

3. CHRISTINA IS RECEIVED INTO THE CATHOLIC CHURCH

Christina left Brussels on 22 September 1655. The archduke, with a brilliant escort of nobles and men of high rank, accompanied her for two miles through the city and beyond. Two companies of his guard followed her. In her suite were Pimentel and Don Antonio de la Cueva Sylva with their wives, and a Neapolitan, Don Francisco Deza, together with her Swedish staff, in all not less than two hundred persons. On the first evening the queen was welcomed by the university of Louvain and spent the night there. The next day she halted at the miraculous statue of the Virgin Mary in Montaigu, to which she paid homage. At Roermond, reached on 25 September, a splendid reception was given by the Count d'Isenghien, governor of the Spanish province of Gelderland: the garrison paraded, cannon thundered and there was a tremendous firework display in the evening. Then the queen went on through Cologne, Frankfurt, Rothenburg, Donauwörth, and Augsburg to Innsbruck, where a date was fixed: 3 November.

Pope Alexander VII had given careful thought to the matter. He was of the opinion that the queen's reception into the Church must have the support of a papal legate. His choice fell on Lucas Holstenius, a canon of St. Peter's, who presided over the Vatican library. This choice was not fortuitous, Holstenius was born a Lutheran in Hamburg, so he, too, was a convert. His intensive studies of the Church Fathers were said to have led him away from Lutheranism, and he was known as one of the most learned men in Italy. Alexander VII admired him and had even dedicated some of his poems to him, and Queen Christina had exchanged letters with him over a long period, in fact there is a possibility that he played some part in her leaning towards Catholicism. In Rome there is an unpublished manuscript with details of contacts between the queen and Holstenius during her last years in Sweden, for among her Italian musicians in Stockholm was a man named Tomasso, who then returned to Rome and played in St Peter's church. Through him Holstenius obtained details about Christina's life—that she read Catholic books and biographies of saints, but that when questioned by the Lutheran clergy, she said they were books of mere poetry; and that she eagerly awaited news from Rome.

No one in Innsbruck knew why Holstenius had come. A splendid and entirely worldly reception had been prepared for the queen, but Holstenius brought with him a letter from the Pope inviting her to visit him, and informing her of the fact that he had formal authority to receive her declaration of faith.

On 3 November, dressed in a simple black dress, adorned with only a diamond cross on her left breast, Christina entered the Court Church. The Archdukes Ferdinand Karl and Sigismund escorted her from the Hofburg. She knelt before the altar and in clear tones—some said, a mannish voice—read slowly and distinctly the Tridentine Creed that Holstenius handed to her. She declared that this was her belief, and was then received into the Church with the usual ceremonial. The archbishop's court preacher, the Jesuit Father Staudacher, preached a sermon in German.

Mass with the Te Deum was followed by a banquet at which pages did a torch dance, and a mythological play was performed.

Christina remained a whole week in Innsbruck and then travelled through Trent and Mantua to Ferrara. Everywhere she went, homage was paid her with elaborate ceremony. It was no easy matter for the Pope to decide on the etiquette required at her reception at the frontier of the Papal States. After studying the ceremonial and earlier cases of precedence, he came to the conclusion that four prelates should be sent to meet her: those chosen were the Archbishop of Tebe, Hannibal Bentivoglio, the Archbishop of Ravenna, and two other high-ranking prelates, Innico Caraccioli and Alessandro Cesarini. These four were rather vaguely given the covering title of nuncios, so that they could rank higher than the Spaniard Pimentel. As "legates" the Pope selected two cardinals, but only cardinals with lower orders, that is, two cardinal deacons, in order to reserve the possibility of conferring even greater honours, in case one day a queen of more exalted standing should come, for instance the French or the Spanish queen, who would then be welcomed by cardinal priests or cardinal bishops. But among the cardinal deacons the Pope chose the most outstanding in the person of Cardinal Giancarlo de Medici, a younger brother of the archduke and son of a younger sister of Emperor Ferdinand II, and also Cardinal Frederick of Hesse, a cousin of Christina's. Before the queen could cross into the Papal States, the Pope was to receive a letter from her, and this letter was duly drawn up as follows:

Most Holy Father,

Now that I have at last reached the goal for which I so ardently longed and have been received into the bosom of our Holy Mother the Roman Catholic Church, I would not fail to inform Your Holiness, and humbly beg you to honour me by bestowing upon me your benevolent commands, which I shall observe with all the respect I owe Your Holiness. I have shown the world with great joy how I left the land in which it is an unpardonable sin to revere You, and set all human prudence aside in order to let it be known that I put more value on the honour of obeying Your Holiness than on the most exalted throne. Now that I am rid of every human greatness, I implore Your Holiness to regard me with the same paternal benevolence that Your Holiness has hitherto always accorded me. As for me, I can but lay my humble person at Your Holiness' feet. Together with my blood and life, I offer Your Holiness my entire person with the blind obedience that is due to you, and implore Your Holiness to deal with me as Your Holiness may see fit, for the greater benefit of our Holy Church. To her, and to Your Holiness as her one true Head, I have dedicated the rest of my life, with the ardent desire to employ it to the greater glory of God. I pray God to grant Your Holiness many long and happy years, as is so supremely necessary for the security and welfare of all Christendom. With the prayer that God may sustain in Your Holiness the great gifts with which He has endowed You, and that He may permit me to enjoy a day I long for, when I may fall and humbly kiss Your Holiness' feet, I beg You to accord me Your Holiness' paternal blessing.

Innsbruck, 5 November 1655.
Your Holiness' obedient daughter,

Christina.

We know the details from Cardinal Pietro Sforza Pallavicino, who wrote a history of the first five years of Alexander VII's pontificate—unpublished till the nineteenth century. After receiving Christina's letter, the Pope called a Consistory and gave the cardinals an account of the whole affair in broad outline.

Fabio Chigi, Alexander VII, had been the Vatican nuncio at the peace deliberations in Münster and had protested in vain against the measures the Peace of Westphalia was to impose. We know from other sources how greatly upset and disturbed he was, observing how the Protestant delegates regarded the Catholic ones as altogether inferior, morally. He himself was a man of quite differenstature from his two immediate predecessors: he took the opportunity to warm the cardinals, in grave tones urging them to see that on the queen's arrival in Rome nothing untoward occurred to scandalize her. "If on the other side of the Alps she may have heard things unfavourable to Rome, she should be able to see it is not so, and that Roman standards are even higher than their renown." The Pope declared he was sure this was true of the cardinals, though in reality we know he was much concerned at the prevailing low standards. He desired them "to keep a watchful eye on the clergy around them, especially at worship and in Church, for curiously enough, people coming from the other side of the Alps were shocked to see little remarks being made, and even official exchanges of views taking place, at the altar." "The Protestants", he continued, "keep a keen look-out for any bad behaviour on the part of Italians, watching every glance, every little thing that they think will provide a clue to their attitude, and they put it all down in their memoirs so that posterity may learn of it." The Pope had in mind some diaries he had seen in Cologne when he was nuncio in Münster: those of noble laymen who always jotted down the events of the day before going to bed. Oddly enough, the Pope seemed to have had access to these diaries, and he now quoted some passages containing very critical remarks about certain cardinals. The point went home. The cardinals were furious, some banded together and drew up a kind of protest stating that the whole College was offended and felt its reputation was at stake, and at the hands of the very man who should uphold it. "But the more conscientious cardinals agreed with the Pope's remarks; they appreciated how irresponsible it would be if a doctor, instead of prescribing medicine, simply declared that his patient was in good health."

It was a paradoxical situation. The Pope was a man of honour, though otherwise insignificant, and he was ashamed of the signs of decadence among the Roman clergy. He did his best to warn the cardinals—but why?—because he took it for granted that his guest, a one-time Protestant, would be a lady of strict moral views, who knew of the Roman Church only its Head, and might be shocked and alarmed on coming into contact with Rome itself. But of course there were no such grounds for concern. The queen was accustomed to speak the proud language of Stoicism and to criticize other people openly, though she would advance sham arguments just as readily as real ones. On one point in particular the Pope was entirely mistaken; he believed she had undergone a religious crisis and had joined the Catholic Church as a result of it.

What a gulf there was, in reality, between Christina's attitude to the Catholic faith and for instance Pascal's; his personal experience of God's mystery occurred in that same year in which Christina abdicated. In one case we have a rational piece of calculation, honest enough in its way but utterly remote from spiritual experience and emotional upheaval, which never for an instant caused Christina to flinch or change her views; in the other, a soul totally and entirely laid open to God, absorbing His grace and undergoing an utter transformation of his whole life. Christina had the heroism of her step trumpeted to the world at large, Pascal never mentioned to anyone at all the greatest and most decisive experience of his whole life; only after his death was a scrap of paper found sewn into his coat, on which he had scribbled down in flaming, apparently disconnected, words what he had experienced in that great moment.

But one or two of the cardinals knew the queen to be quite different. Christina's bold retorts, her cynicism and swearing had caused such a sensation in Flanders that rumours had drifted to Rome. Some of them recommended caution; the whole thing might turn out to be nothing but an insidious political plot. And worried as they were about Christina's Spanish contacts, certain Frenchmen gave the same warning.

Particularly in Venice the plans for Christina's reception caused much bad feeling. At that very time messengers had been sent to the Pope in the hope of obtaining help in the war against the Turks and in the liberation of Crete. The sums spent on the queen's welcome were looked at askance. But as Sforza Pallavicino soberly noted, "No one realized that the money would scarcely have lasted a fortnight if allocated to military requirements." The Venetians forgot that at the same time the Pope granted them a large subsidy for their efforts against the Turks.

Of Christina's appearance and conduct at the time, an entry in the minutes of the city of Bologna's Senate gives us a vivid picture:

> This high-ranking lady was not exactly tall, but certainly not inconspicuous. She had a commanding expression displaying majesty. Her colouring was high, neither blonde nor brunette. Her large eyes glowed with the fighting spirit of her proud disposition. Her well-formed nose gave her face a noble, royal look, softened by the small mouth. Her lips which were of a fine red colour, might have made a Venus of her, had it not been for so many other details of her physique and her bearing, which would have made one swear she was a Mars. And this was further stressed by her clothing, her short hair—she wore amazing wigs which she changed from time to time—and her horsemanship, for she could vie with the most consummate male riders. In brief, she had more mannish traits than feminine ones, her voice and her whole conduct betrayed that she was the daughter of her great father, accustomed to victory and triumph. Such was she.

At the splendid ball given by the city in her honour, she appeared in a different dress. She wore "a blond wig, with heavy make-up and powder, around her neck a kerchief of Genoese lace knotted with fiery red ribbons. She wore a full-length dress of the same colour stitched with silver and gold, and a grey underskirt also adorned with gold and silver stitching. Her footwear was more like a man's."

On 20 November, on the way to Ferrara, at a spot near Melara on the river Po, the queen was met by two nuncios. They handed her a letter from the Pope and presented her with a state coach, a sedan chair and a travelling chair. Christina immediately got into the coach, addressed the cardinals as "Your Eminence"—a courtesy title not required from someone of royal blood—and behaved to them with the utmost politeness. In all the towns through which she travelled, she insisted on being taken first to the church and attending a religious service. Everywhere she visited places where relics of saints were treasured, including Assisi, though she had to make a great détour to pay her respects to the relics of St. Francis. She seemed particularly struck by the "Holy House of Loretto"; she went on there from Ancona, and when the church cupola appeared she got out of the papal coach and walked bare-headed—"in spite of the cold season and her delicate health which made her find the cold trying"—all the way up the long hill to the town. In the church she unfolded a baldachin; she prayed, so it was believed, with such fervour in the holy chapel that those present were moved to tears. Next morning she received Communion, but still in private; she had resolved not to take Holy Communion in public till she could receive it from the Pope's own hand. As a gift for the Blessed Virgin she presented her own sceptre and a crown of massive gold set with a great many large diamonds. Holstenius wrote a distich in honour of the occasion, to the effect that she gave the Mother of God a *spretam coronam*, that is, the crown she had *scorned*; the queen protested and got him to change the word *spretam* to *positam*, the one she had laid down. For never, she said, would she have ventured to give the Queen of Heaven something she scorned, but only what she valued most highly.

On 20 December, the queen came to a villa belonging to the Olgiati family, about a hundred kilometres from Rome. On the same morning the legates selected by the Pope left Rome to meet her on her way. Pallavicino describes the scene: "They formed a cavalcade with such splendid robes and liveries, caparisons and adornments, that the like had never been seen. . . . On leaving Rome they got into their carriages and at Storta, thirty kilometres from journey's end, the queen's majordomo came to meet them and invited them to ride in one of his sovereign's carriages. When they reached the palace in which she had taken up her residence, they saw the queen come down with exaggerated courtesy to meet them, whereupon she preceded them and received them at the door."

For the last stage of the journey to Rome all travelled together in a blue state coach. Sforza Pallavicino, usually so dry in style, here rose to almost lyrical heights: "And the night that fell did not dim the pomp, but rather enhanced it with the torches and lights that were now lit all around."

4. ARRIVAL IN ROME

Where was the queen to live in Rome?

It was considered unsuitable for a woman to be lodged in the Vatican itself. The Pope had all sorts of scruples, recalling the scandal when his predecessor Innocent X had his sister-in-law, Olimpia Maidalchini, there, who kept him under her thumb, and made good use of him. He even forbade Olimpia to show herself during Christina's entry into the city. The queen came to Rome in the cold season, late in the evening. Originally it had been proposed she should reside in the palazzo Farnese, directly next to the Bridgettines' convent. But now it was felt advisable that after her welcome by the Holy Father, she should not have to return through rain, cold and darkness, to the palazzo Farnese, so temporary quarters nearer at hand were sought.

In the extensive complex of buildings that composed the Vatican, there was a house sufficiently far away from the Pope's private apartments, and only connected to them by a very long corridor downstairs and an equally long gallery upstairs. It was not far from the Belvedere Gardens and immediately alongside the Vatican library. So it was decided to lodge the guest here; on account of her high rank, it was permissible for the queen to live under the same roof as the Pope, though as far as possible away from him. The place was splendidly arranged with furniture and other items from the Vatican collections, and with various loaned treasures from friendly or amicably-inclined Roman families. The Pope himself supervised every detail. Among much else the house contained the so-called wind-tower with the different winds pictured on it. The Pope observed that there was a text from Scripture under the north wind, *omne malum ab aquilone* (all

7. CHRISTINA
Engraving by C. de Vischer based on a portrait by David Beck, published by P. Soutman (1650)
Photo: The Royal Library, Stockholm

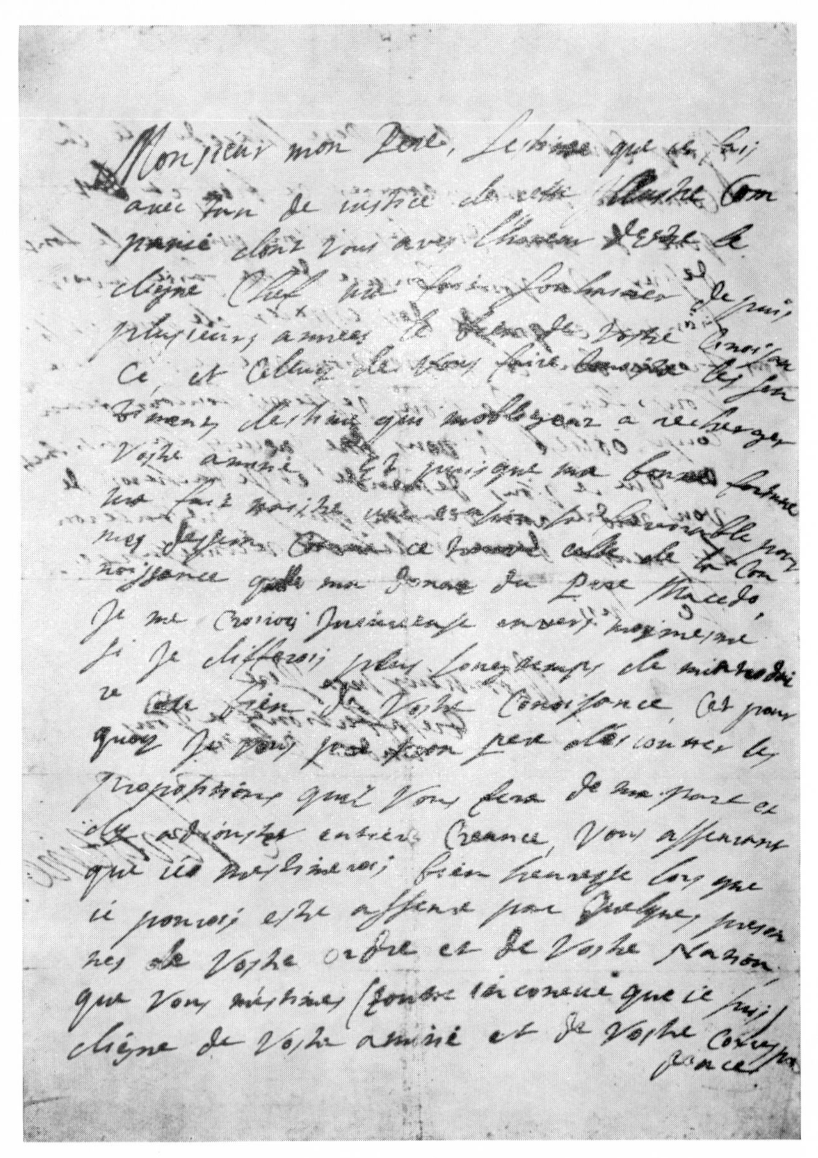

8. The first page of a letter from Christina to the Father General of the Jesuits (September 1651), in the Archives of the Society of Jesus, Rome

evil comes from the north), and he had the inappropriate words painted over, so that neither the queen nor anyone of her entourage could take offence.

Christina reached Rome at about nine in the evening and drove through "the gateway to the public part of the Vatican Gardens, then on to the gateway leading to the enclosed part". Here she was welcomed by the papal Court and retinue and taken to the residence prepared for her, where she removed her travelling clothes and put on ceremonial dress. Then she was escorted along the upstairs gallery to the Pope. All the notabilities, clerical and lay, were in attendance with him. When she caught sight of him on his throne, she genuflected three times and kissed his hand and foot. He stood up at once and offered her a seat, not opposite him, as to lesser royalty, but at his right hand, and—a very special honour—under his own baldachin. She sat on a chair covered with crimson satin but with no arms. After the first word or two of her address, she grew confused and began to stutter. The Pope remained calm, interrupted her with a few kind words, and encouraged her to go on. She spoke for half an hour. Then the queen withdrew to her residence. The next day she visited the Vatican buildings and collections, her knowledge of art making a marked impression.

On 23 December, the legates came again with a splendid retinue to take her away. She was now simply dressed in a dark green mantle stitched all over with silver, and drove with them to Ponte Milvio, outside Rome. There the city governor, with the more distinguished of his officers, gave her an official welcome. He took her to a famous villa built by Pope Julius II, which was often used for receptions. Numerous representatives of the Vatican were there and after a speech of welcome, gifts were presented: an ambling horse, a coach-and-six, a sedan-chair, and an elegant armchair, for Christina. The carriage was built on a model of Bernini's; the queen had displayed interest in him before leaving Sweden, and he was soon to become a close friend. The queen mounted, the two legates, in soutanes and long cloaks, mounted too, and in the midst of a splendid cavalcade of distinguished lords, Christina rode to the Porta Flaminia, where the College of

Cardinals in brilliant robes waited on horseback to form an escort of honour. Cardinal Barberini as senior cardinal greeted her with an address. The legates' duties were now completed and they took their place in the stately procession; the queen rode at a slow pace into the city between Cardinals Orsini and Costaguti, the senior cardinal-deacons.

"The numbers present and their high rank, the pomp and splendour, the beauty and richness of the robes, all created an effect as though of a sea, into which flowed like a great river the lady whom the legates had escorted to Rome two days earlier."

The Porta Flaminia—Porta del Popolo today—was restored under Bernini's supervision: the Vasa coat of arms can still be seen on it; alongside there was an empty space; Bernini let the Pope know how many letters could be carved there, and the Pope himself composed the inscription: *Felici faustoque ornata ingressui anno MDCLV* (done to commemorate a happy and blessed arrival in 1655). Sforza Pallavicino made one of his characteristic entries: "By this means he intended to draw posterity's attention, though without undue stress, to the fact that the inscription was added on the occasion of the queen's arrival in Rome. Here as elsewhere, the Pope ably found a mean between over-stress and reserve; what he did was adequate but not excessive."

The day was officially declared a general holiday; as far as possible all were to decorate their houses and windows. So it looked as though the queen were riding "through a single splendidly-decorated palace". "With the exception of the nuns and the sick", the entire population of Rome had come out to watch; drums beat and trumpets blared throughout the city, and as Christina approached the Castello S. Angelo, the air quaked with thundering cannon. On the next two nights there were firework displays and the city was illuminated.

On reaching the Vatican, Christina went on foot between two cardinals to St. Peter's. She was welcomed at the door by the cathedral chapter and then escorted to the high altar where the sacrament was exposed. The basilica was adorned with tapestries sewn with gold; everywhere there were emblems and symbols referring to the queen in some way. Then she was conducted to some stairs leading from the basilica to the Pope's apartments. On reaching the Sistine Chapel, where the Pope was to receive her in a public consistory, she genuflected three times as ritual required, while the two cardinals on either side of her bowed. At the third genuflection she reached the podium where the Pope was enthroned; she kissed his foot and his hand. Only a few words were exchanged and the ceremony was over.

Two days later, on Christmas day, Christina was escorted by two cardinals and four bishops to St. Peter's, where the Pope was celebrating Mass in person. At Innsbruck she had already said she wanted to take a new name and would call herself Christina Alexandra; this was to be a sign of her devotion to her new Father, the Pope, and some days before she had enquired if this could be done. The Pope, cautious as ever, replied that the idea appealed to him, as the connection was not with his private name but with the one he bore as successor to St Peter. But as, even before her prayer to St Peter, she had done such high honour to the Holy Virgin of Loreto, he would like her to add the name of Maria and place it before Alexandra. This was done. But Christina never used the name Mary. She mostly signed official documents as Christina Alexandra. Knowing of her enthusiastic essay on Alexander the Great, we may suppose that in her mind the name always stood for that ancient glory she admired so much.

Then came Mass, and for Christina her first Communion in Rome, which was at the same time the first official Communion of her life.

The banquet that followed was the talk of the town for a long time to come. The queen sat near the Pope, not at his table but—though under the same baldachin—at a neighbouring table four inches lower. The banquet was watched by a great crowd of onlookers, and during it a sermon was preached by Father Oliva, chaplain to the Pope, and later the General of the Jesuits, and choirs sang.

On the evening of the same day, Queen Christina took up her residence at the first of her homes in Rome, the palazzo Farnese.

CHAPTER TWO

Rome, the Great Metropolis

I. ROME AND SCHOLARSHIP

CHRISTINA had spent years learning about Rome and conditions there. In Stockholm she had in her entourage numbers of Italians, mainly singers and musicians. She zealously studied the works of the Italian renaissance brought back to her as booty by her campaigning generals and ready at hand in her Castle of the Three Crowns. She was in correspondence with Paolo Giordano II, Duke of Bracciano, a poet, painter and sculptor, a musician and patron of many artists. He had even invented a new musical instrument that he called a *rosidra*. He had visited the North too, and raved about the white snow and light nights. In his correspondence with the Queen of Sweden he soon took to signing his letters, "Your slave, shackled to you by chains of iron"; he sent her poems and works of art. Christina for her part sent him a miniature of herself and wrote she wished she could have come in person. The duke was so delighted that he replied with a bad sonnet and a valuable mosaic. After Christina thanked him for the present, he sent her in 1652 his poem *Il Cancionere e le Satire*, and also a copy on enamel of her own miniature portrait. In her further letter of thanks the queen remarked that she looked at least three years younger in it. The duke gladly answered all her questions about artistic and literary life in Rome.

We know too that Christina was much complimented on her expert knowledge of Italian art. It is hard to decide whether this was flattery or seriously meant. But when we remember that in Stockholm she had an Italian opera company and an Italian orchestra, was surrounded by outstanding Italian works of art, was in correspondence with distinguished Italians, and finally, had held intensive converse on serious topics with two learned Italian priests, Malines and Casati, we are entitled to conclude she was in fact very well informed. But it still remains doubtful whether she had a right idea of the cultural milieu in which she was now to live.

Though at the beginning of the sixteenth century Italy still occupied a leading place in the field of scholarship and learning, in the course of the following century nearly all her great talents had departed. In 1660 Giordano Bruno was burnt at the stake in Rome, in 1691 the unbridled heretic and blasphemer Vanini was burnt at Toulouse; in 1616 Copernicus was placed on the Index; in 1633 Galileo had to abjure his scientific convictions to escape lifelong imprisonment or worse; in 1649 Campanella died in France; in 1653 Jansenism was condemned by a papal Bull; ten years later Descartes came on the Index. Between the Sack of Rome in 1527—Rome laid waste by Charles V's soldiery—and 1633, when silence was imposed on Galileo, Italy's intellectual life fell to a low ebb. Nearly all Italian scholars had to flee the country, and Italy was largely dependent on Spain, not only politically but also culturally. In Venice—with the university of Padua—and in the passionate city of Naples, certain attempts can be traced to make a stand against reaction, but they grew weaker and weaker.

The submission of Galileo was treated by the Church as equal to a victory over the Turks. By means of public postings, newspapers and the nuncio's reports, news of Galileo's retraction spread all over the world. The scholars were appalled for they knew it was done under duress and that his own convictions were otherwise. Descartes was so shocked that he destroyed his *Traité du Monde*, a study of Copernicus. A great student of the history of cultures has written: "Now Roman baroque rings in the great hour of Protestant scholarship." Elia Diadoti, Galileo's friend, an Italian Calvinist emigrant living in Paris, gave Bernegger, a prominent Strasbourg Protestant, the task of translating Galileo's dialogues. The book almost became a piece of Protestant polemics. Galileo was under supervision but was able to smuggle out his permission for a Latin and English translation of his work which appeared in 1635. In Paris Hugo Grotius, in league with Galileo's friends, tried to get him to Holland, which after Switzerland was the main refuge for European scholars and intellectuals fleeing from reaction. Grotius described the Dialogues as the most important book of his time. Galileo went on working and sent his writings secretly to Geneva, Strasbourg and Leyden. His *Dialoghi delle nuove scienze*, the first systematic exposition of standard mechanics, was dedicated to the French Comte de Noailles, the one who as envoy—partly in co-operation with Christina's later friend and physician Bourdelot—rescued Campanella from Italy and got him to France.

Practically all Galileo's disciples had to leave Italy. But this did not mean the Church was antagonistic to all reasonable modern science. Even Galileo presented certain discoveries as proved which very soon turned out to be quite unfounded. And to what deterioration free-thinking could lead is best traced in the ideas and life of the intellectual revolutionary Campanella.

He was a Dominican, son of a poor family in Calabria. In 1599 he organized a rebellion against Spanish rule in Naples; three hundred Religious took part in the conspiracy (Dominicans, Franciscans and Augustinians). He spent twenty-seven years in prison, was tortured seven times and finally set free—whereupon he immediately sought contacts in Europe. He offered his services to Galileo, negotiated with James I of England, wrote to the French philosophers Gassendi and Mersenne, and looked for Descartes in Holland, though in vain. Campanella totally rejected Thomas Aquinas and the official Church doctrine, and he considered himself the one true Catholic. He described the ideal State as a "Sun State" which he pictured as a model for a renewed Catholic Church. At its head would stand the Pope with St Paul's Army and St Peter's Fleet, to *compel* people to keep peace. As the centre-point of this State he pictured a Temple of Science and Art. Here ruled *Il Sole*, a priest-emperor, with three exalted princes at his side: Power, Wisdom and Love. All founders of religions—Moses, Osiris, Jupiter, Mercury, Christ, Caesar, Alexander *e tutti li romani* watch over the High Council of this State whose spies bring in news of whatever happens anywhere. The sole duty of the State consists in mobilizing a new humanity, with iron discipline. Men and women are warriors and they wear armour all the time. Merciless terror reigns. During his confinement in the prison of the Spanish Inquisition in Naples, Campanello worked out even worse tortures for his own Sun State. He wanted all the people in it to be State monks following the law of Christ in total poverty and total obedience. He considered his Sun State as an apostolic community in which the new rational and at the same time truly evangelical man was to be produced by means of terror, ascetism, science and *raison d'état.*

Such were the extravagant fantasies that sprang from the brain of a gifted but reckless Catholic friar—it is understandable that the Church was indignant and took powerful measures to protect itself. And there were quantities of these intellectual excrescences which the Church rightly rejected. But though reaction was without doubt justified in these cases, the fact remains that for centuries the Church made disinterested scholarship impossible in Italy and drove nearly all the best minds into exile.

And it was into *this* Italy that Christina now came. . . . True, a lot of water had flowed under the bridges since Galileo's retraction; the younger generation of Jesuits in the Collegium Romanum—above all Casati, with whom Christina had held discussions in Stockholm—began gradually and prudently to withdraw their hostility to Galileo and the modern outlook. When in Stockholm, before her final decision, Christina put questions to the Italian Jesuits on the Church's attitude to the new natural sciences, much of what she was asking was extremely relevant; this was what she had wanted to discuss with Descartes too. At the time she received cautious, reserved answers which seemed to her to indicate that the Church in no way rejected modern scholarship but only certain exaggerations and abuses of over-zealous researchers. After her arrival in Rome she was to discover that only very few priests were intellectually as humane as Casati.

2. OLIMPIA MAIDALCHINI

Another characteristic of Rome in the baroque period was the appalling moral degradation of the papal Court. When we read of all that was liable to occur before a papal election and after a new Pope came to the throne, we are filled with disgust. Even anti-Catholic propaganda hardly succeeded in exaggerating the revolting conditions that prevailed: fact outstripped fiction.

Pope Innocent X is a case in point; his appearance is well-known through Velasquez's brilliant portrait of him in the Doria Palace in Rome. A contemporary described him as a man "of tall, gaunt aspect, with small eyes, large feet, sparse beard, almost olive-green complexion, cold features". He was seventy when in 1644, after the usual political intrigues, he was elected Pope—a mistrustful, uncommunicative man who every now and then quite unexpectedly yielded to magnanimity and friendliness, only to withdraw into his shell again immediately after. His actions were altogether inconsistent. In himself he was a morally upright person, but like his predecessors he took for granted the customary system of "cardinal nephews", whereby the Pope appointed as cardinal a near but often quite undeserving relative of his, piling very lucrative offices upon him. In the Pamphili family to which the Pope belonged there was only one strong personality, a woman, Olimpia Maidalchini, later of notorious fame. Her second husband was the Pope's brother Pamphilio Pamphili and in 1622 she bore him a son, Camillo. Olimpia was not only very gifted, she was also extremely ambitious and lusted for power. She was wealthy but desired to increase her wealth. After the papal election Olimpia soon proved indispensable to the Pope, with the result that cardinals, bishops and other dignitaries started to cultivate the influential sister-in-law, behaving to her with the utmost servility and flattery. There were Eminences who hung her portrait in their rooms. Olimpia's inept son Camillo became cardinal-nephew (without ordination—he was formally designated as *cardinale sopra-intendente agl'affari maggiori*; he was already commander-in-chief of the papal fleet and life-guard as well as governor of the Borgo and other important papal strongholds. Once he was cardinal-nephew he received the Avignon embassy, an abbey in Capua and many other presents and tokens of favour. Camillo's own talents were rather in the artistic and technical fields. For the high offices he now held he lacked all aptitude, they did not even interest him particularly, especially as all decisions were made by Innocent himself. He became acquainted with a pretty young widow, Olimpia Aldobrandini, Princess of Rossano, and wanted to marry her. His mother Olimpia Maidalchini tried with all her might to dissuade him, but did not succeed. In 1647, Camillo Pamphili relinquished the dignity of cardinal. His mother refused to be present at her son's wedding and was later instrumental in causing the young pair to leave Rome.

Olimpia Maidalchini's influence waxed. Irrespective of persons, remuneration was expected for every service and every pressure brought to bear on the Pope; without her highly-paid assistance no one could count on obtaining any ecclesiastical office of any importance. Though otherwise a headstrong and self-willed man, Pope Innocent was wax in her hands. A seventeen-year-old nephew of Olimpia's, Francesco Maidalchini, was soon made cardinal, but to Innocent's dismay he turned out to be of even less worth, if possible, than Camillo Pamphili. This reacted on Olimpia, and the Pope finally grew weary of her intrigues. The measure was full to overflowing when she broke into a hysterical storm of abuse on the occasion of another cardinal's nomination by the Pope: from then on she was forbidden to cross the threshold of the Vatican.

With Olimpia Maidalchini out of the way, Olimpia Aldobrandini's influence grew apace, and her husband, Camillo Pamphili, came back into grace and favour. And now Olimpia Aldobrandini proved herself the stronger: to some extent her influence on the Pope replaced that of her mother-in-law. At that time two younger men were taken into the Pope's entourage, both of whom we shall soon see playing an active part in Queen Christina's life—the nuntius Fabio Chigi, now cardinal (who as Pope Alexander VII was to welcome Christina to Rome), and Decio Azzolino, soon to be Christina's most intimate friend.

Curiously enough—a year before Christina's abdication in 1653—the irrepressible Olimpia Maidalchini came back to the Vatican and was welcomed by the Pope with open arms. . . . And now her influence was greater than ever: she made a firm resolution never to let the reins drop from her hands again. Of her opponents, one fell after another. And now the cunning Decio

Azzolino, cardinal in 1564, came to the fore as her main accomplice. Olimpia Maidalchini's chief aim was to bring about the downfall of Cardinal Chigi so that Azzolino could take his place. But Innocent X died, at the age of eighty, and therewith the unholy influence of this strong-willed, ambitious woman came to an end.

To the very last she displayed incredible energy and recklessness, and when the rumour of the Pope's approaching death spread throughout Rome, there was great rejoicing. Crowds set off to storm the hated palazzo Pamphili. But Olimpia saved the situation by showering coins among them. When the Pope was too ill to deal with matters, the former cardinal Camillo went back into the Vatican and received foreign envoys on his behalf. Meanwhile the ladies were busily occupied on their own account. Olimpia Maidalchini, who knew her time was up, laid her hands on whatever could be removed, and when the Pope fell asleep towards evening, she locked him into his bedroom so that no one could get at the money in a huge chest under his bed. She went back to her palace in a sedan-chair and the lackeys who carried her observed that each time she was heavier than the last—heavy with gold and gems.

Lately her jobbery in political appointments had been so extensive that her takings for ten days were reckoned at half a million *scudi*. Finally a brave man intervened—one who was also to play a part in Christina's story, the Jesuit General Oliva: he forbade Olimpia to enter the dying Pope's chamber.

The Pope remained fully conscious to the last and wanted to appoint Camillo Pamphili's son, seventeen-year-old Giambattista, cardinal—as compensation for a box on the ear he had once given the rascal. This was stopped in time, though the Pope did not die till 6 January 1655 (which meant that Christina had reckoned he would be the Pope she would meet on her arrival in Rome). Hardly had he drawn his last breath than Olimpia Maidalchini invaded his room and with the help of two servants removed the chest from under the bed, before anyone could notice the theft. When she was asked to contribute to the costs of the funeral, she answered that as a poor widow she could not possibly meet the burial expenses of so great a Pope. So the old Pope's body remained unburied for some time, covered with an old blanket, a pewter candlestick beside him, for all the gold candlesticks had been stolen, likewise the table silver, chairs and linen. A shroud and a blanket were all Olimpia had left behind.

For three days the body lay on a bier in St Peter's; no one seemed to have thought of providing a coffin and burying the dead man. The Pamphili family showed not the slightest interest, no more did the cardinals. By the third day the corpse *had* to be removed; it was placed in a closet where the masons kept their tools, bricks and mortar. One of the workmen lit a candle at the dead man's head, another took over the night watch voluntarily so as to protect the body from the rats. Finally a simple wooden coffin was put together and a canon of the church provided the money for the burial.

After these events Olimpia Maidalchini continued her intrigues, working hand-in-glove with Cardinals Azzolino, Cherubini, Gaultieri and the three Barberini's. The group was known as *il squadrone volante*, the flying squadron, a nickname invented by the Spanish envoy. But it did not manage to get its candidate elected to the papal see. In fact it was Fabio Chigi, one-time papal nuncio at the peace conference of Münster, who was elected, calling himself Alexander VII, as we know.

The new Pope began secretly to gather together material that would reveal the extent of Olimpia Maidalchini's criminal activities—he intended to show how her immense fortune had been amassed. Olimpia tried to bribe him with presents and expressed a wish to visit him to kiss his foot, but he refused. Soon after he had her informed that she must leave Rome for Orvieto within a week, and that she was not to go away from that town without his permission. The Pope made a special point of keeping her out of Queen Christina's way as a too glaring example of decadence in the Papal State.

Olimpia died in 1657 at the age of sixty-three, without ever meeting the Swedish queen. But Christina knew her daughter-in-law, Olimpia Aldobrandini, Princess of Rossano, quite well. Before Olimpia Maidalchini's death, Alexander VII had legal proceedings taken against her on account of her jobbery in benefices and offices.

3. MARIA MANCINI

When Christina visited Paris for the first time, she met in the entourage of the young King Louis XIV his lady-love, Maria Mancini, a beautiful girl, one of Cardinal Mazarin's famous nieces. As Christina reported to Cardinal Azzolini:

> He is in love with Mlle Mancini, but with so much reserve and purity I do not believe that in the three years in which he has been courting her, he has so far forgotten himself as to touch her with the tip of his fingers. She is quick-witted and sly and she plays her part as the cruelly-relentless one with great skill, for it pleases her to have one of the greatest kings of the world lying at her feet and sighing deep sighs on seeing her so determined to let him die there, though I do not find this wholly convincing. . . .

Christina spoke to Louis about Maria Mancini and advised him to keep on loving her. But this was not to be. Cardinal Mazarin foresaw that it would never do for his niece to aspire to be Queen of France, for the indignation roused would be directed against him alone. So he set to work to thwart the plan.

This pretty, frivolous creature—"the best and craziest of the Mazarin girls", said Saint-Simon—was married off to a member of the Italian higher aristocracy, Prince Lorenzo Colonna, head of his ancient house. She came to Rome a year after Queen Christina, in 1661.

As early as 1665 the Colonna couple decided to live apart; by that time they had three children. It may have been that they had different interests. The prince was a great chaser of petticoats in the usual Italian manner—through her spies his wife discovered all the places where he had secret access to his mistresses, using rope ladders to reach his more worth-while booty. She herself found an interest in Cardinal Flavio Chigi, nephew of Alexander VII, an outstanding huntsman and man of the world. It was said that the princess once put on his cardinal's robes and burst into his bedroom one morning, laughing gaily.

The princess's house was a centre of interest in Rome and was much visited. For a long time it managed to compete successfully with Christina's salon. Some time later the princess had a visit from her almost equally beautiful sister Hortense Mazarin, who became pregnant after an affair with the Prince de Rohan's equerry. Maria Mancini had the impression that Queen Christina would be ready to take in Hortense and her child as soon as her pregnancy was over, but as it turned out the queen was not prepared to do so—perhaps because Cardinal Chigi, and therefore also Maria Mancini, were enemies of her beloved Cardinal Azzolini. So there was always tension between Maria Mancini and Queen Christina.

Then the *chevalier de Lorraine* came to Rome, a son of Henry of Lorraine and "handsome as an angel"; he had been banished from France by Louis XIV. Very soon the newcomer replaced Cardinal Chigi in Princess Colonna's favour. So Prince Colonna and Cardinal Chigi got together and determined to remove the Chevalier de Lorraine.

First they sent the princess a monk with admonishments and remonstrances, but she turned him out straight away and continued to enjoy herself. In 1672, however, the French nobleman went back to his own country. And now Prince Colonna decided to get rid of his lovely but troublesome wife. After an abortive attempt at poisoning, the princess fled to France dressed as a man. The captain of the ship that was to take her to Marseilles suspected trouble and asked her if she had not perhaps "murdered the Pope" and was fleeing on that account. Although the prince mobilized a large part of the Tuscan fleet, Maria Mancini succeeded in eluding him. Later she travelled incessantly and did not venture back to Rome till after her husband's death in 1689, the very year in which Christina also died.

The lady left her mark, in that she introduced freer French manners into a superficially still fairly puritanical Italian society. Her fate is typical of the cultural world in which Queen Christina found herself after abandoning straight-laced Sweden for Rome. Christina looked upon the Pope's conventional court with as much irony as did Princess Colonna, but she would have nothing to do with her licentious amoral ways. The princess was surrounded by cavaliers and adventurers, Christina by scholars and cardinals. But they shared a deep interest in cultural matters; both loved the theatre, both took a lively interest in astrology. Musicians competed for the favour of dedicating their works to them.

4. RELIGION AND BAROQUE ART

We do not find it easy to place ourselves in the religious atmosphere of seventeenth-century Rome. Perhaps a few concrete instances will help. Of Cardinal Azzolino we know that he was interested in lovely women, wrote verses, engaged in ecclesiastical power-politics, and was not above using purely Machiavellian stratagems on occasion. Once during a conclave he pretended to have lost a slip of paper on which he had noted his choice; but he had in fact written something entirely opposite to what he wanted, with the intention that the slip should be found. On Good Friday 1658, a few years after Christina's arrival in Rome, the cardinal was to be seen in a procession of—penitents!

The procession left St. Peter's Piazza towards eleven o'clock at night. At its head went Cardinals Azzolini, Frederick of Hesse, Carlo Barberini and others, all in sackcloth and ashes, but with liveried servants ahead of them bearing torches held high—so that everyone should clearly witness their humility and self-abnegation. After the cardinals came flagellants with bleeding backs and shoulders, who continued to flagellate themselves all through the procession. Here and there tables were laid where Capuchin friars handed out wine and refreshments. According to eye-witnesses, there were as many as eight hundred flagellants, and there were six hundred torchbearers.

Rome in the baroque period cannot be understood unless we realize that such scenes—common enough in Spain to this day—were daily occurrences and everybody took them for granted. We know further that during Christina's time in Rome it was a common amusement to hold races among cripples or Jewish prisoners, who had to run naked amid a gale of mocking laughter. We may recall Montaigne's description of Roman life some decades before Christina's arrival: scenes of exorcism when nails, pins or great bundles of diabolical tufts of hair issued from the mouths of possessed females. It happened quite frequently that older possessed females spat out horseshoe nails. . . .

Behind baroque splendour and the cult of human glorification lay a cynical indifference towards the suffering of ordinary mortals and people in distress. It is astonishing to find strongly sadistic traits among so much spirituality; and at times this strikes us as repulsive, even morbid. It is not enough to lend an attentive ear to Scarlatti's or Corelli's music or contemplate Bernini's representations of ecstatic women, to appreciate the spiritual climate in which Queen Christina lived for more than forty years; we have to remember the sufferings of the oppressed and under-privileged treated as objects for popular entertainment.

The taste of the period is most apparent in the drawings which a Swede, Nicodemus Tessin the Younger, made of the cardinals' midday meal. They show the famous sugar trophies: pies and pastries representing various scenes from the Gospels, the Crucifixion for instance, Mary transpierced with the Sword of the Seven Sorrows, the Descent from the Cross, the Scourging, etc., the work of ingenious pastrycooks. Queen Christina was evidently present at many of these grotesque banquets, indeed it seems likely that her own table was adorned with similar 'trophies'.

Of course, then as at other times, alongside the unspirituality of high ecclesiastical dignitaries there existed a veritable treasure-house of sincere and genuine religious life. Apart from the broad mass of the Italian people, whose religious life was probably very similar to what it is today, the large number of holy women was characteristic of the times. Many of them were even canonized. We know that Queen Christina often became absorbed in books written by or about such saints, just as she greatly honoured certain noblewomen, as for instance Marie of Savoy who had withdrawn from the world to live in a convent. Catherine Adorna of Genoa played a definite part in Christina's spiritual development, and the first biography of this saint was dedicated to her: she annotated the book with many marginal jottings. Maddalena de Pazzi in Florence, greatly revered by Christina's friend Bernini, was well known to her too, and she must have been acquainted with the life of Margaret of Cortona and of blessed Michelina of

Pesaro; we know she received letters from Spain begging her to use her influence on behalf of St Maria of Sagreda whose book on the Mystical City of God was for some time on the Index; that it was finally removed from the Index may well have been due to the Swedish queen.

Contemplating Bernini's picture of the ecstacy of St Teresa of Avila in Santa Maria della Vittoria, and recalling to mind the many women of similar spirituality, whom Christina came to know either in person or through reading about them, we realize that alongside all the superficiality and worldliness there were many people, specially women, of great spirituality who witnessed to their encounter with a higher reality. In Sweden, Christina had had no clear idea of them—the world of the saints was taboo to Swedish Protestant orthodoxy. But in Rome after her first phase of trials, her first bitter disappointments, were over, she felt drawn to this ecstatic mystical world. That she herself had first-hand experience of spirituality is evident from her Maxims and her remarkable commentaries on Catherine of Genoa.

CHAPTER THREE

First Years in Rome

I. PALAZZO FARNESE

CHRISTINA'S first home in Rome was the palazzo Farnese, today the French embassy. It is not far from the house in which St Bridget of Sweden* lived and where, to this very day, members of the Swedish Bridgettine Order live and work. On Christina's arrival it was the residence of Prince Frederick of Hessen-Darmstadt, who was converted at the age of twenty and became a cardinal in 1652. He was known in Rome as *il cardinale Lantgrevio*. The house belonged to the Duke of Parma; it was built in 1589 and was thus only sixty years old. The duke was in constant financial difficulties and thought the queen might perhaps put in a good word for him with the Pope, if he let her have rooms in his palace.

At the same time, and for a further six months, there lived in it the duke's representative at the Vatican, Marquis Giandemaria. Conscientiously he reported to the duke all that the queen did or omitted to do, and was pleased by neither. It is through him that we are so well informed about Christina's early days in Rome, and according to him her behaviour was that of a sheer libertine.

She was so intelligent, he said, she could form a correct opinion of anyone in an instant. He also noticed her nervousness—for instance she slept every night in a different room. He remarked on a physical defect, one shoulder higher than the other, which she concealed with a large neckerchief. One day, to his horror, she asked to have an ivory statuette of Christ, ascribed to Michelangelo, brought to her bedroom—this was considered extreme profanation. Everyone was dazzled by her erudition. She seldom sat down, much preferred to talk standing up, was extremely cool

* 1302–1373.

and detached to all ladies, though very polite to the daughter of the Duke of Savoy, Marie, a nun; her visits to this lady were so conspicuous that a malicious rumour got about that she was in love with a nun. When it was proposed to cover some of the naked statues on show in the palace, she had the fig-leaves removed at once—whereat the Romans expressed moral indignation. She countered the expostulations of a papal envoy by declaring that she would have nothing to do with such clerical prudery. She also had profane masterpieces hung in the palace, e.g. Caracci's *Danaë*, a picture Camillo Pamphili gave her: it was deemed to be all-too-naked and therefore offensive. Disapproval was expressed again when Christina received the cardinals in a too pronounced décolleté. Soon she was having plays performed in the palace, comedies and operas, and during Lent a weekly "Spiritual Exercise" took the form of recitations from the story of Daniel, with music by Pompeio Colonna, Prince of Gallicano, who was to play an important part in her later life. On 24 January 1656, her first Roman academy met in the so-called Imperial Hall of the palazzo Farnese.

2. CHRISTINA GIVES CAUSE FOR SCANDAL

"While the queen lived in the Vatican, and even later," wrote Sforza Pallavicino, "the Pope's talks with her were a source of great joy to him, even if he was not always free from misgivings." What gave the Pope joy was his impression that the Swedish convert had real and firm convictions. Pallavicino added, "greater minds often pay more attention to what they grasp with their own understanding than what they learn from authoritative sources". Christina told Pallavicino she would be very much ashamed if the Pope, whom she greatly admired, were to outshine her in faith. What was otherwise said of her she regarded as mere flattery, but to stress that point, she said, was to speak the truth.

Doubtless the Pope hoped her example would induce others to come over to the Catholic faith. Count Palatine Christian August of Pfalz-Sulzbach did take Christina as his model and become a convert, but no one else. At first Christina's moral attitude made an impression on the Pope; evidently she still blustered away about her stoical principles: with an inimitable look and tone of voice, wrote Pallavicino, she once declared herself incapable of any improper action, even should God not count it against her, for her own soul could not endure it. Such grandiose modes of speech impressed the Romans at first, and presumably corresponded to her convictions, for her incredible arrogance was still far from being broken. The Pope admired her intelligence, specially when applied to practical matters and political questions, "indeed she scrutinized the designs of princes and prime ministers as thoroughly as though dealing with her own Swedish Court". She had not been in Rome for long before she "grasped the existing situation and could distinguish between the different parties".

On her journey to Rome we saw Christina stopping at shrines and holy places. In early days in Rome she tirelessly visited all the city's show places, mainly of course churches and religious houses, though whether impelled by pious or profane motives is hard to say.

Anyhow, before long the Pope grew dismayed. He saw through her and realized how superficial her religious outlook was, how slight her interest in things of the Church. He observed that she still had "many of the faults which had provoked criticism in Flanders", faults which Pallavicino regarded as too much in evidence, tarnishing the glory of her great sacrifice. He might have said outright that as a libertine Christina was causing scandal. But in his compassionate way he did his best to excuse her, saying that presumably women in the North enjoyed much greater freedom than in the South.

What caused the scandal?

The queen kept company "freely and unconstrainedly with young men, not observing any more reserve than she would were she herself a man of their age". But what most shocked was the lack of any trace of external piety, "such as is usually found connected with a lively faith". She never conversed on spiritual matters, read no devotional books, was neither a zealous churchgoer nor a frequent receiver of the Sacraments—not to mention prayers and mortifications. In spite of his tendency to gloss things over, Pallavicino had to admit that these shortcomings were "truly not small ones", and indiscretion and envy were liable to inflate them still more. But the Pope had no wish to intervene. He realized that admonishments addressed to people of exalted rank "can only be imparted very sparingly". He chose a different tactic: without making any complaint he gave prudent advice for the future, indicating what the world expected of her, and giving her devotional books, "small in size but full of power". He seldom received the queen in audience, but sent people to see her who had her confidence. They tried to make her see that it was no fault or token of hypocrisy to allow a devout attitude to appear in external actions, if done always to God's honour and glory and not as self-glorification. More merit could be gained by praying a single *Ave Maria* in public than a whole rosary in private.

Mazarin's agent reported to Paris that the Pope had reproved the queen for her free and easy ways. When things got so bad that the Pope had to provide her with maintenance expenses from his own pocket, he made it a condition that Christina led a life more likely to bring honour to the Holy See than hitherto. The queen flew into a rage, ranting about empty pieties, cult of relics, sham saints and much else that she loathed—all of which the agents of the French and Spanish courts lost no time in reporting. But Christina did make a slight effort to conform. She learnt to remain still during Mass and not, as she usually did, chatter to her friends; she paid at least outward respect to the Blessed Sacrament, and from time to time she dropped her scientific interests to engage in some kind of religious exercise.

But the pious were not appeased. At that time there lived in Rome a zealous preacher name Zucchi. He attacked her as "false prophetess" and scorned her *scandalosi ministri*. In 1658, in conversation with the Venetian envoy, the Pope too spoke of her in harsh terms, saying she was "born a barbarian, brought up a barbarian, her head full of barbarian notions". And he earnestly complained of her "almost intolerable pride". A few years later, Pope Alexander refused to receive Christina at Castel Gandolfo and suggested she moved away from Rome.

Pallavicino did what he could to convince public opinion that Christina was trying to improve but achieved the opposite:

> Her behaviour is only gradually improving, for this is such a delicate matter that no one dare speak to her about it. With her downright, manly disposition she lacks any sense of obligation to act with feminine reserve and comply with the Italians' own deliberate circumspection. She gives full vent to her natural high spirits and that excitability which makes it impossible for her to stay still for long or maintain gravity of voice and expression, so necessary if people are to respect her and not merely disparage her. The Pope believes that, though bitter to the taste, the fruit is sound at heart, and trusts that time will bring it to ripeness and perfection.

Meanwhile the diplomatic agents continued their reports about Christina's broad joking and *stravaganza*, at least until people grew accustomed to her ways. The Jesuits had done so much for her: she might have been expected to be grateful; but once on a visit to the Gesù church she lost her temper over some point of etiquette, feeling she had been slighted: this was the beginning of a lifelong dislike of the Jesuits. An (undated) note of Pallavicino's to Alexander VII tells how a *disturbatio* arose between the queen and Cardinal Ludovisi, after which Pallavicino said he talked to the queen for an hour and a half, trying to make her see reason; she wept and stormed, but when he left her she had quietened down.

There is a famous picture that shows Queen Christina's carefree pleasure-loving ways during her first years in Rome; it represents a sort of two-storey loggia on the Roman Corso, roofed over with red draperies. Over the queen's seat hung a gigantic royal crown inscribed "Here sits Rome's Queen and Protectress". From this vantage point the queen and her guests watched the carnival and its merry-making, of which some scenes may well have been put on specially for her amusement. A gossipy news-sheet of the day, *Avvisi*, reported that no fewer than twenty-six cardinals could be counted on Christina's loggia, in full view of the thousands of onlookers.

This description is also revealing as to the queen's behaviour: she fidgeted the whole time, got up, sat down again, talked incessantly now to one, now to another member of the Sacred College, displaying marked friendliness to Cardinals Imperiali and Azzolino. To Cardinal Borromeo (a member of the family of St Charles Borromeo), she remarked with a laugh that saintliness was not an inheritable trait. . . . She scattered witty or pointed remarks at random, *concetti di grasso e di magno*, and although she was a lady, "it was hardly noticeable, for in dress, hair style, behaviour and voice, excessively loud and deep, she is like a man".

From the same source we learn that Cardinal Albizzi prepared a serenade for the queen on the last day of the carnival. During the performance the vesper-bell of the Jesuit church was heard ringing, a signal that the carnival and its merry-making had come to an end. The cardinal, however, ordered the ringing to be stopped—it spoilt the music. . . . There was a good deal of indignation in consequence of this and similar episodes, and protests were made. It was said that "the Sacred College" should not meet in "consistory" to enjoy secular theatricals, or at least not as a lady's guests.

Tessin the Younger's pictures give a good idea of the popular entertainments of the time: a very elegant drawing of his shows cavalry and infantrymen forming a long lane right down to one of the city gates. Through this lane a crowd of people come running in panic, chased by a band of excited beasts—horses, mules, billy-goats. Perhaps the danger was not so great, even though the runners were spurred on by men on horseback, but what makes the whole thing so repulsive is that the hunted are naked. On a raised platform sit noble lords and ladies—perhaps the queen is among them—much amused by this sadistic scene. We mentioned the races run on similar occasions by Jews and cripples—also naked. Such cruelties must be remembered when we try to form an opinion about aristocratic baroque culture: this offensive trait of brutal inhumanity is to be found everywhere. Christina herself often spoke of having people whipped, even to death, and her indifference to Monaldesco's fate is in the same context—stabbed by her own servants at Fontainebleau.

There is no knowing what feelings were aroused when Christina once went with an escort of thirty torchbearers to call on the

French ambassador, dressed in a black velvet jacket with diamond buttons, *alla Valona* breeches, an ostrich feather in her hat and a sword at her side. The queen dressed conspicuously on purpose, and liked to draw attention to her special position; not on any account would she appear as befitted an ordinary woman.

She could display quite virile qualities when she wanted to. She is said to have paid a visit to *Madame la conestabile*—Princess Colonna, i.e. Maria Mancini, and was taking leave; when her hostess did not accompany her as far as she thought proper, she seized her hand and dragged her along. . . . When she visited the town of Lucca and a salvo of shots was fired by way of salute, it did not startle her at all and she went on chatting with her entourage on the arts of fortification and strategy, "like an old campaigner". In Lucca, too, she told with a laugh how in Paris the only mask she could find that would fit her noble nose was King Louis XIV's.

Queen Christina had expected to find much greater toleration in Rome than in Protestant Stockholm, but she was utterly mistaken.

The Italian libertines—any that could be taken seriously—had been driven out, and it was not easy to find people even half way to free-thinking. Pastor, the author of the great history of the popes, assumed that Christina was a typical renaissance lady who, due to her upbringing in backward Sweden, had no idea of the neo-Puritanism reigning in Rome. But that was hardly the case, Christina was "modern" rather than not, she belonged to the Catholic free-thinkers so characteristic of her time, and counted on meeting in Rome the same type of enlightened intellectuals, though in ecclesiastical circles, as among the French she collected around her in Stockholm. It was a bitter disappointment to find herself in an ecclesiastical atmosphere as strict as the Swedish Lutherans, and she made no secret of it.

Soon after her arrival in Rome, Queen Christina made the acquaintance of Pompeio Colonna, Prince of Gallicano, and later became his close friend. He was a cultured man with literary and artistic tastes, able to discuss with the queen most of the questions that interested her—though not, perhaps, theological problems and religious topics. He had come to the fore as a politician, or at least a political adventurer. From 1501 till the eighteenth century, Naples belonged to Spain, was ruled by a Spanish viceroy and had its own unique Italo-Spanish style of architecture, which is still in evidence to some extent. The prince was much disliked by the Spaniards, since more than once he had taken an active part in the Neapolitans' struggle against Spanish rule. A French diplomatist and adventurer, Marc Duncan de Cérisantes, for a time in the queen's service, was killed during a riot in Naples, but it was presumably the elegant, imperturbable Prince of Gallicano who first acquainted Christina with conditions there. It is easy to see how most of the men with whom Christina came into contact during her first years in Rome, acted out of pure self-interest; it is even true of Cardinal Azzolino, but most of all of the Prince of Gallicano, whose main concern was to grasp any means that might conceivably be of use in ejecting the Spaniards from Naples. So he cultivated Christina's society and gave her very sensational descriptions of the conditions that obtained there. He was a member of her first academy, founded in 1656, and played a considerable part in it, and his contacts with the queen roused the greatest displeasure among her Spanish entourage. Spain considered herself the first of Christina's protecting States and naturally supposed she would support Spanish policy in Italy. Before settling in Rome, she had hardly looked into the problem at all, but once there soon made herself acquainted with the question. The Prince of Gallicano pleased her and seems to have influenced her. There was also the fact that the Spaniards around her were second-rate men; she soon felt inclined to get rid of them.

Sforza Pallavicino admits that Christina came to hate Cardinal Giancarlo de' Medici, and he was at the head of the Spanish party among the cardinals. It was not long before she had made an enemy of the Spanish envoy too.

Presumably Christina would have had to break with Spain in any case, sooner or later. But the break was speeded up by the presence of the Duke of Terranova, a grotesque caricature of Spanish pride, a foolish creature with no powers of discrimination, who, unhappily for his country, was Spanish envoy in Rome.

There were many unsuitable silly men among the diplomatists of the day, but none as foolish as he.

On the face of it, the situation was extraordinarily favourable to the Duke of Terranova: the Spanish king had helped Christina in her conversion, giving her all the practical aid she needed—though with the tardiness that always characterized Spanish policy—and he instructed Terranova to treat Christina with every sign of respect. The Spanish king knew that the Queen of Sweden could be a valuable ally of his politically, or in the ecclesiastico-political field, because in Rome the cardinals friendly to Spain were always in conflict with the neutral groups and those of French leanings, and stressed the need to avoid trouble between the rival parties.

At the beginning Terranova wrote favourably of Christina's intelligence and personality, but his own capacities were limited, and he was indignant to a degree when she made no attempt to conceal her libertine views. Her lack of outward piety gave offence, so did her sharp retorts and preference for the company of amusing and entertaining people rather than prelates and the pious. In January 1656, only a few weeks after her arrival, he was saying: "Italy suits Christina as ill as Christina suits Italy."

Curt Weibull called Terranova a "choleric stickler for etiquette" and he is absolutely right: the man was a conservative of the old Spanish school.

There was trouble when Christina was to receive her first Communion in public. One of the godparents required to attend should by rights have been a Spaniard. Terranova came forward, but so did Christina's friend Pimentel. The Pope passed them by and let Cardinal de' Medici, with his Spanish sympathies, function as godfather.

Christina soon made friends with a Frenchman, Hugues de Lionne; as he was not formally an envoy, Terranova was indignant. He complained about a breach of etiquette: Lionne was permitted "to speak to the queen with his head covered".

But there was worse to come. Terranova in all his glory, together with the Spanish grandees of the Church States, was to be received by Christina in the palazzo Farnese. At such audiences the

Roman cardinals had a long-established right to sit in armchairs, while the envoys had to put up with ordinary chairs. Terranova knew this, but his pride could not admit to his entering the same room as a cardinal and taking a lower place. So it became impossible for him to visit Christina at all, though his powerful monarch had expressly commanded him to do so; here was a most delicate collision of duties to plague him, but by dint of putting all his wits together he found a solution: he would pay his respects to Christina, but not in her official audience hall, in one of her salons instead. There she would sit on a sofa and not on a throne, and he himself, hatless, would accept an armless chair. We may be sure he then fell on his knees and thanked God and all the Spanish saints for this inspiration.

But soon he was driven once more to despair.

In Italy Christina had an old friend, the Duke of Bracciano, with whom she used to correspond diligently from Stockholm—as we saw. Now he was a very eccentric gentleman: Bernini painted a most amusing portrait of him. Among a variety of other insignia, for some reason or other he also possessed the rank of a Spanish grandee. Christina had made a cautious enquiry of the expert, Terranova, on how he was to be treated. As Spanish grandee, he had the right to keep his hat on during an audience, Terranova declared, but Alexander VII did not agree. He informed the queen that she should make no distinction of rank between Spanish grandees and Roman barons—and would she kindly observe the same rule as he did himself: all grandees to take off their hats at an audience. Now a bitter quarrel ensued. Christina followed the line suggested by the Pope, not the Spanish duke. This meant that no Spanish grandee could set foot in her palace....

At the time, all this was regarded as a real political defeat. Terranova saw it as a sign of the Pope's firm resolve to demonstrate against Spain.

But in Madrid there were more sensible heads than Terranova's. The episode was considered with the usual deliberation and Terranova was found to be in the wrong. On the other hand, offence was taken at the Pope's and Christina's indifference to the

Spanish grandees, and it was hoped that the queen could be persuaded to apologize—after all she owed Spain a great debt of gratitude. That only showed how little they knew Christina. In Madrid the thing was taken so seriously that it was thought Terranova might have to leave Rome, which could lead to a breaking-off of diplomatic relations between the Pope and Spain.

First, the Spaniard put the blame on the Pope, but he was after all experienced in such matters. So he blamed Christina, though he knew quite well she had acted perfectly correctly; had she complied with Terranova's demands there would have been a rift with the other envoys in Rome.

But the worst of it was that Christina so demonstratively favoured the man held to be Spain's most dangerous enemy in Rome, namely the Prince of Gallicano, whom the Spaniards regarded as a arrant rebel against their legitimate rule in Naples. Christina had received warnings from Madrid about this dangerous gentlemen, on her journey to Rome, but she preferred his easy libertine manners to the etiquette-bound formality of the austere Spaniards. She let him get up and speak in her academy—which started merely as a regular evening gathering; she listened to the Spaniards' expostulations with a bored expression, but brightened immediately when the Prince of Gallicano, undaunted by the presence of the Spaniards, told of his own various activities and called the Spanish terror in Naples by its proper name.

Christina was attacked from another side too, for the group of cardinals which Terranova had once spitefully called "the flying squadron", criticized her undignified behaviour. Terranova's nickname stuck and almost became the official designation of the group of cardinals who did not wish to go in either Spanish or French leading-strings. One of the more outstanding members of the group, young Cardinal Decio Azzolino, took care that in spite of their criticisms the queen was invited to a series of banquets given by the cardinals, and soon he was higher in the queen's favour than the Prince of Gallicano himself.

As we saw, Christina was also friendly with a Frenchman, Lionne. Sometimes she talked to him for three or four hours on end, which was duly reported to Terranova by her entourage, still dominated by Spaniards. Of these, it was Don Antonio de la Cueva who had the strongest influence on Christina.

The queen openly showed her dislike of many Spaniards, as was generally observed, and treated them very badly when they proffered advice on lines of conduct. Terranova had never met a queen of such independent habits and was forced to the conclusion that she was but a pawn, wax in the hands of his opponents. That she was by nature quite inflexible passed his comprehension, and we have to admit that in those days there was no other queen of such lofty, domineering ways.

"The Spaniards' tyranny does not please her," wrote Lionne to Paris in high glee.

"The queen's behaviour is more and more disadvantageous to us, she has made herself patroness of the 'flying squadron', has taken a great fancy to Cardinal Azzolino and admires all his friends. She has completely broken with the Spanish cardinals and diplomatists and definitely turned to the friends of France who are here. Thus she has struck a blow at Your Majesty and insulted us all"—so wrote the indignant Terranova.

But as we said, there were in Madrid wiser men than he; they found him inept and reprimanded him. They considered it only natural that Pimentel and della Cueva—the two Spaniards in her entourage—should leave her. And the Duke of Terranova was given to understand that henceforth he must cease to interfere in the queen's affairs.

So it was recognized in Madrid that Terranova and his fellow-countrymen had played their hand badly and failed to win Christina's support for Spanish interests in Rome.

Terranova was raging with fury at this personal defeat. Instead of concentrating on his country's true interests, he acted solely for reasons of personal prestige. He began to malign Christina: "The queen's extravagances get more and more unbearable every day, and it is believed that His Holiness will wither this incorrigible woman with his scorn and tell her she does not suit Rome; or he will compel her to enter a convent."

Meanwhile Terranova had had information about the queen's distressing financial situation—one fine day, utterly in debt, she will, he thought, have without doubt to beg for permission to reside in the Spanish envoy's palace.

Now the rumour was spreading that Christina had illicit relations with Cardinal Azzolino and other men—the former had to defend himself in a letter to the Pope, and della Cueva called the queen "the biggest *putana* (harlot) in the world".

Then it was the queen's turn.

When della Cueva and his wife appeared at Christina's palace on a farewell call, he begged her pardon, as was customary, for not serving her as well as he should and would have done: Christina drew herself up and retorted that his conscience must decide, but he should take note of the fact that she would always reward a man of honour and punish a rogue. If she knew—and by that time she did know—that he had maligned her, she would deal with him according to his deserts. To his wife Christina said in condescending tones, that it did not matter to her in the least if she too had shared in spreading evil rumours—for she was after all only a woman.

Immediately after this scene—one can imagine how the thirty-year-old queen was boiling with rage—she let the Spanish king know, through Pimentel and Cardinal de' Medici, that it was only out of respect for his person, and for della Cueva's rank as Spanish general, that she refrained from having him flogged to death.

That was unmistakable language, of a kind Christina was often to have occasion to use in Rome. Terranova became more and more spiteful: "The intolerable follies of the Swedish queen go so far that one cannot describe them," he reported. Her old friend Pimentel wrote to Madrid that she must be ill; perhaps the heat had something to do with it, since she was not used to it. And he wondered what she would be like when midsummer came and the heat increased.

The Pope admired Christina but was, as we saw, uneasy. When he asked her to mend her ways as a condition of financial support, she found a way of retaliating: Alexander VII had originally renounced the custom of providing his relations with well-paid sinecures, he had in fact abolished nepotism. But for some reason he changed his mind and gave his brother and both his nephews "nephew" status. This aroused general opposition. But Christina seized her chance, welcomed the favoured men to her palace with open arms, and treated them exactly as though they were proper cardinals. The Pope proved grateful and let Terranova know that he disliked his measures against the queen, and in fact would consider any insult to Christina an insult to himself.

Christina now issued a manifesto explaining things to all and sundry and stressing her own victory. In this self-confident and carefully-worded document she told how della Cueva and his wife had treated her on their farewell visit, how she had been tempted to have him flogged, and had imparted a severe reproof to Cardinal de' Medici. Incredible though it may seem, she said she would like Duke Terranova to know she had brave and honourable people at her court who were ready to prove their quality if the duke did not conduct himself in a way more appropriate to his position as Spanish envoy.

She concluded scornfully: "The following day Don Antonio Pimentel was ill, or at least he said he was, and had the queen informed that the Duke of Terranova had never spoken of the queen without the respect he owed her . . . indeed he was her obedient servant."

Now the Duke of Terranova was near breaking-point. He reported all the current rumours to Madrid: that Christina was pawning her jewels to the Jews, that she was not of royal blood at all but the child of a rebel against the Danish king, and for lack of better, he mentioned two admonishments of Saint Bridget's taking certain sovereigns to task: he, the duke, knew for certain that these revelations referred to Christina.

In Madrid the surprise was great. But Christina carried on her warfare, sending the Dominican Father Guemes to Madrid with a letter, a masterpiece of its kind. The cleverest trick of all was that before he left, Guemes was sent to the Duke of Terranova for a letter of recommendation. The foolish duke gave him one, describing him as completely trustworthy. Thus equipped, Guemes appeared in the autumn of 1656 before the Spanish king, to whom he handed Christina's devastating accusations against the very duke whose recommendation had been his passport.

King Philip IV capitulated. He agreed to give the Duke of Terranova the discharge for which, as the Council would recall, he had once petitioned. . . .

Christina's victory was complete.

This episode, which the Swedish historian Curt Weibull has so ably brought to light, shows one of Christina's most brilliant *coups*. She was in a difficult situation, unpopular, short of money—there seemed nothing for her to do but give in and swallow her humiliation. But it was not in vain that she had had lessons in politics from Axel Oxenstierna. Her quick wits, courage and strength of will came to the rescue and she won. Now she could cut a very different figure in Rome, and everyone was filled with admiration, for she had shown in a single stroke what a power factor she was.

CHAPTER FOUR

The Monaldesco Affair

I. PREPARATIONS

CHRISTINA took to the warpath against the Spaniards because they had offended her honour. But behind her action there were without any doubt deeper political motives. On her departure from Sweden and afterwards, she had constantly insisted she sought peace and quiet above all—so as to devote herself to her cultural interests; as she wrote to Chanut in 1654, she wanted to spend the time ahead of her in meditating on her past in philosophical tranquillity, and ridding herself of her faults, but "with neither consternation nor remorse". From a sheltered haven she desired to watch poor folk tossed hither and thither on the wild sea-storms. Her sole purpose was to make herself comfortable and happy, leading a purely private life.

Whether Christina really imagined this is what she would do, we do not know. The fact remains that immediately on her arrival in Italy she became involved in the most subtle and intricate political intrigues, on a European scale. While she employed her utmost skill to disengage herself from her Spanish commitments, she already had other projects in view. In Rome she soon gave ear to the counsels of two men, the Prince of Gallicano with the Neapolitan rebels behind him, and Cardinal Azzolino. Both men knew what they were about and both influenced her actions; in fact the part they now played in her life was comparable to that of Johann Adler Salvius in Sweden, or such is the impression gained both from her correspondence with Salvius and from her link with revolutionary circles in Naples and conversations with Cardinal Azzolino. To some extent she was a pawn in the hands of astute political intriguers. Where Cardinal Azzolino is concerned, her dependence is readily demonstrated. But for an understanding of her attitude to the Neapolitan question we must turn to some still-unpublished State papers.

That Christina aspired to the royal crown of Naples, and that Monaldesco was executed because he abused her confidence, is known since the publication of Azzolino's letter to Monsignore Marescotti, papal nuncio in Poland, dated 13 April 1669.

After breaking with the Spaniards, Christina attached herself to France, in particular to a man who was later to achieve fame, Hugues de Lionne, at that time in Rome, whom we met briefly in an earlier chapter. He was intent on driving off the field Mazarin's dangerous enemy and rival in the struggle for power: Cardinal de Retz, and was Christina's match in political skill. De Retz, a friend of Azzolino's, introduced himself, and with his well-known charm rapidly won her over. She soon had the situation under her complete control.

She planned to be Queen of Naples, but could only succeed if she gained the complete confidence and support of France. For a while she wavered. She was not sure whether to rely on the man at the helm, Cardinal Mazarin, or on Cardinal de Retz, whom many—including Alexander VII himself—regarded as his probable successor. With consummate skill she played her double game: with Lionne she drew up a scheme (immediately communicated to Mazarin), promising to use her powers of persuasion to induce Cardinal de Retz to relinquish his claims to the archiepiscopal see of Paris, in return for certain services. At the same time she handled de Retz so ably that the possibility of his eventual victory remained open. The details of this double-dealing are to be found in Lionne's reports to Mazarin, as well as in certain jottings of de Retz's which have not yet been properly scrutinized. However, though she played it with the utmost subtlety, Christina's game was finally detected by that sly man, Mazarin. The procedure of the three reckless intriguers, Christina, de Retz and Mazarin, each seeking to outplay the others, is as exciting as a detective novel. Though he was Mazarin's agent, Lionne was watched by his spies; he promised Christina to trick de Retz, who for his part promised her to hoodwink Lionne. She prophesied to Pope Alexander VII, whom Cardinal Mazarin hated, that he would become the pawn of the

Spaniards if he did not make de Retz give way to Mazarin. To Lionne on the other hand, she said—for Mazarin's ear—she expected his powerful support for certain plans, if she did France the service of putting that dangerous man de Retz out of action. That the object of her plan was the crown of Naples, we know from a number of sources.

We have to remember that Christina was not acting without authority. As she saw it, and in the general view too, she was the victor of the Thirty Years War, the sovereign who dictated the Peace of Westphalia. She regarded herself as a European peacemaker, often insisting that the keeping of peace was the main incentive of her policies, both in Sweden and afterwards. She was a force to be reckoned with and everyone admitted it. But from personal experience Mazarin knew what curious motives are sometimes operative in politics. He too was a double-dealer. He pretended to believe her, flattered her, but was fundamentally extremely distrustful of her.

Perhaps she overplayed her hand. At all events Lionne's plan fell through: Cardinal de Retz persisted in his claims. But to Mazarin it was clear that Christina was no negligible factor, and her Neapolitan project was bound to interest him; he too had attempted more than once to capture Naples by storm. But he had always failed.

To Lionne, Christina used derogatory terms in referring to the Pope who had given her such a splendid reception on her arrival in Rome. "To rule the world more is needed than mere holiness," she remarked cynically. "Holiness is at times of a harmful nature. When the Pope says *Dio ci provedera*, he believes he has done all he can, and then puts his entire trust in Providence. But the Spanish have a finer saying, *A dios rogando y con el mazo dando* (pray to God but hit out on your own)."

She compared Alexander VII to his weaker predecessor, Innocent X, fully aware though she was of the latter's dependence on Olimpia Maidalchini, and very critical of it. Innocent believed the world ruled itself, Alexander believed God alone ruled all, both drew the conclusion that things could be left to run their course. "I am aware", said Christina, "that Pope Alexander's attitude is incomparably the better, but I am in doubt as to whom I should believe when politics are discussed."

Who was to be the future ruler of France, de Retz or Mazarin—the latter being eleven years older and likely to die before his rival—was not of great concern to her. Support for her own plans was the one thing that mattered. To Alexander VII she hinted at her great European peace programme and tried to convince him that sooner or later he would have to come out on France's side, France, the rising sun among European powers—and throw over the retrograde Spaniards. Certainly her motives were sincere so far, for she had had enough of the Spaniards. But part of the plan was to drive the Spaniards out of Italy, over which they had had a stranglehold ever since 1500. Where France had failed, with French and Italian help she might succeed.

As a Swedish scholar observed:

> Christina's plan to smooth away hostilities between France and the Papal See was in its way a politically sound and clever idea. When, after Marazin's death, de Retz made his peace with Louis XIV, it was a consequence of Christina's proposals in 1656. And Alexander VII was bitterly to rue the fact that he did not follow Christina's advice and do more to win Mazarin over: when it came to a settlement between France and Spain, the negotiations which in 1659 led to the Pyrenean Peace were conducted without the slightest sign of papal participation.

2. SUMMARY JUSTICE AT FONTAINEBLEAU

In spite of the failure of his intrigues against Cardinal de Retz, Mazarin kept his eye on Christina and sent one of his best men to Rome to intensify their co-operation. In spring and summer 1656, a year and a half after her arrival in Rome, Christina was engaged in close negotiations with Mazarin. No one knew anything about it, presumably not even Cardinal Azzolino. The plan was for Christina to become Queen of Naples, and after her death the throne would pass to Louis XIV's brother, Philip of Anjou. A few months earlier, leading Neapolitans had been to Paris and discussed with Mazarin who should be their king: their preference was for a French prince. At that same time Christina broke with the Spaniards, and now the marquis Gian Rinaldo Monaldesco entered her service. He had been in command of one of the volunteer corps formed in Rome to support the Duke de Guise's attack on Naples in 1654. He and the Prince of Gallicano were probably the first to think of Christina as future ruler of Naples.

She met Mazarin at Compiègne and on 22 September signed a formal agreement with France. (This document was unearthed by Martin Weibull in Paris, towards the end of the last century, and later published by his son Curt Weibull.) It put Christina in charge of the *coup de main* in Naples.

She then came back to Italy to make her preparations and ensure the support of the Italians. She had a triumphal return journey through France; she was honoured and admired, though she gave offence to some.

On 19 November she stopped in the little town of Pesaro, and to everyone's surprise remained there for eight months. No one knew what she was up to in Pesaro, it was thought she feared the Pope in Rome; it was also supposed she wanted to live cheaply because her allowance from Sweden did not come on time. In reality she was putting all her energies into the coming campaign.

On 29 March 1657, she informed Mazarin that she needed another talk with him. She would go to Avignon and wait there for the right moment, but she gave him to understand that various difficulties had arisen. The real trouble did not lie with the Spaniards but with Mazarin himself, whom she believed to be no longer wholly in favour of her plans.

She left Pesaro on 21 June and finally took up residence in the castle of Fontainebleau, south of Paris.

It is Father le Bel, prior of the monastery of the Holy Trinity, who recorded what took place there on 10 November 1657:

> On Tuesday, 6 November, at a quarter past nine in the morning, I was standing at the monastery door looking at the labourers out in the fields. Then came a lackey of the Queen of Sweden who was staying at Fontainebleau, living in the castle *conciergerie*: he asked for the prior. I replied, I am the prior, whereupon he said his queen wanted to speak to me. I replied I would gladly go with him to learn what her Swedish Majesty wanted. Then I shut the monastery

door. So as not to keep the queen waiting, I took no one with me but went alone to the castle with the lackey. After a short pause in the ante-room he took me to the queen. I bowed deeply and enquired what Her Majesty desired. She said we would go to the *galerie des Cerfs* to talk undisturbed.

In the gallery the queen asked if she had not met me once before. I answered, I only had the honour of waiting upon her and putting my services at her disposal, and she had been so kind as to thank me for this. Then the queen said the habit I wore gave her a guarantee that she could depend on me. And she made me swear to regard everything that she told me as said under seal of confession and not to be repeated. I replied that in regard to confidential matters I was deaf, dumb, and blind, even in dealing with ordinary people, how much more so when some one of royal blood desired it, of whom it is said, *Sacramentum regis abscondere bonum est.* Upon this the queen gave me a little packet of papers sealed with three seals but with no address. She told me to give it back to her when she wanted it, whoever was present at the time. This I promised to do. The queen further begged me to note exactly the time—day and hour—and the place, when and where, she handed me the packet. Apart from this the queen said nothing. I took the packet, bade farewell to the queen who declared she wished to remain in the gallery, vowed silence once more, and was back home before ten o'clock.

On Saturday, 10 November, at one o'clock in the afternoon, just after I had been shaved, a chamberlain of the Queen of Sweden came to take me to the castle. I first went into my inner room to fetch the small packet the queen had entrusted to me, I assumed she had called me to ask me to return it. I followed the chamberlain who led me across the *cour du donjon* to the *galerie des Cerfs.* As soon as we reached it the chamberlain at once shut and locked the door. I was rather taken aback. In about the middle of the gallery I saw her Swedish Majesty speaking to someone whom she addressed as *Marquis.* Later I learnt that it was the Marquis Monaldesco. I approached and greeted the queen. In addition to the marquis, there were three men in the gallery: two stood a good four paces away from her, the third quite near. In the presence of these four men, in a rather loud voice the queen requested me to give back the packet she had entrusted to me. "Reverend Father," she said, "I wish to have the packet that I gave you." I pulled it out of my pocket and handed it to the queen. She took it and examined it carefully. When she was sure it was in the same condition as when she gave it to me, she opened it. Then she handed the letters and papers it contained to the marquis, whom she asked with gravity and deliberation if he knew these documents. He denied it, but his voice trembled. As he refused to recognize the letters and papers, mere copies the queen had had made, she produced the originals. She showed them to the marquis, called him traitor, and finally brought him to admit to his own handwriting and signature. She, the queen, put further questions to him; he excused his actions and accounted for himself as best he could, putting the blame on others. Finally he threw himself at the queen's feet and begged for pardon. At that moment the three others present drew their swords. They were not to replace them in their sheaths until they had completed the marquis' execution.

The marquis now got up. He drew the queen from one end of the gallery to the other; he implored her to listen to him and hear what he had to say in his own defence; the queen did not refuse but listened with great patience and without a sign of emotion, nor showing any trace of anger.

Over and over again the marquis tried to persuade the queen to hear him. But now she turned to me: "Reverend Father," she said, and leaning upon a small ebony cane she advanced one step towards the marquis, "see for yourself, and be my witness, I am not precipitating things or dealing with this man too hastily, but allow this traitor, this faithless man, time sufficient and more than he has any right to claim, to justify himself to me, if he is in a position to do so, for he has failed in his duty". As the queen pressed him, the marquis finally handed her a few papers and two or three little keys tied together which he held out to her. At the same time, some silver coins fell out of his pocket: I do not remember which of us picked them up, which of the four, that is, who, in addition to the marquis, were with the queen.

The interrogation had lasted a good two hours. The marquis' defence had not succeeded in convincing the queen. Now she came towards me. With a slightly raised but quiet, grave voice, she charged me: "Reverend Father, I shall now withdraw and leave this man to you; prepare him for death, take his soul under your protection."

Had her verdict fallen on myself, my sorrow could not have been greater. At the queen's final words, the marquis and I both fell at her feet. I begged for mercy for the poor marquis, but the queen answered, turning to me, it was impossible for her to let mercy prevail. The traitor was the more guilty, indeed the more criminal as he knew very well, for the fact that as her loyal subject she had entrusted much of her business to him, many of her ideas and secrets. Not to mention the benefits she had showered upon him: greater than she could have bestowed on a real and well-loved brother, for as such she had regarded him always. For this ingratitude alone his conscience must smite him. With these words the queen left the *galerie des Cerfs*. She left me alone with the three men who stood there with drawn swords ready to execute the marquis.

As soon as the queen had gone the marquis threw himself at my feet and adjured me to follow her and obtain her pardon. The three men threatened him with their weapons but without touching him yet; they wanted to force him to make his confession; with tears I implored him to plead for God's mercy. The situation aroused the pity of the leader of the three men, who went out after the queen, but he came back in great distress: the queen commanded him to hasten the execution. In tears he said: "Marquis, consider your soul; you must die!"

At those words the marquis was beside himself. Once more he threw himself at my feet and implored me to hasten to the queen. This I did. I found the queen alone in her chamber, her face was as calm and majestic as though nothing had happened or was happening. With tears and sobs I fell at the queen's feet. I begged her by the wounds of Jesus Christ and his Passion to show mercy to the marquis. The queen assured me how much she regretted not to be able to grant my request, in view of the inhumanity and infidelity of which this miserable criminal was guilty; she added that she had had many evil-doers broken on the wheel who deserved it far less than this traitor did.

I put it to the queen that she was in the French king's palace and must be aware of what she was in the course of doing. She should consider whether the King of France would approve. The queen replied that she would give the same verdict before the altar itself; she called God to witness that she was not dealing with the marquis as a person but with his infidelity and betrayal which were beyond compare and concerned the whole world; moreover, it was not as a prisoner or as a refugee that the King of France was entertaining her in his palace; as ruler in her own right she could hold judgment over her subjects anywhere and at any time; she had to account for her actions to no one but God alone. What she was now doing was by no means without precedent, I replied, but there was a difference; if a King of France committed a similar act, he would at least be doing it at home and not as someone else's guest. But no sooner had I said these words than I regretted it. I feared I had gone too far and continued: "Your Majesty, by the respect and honour you enjoy in France, by the hope that all good Frenchmen entertain that the outcome of the negotiations in which you are engaged will be of great benefit for the whole of Europe, I entreat Your Majesty in all humility to desist from such an act. However justified from your point of view, in the eyes of the world it will still appear as an act of violence and precipitation. Show the poor marquis noble mercy! Or at least place him in the hands of justice: let there be a proper writ issued against him. By this means Your Majesty will herself gain satisfaction, and will maintain her reputation as a woman worthy of admiration, a reputation which Your Majesty has hitherto enjoyed universally, as due to your thoughts, words and deeds."

"What on earth are you proposing, Reverend Father," the queen exclaimed. "I who have the right to execute judgment over my subjects should submit and conduct a lawsuit against a traitor in my own household, a man of whose crime, infidelity and betrayal I have evidence, written in his own handwriting and signed by him?"—"That is true, Your Majesty," I objected, "but Your Majesty herself is a party to the affair!"—"No, no," the queen interrupted me, "I shall inform both the king and Cardinal Mazarin. Go, Reverend Father, go back and see to the saving of the delinquent's soul! On my honour and conscience, I cannot grant what you ask."

The queen sent me back. But as her voice faltered over the last words I was aware that she would doubtless have put off the execution and chosen another spot for it, had it been possible. But the thing had gone too far to make any other decision without running the risk of the marquis' escape. That is why she sent me back. So I found myself between two millstones. I did not know what I ought to do and what I should resolve upon. I could not simply go away, and even if I could, duty, honour and conscience bade me assist the marquis in the saving of his soul.

I returned to the *galerie des Cerfs*, I embraced the marquis, wept, exhorted and charged him with the best and warmest words at my command, and as God inspired me, to prepare for death and think of his salvation. There was no more hope for him in this life, but if he suffered now, and suffered in the name of justice, he would find again in God the life he lost on earth. On Him alone should he set his hope of eternity; from Him he would receive consolation. At these words the marquis uttered two or three loud cries. I had sat down on one of the benches in the gallery. The marquis sank down at my feet and began his confession. He did it in Latin, French and Italian, in whichever in his anxiety he found it easiest to express himself. Just as I was putting a question to him to clear up a doubtful point, the queen's court chaplain came into the gallery. The marquis immediately rose and went over to him without waiting for absolution.

Hope for pardon was again aroused. The marquis and the court chaplain drew aside into a corner, held hands and spoke together for some considerable time.

Then the court chaplain went out again and with him the leader of the three men. But the next moment the latter returned. "Marquis!" he exclaimed, "pray God for forgiveness, for you are to die without delay: you have made your confession." At the same time he pushed him to one end of the gallery, exactly under a painting of the château de Saint-Germain on the wall. I turned away but saw how his sword struck the marquis in the stomach. He tried to parry the blow and seize the blade with his right hand. But the man withdrew his sword and in doing so cut off three fingers of the marquis' hand. The blow had bent the sword and the man who struck it turned to the others and said he thought the marquis must have armour under his clothing. And indeed he did have on a coat of mail weighing nine pounds. The next moment the same man struck a blow at the marquis' face. He called out, "Father, Father!" so I went to him. The other man considerately withdrew a pace or two. With one knee to the ground he begged for pardon and said a few words to me. I gave him absolution and as penance for his sins recommended him to suffer patiently and forgive all who were causing his death. He accepted his absolution. Then he threw himself on the stone floor and one of the men—not the first—applied a blow to his head which knocked out a piece of bone. Stretched on his stomach, the marquis made signs to strike him in the neck. The same man struck at his neck two or three times but without doing much damage. The coat of mail had slipped up and that and his collar made the blows ineffective. I exhorted the marquis to remember God and bear it in patience. The leader then turned to me and asked if he should continue. I retorted indignantly, "I have no counsel for you on this matter; life, not death, is what I desire!" He apologized and admitted he had no right to put such a question to me.

While the poor marquis was awaiting the last, mortal blow, he heard the gallery door open. He pulled himself together, turned and saw that the queen's court chaplain had come in again. He dragged himself along the wainscoting till he reached him and asked to be allowed to speak to him.

The court chaplain placed himself on the left of the marquis, I stood on his right. Then the marquis turned to the court chaplain, seized his two hands and said a few words of confession. The chaplain admonished him to beg God for forgiveness and asked me for permission to give him further absolution. This he did. Then the court chaplain left the gallery after requesting me to remain with the marquis, and went back to the queen. The man who had formerly struck at the marquis' neck placed himself on his left. He ran his long, narrow sword through the marquis's throat. He fell to the right, where I was standing. He spoke no more, but his death throes lasted for another quarter of an hour. I exclaimed, "Jesus! Mary!" and other holy words.

His blood ceased to flow. The marquis breathed his last at a quarter to four o'clock. I prayed a *De profundis* and a prayer for the dead. The leader of the three men then seized the dead man's arms and legs and shook them, unbuttoned his breeches and underpants and felt in his inner pockets. He found nothing there and in the other pocket merely a prayer book and a small knife.

The three men then went together to the queen. I followed. The leader announced the marquis' death in my presence. The queen heard the news, expressing regret that she had been compelled to perform this execution. But, she said, his crime and his betrayal had met with justice; she prayed God to forgive him.

The queen charged me to see to the removal of the corpse and its burial: she promised to have many Masses said. I carried out the queen's command as quickly as I could. I sent for a bier, had the corpse placed on it and taken on a cart to the church of Avon. It was now twilight; the corpse was heavy and the road bad. The funeral procession consisted of my sub-prior and chaplain, accompanied by three men. The chaplain was to bury the dead man in the church, near the holy-water stoup. This was done without attracting attention and without disturbance. It was then a quarter to six.

Two days later, on Monday, 12 November, the queen sent two chamberlains to the monastery with a hundred pounds for prayers for the marquis' soul. The money was handed to the procurator of the monastery who issued a receipt for the sum, and on the evening of the following day a repeated ringing of bells let it be broadcast that Masses for the marquis had begun.

On 14 November, at ten in the morning, in the parish church of Avon where the marquis was buried, a solemn Requiem Mass was celebrated. All the priests of the church were there and took part in the Masses; the Superior of the monastery sang the last Mass himself, made a generous donation to the church and those officiating, and gave alms to all the poor who were there. For the thirty Masses held there the church was appropriately illuminated. And on Monday, 19 November, all the monks once more read Holy Mass in the great church of Fontainebleau, one after the other, at an altar set aside for the purpose. They prayed that God in his mercy would admit the soul of the dead man into his holy Paradise. Amen.

Christina's own description of the event is not without interest. We give a transcript here, with a few abbreviations:

Since about October, the Queen of Sweden had begun to suspect the marquis . . . and her suspicions grew daily stronger as further signs of his disloyalty turned up. She watched his every step, scrutinized the letters he received, and discovered he was in fact betraying her, and in so despicable a way that he was ascribing the misdemeanours of which he alone was guilty, to someone else who was then absent, but was also in the queen's service. She pretended the other man was the real traitor and assured the marquis that she in no way suspected him, so as the better to unravel the plan. The marquis deemed his scheme had succeeded, and one day said to the queen: "You are betrayed, Your Majesty, and the traitor is the absent knight whom Your Majesty knows; it can be no other, soon Your Majesty will be convinced of it, and then I beg Your Majesty not to pardon the culprit." The queen replied: "What does a man deserve who betrays me in this way?" The marquis answered: "Your Majesty must have him executed at once, without mercy; and I offer myself either as avenger or as victim: justice is at stake!"—

"Well," answered the queen, "do not forget your words; I assure you I shall not pardon him." But she had sealed the intercepted letters addressed to the marquis, and now handed them to the Prior . . . in Fontainebleau, to lay them before the marquis in due course.

The latter noticed that post often came in, but with no letters for him, so he began to be suspicious and tried to arrange better postal connections through Lyons. As an alternative he indicated that he was contemplating flight. The queen intended to forestall this possibility, and on 10 November she had him summoned to the *galerie des Cerfs* of which she had the use. The marquis kept her waiting a little, when he came he was trembling and pallid. The court had noticed how his expression had changed a few days earlier. First the queen put a few ordinary questions to him. The prior whom she had requested to come to the gallery now entered by a door which was immediately shut behind him; through another door came the captain of the guard with two soldiers. Now the queen began to speak more sternly; she asked the prior for the marquis' letters, showed them to him and accused him of blackguardly action and abysmal treason. Then she pulled out of his pockets all the papers he had in them and found two forged letters, one to the queen and the other to the marquis, indicating further treason, worse than the first: these letters were intended to intensify the suspicions against his friend. Among the letters were originals in the marquis' own hand.

At his wit's end, unmasked as traitor and forger, he threw himself at the queen's feet and admitted that a few days earlier, in that very room, he had pronounced his own death sentence. The queen now requested the prior to hear the traitor's confession and commanded the captain to carry out the sentence. Monaldesco fell into a panic and threw himself once more at the queen's feet and begged her to turn the death sentence into lifelong banishment from Europe, but the queen answered it was better for him to die than live on dishonoured. Then she turned and went out with the words: "May God be merciful to you, I am doing you justice!"

The execution was delayed because the confessor made several attempts to persuade the queen to save the marquis' life, for he stubbornly refused to make his confession; but when he saw that there was no more hope for him, he expressed the wish to confess to the queen's court chaplain who was an old friend of his. The queen agreed. When the priest appeared he found the marquis in a great state, who begged him to speak once more to her Majesty. The chaplain did so, with tears in his eyes he knelt before the queen—now for the third time. But she remained impassive. Then the marquis turned to those present and said: "My friends, see my unhappy lot and learn from my fate: never do anything wicked!" Now the order for the execution was repeated so he confessed to the priest. . . . His mean treachery did not even strike the queen as surprising, for he had proved himself disloyal to his natural lord, Pope Alexander VII, too, composing satires and pasquinades at his expense, which were later found on him. . . .

3. WHAT DID MONALDESCO BETRAY?

Monaldesco betrayed Christina. Her contemporaries were convinced she had had an affair with him—this was still believed in later years—and when she grew bored with it she had him killed. This betrays a complete lack of comprehension of Christina's character. All her life long she never had intercourse with a man. All she was doing was taking advantage of the right she had to exercise formal jurisdiction over her subjects, namely those in her service. Monaldesco was a criminal who admitted his crime and was duly punished. No one could object to that.

The Pope was shocked and let her know she had fallen in his esteem—in fact he suggested she should stop in Avignon, which still belonged to Rome. He also announced he would take legal proceedings against Monaldesco's murderers. Christina seems to have remained unmoved.

Chiefly it is her haughty calm that most amazes and impresses us: she had once threatened a Spanish general with a flogging; now, in a foreign country and at a French king's castle, she had an Italian marquis executed without heeding the inevitable gossip and ill-intentioned rumours, though for a long time, and even after her death, they were the source of a whole spate of spiteful literature on her vicious nature. Cardinal Mazarin was horrified and sent her old friend Chanut to her to remonstrate. She retorted with one of her most arrogant letters, a model in its way:

Cousin,

Monsieur Chanut whom I count among my best friends, will tell you that I welcome with respect all that comes from you. If he did not succeed in causing me to panic, that was not because his eloquence was incapable of painting my presumed atrocity in suitable colours. Truth to tell, we Northerners are rather ferocious people and not very timorous by nature. You will therefore excuse him if his message did not have all the success you would have desired. I beg you to believe that I am capable of doing anything to please you, except to feel afraid. As you know, no one over thirty years of age is afraid of tittle-tattle. I myself find it much less difficult to strangle a man than to fear him. As for what I did to Monaldesco, I tell you that if I had not already done it, I should not go to bed this evening without doing it, and I have no reason to repent and more than a hundred thousand reasons to feel satisfied. Those are my feelings on the subject. If you accept them, I shall be delighted; if not, I shall not cease to have them on that account, and shall remain all my life,

Your affectionate friend,

Christina.

She was convinced she had done what was right—morally, and legally. Utterly without misgivings she trod the path that seemed good to her.

What had Monaldesco betrayed?

We have no clue from letters or other papers and must fall back on hypothesis. Obviously it was something to do with Christina's political plans. We know that rumours were abroad as to her intentions in Naples. The papal nuncio in Naples reported to Rome,

. . . "From very well-informed people too, I have heard that the intention exists to attack Italy from the sea; the Queen of Sweden is said to have a part in the negotiations. It is generally believed that the attack will be against the kingdom of Naples"—whereupon he described the exact plan of strategy.

It is true that the plan became known prematurely. Monaldesco's execution took place on 10 November; on the 6th the papal nuncio in Naples reported that the Spanish viceroy was preparing for an eventual French attack, which he would hardly have done had he not received information about France's intentions. As early as August there were already rumours abroad as to Christina's and Mazarin's plans. Spanish spies had every opportunity to watch the manoeuvres and preparations of the French fleet.

So the plan was known. News had leaked out. But had Monaldesco betrayed it? After all, he was an ardent Neapolitan patriot, he regarded the freeing of Naples as his life's mission; he took a personal part in the preparations, and his whole future hung on the successful outcome of the project. After victory he could aspire to a very high place in the new State of Naples.

In such a situation, was he deliberately guilty of an act described by Christina as "an enormous felony and unbelievable treachery"? According to her own words he had "betrayed the interests of the queen his sovereign". Christina held that his treacheries were without parallel and concerned everyone ". . . n'eurent jamais de pareilles et touchaient tout le monde." She told Monaldesco she had had many men broken on the wheel who deserved their punishment less than he did. The object of her betrayal—those "interests" of hers—were known at her court only to Monaldesco and Francesco Maria Santinelli.

It must have concerned her Neapolitan plans. But if so, the problem is knottier than ever; no Neapolitan patriot would have truck with the Spaniards, surely; what could he expect to gain? And he could have gone to Spain, instead of lurking at such risk at the queen's court and writing his hazardous reports under her very nose.

The Spanish archives contain nothing to suggest that reports were being received from Monaldesco to account for the strengthening of defence measures in Naples. There is much to suggest that such measures were taken after the arrival of other reports: what the Paris nuncio knew was soon common knowledge at the Curia.

Certainly Monaldesco did betray matters that the queen considered extremely confidential and important. But a *coup d'état* against Naples did not concern "everyone": in a wider context, the whole affair was trivial enough.

For some time Queen Christina had noticed that Mazarin was wavering, showing but little interest in her plan. When he originally gave it his approval, Christina was jubilant: "I owe no one such a debt of gratitude as Cardinal Mazarin," she wrote to

Karl Gustav. However, during her stay in Pesaro she noticed that Mazarin's mind was set on making peace. So in her most grandiloquent style she wrote: "Today's news threaten the world with peace and tranquillity. *I love storm and dread it when the wind falters.*" She entreated Mazarin not to procrastinate: "The opportunity is favourable, I fear all that delays the fulfilment of my wish to see the French king triumph and Your Eminence overwhelmed with honours." (8 November.)

But Mazarin continued to hedge. By now he had more important business to attend to: on 23 March he had concluded an alliance with England against Spain, and the two nations were planning joint action against Spain in Flanders, with a view to conquering the main Spanish strongholds in Flanders, Dunkirk and Gravelines. The Naples plan consequently fell into the background. In March he told the queen that many difficulties had arisen, though he had September in mind. Christina's subsequent journey to Paris was for the purpose of applying some personal pressure to induce Mazarin to get on with the execution of the plan.

Christina suspected Monaldesco as early as October. Once, in a letter to Mazarin, she mentioned that Monaldesco's betrayal "concerns that matter in which they are both interested". Azzolino wrote that Monaldesco had "betrayed negotiations that he himself had conducted with Cardinal Mazarin and others, in the queen's name".

Then Mazarin deliberately spread a false rumour, making out that the queen had no part in the murder, the whole guilt lay on her servant Ludovico Santinelli. He did his best to get the queen to comply with this version of the story, but she retorted haughtily: "I know no one, however exalted and mighty, who could make me deny my conviction or oblige me to disavow my actions. I am not telling you this as a secret that I confide to you as a friend, but as a conviction I am prepared to declare to the whole world and no one can stop me from holding it, no one can conceal it but by robbing me of life."

With the material at present at our disposal we can come to no firm decision. We have to remember that Mazarin was playing a double game all the time and was no longer particularly interested in the Naples plan—even if he did not want to drop it altogether, and that it was with him that Monaldesco dealt. There is every possibility, as was suggested, that Monaldesco worked for Mazarin's interests rather than Christina's and that he was employing delaying tactics, or toyed with the idea of replacing Christina by another claimant to the throne of Naples, one more likely to carry Northern Italy with him. Behind her back he may well have been repeating to Mazarin all her ideas and plans, perhaps even her derogatory remarks about his insincerity and procrastination. When the queen stated that Monaldesco sought a safer postal connection through Lyons, there is no compelling proof that it was so, or that Spain was involved.

What she herself said about Mazarin after the catastrophe is relevant; never in a single word did she hint that plans of hers had been betrayed to Spain, and surely, with all the copious material at our disposal, letters, jottings and private notes, it would be known if were it so. Nor is there any Spanish allusion to it. The fact remains that Christina always spoke disparagingly of Mazarin, and after the episode treated him with withering scorn.

These are suppositions, not facts. The one thing we know for certain is Monaldesco's outright treason, whereupon the queen exercised her formal right to punish.

CHAPTER FIVE

Pallas in Love

I. A REMINDER OF CHRISTINA'S ATTITUDE TO LOVE AND MARRIAGE

ALL her life long Christina's attitude to marriage was negative. In her maxims—written over a number of years, though not revised and copied till the beginning of the seventeen-eighties, the only form in which they are now known—she returns to the theme with remarkable frequency: "Love and marriage are practically incompatible"; there could be no happy marriage, for married people could never love one another. People got married without knowing one another. As soon as they knew one another they were bound to hate each other. It would be altogether excessive good fortune to be at the same time married and in love. . . .

Nor was this all. Christina considered woman's position in marriage as undignified and humiliating: "Nuns and married women are equally unhappy, if in different ways." The courage of married couples was to be admired, but as a rule people married without knowing what they were doing.

According to Christina, women married mostly to indulge their lust, even preferring an old man to none at all. But in reality more courage was needed to marry than to go to war.

Already in her Swedish days Christina had concluded that women were wholly unsuitable as rulers. She recognized the right of Karl Gustav's male heirs to the throne, but not that of his equally probable female offspring. To Whitelocke, the English ambassador, she declared outright that women are not capable of reigning.

This curious view must have had a reason. In the first part of this book we saw her purely personal grounds for rejecting marriage: her special constitution, her virile upbringing, her contempt for women (not unconnected with her mother's hysteria), and her medical studies which we can trace by the underlinings in her books. But we must also take into account the attitude of her age: Christina was by no means the only lady of the seventeenth century who had such a negative view of marriage; though her personality and habits have apparently very little in common with the *précieuses* of her day, she none the less shared their attitude.

Christina once remarked about her friend, the literary Madame de la Suze, that she had gone over to Catholicism and parted from her husband so as to be sure she would never see him again, either in this world or the next. . . .

2. THE SUPERWOMAN—PALLAS OF THE NORTH

The characteristics that most struck the French ambassador Chanut, when he made the acquaintance of young Christina in Stockholm, were her cult of virtue, her high moral standards and her self-control. Christina's attitude was all the fashion at that time in Sweden; in the earlier seventeenth century, nearly all cultured people were strongly under the influence of classical Stoicism. The highest consideration went to whoever by sheer intelligence and will-power could master his passions: all this naturally within the framework of Christianity and the Church—not till a century later did faith in man as such, outside Christianity, become dominant. It is amazing to see what discrepancies and tensions were thereby completely overlooked. A modern cannot disregard the glaring incompatibilities that exist between Stoicism, which holds that man is perfectly capable of leashing the common impulses within him by his own efforts, and the Christian recognition of man's helplessness without the support of grace. But in those days it was not so. You could be a "Christian Stoic".

In Christina the cult of what can be called the stoic superman was the very end for which she lived. She believed herself invulnerable. All round her she saw weak, yielding women—men too —who all sooner or later gave in to their passions. She alone was superior, she was the Pallas of the North, guided by wisdom and will-power: for over a decade poets had sung it, flatterers had whispered it in her ear, and she had come to believe it.

Father Malines, too, found in her a creature "who had freed herself to such a degree from the vanity of human grandeur, and possessed such an unerring view of everything, that one might suppose her to have penetrated to the very core of classical moral philosophy". Descartes, at first anyhow, gained the same impression of sovereign superiority.

In her youth she never venerated a saint, and it was the superman-cult that she expounded in her maxims; she belonged to the then dominant school of neo-Stoicism, whose best representatives were Justus Lipsius and Guillaume du Vair. She was thoroughly at home with recent editions of Seneca and Epictetus, and well read in the current stoical philosophy popularized by numerous anthologies of moral teaching, not all of a high standard.

Her proud self-sufficiency was enhanced by her belief that being a crowned and anointed sovereign, she was God's representative on earth, responsible not to men but to God alone, and belonging to a sphere high above mere human petty affairs. "The sea is an image of a great mind," she once wrote, "however much it may appear to move, it is motionless in its depths." And another time, "There is a star that unites all great minds, independently of the lands and the centuries that part them." In her essay on Alexander the Great she mentioned "the divine fire that inspires great minds", and worked out a whole theory of how Providence exalts the superman and endows him with historic significance.

Obviously with herself in mind, she advanced the idea that Providence only occasionally "bestows" such supermen on the people; they are born rather to be a scourge and punishment, "but always an honour and a blessed event for their age and for all their subjects". They make their appearance like comets; it seems as though after producing these demi-gods nature wanted to "rest awhile . . . so as not to destroy the order established by Him who alone is Lord over throne and sceptre according to His pleasure".

One of her maxims that she tore out eventually, but evidently found it hard to part from, for she entered it again, only to delete it in the end, gives an admirable idea of the type of superman to which she believed herself to belong:

"Confessors of princes are like men engaged in taming tigers and lions: they can induce the beasts to perform hundreds of movements and thousands of actions, so that on seeing them one might believe they were completely tamed; but when the confessor least expects it, he is knocked over by one blow of the animal's paw, which shows that such beasts can never be completely tamed."

A book about Sweden, published in 1682, preoccupied her at one time: she found part of it was about Karl Gustav, whereupon she observed that he was a king she herself had created—"even as (though without intending a comparison) God created the first man".

For sheer arrogance, these two quotations can hardly be surpassed: here is the culmination of her proud conception of the superman, based on the current assumptions that a prince was an exalted representative of God, set high above common mortals.

Christina read Corneille with ardour, and in his play *Agésilas* he wrote:

> *Un roi né pour de grandes actions*
> *Dompte jusqu'à ses passions*
> *Et ne se croit point roi, s'il ne fait sur lui-même*
> *Le plus illustre essai de son pouvoir suprême.*

3. CHRISTINA AND FEMININE BEAUTY

In French diplomatic correspondence from Rome there is a not exactly pleasant report which ought not to be wholly disregarded. Its author is a well-known diplomatist, Abbé Servient, a relation of Lionne's, whom we infer from other sources to have been well-informed and not without experience; Saint-Simon describes him as "renowned for his moral lapses". In November 1680 he reported to Croisy that four years earlier the queen had occasion to believe she was changing into a man. This had proved to be an error, and it would be legitimate to regard the whole report as false; there were other tasteless details in it which we will of course ignore. But the supposition might have endorsed a secret hope of Christina's, for on many occasions she expressed her scorn for women and her admiration for the male sex to which she would have loved to belong; she was fully aware of the strong virile traits of her own physical and mental constitution, and doubtless would have considered it a great mark of grace had she really turned into a man.

During her journey across France she was everywhere greeted as "the splendid daughter of the great Gustavus", "the tenth Muse", "the Sappho of our time", "the pride of her sex". As she exclaimed bitterly to her friend Bourdelot: "It is dreadful how hard people are trying to let me know I am a woman! I know it myself all too well. . . ."

There are many accounts of Christina's interest in female beauty during her Italian years, most of which can be disregarded, but not all. At times she expressed herself with the utmost frankness. On 29 August 1668, for instance, she wrote to Cardinal Azzolino that she had heard the French ambassador was leaving Rome and would be replaced by the Duc de Vieuville. She regretted the ambassador's departure but consoled herself with the prospect of meeting his successor's wife again, for she had made her acquaintance on her journey to France and she was sure she would become her intimate friend. She continued: "I know her very well, though not her husband, and I can assure you that she will be an embellishment to the Roman Court, for she is beautiful, bewitching and *galante*, a woman of distinction, belonging to the *grand monde*. I was informed that Cardinal Chigi paid much attention to her during his stay in France. You may tell him in my name that I am thinking of becoming his rival."

After her early simultaneous passion for Ebba Sparre and Count Magnus de la Gardie—a double faculty which she developed over the years—she still got excited about lovely young women, and in given circumstances got more deeply involved, but she was also susceptible to masculine beauty. On top of that—to her own amazement—she was soon to be in the throes of an all-devouring passion for a man.

4. THE CARDINAL

Christina came to Rome in 1655 and was greeted as the stoical superwoman she had proclaimed herself to be. We saw how Rome soon discovered something else about her, that she was a libertine with a sharp tongue, imperturbably transgressing conventions and taboos and callously brushing aside the current conceptions of how a devout and modest woman should conduct herself; she preferred the company of men and showed a perverse scorn for many of the external forms of ecclesiastical life. Worse still, rumours went from ear to ear that she was by no means the virginal queen she was supposed to be; as we have seen, a petulant Spanish diplomatist described her as "the biggest harlot in the world", and long before Monaldesco's execution, which finally convinced the world of her low moral standards, it was whispered in Rome that she was in love with a Roman cardinal. Posterity did not take these rumours too seriously, till in 1899 Carl Bildt, Swedish ambassador in Rome, rediscovered the letters written at the time of her stay in Hamburg in 1666–8, letters containing evidence of ardent feelings of personal devotion.

Who was this Cardinal Decio Azzolino?

His biography is still incomplete, for shortly before his death he destroyed a great part of his papers, and specially the letters he had written to Queen Christina in Hamburg. Among the queen's papers, however, there are large numbers of shorter letters and notes which they exchanged, and these provide good insight into the cardinal's character and the scope of his interests.

A former patron of Azzolino as a young priest was Cardinal Barberini; he found him a post as secretary to Cardinal Pansirole who took him along when he went to Spain as nuncio. There Azzolino showed powers of "quick judgment and a good diplomatic eye". Cardinal Pansirole was exceedingly pleased with him; he came back to Rome with the cardinal and found a post in the papal secretariat of State; there he was code-secretary too. Pope Innocent X noticed his "liveliness and intelligence". At that time—like all other ambitious papal diplomats—he had to take care to be in the good books of the Pope's powerful and unscrupulous sister-in-law, Olimpia Maidalchini: he succeeded admirably. His enemies talked of an affair, his friends merely regarded the relationship as a very close one. When in 1654, just before Christina's arrival in Rome, he was made cardinal, Olimpia wanted him to be appointed secretary of State. But Innocent X could not be parted from Cardinal Chigi, whom Olimpia opposed at every step. She won the point, however, that Azzolino was to be present at every audience granted by the Secretary of State.

There were many rumours in circulation about Azzolino's private life, but there is no reason to believe them. We have no knowledge that he led a loose life in contravention of his priestly duties; but he was elegant and fond of cultivating feminine society. Ludwig von Pastor, the great historian of the popes, observes severely: "he had no purity of morals". One of the best-known chroniclers of the time, Angelo Corraro, wrote in a book published in 1663, that Azzolino "wasted his time in love affairs", and that nothing he did had positive results: "He seems never to have had enough time for his pleasures." The only pleasures of which we have any definite information, were art and the theatre. Apart from that, ecclesiastical politics seem to have had a strong hold on him: he played a leading part in no fewer than four papal conclaves.

Queen Christina occasionally made bitter allusions to his interest in pretty actresses; naturally it was only a pastoral interest, she remarked spitefully.

Somewhat more dubious was his behaviour during the 1669–70 conclave; we saw how he pretended to lose a slip of paper on purpose to mislead his enemies; but the little trick proved completely ineffective.

Most of his friends, and his enemies too, praised his elegance, his flexibility, wit and industry, but these traits may have been only a façade. In his letters he is seen to be sober, energetic and totally without humour; he never gives an impression of possessing real moral or intellectual quality. More likely, he was a skilful, unscrupulous political realist, but for all his abilities he never achieved any major political success.

To his credit let it be said that he was wholly and in every respect devoted to the queen, he steered her through a number of difficult situations, mostly of a financial nature. How far his helpfulness was based on real friendliness or was rather dictated by politico-ecclesiastical considerations, is hard to say. At all events not a single shred of evidence exists today of genuine deep feeling for Christina on his part.

It is not easy to visualize Christina's relationship with this powerful cardinal during her first years in Rome. Soon after her arrival she evidently knew him well. Giandemaria chattered on about him in his letters to the Duke of Parma and declared he turned up "at the most impossible times of day". When for reasons of prudence the Pope issued a ruling that the cardinals were not to visit distinguished ladies nor appear in Rome *incognito* (i.e. masked), Christina took action and obtained an express repeal of the ruling that Cardinal Azzolino was not to visit her otherwise than in the presence of witnesses: "and now he is almost always with her", it was said. It was also Giandemaria who wrote: "when I last saw the queen she kept on pulling a picture out of her pocket, but I could not see whom it portrayed, though I supposed it must have been our good Azzolino" (*esser quel della bon'anima Azzolino* —the cardinal's name written in cypher).

In the Chigi archives there is a letter from Azzolino to the Pope, dated 22 March 1656, that is, very soon after the queen's arrival. He wrote to explain his conduct: there were rumours circulating about his "long and frequent visits to the queen" and the many letters they exchanged. He therefore desired to state expressly that he had only received a very few notes, except in one special and precisely-indicated connection.

So the Pope was already uneasy about Azzolino's friendship with the queen, even at this early stage, and the relationship was spot-lighted with ill-intentioned zest by the cardinal's many enemies. The Pope, however, saw the thing in its true proportions: notes or no notes, the fact remained that Christina had strong feelings for the young cardinal that were likely to develop into passionate ones before long. During the next ten years the rumours became more and more circumstantial. One took the form of a libel entitled *Il concubinato scandaloso e publico in Roma del Cardinal Azzolino con la Regina di Svetia*. Azzolino set up a thorough search for the culprit: today we have sufficient material to know that he found him and had a shrewd idea of who was behind it all.

5. IN THE THROES OF PASSION

In the years 1666–8 Christina's bad financial situation took her to Hamburg and Sweden. For various reasons, the generous Swedish financial allowance allocated to her was not being paid in full. From her residence in Hamburg, in the Krayenkampstrasse, opposite the church of St Michael—her business-manager Texeira had a house there—Christina wrote a series of letters to Cardinal Azzolino, largely on business matters and her Swedish plans, but other passages in these letters breathe a passion so powerful that they astonish anyone knowing Christina's scorn for her passionate mother, and indeed for all who let themselves be carried away by their baser instincts.

Obviously Christina was deeply in love with the cardinal for a long time. There had been a happy, relatively stormless period in their friendship which now, for some unknown reason, had come to an end. So she wrote from the fullness of her distress and extreme predicament. Her nerves were shattered, more than once she sank below her true self, became jealous and hysterical, and almost a figure of fun. In a word, she was in a very excited condition—a prey to passion: but passion, according to her stoic philosophy, was not compatible with the more exalted levels of human life.

Azzolino was evidently left in charge of her affairs in Rome. In her very first letter she gives him a kind of blank authority but tells him that she unfortunately cannot send him the promised money. Azzolino must have been in a serious dilemma and his patience ran out. Again and again he gave her severe warnings, but as a rule the only answer was that he must wait.

Christina longed to be back in Rome. The cardinal wrote that he had heard she did not want to stay in Rome but return to Sweden, to which she replied: "How so? Do you not want me to come back again, or can you believe I could ever make up my mind to leave Rome for good? . . . Believe me—I would rather live on bread and water in Rome and have only one chambermaid to wait on me, than be elsewhere and possess all the kingdoms and treasures of the world."

She thanked him for the "loving sentiments" expressed in his letter and added: "I can assure you too that I deserve your friendship, because of the most tender passion and greatest L. in the world. I know not if I shall ever be happy again but I do know that I shall R. you till death. Farewell."

In Christina's code, L appears to mean Love; R. must be the cypher for to love. We observe here that she already spoke of *his* friendship and *her* love.

She also thanked him for sending her his poems which had brought her much consolation, and denied the rumour that she had tried to sleep on her departure from Utricoli: "I was weeping for my sad lot. My eyes were filled with tears, not sleep."

In her next letter, on 30 June 1666, she wrote that it gave her infinite sorrow to be away from Rome, and the cardinal. She inferred from his letter that many people missed her, and she would like more details about this. She thought, however, that he had been deceived, for it was after all "a matter in which your interest is known to everyone".

On 14 July, Azzolino had written that his feelings for her were warmer than she could imagine, to which she replied that he could never properly imagine what feelings she nourished for him. Indeed she was all restlessness.—On 21 July, she was persuaded it was impossible he would ever forget her, and she waited impatiently for his letters from Rome—"to know if they bring me death or life". She assured him: "The affection I feel for you will have no other end or bounds but those of my life itself."—On 4 August she wrote that their exchange of letters was the only joy left her, and their *amitié* could not and should not cease till death—"I should be only too happy if I were allowed to see you once more before I die."

On 15 September she wrote a letter from which we infer that Azzolino had asked her to get a newly-published French devotional work, *L'Intérieur chrétien*. It mattered little to her that severe Roman priests avoided her—one thing alone was important: "my heart which will be true to you till death".

It is apparent that she was disturbed at his relative coolness. On 29 September she wrote: "Whatever changes may occur in your heart, they cannot alter my own heart; I shall keep unbroken troth to you till death."

In the following letters the situation became more acute. She refused to answer the coded parts of his letters, "for I can neither alter my feelings nor tell you of them without hurting you". Azzolino had evidently forbidden her to make declarations of love. She began to realize that he by no means returned her love. On 23 October she let the cat out of the bag: "All your coolness cannot stop me from worshipping you until V." (V: death).

At that time, anxious to find something to distract her, Azzolino challenged her to write her autobiography.

During this period in Hamburg Christina was ill nearly all the time.

She complained of pains in her side, she grew thin, was constantly thirsty and in a perpetual state of deep melancholy. She remained all day long in her room, an icy cold one, and slept, worked and ate there and had Mass said there too. She even received her visitors in the same room. In the evenings she sat close to the fire reading. When the doctors ordered a milk cure, in one day she drank ten jugs of milk. She became more and more mistrustful of Azzolino and believed he was afraid she would come back to Rome. She hinted to him that it was not so certain she would come back again: if he did not return her love, she had nothing more to do there.

Azzolino sharpened the tone of his letters, accusing her of not following his advice in political and financial matters. She answered with dismay that his ideas and advice were her oracles and it was merely external things that stood in the way. This same letter, dated 26 January 1667, contains her most outspoken declaration:

> *J'ajouterai toutefois que mon intention est de n'offenser jamais Dieu, avec sa grâce, et de ne vous donner jamais sujet d'offense; mais cette résolution ne m'empêchera pas de vous aimer jusqu'à la mort, et puisque la dévotion vous dispense d'être mon amant, je vous dispense d'être mon serviteur, car je veux vivre et mourir votre esclave.*

This forthright declaration of love needs closer scrutiny, there is possibly an ironical undertone to it. If it was the cardinal's *dévotion* that kept him free and entitled him to say No, what did Christina mean by *dévotion*? I used to believe that with no irony at all she meant his Catholic faith and ecclesiastical outlook. But this does not seem to fit. Indeed in other places in her letters Christina used the word quite evidently in an ironical sense. On 9 February 1667 she wrote:

"You have taken the story about the doctor in a way that would have wounded me on another occasion; but as I know you are *dévot*, it no longer surprises me; for it is an effect of *dévotion* to make God responsible for all the silly things people do; but I, who am not so much at home in *dévotion* as you are, take it all in quite a different way." This seems to indicate that for Christina the word signified a conventional or false piety, perhaps even a mere ecclesiastical convention.

On 9 March she wrote him an extremely sardonic letter:

> You edify me with the theological and moral meditations you draw from whatever happens, and I do not doubt for a moment that your mind was, as usual, turned to God when you listened to a comedy being read at the French ambassador's, and the two young ladies who recited, used as they were to giving some degree of pleasure to the whole of Rome, did not inflict mortification on you by attracting your glances to themselves. But no doubt you were following our Lord's example, in order to convert them . . . for when I consider what a scruple prevented you from going to watch the fireworks at the Spanish ambassador's, I conclude that it was a pure effect of that *dévotion* of yours that preoccupies your mind at present, and attracted you to the French ambassador's. . . .

What scathing tones! If here the word is undoubtedly used in irony, why not also in the great love-letter of 26 January 1667? It would then mean something like this: ". . . as it is ecclesiastical convention that prevents you from being my lover . . . ", consequently, he had no urgent reason for rejecting her love, and she really did reckon with physical union and had no objection to it.

However, the word *amant* is a difficulty. It does often mean "lover" in the physical sense, but in that century it did not necessarily do so. It is hard to decide which is intended here.

At all events, this letter is the most important document in the story of Christina's life. The superwoman had collapsed, there was nothing left of her proud assurance that she would always remain mistress of her passions. Here she was singularly like her own much-scorned mother, Maria Eleonore, who begged for Gustavus Adolphus's love in exactly the same way, without ever winning it. Christina, who had always assured herself and her entourage that she was born to rule and could never accept a subordinate role, was now pitifully begging for love, and if her friend was not to be her lover, she wanted at least to be his slave for ever and ever. It was complete capitulation.

We do not know Azzolino's answer, but he must have been a good deal perturbed.

In her letter after the one dated 2 February, Christina wrote amenably: "*On est trop heureux quand on a quelque part en votre approbation et en votre estime*" (overjoyed to have some share in your approbation and esteem)—a minimum of appreciation. She knew she could not be the one and only being in his affections; she had to be content as one among many whom he esteemed and on whom he bestowed his gracious approbation. But how humiliating that was for her.

Now she began to speak pathetically of her approaching death. What was she to do in Rome if he did not want her there? "I think you hate nothing so much as my presence," she wrote on 16 February 1667. In search of distraction she tried the dubious solution of giving a great banquet; she was so exhausted by it that afterwards she had to let the doctor take half a litre of blood. Azzolino was up in arms at the unnecessary expense. Then on 9 March she wrote her furious letter about his visit to the French ambassador's where he admired the pretty actresses. Now she really was humiliated, plagued by jealousy she mocked and reviled her beloved; how horrid of him to tell her and betray his attraction for the two girls. The simple logic of a commonplace love story takes over: If you do not love me, I hate you; if you love another, you are a bad man. She ended in icy tones: "May God grant you long and happy years!" Not a word more of her own feelings. The game was lost.

In her next letter she wrote bitterly:

"I am not answering your code letter. I do not want to change either your feelings or my own. You are right, and I am not wrong. I do not complain of you. So please do not you go on complaining of me."

This outburst must have been caused by a letter of Azzolino's accusing her of hysteria and begging her to control her jealousy. She submitted—rather be his slave than lose him.—On 30 March she continued: "I beg you to believe that you have unlimited power over me and that being obliged to you in the way I am, your will shall be an eternal law to me against which I shall never demur." So she accepted her "slavery", humiliating though it might be; indeed with her new attitude she could adore him more freely than of old. When he achieved success, she rejoiced more than he himself, he was born to great things, God had chosen her to tell him what great things still awaited him: "Courage, follow the splendid career that heaven opens before you, follow it to the end, and be assured that you are destined to be the greatest and happiest man of the world—in merit, virtue and good fortune. You will know one day that I speak the truth."

Christina believed that the way lay open to the papal see. But she herself had no desire to return to Rome (20 April 1667): her self-pity emerges from the extensive account she sent him of her physical condition (27 April 1667)—if only in order to excite his sympathy. In Rome he was still having to deal with her bad financial situation: "I am in despair that you have no money, but sell and pawn, borrow what you can, and fear nothing." She hoped not to live much longer: "I do not care what happens, for in my present state I do not like life enough not to concur joyfully, were it taken from me. And since I have made a resolution, too, never to see you again, there is nothing more in life to hold me. . . ."

We need but consider how twenty years earlier Christina would have judged a woman who behaved in the way she was now behaving. Her poor health grew worse, and her unhappy love was the main cause of the deterioration. The Italian doctor Macchiati could make nothing of it, but a French cook turned up and cured her, just as Bourdelot had cured her in Sweden. His recipe was French and very effective—he gave her an excellent strong broth (*brodi molto galanti, all' uso di Francia*, wrote Macchiati, much impressed) and took charge of her peculiar diet. Then a French doctor came from Copenhagen and bled her. Very soon she was well again.

On 13 May 1667, Christina wrote from Sorö in Denmark:

"I do not think I have long to live. If I had only paid my debts I should die contented, regretting nothing but the fact of having lived two years too many, *car c'est à plus près de ce temps et ceux* . . ." —the letter stops abruptly as though it had ended in a burst of tears: two years earlier, in spring 1665, she was happy—at that time she still had hopes of Azzolino's love.

Now she looked round for other interests. The Polish throne was vacant, she devoted an immense amount of effort to her candidature; both Azzolino and the Pope supported her. She celebrated the enthronement of the new Pope Clement IX with a great banquet in Hamburg, which ended, however, in a tumult with a shooting incident.

We observe how eager she was to seek out new things to do, new interests; for instance she spent a lot of time just then on alchemy. But her bitterness overshadowed it all. When Azzolino sent her a comedy he had written—it was not quite finished—she wrote a commentary on it that was really about herself.

She was still to some extent obsessed with him: "All your cruelties and your bad treatment of me will never change the constant faithful affection that I shall feel for you till death"—but of love there is not a word. Evidently Azzolino had categorically forbidden her to mention it. The customary declarations now took the following form: " . . . I beg you to be persuaded that your friendship alone will always constitute all the glory and all the felicity of my life and my death."

Every now and then she got annoyed with him, however, as on 22 August 1668:

> I am sending half your last letter back to you; please forgive me if the answer displeases or shocks you. I have so high a consideration for you that I say no more; if you had as much consideration for me, I would not receive from you the unworthy treatment

9. Cardinal Decio Azzolino
Bust by Lorenzo Bernini in the National Museum, Stockholm
Photo: National Museum, Stockholm

10. Pope Alexander VII, of the wealthy Chigi family, who received Christina into the Roman Catholic Church

11. Cardinal Sforza Pallavicino, who wrote one of the first descriptions of Christina's conversion

12. Cardinal Mazarin, Christina's most difficult political adversary

that I have so often received, and borne with a patience that ought at least to deserve some consideration from you, though an unhappy friendship of twelve years' duration has not been able to elicit it. I have directed the marquis to tell you what I think about the matter; please welcome him as a final gesture from a friendship on which you have never laid weight, and then decide. If this friendship is importunate, I protest that I shall seek death to deliver you from it, and that death will be less unbearable than the disdain and scorn you show me.

But already on 12 September things were better: "I am delighted that you are pleased with me. I shall try to live in such a way as to deserve to please you always."

On 10 October her bitterness broke out again:

I hope you will understand that my misfortunes have not changed my heart. I know that I shall be all the more odious to you on that account, but what am I to do? Such is my lot. I shall, however, manage my stay in such a way as not to be importunate to you—perhaps fate will take over and part us again. Whatever may happen, I shall remain always the same till death. I beg your pardon for venturing to say things disagreeable to you; I speak from the fullness of my heart. No need for anxiety, you shall have the pleasure of seeing in me the unhappiest person in the world, without my complaining of it. And in the places where everything will remind me of past felicities, I shall wish for nothing but death. I hope my suffering will bring it on, and I should be too happy to die unhappily in Rome at a time when all other people will live there happily. Adieu.

This is mere verbiage: in reality, on the point of returning to Rome, Christina was positively intoxicated with joy: "It will give me measureless joy to see you again."—"I am leaving at last with the same joy that souls experience on leaving purgatory."—"I await with extreme impatience the happy moment when we meet again."

6. AFTERMATH

Cardinal Azzolino remained adamant—we possess no single letter of his with a hint of love or even sympathy. On the other hand he remained all his life the queen's faithful friend; they worked together splendidly for years on end, most intensively and best of all during the papal conclave of 1669–70.

Christina's love never died. This is evident from the many little notes she sent by special messenger after she came back to Rome; it is most striking to compare his matter-of-fact missives, often written in a peremptory tone, with her strongly personal answers written with a bleeding heart. Among her papers we found the following undated note:

> Today is for me a specially unhappy day, for it will not allow me to see you. What are you thinking of doing to compensate me for all the suffering caused by the cruel law you imposed on me? Your note has the advantage of consoling me a little, but please think of my feelings when I received it instead of you; I sincerely admit that I never thought I would have to accept a letter from you with dismay, and yet I felt a strange tenderness and sadness along with the consolation it brought me. My lot it is never to experience other than imperfect joys.... I shall never love anyone but you, and you are determined to make me for ever unhappy. Farewell!

During the papal conclave in 1670, Christina received another communication from Azzolino and saw it was marked with the initials S.M., which, formally, would mean *Sa Majesté* or *Sua Maestà*. What did they mean here? We do not know. But the note caused her to break into tears of joy and gratitude, so it must have signified that he was still capable of the fond feelings he had shown five years earlier: "If I could describe to you the joy those initials give me, you would somehow regard this form of address as worth while, while I even prefer it to the title of Queen of the Universe. But I must have forfeited the right to it, since you deprive me of it. Act as you find best! I am so much yours that without being unspeakably cruel and unjust, you cannot doubt that you owe me an SM."

What did SM stand for? *Semper mea, sempre mia*? (always mine). There must surely be some hidden tender meaning to these initials. A well-informed German writer, Oskar von Wertheimer, though unacquainted with the bulk of the material, has done a good character sketch of Christina, and he has his own hypothesis, which may be right: It might be, . . . he said, that the cardinal's feelings changed at that time from strong platonic love to outright *amitié*.

We know nothing of later conflicts. Christina's passion seems over the years to have passed into quiet friendship. Here as in all other fields she had to accept resignation—her whole life in Rome was a ceaseless relegation into the background of her too exalted claims and demands. In her correspondence from Hamburg she betrayed conspicuous coolness and indifference to the challenge of religion, though constantly referring to it; scoffing at Azzolino as sham moralist—but later, at Azzolino's side, she was caught in a strong religious upsurge that came upon her quite unexpectedly, via Quietism.

Her spiritual life thus ultimately acquired gravity and depth, and she succeeded in letting go of many another stubbornly-held hope for personal happiness, with the result that a certain peace and calm invaded her tempestuous soul.

7. A NEW CONCEPTION OF MAN

Christina's personal destiny certainly followed its own laws. But no one can live uninfluenced by the great trends of his day. We saw how young Christina's headstrong self-assurance rested upon the current stoical ideal, and how it broke down under stress of her experience of passion. She kept her pride, but it was no longer so unconditional—she acquired a first-hand knowledge of the hardships of life, and her confidence in the supremacy of will-power and sovereign self-control was shattered once and for all.

It is remarkable how Christina's individual development ran parallel to the great changes that were then taking place in the European cultural outlook. By the middle of the seventeenth century the tide had turned and people were on the defensive against the high claims of Stoicism. Saint-Evremond's outcry against Seneca is typical, dubbing him a charlatan, "a big-mouthed fellow quaking in fear of death and trying with all his might to keep himself under control as he cut his arteries open . . . a man not over-convinced of the truth of what he was saying". Typical, too, is the engraving often to be found in books of the period—as for instance in the first edition of La Rochefoucauld's *Maximes*—

showing Seneca with a mask over his eyes which a child is trying to snatch away. Corneille went on and on presenting his dramatic interpretations of the stoic faith, but those same rhetorical speeches which once brought the house down in *Le Cid* were now, in *Oedipe*, *Sophonisbe* and *Agésilas*, regarded as boring.

This reaction against Stoicism had several causes. As general background we have the sobering effect of the aftermath of the *Fronde* in France. Just as the aftermath of the wars of religion made some people sceptical of all religious doctrines when used as weapons against their fellow-men, the disillusionment and disarray after the *Fronde* troubles opened people's eyes to man as he really was—not at all Seneca's or Corneille's noble, controlled, self-disciplined superman, but essentially subject to impulse and motivated by self-interest.

A powerful drive in the same direction came from the Church and classical Christianity. There had always been a certain amount of Christian disapprobation of Stoicism, as a distorted view of man and the human condition. But it was Jansenism that caused the decisive turn away from it. With Jansenius's *Augustinus* in mind, the Port-Royal theologians had never, when occasion arose, refrained from castigating the tendency of the earlier part of the century to set man upon a pedestal. Another representative of the new trend was Pascal, the greatest opponent of the Stoics. His attitude and the consequences he drew are clearly set out in the famous *Entretien sur Epictète et Montaigne* conducted with M. de Saci; in his *Pensèes* he more than once criticizes Montaigne.

Epictetus' greatness, said Pascal, is to have recognized man's obligations. His weakness is not to have seen man's imperfection.

Pascal rejected the *principes d'un superbe diabolique*; the ancient philosophers knew nothing of man's wretched state after the Fall and did not grasp the difference between man's present state and his condition before the Fall. The Stoics had observed certain indications of an earlier greatness, but were ignorant of man's corruption, so they assumed that nature was sound and needed no Redeemer, an attitude that could only engender pride. The Epicureans, for their part, clearly perceived the present wretchedness of man, but knew nothing of his original condition and therefore treated nature as necessarily sick and incurable, which is enough to make man despair of ever reaching his true Good, and to drive him into a state of indifference.

Of these two philosophies, the one is conducive to pride, the other to laxity. Whereas the Christian faith taught something quite different, that human weakness and human strength belong to two separate spheres, weakness to nature, strength to grace.

So Pascal rejected the stoical attitude: man lives in indescribable wretchedness, he can reach neither truth nor goodness on his own, but "this whole wretchedness proves his strength. It is the misfortune of a great lord, a king dethroned".

As for the ancient philosophers, he says, either they convey an impression of pure greatness—and that is not the true condition of man; or they convey an impression of utter degradation—and that is equally not the true condition of man. The dichotomy is resolved by Pascal in a new concept that comes nearer to the true paradox of human nature. At that time the new psychological realism—in Pascal and others—was accepted with a great sense of relief.

La Rochefoucauld, too, is to some extent dependent on Port-Royal, though we have no right to call him a professing Christian. He had personal experience of the prevailing chaos after the Fronde, and together with other noblemen he suffered humiliation and was committed to silence and compromise. It took a great effort of self-control for him to sit uneasily at the side of his mortal enemy Mazarin and make a pretence of loyalty. His sharp censure of the whole scale of noble classical virtues, branded as cynical self-esteem, was aimed at the aristocratic divinization of man to which Corneille had subscribed. He, too, kept aloof deliberately from Seneca; to the Chevalier de Méré he once remarked: "I believe that in ethics Seneca was a hypocrite and Epicurus a saint." A typical work of the times was the great catalogue entitled *La fausseté des vertus morales* published by Jacques Esprit in 1677; Seneca and Cicero were rejected out of hand.

The new literature that appeared in Louis XIV's time kept aloof from the view of man attaining greatness through the exercise of his natural faculties and preferred to expose him in all his wretchedness and need. We can only understand this new trend if we know the true state of society at that time: apparently brilliant and privileged, the nobles were in reality reduced to absolute indolence and impotence. Not even the most exalted of them dared decide for themselves whom they would marry and where they should live. They were pawns in a ghostly, unreal Court-world of empty forms and etiquette. Only the most naïve were taken in; the true psychologists, Saint-Simon and La Rochefoucauld, saw through the paltry and humiliating masquerade and scorned it.

Again, in reaction to the earlier unequivocal classical conception of man, a new understanding developed of human nature as something mysterious, undependable and intricate. Pascal constantly wrote of the undependability and oddity of human nature; La Rochefoucauld made the same observation: "Our imagination cannot picture how many contradictions there are by nature in every human heart."

Christina underwent precisely the same evolution, as her maxims reveal. She no longer believed in Stoicism, impassive and indifferent: "imaginations neither change men nor make them better", she wrote; and almost in Pascal's style: "Man is an abyss of unhappiness and ignorance; he knows neither his body nor his soul, he is aware of being truly Nothing, clothed in a little life; but this knowledge does not make him wise, only unhappy, for philosophy can neither change him nor make him better." The philosophers—she always meant the ancient moral philosophers—were either deceivers or they deceived themselves, they had not the slightest proof of the rightness of their doctrines. "The calm on which the philosophers prided themselves was a pose; they were braggarts and deceivers" (this is worthy of Saint-Evremond himself). It is totally incorrect that by choosing the Stoics as guides you achieve such indifference to the difficulties of life, or acquire such superiority to them, that you no longer feel your anguish. Man has to acknowledge the existence of suffering on earth, and realize that he cannot escape from it. "The philosophers may say what they like, I believe that poverty, illness and physical pain are really evil things which reason cannot conjure away from us. Only religion assures us of acceptable consolation in the midst of all the evil of this life." Christina now believed in virtue only as the effect of divine grace; all other virtue is introverted: "Virtue that has not God alone as its goal is no virtue but pure vanity." A close reading of her maxims even reveals literal transcriptions at times of maxims of La Rochefoucauld and Jacques Esprit.

From the new psychology of contemporary literature Christina also learnt that "people are as much unlike themselves, at times, as they are unlike one another", which is exactly what La Rochefoucauld declared, and in the margin of her copy of his work she added a note to this maxim: "Perfectly right and splendidly formulated." So we can track down in Christina's maxims how she gradually discovered the true nature of human life, after indulging so long in prejudices and clichés, and assuredly this change was due to the influence of the great French moralists. Christina pondered over La Rochefoucauld's notion of a hidden mechanism behind the conscious will-controlled ego, and particularly over his theory of the dependence of the soul on the body and its passions; also Jacques Esprit's doctrine of virtue on the Jansenist model was not without effect on her.

However, most emphatically of all, Christina adopted the modern idea of the passions as held by Nicole, Maldonnat, Coton, François de Sales, Camus, Senault and others. In some of her maxims, presumably those composed towards the end of the seventies, she dwelt on the subject at some length. She had changed her mind since her young days when she was so proud of "the power she had over herself and her emotions". "If we conquer our passions, it is because of their weakness rather than our strength," said La Rochefoucauld: Christina noted in the margin, "This is perfectly true", and moreover she entered this maxim among her own: "We triumph over our passions only when they are weak." She who formerly scorned the passions as unworthy of man, now described them as "in themselves innocent and natural"—and we recall P. Senault's remark: "It must be understood that the passions are neither good nor bad." The philosophical calm so highly vaunted by the Stoics was now scoffed at: "This tranquillity on which the philosophers preen themselves is a turbid and meaningless state".

Now, on the contrary, she held that the passions were "the

salt of life": we are happy or unhappy according to whether we have strong or weak passions.

All these novelties would have been completely outside Christina's scope had she not herself experienced the overwhelming power of her own passions in her relationship with Cardinal Azzolino, an experience which contributed greatly to the process of undermining her self-assurance and pride. She had a long way to go, and she was to fall a victim to many other illusions, but to her earlier stoical self-assurance she would never return.

That was the most important thing she learnt from her tragic love.

CHAPTER SIX

Christina and Art

1. CHRISTINA'S PALACE

IN summer 1659—four years after her arrival in Rome—Christina moved into the palazzo Riario. It was only two years after the Monaldesco scandal, and when she came back from Paris she was the object of sharp censure, including the Pope's. In an animated talk with her he suggested she had better leave Rome, and she never forgave him. But Cardinal Azzolino poured oil on the troubled waters, and with his innate gift for diplomacy straightened things out for her; the way he did it, and her strong sense of gratitude to him, certainly contributed to a deepening of her liking for him.

After that, Christina lived in the palazzo Riario till the end of her life, but for the two journeys to Germany and Sweden in 1660–2 and 1666–8. In 1670, for a few months she rented accommodation in the palazzo d'Inghilterra, the present-day palazzo Giraud-Torlonia on the Borgo Nuovo (today the Via della Conciliazione), for the somewhat odd reason that she wanted to be as near as possible to Cardinal Azzolino during the conclave that was then taking place. For shorter periods she retired to various convents, for instance the neighbouring Aracoeli convent where she had good friends among the Carmelite nuns. She took elegant furnishings with her for the cell she was to occupy: asceticism meant nothing to her, as her maxims show. Nor did she find simple convent cooking acceptable, but had her food brought in two baskets covered with red leather and adorned with her coat of arms.

The palazzo Riario—summer residence of the Riario family—was on the Lungara, the long street (then only a path) linking the Borgo and Trastevere, two Roman districts on the right bank of the Tiber. The palace is at the foot of the Janiculum and its grounds once ran to the top of the hill; where today stands the great Garibaldi monument, there was then the *casino*, a three-storey building with nine rooms where the queen lived till the palace was ready for her. It was not till 1663—Christina was then thirty-seven years of age—that she finally moved in.

The palazzo Riario cannot be compared to the great family palaces in Rome, at least not from the outside, though today it has a new façade and has been enlarged. But if we compare its furnishings and art treasures in Christina's time with those of other contemporary palaces, we find to our amazement that the Swedish queen's home was one of the most opulent, and possibly the most tasteful of all.

We know from Tessin the younger's description exactly what the queen's home looked like. Its splendidly-furnished rooms contained many valuable works of art from antiquity and the renaissance and baroque periods: sculptures, pictures, Gobelins and other tapestries, a famous collection of coins, medals, cameos and gems, a carefully-selected library and a picture gallery containing many works of great masters. In the library there was a collection of manuscripts that now belongs to the Vatican and is in its own way considered to be one of the best in the world. Even in Sweden Christina used to collect classical and oriental manuscripts with considerable flair, advised by the best connoisseurs of the day. Perhaps that is where her keenest interest lay: these volumes splendidly bound in red leather or parchment with the Vasa coat of arms in gold relief, are today scattered all over the world. Many can be found in a number of European libraries, often containing marginal notes in Christina's hand, and these often reveal much of her inmost thoughts.

In the palace garden there was a riding-track, but Christina seldom used it. The lower, flat part of the garden was lavishly laid out with trim hedges and flower-beds. Three long alleys of oak and laurel provided protection from the sun and the gaze of the curious: they led through the lower part of the garden to the slopes of the Janiculum. Here, the garden was more like a park, a shady grove of oak, chestnut, plane-trees, pines and acacia, with magnolias and cypresses, covered the two terraces of the slope, adorned with steps and fountains here and there.

The acquisition and care of her art treasures must have occupied a large part of Christina's time. It can be said without exaggeration that her artistic activities played as great a part in her Roman life as her theatrical and musical interests. She was always up to date in her information about current archaeological excavations, and knew exactly where in Rome the antiquities they unearthed could be purchased. If works of art attracted her, she ordered casts, and she possessed among other things, busts of Alexander and Caesar. She wrote essays on both these heroes of hers, based on Plutarch among other sources. Christina had excavating done on her own account in the hope of finding coins and sculpture. Only two years before her death, a shaft was dug at her command in the neighbourhood of the Baths of Diocletian, not far from the present central railway station, but only three fragments were found. Another time she had excavations done near San Vitale—in the middle of today's via Nazionale—but with no success.

The best connoisseurs of Rome were employed as restorers and custodians of her treasures. A pupil of Bernini's, Ercola Ferrara, restored a number of pieces for her, and so did his pupil Balestri Sanese, known as Pietruccio. The archaeologist Giovanni Bellori served her as custodian and adviser, and she seems to have been on friendly terms with him; he was one of the outstanding art historians of his time, a Winckelmann of the seventeenth century. Bellori also taught Christina to admire Raphael, whom he regarded as the greatest reviver of antiquity. In one of his books he attacks different forms of mannerism—a parallel to Christina's own battle against mannerism in literature. Bellori was also a friend of Poussin's; a man of manifold interests, he looked after Christina's library. It does not seem to have worried her unduly that he did not share her high opinion of Bernini. He was in addition official custodian of Roman excavations, and Christina's palace became a meeting-point for all the artists and connoisseurs, archaeologists and collectors of Rome.

2. BERNINI

Bernini was one of the first great Italian artists with whom Christina came into contact; she was interested in him in her Stockholm days, as we saw, enquiring about his current work on the piazza Navona fountain and elsewhere. He designed the gala carriage in which she entered Rome, and on the same occasion restored the porta del Popolo in her honour. We are told that at their first meeting she recognized him at once; soon after she paid him a visit in his workshop, admired his work, congratulated him. She came again and again, and Bernini greeted her in the rough red overall he wore when working in marble. The queen took no offence and fingered the overall with her "own gracious hands", which was taken as a sign of special friendliness and favour.

There is any amount of evidence that she went on admiring Bernini and giving him practical encouragement for many decades; in a laudatory letter to King Louis XIV she mentioned him specially, recommending the king to employ him in the reconstruction of the Louvre which he was planning. We know that Bernini did indeed go to Paris and make a number of drawings and sketches, which were indirectly to influence the rebuilding of the Stockholm palace—through Bernini's friend, Tessin the younger. But on his departure from Paris all his draft plans were discarded. In 1675, Christina wrote to Angelo Morosino: "I have such a high opinion of the said Bernini that I gladly take every opportunity to do him a good turn, for he has proved himself the greatest and most outstanding man in his craft who ever lived."

After Bernini's death, Christina got Filippo Baldinucci (of her entourage) to write his biography: it appeared in 1682, dedicated to the queen; a great deal of the subject-matter was later borrowed by the painter's son, Domenico Bernini, for his biography of his great father. In both works there is frequent reference to the close and friendly relations that existed between Bernini and the Swedish queen. From another, admittedly later, source, we learn that when she heard that on his death he only left 40,000 *scudi*, she exclaimed: "Had he died in my service I should have been ashamed that he had so little to leave."

Bernini had a very high opinion of Christina's taste and judgment in matters of art. According to Chantelou, he declared in Paris, in 1665, that the queen was one of two ladies with the capacity to appreciate his art. His sculpture, in particular, she understood quite as well as he did himself—"down to the most delicate touches".

Tessin the younger, a Swede who visited Rome twice, in about 1670 and 1688, tells us a good deal about Christina's relations with Bernini. He catalogued the queen's art treasures, and to him we owe the information that Christina purchased several of Bernini's works, among them a bust of herself: it is doubtful, however, if it is the one now in the Stockholm National Museum. She also bought the head of a woman—probably a youthful work—some paintings, and finally a marble figure of Christ, his hand outstretched in blessing, long supposed lost. According to Baldinucci, Bernini wanted to give it to Christina as a gift, but she refused, for it would be utterly impossible to find him a suitable present in return. So, the story goes, Bernini was to leave it to her as a legacy. However, though there is no mention of the statue in his will, somehow—at the artist's express wish—it did become the queen's property.

There is another matter connected with this bequest which has never been cleared up before: Baldinucci tells us that when he felt death approaching, Bernini begged Cardinal Azzolino to ask the queen to pray for him, and for this reason: he was convinced the queen spoke a language that God understood specially well, while to her God used a language which she alone could properly interpret. Italian scholars, in particular Stanislao Fraschetti (1900), scoff at this—a perfectly natural reaction, seeing that at the time the queen was only known in the caricatured form provided by most biographies, whether older or more recent. Fraschetti commiserated with Bernini ironically: "Poor Bernini, not to have found a better advocate before God! I do not believe that he will have got much benefit from Christina of Sweden's 'special language'." Like many others, Fraschetti believed Christina had remained the cynical libertine of former days; so she was, in most people's minds, thanks to the libels spread about her; she was said to have one love-affair after another, executing her lovers (as demonstrated by the Monaldesco story) when she wearied of them. Frascetti must have heard of her habit of using coarse expressions, too. But we now know for certain that Christina never had a lover in the common sense of the word, that all talk of her lustful ways was pure invention, and that she did eventually, though not at the time of her formal conversion in 1654, undergo a religious crisis at the end of the seventies, which enabled her to live a genuine spiritual life. On that point we are fully informed today, thanks to jottings in her own hand, newly discovered in the Roman archives; these throw new light on her maxims and reveal how strongly she was influenced by the quietist movement in Italy, of which the most outstanding representative was the Spanish priest, Miguel Molinos. Of great significance too is Christina's familiarity with certain saints; Catherine of Siena, for instance, made a great impression on her.

So Bernini's request for prayers on his deathbed is not in the least ridiculous. He meant it quite seriously and knew what he was doing. Like so many of Christina's closer friends, he was convinced that her religious experience was valid and that she possessed great, if not unique, understanding in these matters. All her contemporaries knew she was at the very heart of Molinos's widespread movement and we know now how trustingly the radical religious circles in Italy and Spain turned to her for support.

Christina responded to Bernini's request with dignity and modesty. He was told that she promised to do all she could to carry out his wish, on condition that he for his part undertook to pray for her, "that God would give her the grace of his perfect Love, so that one day we may be united in the joys of the Love of God and belong to God in eternity".—"And tell him, please, I have done all I could for him, and shall do so in the future too."

Bernini's request throws a new light on his own last phase; Fraschetti was rather perturbed at Bernini's intense preoccupation with religion in the last years of his life, writing of his "morbid mysticism" and of how he liked to depict scenes of revolting cruelty and martyrdom. But his mystical trend was genuine. In his youth, Bernini was notorious for his very loose erotic life, but later on he lived almost like a monk; he did not marry till 1639, and then only because ordered to do so by Pope Urban VIII (the Pope whose simple, expressionless features he portrayed in some masterly busts that are true likenesses). During his whole life he was in contact with Jesuits, participated in their religious exercises, illustrated the works of the Jesuit General Oliva, and restored chapels and churches at his own expense. It was under the sign of religious faith that he and Christina came together. At their first meeting she would have nothing to do with mysticism, but in due time, through a variety of causes, she learnt to change her mind.

In some respects Bernini's art shows the same dichotomy as Christina's taste: alongside a large number of strongly sensuous paintings of naked figures, her collections also contained the most naive and worthless religious pictures. It was said she had much admired a sculpture of Bernini's called *Truth*, not a particularly interesting work, representing a somewhat affected female figure with no trace of spirituality. At the same time, however, both were susceptible to true religious feeling, and as the years went by a vein of mysticism became apparent. It is no accident that Bernini wanted to give Christina his last great work, the statue of the Redeemer, and finally did so. This statue exists no more. But there is a drawing of it from which we can picture what it was like: on the left side of the drawing the statue is shown in outline but headless: this was Bernini's own work; while the right-hand drawing, showing the head, is executed in a different style and is not his work. However, the two sides together give a good idea of the complete statue. Bernini had by now abandoned his former manner of representing saints, for instance St Sebastian, where it was not clear whether the work was of religious or purely sensuous inspiration. His later years show greater maturity.

So Bernini's confidence in the queen rested upon his appreciation of her religious outlook. Similarly, his own last works tell us something of Christina's spirituality. Now and then a maxim turns up in Christina's manuscripts which inevitably recalls one of Bernini's earlier pictures of mystical women saints, above all the one of St Teresa pierced by the arrow of a smiling cherub, in the

Cornaro chapel of Santa Maria della Vittoria, and the wonderfully fine sculpture of St Lodovica Albertoni dying in ecstasy, in San Franscesco a Ripa. There are numbers of maxims appropriate to this theme; we will quote but one: "Our true worth and our blessedness depend wholly on the last moment of our life: all the rest vanishes like smoke that disperses and is scattered by the wind. But in this last terrible or happy moment, God lets us know what we were and shall remain for all eternity, before the whole universe, and in God's own sight."

The atmosphere in which Christina lived in Rome was largely created by the composers she admired and who to some extent were in her employ—Arcangelo Corelli and Alessandro Scarlatti the elder. But the more important of her maxims reveal a mystical vein, a powerful yearning for God and complete acceptance of His will, which we can best appreciate by deeply contemplating those pictures of the death of holy women painted by her friend Bernini.

And we can perhaps come even nearer understanding Christina's relationship with Bernini. In his last years, Bernini liked to have hanging over his bed a drawing, or a painting, showing Christ on the cross, soaring above a sea of blood that covered the world and washed it clean; at the foot of the cross His Mother swayed in prayer, and above it appeared God the Father. Bernini's son wrote: "By this sea, said my father, all his sins were covered over, and divine justice could redeem them by no other means than by the blood of Jesus Christ, for by this blood they would be transformed, and through its merit find pardon."

Under the picture in either form, in addition to a Bible text (Heb. 9. 14), there was a quotation from an Italian mystic, St Maddalena de Pazzi: the sins of the world will be washed away by the blood of Christ, she said.

Without much success, scholars have attempted to trace the source of inspiration of this work. Curiously enough, the Quietist, Molinos, has been mentioned as a possibility. No less a critic than Taine in his *Voyage en Italie*, mentioned Molinos's *Guida spirituale* as accounting for Bernini's *Teresa*, for instance. But this is quite incorrect. Molinos's book was certainly to some extent influenced

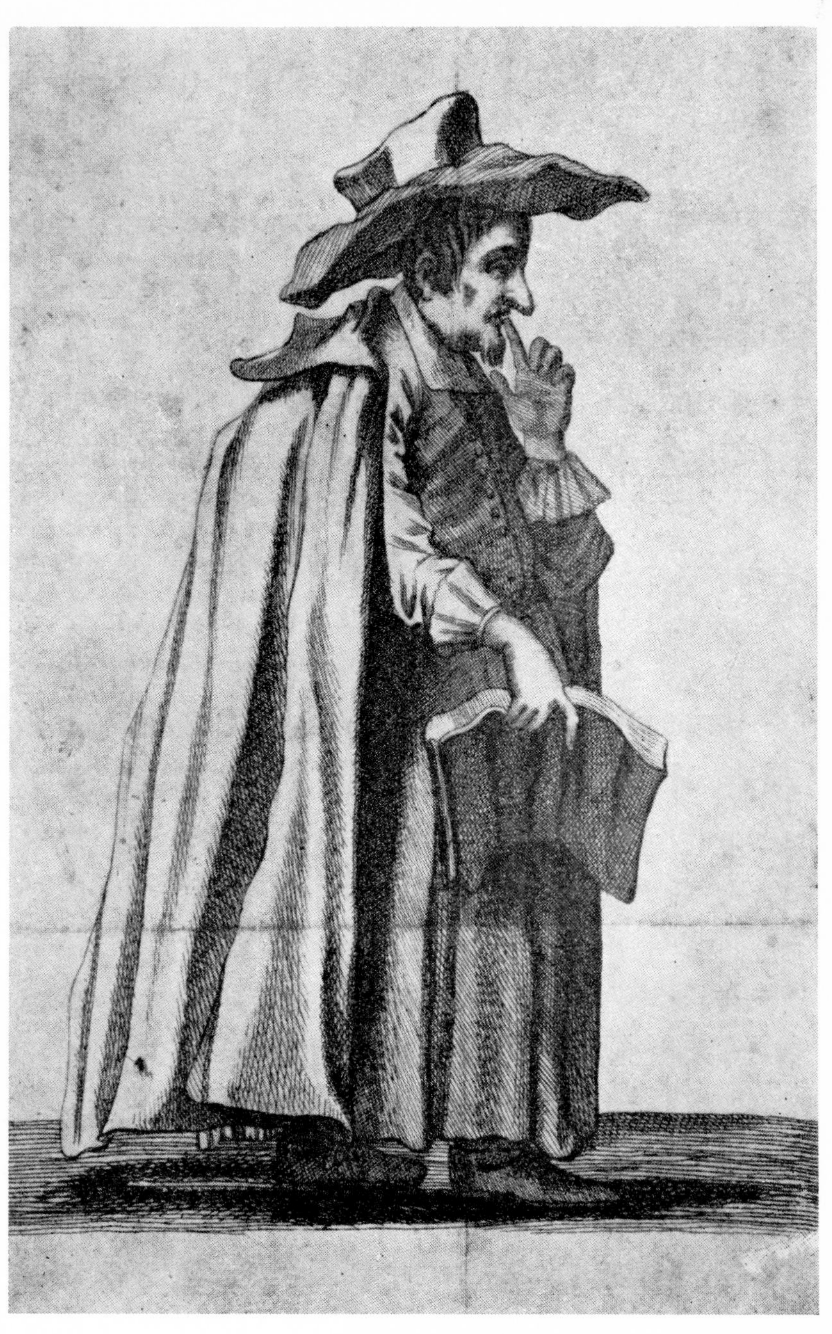

13. MIGUEL MOLINOS
Contemporary engraving by Arnald van Westerhout

14. CHRISTINA in 1670
The painting, attributed to L. Lamberto, is in Mora, Sweden
Photo: Svenska Porträttarkivet

by St Teresa's mysticism, though in quite a different way; but Bernini was directly under her influence. After that, another scholar cited Molinos as the inspiration of Bernini's sea of blood, but this cannot be correct either; all his life long, Bernini was in contact with the Jesuits who were relentless enemies of Molinos, rejecting his views out of hand: proof of this is the polemical work against Quietism by the Jesuit Segneri. In Jesuit circles in Rome, Molinos was regarded as a charlatan, so it is hardly credible that Bernini's picture was inspired by the Spanish quasi-mystics.

On the other hand, baroque art frequently depicted Christ's blood washing the world clean, and often saw grace as a billowing sea, sometimes as a sea of Christ's blood. It is a recurrent theme in Catherine of Genoa, beatified in 1675 (but not canonized till 1737). For Catherine the sea was always a symbol of grace; she sank in "the sea of divine love", and God is "a sea of love": it is in this saint that we find Bernini's inspiration. Here is an interesting account of a vision she had: "One day when she was at home, in a vision she saw Jesus Christ Our Lord covered with blood from head to foot. It seemed to her as though the blood flowed out from His body over the whole world, wherever He went. A voice said to her: 'Do you see this blood? It is shed for love of you, to wipe away your sins.' "

Another time she wrote: " . . . this sea of hidden love, so great that everyone is overwhelmed and dies who gives himself into the power of this sea". And in a third passage we read: "I am so washed in the tide of his measureless love that I seem to be below the surface of a sea and cannot touch or see or feel anything around me except its water."

Christina was a great admirer of Catherine of Genoa. Her copy of *La vita della B. Caterina Fiesca Adorna Dama Genouese* (1681) still exists, dedicated to her by the author. Christina underlined many passages and wrote a lot of marginal notes that give a better idea of her religious development than even the maxims. She expressed herself quite personally and without embellishment, admitting *expressis verbis* what she regarded as her sins. In a later chapter we shall see that Christina did try to preserve some shred of her former stoical faith in man, but finally, in fear and joy, she surrendered to a God who required of her perfect humility and self-renunciation with full admission of sinfulness.

This long parenthesis arose from the need to counter the views of the Italian scholars who regarded Bernini's deathbed request for Christina's prayers as ridiculous. Bernini knew something that Italian and other scholars refused to admit: under the influence of certain saints, and strongly affected by Molinos and his Quietism, Christina had herself become something of a Christian mystic. So it was in fact quite natural for Bernini to appeal to the sorely-tried Swedish queen, now at last a deeply-religious woman, and to want to bequeath to her this last work of his, the statue of the Redeemer—and indeed, even to beg for her prayers.

CHAPTER SEVEN

Drama and Music in Rome

I. THE THEATRE

FROM her Swedish days onwards, Christina always took a lively interest in the theatre. In 1652, as we saw, she sent for an Italian opera company to come to Stockholm. Then to her great surprise she discovered that there was little theatrical life in Rome, owing to the strict orders of Pope Sixtus V who had prohibited the appearance of women on the stage; so the focus had shifted to the Medicis in Florence, the birthplace of Italian opera and musical melodrama towards the end of the sixteenth century. Early in the seventeenth, under Paul V, a Borghese, Rome's strict puritanism relaxed to some extent; 1620 saw the first opera, *Arethusa*, composed by a priest, Filippo Vitalis, and performed by seminary students; in the same year Cardinal Lancelotti put on some comedies. He circumvented the statutary prohibition by having female parts played by men, but male parts by women. . . .

Urban VIII was culturally open-minded. His nephews, Cardinals Francesco and Antonio Barberini, as well as Taddeo Barberini, Prince of Palestrina, set up a proper theatre, designed by Maderna and Bernini, in the rambling family palace. It opened in 1634 with a melodrama, *Sant' Alessio*, written by young Giulio Rospigliosi, later Pope Clement IX, a good friend and well-wisher to Queen Christina. This theatre gave regular performances all through the Carnival season. It is said there was room for three thousand guests, but admission was by invitation only, there were no tickets for sale.

Guilio Rospigliosi had real literary talent and wrote a few more melodramas for the same theatre, *Santa Teodora* and *Chi soffre speri*. The performance of this melodrama was described by no less a person than John Milton, in a letter of 30 March 1639 to

Christina's friend-to-be, Lucas Holstenius; the stage showed a market in Farfa, a horse race and a sunset.

But when Urban VIII died in 1644, his culture-loving nephews had to go into exile, and for full ten years the great Barberini theatre remained closed, to the great sorrow of all Rome. But opera flourished in Venice, where Claudio Monteverdi set the tone—for Rome had only individual performances in private houses like the Prince of Gallicano's or that of the French ambassador, Cardinal Michele Massarino, brother of the great Mazarin.

On the other hand, comedies could be seen; Salvator Rosa and Bernini wrote comic plays which they stage-managed themselves, sometimes taking parts as actors; they painted the décor and paid for the production. Some years before Christina's arrival there may have been a real comedy theatre where tickets were sold for admission. In 1653 the Barberini theatre reopened with another melodrama by our industrious friend Giulio Rospigliosi, who in the meantime had been nuncio in Spain. The play was entitled *Dal male il bene*, with music by Marco Marazolli, Rome's best-known composer and leading papal tenor.

2. WHEN CHRISTINA CAME TO ROME

Christina's arrival in Rome was the occasion for many celebrations and theatrical performances. The most brilliant was on 31 January 1656, at the city's leading theatre, the Barberini. Once again Rospigliosi wrote the libretto for a play entitled *La vita umana* or *Il trionfo della Pietà*, with music by Marazolli. The prologue, sung by Aurora, honoured the "great-hearted queen" Christina. In the second act, Innocence sang a hymn of praise to Bridget, "glory of the Swedes and Nericia".* Innocence and Life sang a duet promising Christina, "the new star of the Vatican", more splendid crowns and higher honours than those she had laid down in Sweden. Grimaldi's décor inspired Galestrucci's fine engravings which enable us to appreciate something of the magnificence of the spectacle. At the beginning of the performance the stage was dark, then the sun rose over two cities, the strong-

* Bridget is still known in Italy as Princess of Nericia: Nericia (Närke) being a district of Sweden.

holds of Voluptuousness and Reason. Aurora made her entry on a silver chariot, scattering flowers. The last act showed the banks of the Tiber, Castello S. Angelo, and fireworks.

Christina was welcomed to the theatre with great pomp, she sat with her suite among eighteen cardinals and many other prelates, and was so delighted with the performance that three days later she came again, but incognita, hidden in a box. The play lasted from half past nine till three in the morning. In fact she came a third time, and by now she was so greatly impressed that she resolved to found her own theatre.

In due course a number of Rospigliosi-Marazolli melodramas appeared at the Barberini. But Christina saw other dramatic works too: at the house of the Prince of Rossano, husband of Olimpia Aldobrandini, the court ladies themselves performed in some minor melodramas, and at the Pamphili's home Christina attended plays and an oratorio, *Daniele*, produced by the author, the Prince of Gallicano. She also saw religious plays, e.g. *Il sacrificio d'Isacco*, an oratorio by Carissimi she had enquired about in a letter from Stockholm. In her own palace she gave concerts and even took lessons from Loreto Vittorio, composer and male soprano of the papal choir; she usually devoted three to four hours to her singing lessons after dinner; she had a small mezzo-soprano voice, but both she and her singing master were disappointed at the results. She heard music at the homes of Cardinals Savelli, Costagutti and de' Medici, Princess di Butera and the Duchess of Bracciano.

Sometimes Christina's inconsiderate manners annoyed the audience and disturbed the singers and players. She would read a book intermittently during performances or chat with her entourage "in loud, penetrating, strong tones". In fact there were times when the public hissed her outright.

She was soon to become involved in hazardous political intrigues; with the French diplomat Hugues de Lionne, she saw a performance of Corneille's *Héraclius* at Mazarin's palace, and this may well have been the queen's first introduction to contemporary French drama. Her interest was roused and she declared she would have this master's plays performed on her own stage soon.

As we saw, at first Christina lived in palazzo Farnese, the property of the Duke of Parma. She had a theatre installed, employed actors, and according to a not very trustworthy source (which, however, may be correct in this case), gave performances at least once a week.

During her sojourn in France also Christina saw some plays, but they did not please her much. She had already begun to hate the Jesuits and poured scorn on a very poor dramatic performance at a college of theirs. The Fathers were much distressed, and the king's confessor, Father Annat, assistant of the Jesuit General in Rome at the time Christina wrote to him, tried to mediate. Christina answered him gravely: "I know the power of the Jesuits all too well and would rather have a mighty prince as my enemy than your Order. So I will willingly make my peace with you, but on condition that I shall never have to choose one of you as confessor—or appoint one of you as actor."

An Italian troupe too failed to win her approval; someone stood up for the actors, saying they usually played much better: "That I can well believe," said the queen, "for otherwise they would have been dismissed long ago." On the other hand, French drama greatly appealed to her. The audience used to gape at her during performances, for all the time her face reflected what was going on on the stage. At the finest passages she uttered loud cries, and was so absorbed that she did not even hear when the dowager queen spoke to her.

3. AFTER HER FRENCH JOURNEY

In 1657, when Christina came back to Rome, she found that the Monaldesco scandal had made her very unpopular. She had to move with circumspection and ceased to give public performances of her own. But we know she had her musicians or at least a small orchestra; Marco Marazolli dubbed himself chamber *virtuoso* of the queen, so he must have had a permanent appointment. At all events Christina was always eager to attract the best conductors, singers and musicians to her court, and in her correspondence we sometimes find quite comical evidence of her efforts.

Alessandro Cecconi was employed by her, and in 1658 he died of apoplexy at her home on the Quirinal. Immediately the rumour got about that she had murdered him, and indeed for the same reason as Monaldesco—because he had been her lover. A revealing episode: evidently Christina's contemporaries had no great opinion of her artistic tastes and always saw some sinister intention in whatever she did. In 1656 Christina apparently took on another famous singer, Guiseppe Bianchi, which later led to a rumpus with the Duke of Savoy who was also very musical. During Christina's absence in 1661, Bianchi sang to the ducal court for the special benefit of the duchess, Christine of Savoy, who then tried to keep him in Turin. Queen Christina protested. But when she could not get her singer back immediately, she made another proposal: in 1656 she had seen in Turin a collection of about thirty volumes of Pirro Ligorio's work and was eager to acquire them; now she requested the loan of these volumes, to have copies made. She seems eventually to have succeeded, for the copies are still to be seen in the Vatican's Ottoboni collections.

In 1665 Christina was able to designate as "her musician" the singer Antonio Rivani, known as Ciccolino. Guiseppe Maria Donati, a Bolognese, was a singer at the Tordinona theatre in 1673; a year later Christina had him taken on in the papal choir; *musico primario della regina*, he termed himself. We could name here nearly all the principal singers of Italy—Paolo Pompeo Besci, G. B. Vulpio, Vincenzio Dani, Nicolo Coresi and his wife, the great singer Antonia, to whom Christina once gave Correggio's *Leda with the Swan* (only a copy, though, done by Carlo Maratta).

Another interesting point hitherto insufficiently studied is that Christina had a theatre installed in the palazzo Riario: we know of it from some drawings or coloured sketches done or copied by Nicodemus Tessin the younger. Here the queen had an opera of Alessandro Crescenzi's performed, for which Cardinal Azzolino composed the prologue. Azzolino also wrote comedies, a comedy of his is mentioned in his correspondence with the queen during her stay in Hamburg, but it is not extant; it evidently had a moralizing slant which seems to have irritated her. Before the journey to Hamburg she had a series of secular plays performed on her stage; we do not know the entire repertory, but from other sources we can get a good idea of her taste in such matters: in 1666, Lionne was told in a letter that they were *des pièces un peu lestes* (rather spicy ones). The Pope was worried and had special prayers said in his private chapel, for all Rome was scandalized. Several cardinals are said to have seen these performances and witnessed the "lascivious and sinful comedies" the queen put on alternately with opera and melodrama.

Naturally there was no question of immorality as we understand it. In puritanical Rome, people were not used to seeing profane plays censorious of the *status quo*, such criticism was usually left to rather dubious writers like Pasquino and Marforio,* or to popular comedies. But to allow social problems or ecclesiastical matters to be discussed on the stage, in the presence of noble personages, was unheard of.

In Paris conditions were completely different. As we saw, it was Hugues de Lionne who introduced Christina to modern French drama. On 15 January 1666 he wrote to Cardinal de Retz, his old rival, then in Rome: "I am sending Your Eminence a play that has aroused great interest here and may provide you with a few hours of entertainment" (it was Racine's second play, *Alexandre le Grand*, fresh from the printing press), and requested the cardinal to pass it on to the queen if he thought it deserved such an honour. He also wrote to Queen Christina a letter that has come to light three hundred years later. "I am sending Cardinal de Retz a play that has aroused great interest here: the author is only twenty-three years old, and some think he has at his first attempt begun where Corneille as an old man has stopped. Should Cardinal de Retz find it worth passing on to Your Majesty after reading it, then Your Majesty will have unique first-hand news of how we view this rivalry between the poets; for after so many

* In a Germany library there exists a remarkable manuscript entitled *Dialogo tra La Regina di Suetia e Donna Olimpia Maidalchini: tra Pasquino e Marforio*, in which the queen complains bitterly of the criticism to which she is exposed in certain books. Olimpia Maidalchini (with whom Christina probably had no contact at all as she was in disgrace in the latter part of her life, banned from Rome by her mortal enemy, Alexander VII) tried to justify the Roman habit of openly criticizing princes and clerics. It is of course a forgery.

victories the old champion could hardly have expected to be beaten by a young rival."

Lionne was some years out in saying Racine was only twenty-three, he was in fact a few years older, being born in 1639, but that is no great matter. We know from Cardinal de Retz's reply how Christina reacted. On 16 February he wrote to Lionne: "On Tuesday I forgot to thank you for the Alexander play, it is excellent. The Queen of Sweden was on tenterhooks and begged me to send it her even before I had time to take it to her myself. Then she greatly admired it." In fact she had the play put on at once.

Christina's taste was so unerring and so modern that she shunned mediocre plays and instantly recognized a masterpiece by a young French author. At roughly the same period she was interested in another, much more tendentious, play, Molière's *Tartuffe*, which she also wanted to have performed, in fact she expressly requested permission to do so. But *Tartuffe* had already caused a scandal in 1664, when the first three acts were performed in the presence of Louis XIV. Lionne naturally knew of Molière's difficulties in obtaining the right to public performance, for a number of highly-placed personages had condemned it outright. It was performed unabridged on 29 November 1664, at the château of the Prince de Condé, whom Christina greatly admired. But its first performance at the royal palace was not till 1667, when it was immediately banned; its great success only came two years later.

So Christina planned to present a masterpiece of world literature, Molière's *Tartuffe*, a play that could not at the moment be put in on Paris. Lionne's answer was addressed to d'Alibert, who was then in charge of the queen's correspondence and was most circumspect: he recalled that although Molière had produced the beginning of his *Tartuffe*, it was still not finished, and he found the queen's plan impracticable, for Molière wanted the play reserved for his own theatrical company and would demand twenty-thousand *écus*. Indeed, after banning the play the French king would be unlikely to agree to its being put on on Christina's stage. So no performance of *Tartuffe* took place. The episode as such is significant enough, for it shows the queen's courage, utter indifference to the views of other potentates, and eagerness to applaud the unmasking of hypocrisy.

Presumably she had other French plays performed. One of her secretaries in Stockholm, Gabriel Gilbert, later Swedish ambassador in Paris, was himself a well-known dramatist, who in the years 1657–67 was at the height of his renown. It can be assumed that Christina discussed French drama with him. In her youth she no doubt recognized her own Stoicism in Corneille's plays depicting great and noble souls who conquer their passions and sacrifice their lives; Christina was convinced that she herself had made the greatest sacrifice when, as a stoic superwoman, she had given up her throne. In later years, after learning the force of real passion and how irrepressible it is, Christina will have read Racine with special interest. Perhaps it brought her to a better understanding of her mother's violent passion for her husband even after his death—a passion which Corneille the Neo-Stoic would have quelled and young Queen Christina despised, while Racine, with his deeper psychology and knowledge of female emotions, could present it convincingly.

It has been suggested that Monaldesco's assassination may have inspired Racine's *Bajazet*; though probably this is not so. But today we know that all her life long the queen was greatly interested in French classical drama. Evidently Christina's enthusiasm for the theatre reached its climax in 1666: it was then she set up her own stage as soon as Court mourning for Anne of Austria was over. A Frenchman wrote to Lionne: "Count de Saint Paul and Chevalier d'Harcourt are here and are amusing themselves seeing the sights of Rome, in the evening attending plays at the Queen of Sweden's." Then Christina rented a house on what was formerly the piazza San Marco, and it was there she watched that rollicking carnival procession. As we read in a contemporary report: "Yesterday the queen welcomed twenty-three cardinals to watch the masked procession: in full view of her guests she herself mounted a horse"—so it looks as though Christina rode in the carnival procession and thereby gave offence, especially as she was dressed more or less like a man. There was a pretty strong reaction to this scandal and to her supposedly immoral plays, but we learn that the queen was not at all perturbed and went on having her plays performed as usual. In a letter to Cardinal Azzolino from Hamburg she wrote: "I beg . . . you to have Father Zucchi's sermons copied out for my edification, but not in code: I shall read them with pleasure; I shall now be relieved of the onus of visiting the Jesuit church when I come back to Rome." She also wrote: "I beg you to inform Father Fozio he is wasting his time praying God to turn me into a saint; I shall never be virtuous enough to be a saint, nor infamous enough to pretend to be one." Here we recognize the old tone and realize how it would have delighted her to have Molière's *Tartuffe* performed on her stage.

4. CHRISTINA AS THEATRICAL MANAGER

In 1668, when Christina came back from her journey to Germany and Sweden, her friend Giulio Rospigliosi was Pope. It was to express her pleasure at his election that she had given her great banquet in Hamburg. Clement IX was the only Pope she knew whom she wholly liked; he was friendly, tolerant, interested in cultural matters and drama, and dealt with her with great understanding, welcoming her with demonstrations of affection and raising her prestige so high that the wretched Monaldesco affair soon lapsed into oblivion.*

As nuncio in Spain, Clement IX had known the Spanish playwrights personally, Lope de Vega for instance: he was greatly impressed and even after becoming Pope he went on composing librettos for melodramas and operas. In 1668 his melodrama *Baltasara, or The Actress in Heaven* was performed with Sabatini's music and décor by Bernini, but he was only nuncio when he wrote it. The story is significant: a Spanish actress Baltasara abandons her lover, her art and the world, to live a hermit's life in the wilderness where she successfully withstands all temptations and is finally

* Christina had a certain liking for Alexander VII, but was aware of his faults. In a conversation with Lionne soon after her arrival in Rome, she said the Pope talked nonsense and wasted his time on trivialities; she would gladly have given her life to see him act otherwise, she added with typical baroque excess. Another time, "It must be taken as proven," she said, "that the Holy Spirit guides His Church in Person, seeing how hopeless the popes are."

taken up to heaven. It was performed seven times with great applause and made such a strong impression that a young lady-in-waiting, full of emulation, disguised herself as a man and set out to live a hermit's life in the mountains. . . .

Christina was not in Rome at the time, but on her return from Hamburg she resumed her cultural interests with the same enthusiasm as before. She now appointed as theatrical intendant the French adventurer, Jacques d'Alibert, whom we mentioned earlier. He had done a variety of jobs for her ever since 1662, and she was to remember him in her will. To some extent he played the same part in her life at this stage as Bourdelot had done in Sweden. As a diplomat in Paris he had been found at fault, but that did not worry Christina. From Hamburg she begged him to send her all the Roman gossip—about cardinals, hunts, masquerades and other *choses galantes*, and he was to tell her of current female intrigues. "I shall consider it a great favour if you will keep me informed of these things," she wrote.

After the 1669 Carnival Christina became the leading light in Rome's theatrical world. In her palace, performances of Italian plays were given on Feast days, Spanish plays on Sundays. The Italian plays were done by a company of the Tordinona theatre under the management of Tiberio Fiorilli, known as Scaramuccia, writer and actor. Then Christina rented the Tordinona theatre and on 17 and 18 February had Filippo Acciaioli's *Elysian Fields* performed there (he also ran a well-known puppet theatre).

In 1670 Christina gave further scope to her passion, she rented the Tordinona theatre for an indefinite period and at once had it rebuilt. The Romans found it very amusing when she had a magnificent royal box adorned with a crown and the Vasa arms. Within a year the new theatre was opened with a performance of the opera *Scipione Affricano*, dedicated to the queen. *Jason*, intended for Maria Mancini, came next. Both operas were presumably composed by Francesco Cavalli. The order forbidding actresses to appear on the stage had in the meantime been rescinded; but not even Pope Clement IX, broad-minded and tolerant though he was, could allow plays to be put on all the year round—in the forty days of Lent there could be no theatrical season, and that was the rule for the future too. In 1675, Le Spon wrote in his *Voyage d'Italie*: "Every day concerts can be heard in the churches, at the Queen of Sweden's and at the Cardinals'—with the best singers in the world."

But 1675 was a Holy Year and the theatre had to remain closed. Papal etiquette forbade Christina to have plays performed even on her own stage in palazzo Riario. The next year was even stricter, when Clement X died and a man succeeded him who had formerly often had a seat in the queen's box, but, as Pope, became bitterly hostile to the stage; it was the great Pope Innocent XI, the greatest of the four popes under whom Christina lived, but unfortunately also the one who least appreciated her and with whom she had grave differences. He forbade all public performances, he would not let singers appear in churches who also sang on the profane stage, and he again prohibited actresses. Also the partitions between boxes in the theatre were to be removed so that no love-making could occur—there was such a fear of love-scenes on the stage, it was felt that at the mere sight, men and women would fall into each other's arms.

The prohibition against women players was countered by the employment of *castrati*. We have a letter to the Pope from Christina, tinged with irony, in which she admits to having allowed d'Alibert to put on theatrical performances of the forbidden sort, and announced she would consider it her duty to have the theatre burnt down if entrance money was charged for these performances. . . . In 1678 she wrote in protection of Don Benedetto Pamphili who was out of favour with the Pope: he had engaged papal singers who had appeared on the stage as ladies. . . .

In the long run, being in serious financial difficulties, Christina had to close the Tordinona theatre.

5. CHRISTINA AND MUSIC

That did not mean she stopped having plays performed. When she dared not put on an opera in her own palace, she rented a boys' school for the purpose. We also know that in 1680 an opera was performed in Bernini's little theatre, to some extent the successor of the Tordinona. But in her latter years the queen mainly gave musical evenings—operas and concerts. After being the dominant factor in Rome's theatrical life for a number of years, she now formed the centre of the city's musical life. She enlisted the most outstanding composers, conductors and singers of the country, and at certain periods had a large orchestra at her disposal. Distinguished visitors to Rome were much struck by the quality of those musical evenings in palazzo Riario itself or in its grounds on the slopes of the Janiculum.

One of the great musicians of Christina's entourage was Alessandro Scarlatti. Before he was nineteen, he wrote the score for a musical play, *Gli equivoci nel sembiante*, to a text by Domenico Filippo Contini (1679): Christina heard of it and had it performed at the teatro del Clementino on the Piazza Nicosia. A current number of the *Avvisi* had the following notice: "On Sunday Her Majesty was so delighted with Contini's play that she wanted to hear it done at the Collegio Clementino. But as the papal Swiss Guard refused to admit Cardinal Colonna's lackeys who had been placed at her disposal, she ordered them to force their way into the hall; this they did, and many blows were struck at the Swiss Guard. It is widely known that the author of this play is a Sicilian: he is in very bad odour at the papal Court because of his sister's secret marriage to a priest. But the queen had him fetched in her *calèche* and he played in the orchestra, even though the cardinal-vicar was among Her Majesty's guests." This report interests us in showing how Christina conducted her life—imperturbably and energetically grasping the nettle in any difficult situation and making sure that she got her own way.

It shows too how strong was her love for music and the theatre. She gave Scarlatti a job, and while he was in her service he produced some very good works. In 1680 Christina had an opera of Scarlatti's, *Honestà nell' amore*, performed at Bernini's theatre on the Corso; he was now her *maestro di capello*. Scarlatti then composed several works in rapid succession, some of which he dedicated to the queen; she had most of these operas performed. After four years of honourable service, the queen's wonderful composer and conductor transferred to the Court of Naples. Italy's most famous singer, Giovanni Francesco Grossi, was also in the queen's service and collaborated with Scarlatti.

Bernardo Pasquini is also mentioned as a *maestro di capella.* He was an outstanding composer and had written the music for a work that was performed in honour of Queen Christina on her arrival in Rome. One day Christina saw him in the street and immediately stopped her carriage to speak to him. For the Tordinona theatre he wrote *Amor per vendetta, ovvero l'Alcasta* (1673) dedicated to Christina. His work *Il Lisimacho*, with libretto by Baldosino (Giacomo Sinibaldi), performed in 1681, was also dedicated to her.

Two years before her death, Queen Christina celebrated the accession of King James II to the throne of England for no less than three days on end. For this occasion she ordered an *Accademia per musica*, a cantata with a text written by Cardinal Albani (later Clement XI) in collaboration with the poet Guidi, and music by Pasquini. We know it involved over a hundred singers and soloists lent by the Pope and an orchestra of a hundred and fifty strings. There were seats for a hundred and fifty ladies and the number of gentlemen who listened standing was even greater. The conductor on that occasion was Arcangelo Corelli, of the queen's closer entourage, who in 1681 dedicated his first work to her, a violin sonata. Never before had such a magnificent musical occasion occurred. The English envoy, Lord Castlemaine,* was most enthusiastic. Corelli as conductor was the first to build up huge orchestras in Italy. It must have cost a mint of money.

6. CHRISTINA'S PART IN ROMAN CULTURE

In Rome, Christina founded two, if not three, academies to which she invited prelates and theologians, composers and poets, philosophers and scholars, and of course members of the Roman aristocratic families. She encouraged people to discuss questions of ethics and scientific problems. Such discussions were not necessarily of a very high standard, nor were the lectures, only part of which have survived in writing. The more decisive and controversial questions raised by Galileo were still taboo; slighter and less explosive scientific topics of current interest had to suffice. What is more relevant is that Christina sought out a whole suc-

* Viscount Castlemaine, husband of Barbara Villiers, mistress of Charles II.

cession of scholars eminent in various fields of learning. She had an almost passionate liking for astrology and alchemy and was a patron of all sorts of charlatans as well as real scholars, for instance the Dane, Ole Borch, whom she employed to make gold for her, and with whom she conversed on "the study of an experiments in secret chemistry". Borch was an admirer of Borris whom Christina likewise patronized and consulted. She had an observatory in her palace with two permanently-employed astronomers, and a *destillarium*, i.e. a laboratory. To this day her archives contain drawings in her own hand of scientific apparatus and drafts of a larger work, *Il laboratorio filosofico* or *Paradossi Chimici*, as it was to be entitled. She frequently visited Palombari's laboratory on the Esquiline, was a friend of Borelli, the physicist, who was a member of one of her academies and drew an annual stipend, and she held discussions with scientists of standing like Viviani, Cassini, Torricelli, Marchetti, Quartarono, Bandiere and Ciampini. A son of Otto von Güricke sent her from Magdeburg his father's book on experiments with the air-pump, but pointed out that similar experiments had been made in Paris, London, Florence and Rome. Christina naturally encouraged scholars in the humanities too, historians and archaeologists; a remarkable number of learned works are dedicated to her.

Only when we take a bird's-eye view of all this can we appreciate her position in Rome between 1660 and her death: her scientific interests, her role as foundress of academies and as cultural Maecenas, and the leading part she played in the artistic, theatrical and musical life of Rome.

And there is more, for she was influential in important and decisive questions of ecclesiastical policy, though that is a topic we can do little more than mention in this book.

CHAPTER EIGHT

Christina's Spiritual Evolution

1. CHRISTINA AND THE RELIGIOUS REVIVAL

In Rome Christina was not only taken up with music, art and scholarship but also, and increasingly, gave her mind to problems concerning the Church. The free-thinking ideas of her younger days seem to have faded into the background: in the main she came to terms with Church conventions. One might believe—and that is the view commonly held in previous books about her—she had more or less passively accepted the Church's doctrine and consequently rejected contrary tendencies.

That is only partly correct. The great contemporary French Catholics were astonishingly remote from her experience. The most controversial religious movement of the day was Jansenism; it kept popes and cardinals alert for decades on end, till it was finally overthrown. Christina must have known the movement quite well, but she was evidently in no way influenced by it. We know that on her first visit to Paris the great Jansenist Arnauld let her see the first twelve of Pascal's *Lettres Provinciales*; such acute criticism of the Jesuits must have appealed to her, but we have no reliable information about it. Later she occasionally expressed an opinion about the Jansenists, for instance in 1679 she wrote to Paris to her old friend Dr Bourdelot, a man with whom she had always enjoyed a chat: "I am astonished to hear from you that MM. Arnauld and Nicole are in Rome. They are unimpeachable gentlemen, apart from their Jansenism; but even if they were sheer devils, one could not refuse to do them well-merited honour. As far as I know, there are no Jansenists in Rome. If there were, they could only be rash fellows or unknown men. I myself have a blind faith in the doctrine of the Roman Church; I believe unreservedly all that its supreme Head proclaims."

When in France, Christina had a clash with the Jesuit Father Annat, and was summoned by Anne of Austria, Queen of France, who warned her against the Jansenists: in Paris at that time, anyone criticizing the Jesuits was immediately dubbed "Jansenist". Christina retorted she had never so much as met a Jansenist.

So apparently she took no interest in the great conflict over Port-Royal. St. Augustine's strict rule as interpreted by Jansenius and Arnauld might even have seemed quite foreign to her religious attitude at the time. None the less she was well-informed on all the more controversial issues, for her friend Cardinal Azzolino sat on the Roman commission which in 1667 was to reach a decision on Jansenism. To him and to Christina the Duchesse de Longueville turned repeatedly for support for Port-Royal, and it was thanks to a letter of recommendation from Madame de Longueville to Christina that the Oratorian Father Boisson gained access to the highest circles in Rome, when he went there to try to rouse sympathy for Jansenism.

This same strange, in fact inexplicable, indifference was typical of Christina's attitude to all the great figures of the religious revival in France. There is no trace in her of any influence of François de Sales, Vincent de Paul, Cardinal Bérulle and the "French School", the French Jesuits, the women mystics and the Enthusiasts, who were all frequent topics of conversation at the time. These figures, who make the seventeenth century one of the most interesting periods in the history of the French Church, and in fact of the whole history of religion, were subjects of lively controversy; there was some hard fighting and in some cases the outcome was tragic—we need but remember the fate of Port-Royal and Madame de Guyon's Quietism. Certainly Christina must have had some knowledge of all this. But it appears to have made no impression, at least not in the first years of her exile.

This does not necessarily mean that Christina was religiously passive. In her letters she naturally did not mention such delicate matters, but fortunately we have other sources of information: the queen had the reprehensible habit of annotating even the most valuable books with underlinings and remarks, often in ink; from these annotations we can often deduce her own views. But they are usually only to be found in books she came across later in her life.

2. THE BLIND WISE MAN OF MARSEILLES

As a rule, the queen was utterly indifferent to the new religious currents in France, but there was one exception: a most surprising one. Christina's very idiosyncratic Catholic faith was satisfied with fundamental loyalty to the Pope and the claims of the Roman Church to be the one and only one to preach the true faith; towards several of the major dogmas she showed considerable scepticism. In certain respects, a deeper personal piety did ripen in her, but this was not brought about by any theological system or religious leader of genius, as one might have imagined, but by a movement the Protestants called Pietism, the Catholics, Quietism. It provides some sort of evidence of the void concealed behind her intellect and energy: deep down inside her she was unsatisfied.

Much has been written about Christina's journeys to France in 1656 and 1657. The most important episode was neither the assassination of Monaldesco nor her encounter with the French Court and the élite of French culture, but her first meeting with an unknown blind mystic in Marseilles, François Malaval. "That remarkable Provençal", as Abbé Brémond calls him, came from a middle-class family and studied under the Oratorians in Marseilles. Later he continued his study of canon law and theology under the Dominicans and obtained his doctor's degree. The Bishop of Marseilles had a high opinion of him. He knew a number of priests but remained a layman, and in spite of his blindness continued his studies, which was in itself a remarkable feat. People visited him and he set many enquiring souls on the right path. His interests were many-sided. The natural sciences absorbed him; he was in touch with Gassendi when the latter came to Toulon in 1650. From his later correspondence with Christina, now accessible in various European archives, it emerges that they discussed the early mystics and their relation to the primitive Church. In Marseilles, scholars and literary men alike regarded him as a sort of oracle. He wrote a book on prayer in Latin and showed it to a few friends; at their wish he translated it into French. It was thus that his *Pratique Facile* (1664) came into existence, later to be so famous—but he was not yet known as a writer when he met Christina. Later on he dedicated the Italian translation to her. It had a great success in Italy.

Malaval wished to show how contemplation, the longing to know God and achieve union with Him, is grounded in faith, and to explain its nature and characteristics in so crystal-clear a manner as to enable people of small intellectual powers and average understanding, if they happened to pick the book up, to grasp its meaning quickly and, with a modicum of good will, follow it.

Malaval began by recognizing that the soul "is high above the senses and passions", and that "by God's special grace we must free ourselves completely from the senses and passions if we are to experience contemplation". We need not be learned by any means to attain to this state, which alone can bring peace to the soul: "the most stupid and simple people are sometimes called to contemplation". In particular Malaval differed from certain "modern" authorities on the life of the soul, who believed that something could be done by means of a variety of carefully-elaborated exercises, violent efforts being made to force our reason and the powers of our soul to achieve contemplation.

The book is written in dialogue form, the "director" initiating Philothée into his method; the important thing is that a soul should really desire to listen to God, "suppressing every thought, every movement of the will, every conclusion", for God speaks "more quietly, more effectively, intelligibly and often, than any preacher, confessor or book of edification".

For the true Quietist, prayers, sermons and pious thoughts were not what is most essential for the soul, but should rather lay a foundation of inner peace and recollection. When contact is attained, when all intellectual and emotional stages are left behind, it is enough to make the sign of the cross with the one thought: "My God, You are my all": the Holy Spirit will see to the rest; we may remain passive at this point, in fact any personal effort might do harm. Never should we read a devotional book without constantly breaking off our reading "to recollect ourselves in God".

Malaval was aware that many confessors would not like his book and would prefer to recommend their own exercises, so he was all the more eager to demonstrate how it agreed with the teaching of Dionysius, Augustine, Gregory, Bernard, Thomas Aquinas, Bonaventura, François de Sales. This book, *Pratique facile*, seems harmless enough, even rather attractive. But why did the queen esteem its author so highly? We have to remember her strong distrust of outward devotions, veneration of relics, worldly cardinals and the Jesuits' involvement in power-politics. Here she met something entirely new, a gentle, quiet way to inner peace. At her first meeting with Malaval there was no close exchange of ideas, but he was perhaps the first to indicate to her an utterly different way to religious peace, as compared with the traditional religious exercises which obviously bored her—a direct way to God without external aids.

No more than anyone else could Christina foresee that these ideas were suspect, and indeed were the germ of one of the most hazardous movements that ever shook the Church in France and Italy. Suffice it here to say that Malaval's book was to be of decisive importance to Madame de Guyon, around whom the great controversy about Quietism was to arise between Bossuet and Fénelon, before the end of the century; moreover, Malaval must be reckoned as one of the main influences on a man later known as "theologian to her Holy Majesty Queen Christina of Sweden"—Miguel Molinos.

3. A NORMAN HERMIT

We know very little of Christina's spiritual life in the years following her meeting with Malaval; her whole interest seemed centred on her cultural hobbies, or on her passion for Cardinal Azzolino. In a letter to Cardinal Azzolino written from Hamburg on 15 September 1666, it appears (cf. p. 255) that in Rome she was subject to harsh criticism from the stern Jesuits. In the same letter there occur the following words: "I shall hasten to acquire the book, *L'intérieur chrétien*; as soon as I have got it I shall send it to you." The cardinal had apparently asked Christina to get hold of a book that for some reason had caught his attention. Perhaps, alarmed at the censorious attitude towards her of the Roman theologians, he advised the queen to read it herself.

L'intérieur chrétien was one of the more controversial devotional books to appear in France in mid-century; its author was Henri de Bernières de Louvigny, and it was published in 1659; the Italian translation appeared in 1666, at that very time. The author lived near the town of Caen in Normandy, in a hermitage near an Ursuline convent founded by his sister Jourdaine and still ruled by her. The book soon ran into several editions. Surprisingly enough, it became very popular again much later—in Sweden, where it was published in 1817 at Gothenburg, under the title of "The hidden life with Christ in God, by Jean Bernières de Louvigny, after the German translation by G. Ter-Stegen". Like so many other purely Catholic books of prayer and edification, it was welcomed by the Swedish Lutheran clergy, and *L'intérieur chrétien*, in Sweden as in Protestant Germany, became a popular book of devotions, its readers having no inkling that it was the work of a papist. The Swedish people made the acquaintance of Thomas à Kempis in the same way. When Molinos was condemned as a heretic in Rome, it was not long before his *Guida spirituale* appeared in a German translation and likewise became a popular devotional book for pious Protestants. But as far as I know, 1666 is the first year in which a pietist or quietist book is mentioned in Queen Christina's correspondence.

In due course *L'intérieur chrétien* too was placed on the Index (1689); its author was regarded as one of the more dangerous Quietists, and it was on his account that Bossuet entered into such violent controversy with Fénelon, his match in the spiritual field.

4. CATHERINE OF GENOA

Before we look at Italian Quietism and the decisive part it was to play in Christina's spiritual development, we may look somewhat further ahead to her relations with an Italian saint, and shall see how her old attitude changed and new experiences came to prevail.

One of the more important sources for a study of Christina's spiritual and religious development is her annotations in a book that appeared in 1681, about St Catherine of Genoa (1447–1510); the joint authors had dedicated it to the Swedish queen. By that time, after her friendship with the Spaniard Miguel Molinos and their earnest discussions together, Christina was familiar with the phenomena and claims of religious mysticism.

We know how, earlier in her life, Christina found it so difficult to believe in the doctrine of purgatory. Only a few years after she came to Rome, she wrote to a friend of Azzolino's, whom she knew was keeping an eye on her: "Although belief in purgatory is an article of faith, I do not believe a word of what you say about it." Catherine of Genoa was, however, intensely aware of the necessity of purgatory—she wrote a whole book on it. To Catherine's descriptions of peace and joy, which can also be dominant in purgatory, Christina noted: "In God's sight purgatory is turned into paradise."

Even as late as 1681, Christina was still addicted to many of the ideas of her stoical period. Before discussing this dichotomy in her mind, a more general remark has to be made.

Converts, or religiously immature souls, tend to identify themselves prematurely or too rapidly with the greater saints; they make their experiences their own, identify their (small) experiences with those (greater ones) of the saints. That is why wise priests often advise converts, or people who have only recently become acquainted with the Church and her mysteries, not to read the mystics or books by saints. We should therefore treat with caution Christina's marginal notes, and not believe every word she puts down. Which are the more convincing remarks is hard to say. The methodical way to discover this would be to take as authentic any point of criticism revealing insufficient comprehension on the part of the critic, but to regard with caution any too eager comparison between the writer's own spiritual condition and the saint's. If in exceptional cases we want to run the risk of taking some positive statement for an expression of sincere and deep sympathy, then we must look for certain special conditions to be fulfilled. Context, style, tone and approach must all be probed for evidence of deep conviction, specially in comparison with other authentic notes. Here expressions of sincere contrition, shame, an admission of sinfulness, a natural longing for deliverance, are particularly indicative.

As long as possible, Christina strove to maintain her proud youthful belief in the unbounded capacity of the soul to stand fast, to shape its own destiny, to conquer its foes. Where Catherine of Genoa describes a conversation between the soul and self-love and the body, and the soul tells the body how it has lived in such a way as to become, gradually, the slave of the body, unable to do anything the body does not want, Christina expressed vehement disagreement in the margin (in Italian). A little further on she noted, even slaves can do what is right and have to observe the rules of morality.—When Catherine makes the soul tell God it knows that of its own powers it can do nothing to correspond with God's will, she objected: "Not so."—And when Catherine declares the soul is in itself nothing, Christina observed: "What can a nothing do?"—how could the soul, being nothing, produce love?

But when Catherine stresses man's God-given qualities, the margin is filled with remarks of enthusiastic approbation. In apparent contradiction to what we saw just now, Catherine says the soul is furnished with such strength and dignity that it could not be overwhelmed except at its own desire. "That is true," noted Christina. Likewise she eagerly approved of another statement of Catherine's, that God so much respects the will of man that He never puts restraint on him. At a mention of dependence, Christina remarks that "will-power and grace" (mark the priority!) can also redeem him. Indeed even in her most religious period Christina always displayed a great respect for the human will. She disliked any vagueness of expression and insisted that religion must have its active functions, noting for instance that grace makes a man "to the highest degree active". Man, she held, needs his will to love God; this is quite unlike Luther's idea, that to a completely helpless man everything comes as grace: "Where there is no will there is no true love," she said.

She rejected strict asceticism too. It is not right—at least not for everyone—to sacrifice secondary things for the sake of primary ones. Two remarks of hers illustrate this point: "Is it a fault to enjoy conversation?"—"There is no need to lose the greater for the sake of the lesser thing."

Sometimes, when Catherine describes a condition of depression and despair, Christina finds a physiologico-medical explanation. According to Bourdelot, in Swedish days Christina already had a good knowledge of medical literature. At such passages she would note, "*Humore malinconico*" (melancholy temperament).

On ascetic exercises she wrote: "It is unjust to God to believe that such nonsense pleases Him." Where Catherine deals with the destitution of the soul, Christina was obviously irritated: "Such destitution may or may not take place—but what purpose does it serve?" And in her view too much fuss was made of doing good.

Her own ideas are clearly evident when she endorses Catherine's picture of the soul, freed from all earthly beauty, turning to its source: "This is the only principle of our life and its only goal."

It is chiefly in the earlier part of the book that a critical or arrogant tone is apparent, but not very frequently. Christina's first reaction was a natural shrinking from the strange world of the saints and their experiences, then bit by bit she attempted to link up her own experiences with this, to her, new mode of expression. These annotations reveal her more freely and personally than her maxims even. Apart from her comments on Molinos's trial, found in an important manuscript in the Vatican, there is hardly another document that gives us so intimate a picture of Christina's spiritual life.

When Catherine says the soul is surprised to discover what a poor specimen of creation it really is, Christina commented: "Very remarkable indeed!" In passionate words the saint shows how the soul sees physical and spiritual death on either side of it, surrounded as it is by so many foes that it "feels like a beast driven to the slaughterhouse". Christina, not in the least taken aback by this outburst, merely noted: "Many others have none the less fought their way through."

Then come Catherine's observations on the soul's increasing awareness of its wretchedness: the deeper Christina went, the more disturbed did she become. At a passionate reference to the soul in need, the queen noted: "That is my case: poor thing that I am!"—

how strikingly different from the usual tone of her letters and maxims. But the queen was reading on breathlessly, and the saint's following words elicited this from her: "As far as I know I have committed no such theft . . . but I have to do penance for many other sins." This strikes quite a new note: no one knew anything of this strain in her. We witness the complete submergence of her earlier faith in man: "I am nothing, can do nothing, and crave for nothing."

Marginal notes such as *questa è l'historia nostra* are recurrent. When Catherine has the soul describe its plight, entangled in its despondency and not knowing what to do, finding no spot to rest in either heaven or earth . . . Christina noted: "Blessed Catherine is not the only one to have endured such martyrdom." The soul complaining that its bondage to the earth makes it despair, elicits from Christina: "My own case?" And further on likewise, *caso nostro in terminis*. "May God protect me from myself!"—a sheer cry of distress. But she had not lost hope, and when the soul reaches an important stage in its progress, "That I shall achieve by God's grace!" wrote Christina. A passage on the highest moment of mysticism drew from her the remark: "These moments are more worth while than the whole of life, however long it may last." Another passage that runs: "O my God, defend me from myself and do with me whatever you please; I shall endure all things, if only you will save me from the wretchedness and dangers in which I find myself", prompted Christina to note: "My own case, for many years now. . . ."

These marginal notes bring us nearer to Christina than any other attainable source. Though she tried to keep at least a vestige of her earlier confidence in man, she finally capitulated, anxiously or in joyous adoration. Here we follow at first hand the final collapse of her former attitude and the steady penetration of her personality by the new awareness of sin in the light of Christian realism.

In her notes to the report on Molinos's trial, to which we shall come presently, Christina made some very unfriendly remarks about the Jesuits: "Their spiritual exercises contain nothing but arrogance and self-assertion." She was equally severe on sentimental piety: *gerghi de bacheton* is an expression of scorn to which she often resorted, it means something like "pious twaddle". A letter from an unknown priest was peppered with irate remarks, of which we cite a few telling samples: "Who asked you for your views?"—"please stop school-mastering me, since my ninth year I have not let anyone do that!" (Curiously enough Christina often mentioned her ninth year as a sort of boundary after which she went her own way.)—"Schoolmaster, tutor, controller, precentor—all such canaille I abhor."—"Cheeky hypocrite, he deserves a good beating rather than a written answer!"—"Lies—if anyone believes such a thing I shall have him beaten to death."—"Do you suppose I am so unworldly as not to know what goes on in Rome and what devilry is done?"—"When the devil sends you to penal servitude, don't come and make out it's my fault!"—"If God was a monk, woe to the world!"—"As soon as you reach eternity you will see what a monster you were here on earth; and God only knows where you will end up."

In conclusion, we can say that already in Sweden Christina abhorred all the trappings of external piety; in Rome her abhorrence waxed. There was also her natural independence, making her reject any sort of pressure, specially when it took the form of advice or suggestions from a confessor. With her self-assured confidence in a Christian sovereign's responsibility to God alone, she regarded the dependence of certain monarchs on confessors from the Jesuit Order as revolting and humiliating. She had come to Rome in search of spiritual and intellectual toleration. To her great disappointment she was to experience that Rome was no Padua or Florence where free enquiry and independent thought were highly honoured: nearly all outstanding scholars had had to leave the Papal States, and she had landed in a priest-ridden centre where worldliness, poltroonery, servility and career-mongering were rife. She was not at her ease in Rome. The only man who met her requirements was Cardinal Azzolino, but her enthusiastic or loving outbursts in praise of his genius lacked all spiritual impulse: she always spoke of him as though he were a statesman, not a priest.

This was the background to her interest in an utterly different kind of religious feeling, more popular and emotional in tone, than what she had hitherto known. Through force of circumstances Christina became involved in a religious movement that—so one would think—was utterly foreign to her proud, aristocratic nature: Spanish Quietism, in its Italian form. This phase in Christina's life has remained as good as unknown till now, and yet it concerns what is in some respects her most remarkable experience, occupying nearly two decades of her Roman period. This is how we came to know about it: through an Italian journalist, Bandini, who discovered that Christina had been interested in Molinos's trial: but, knowing neither her maxims nor her religious viewpoint, naturally he was led astray by the distorted picture current in his day; he could not realize to what an extent she was personally involved.

5. QUIETISM

From the second half of the seventeenth century onwards, there spread throughout Spain, France and Italy that curious religious movement which soon came to be known as Quietism. There is a large amount of literature on its development and leading personalities, particularly Madame de Guyon and Fénelon in France. The Protestants usually held it to be wrong to persecute the Quietists, and Henri Brémond, a former Jesuit, thought likewise. But Catholic opinion regarded Quietism as one of the most perilous distortions of doctrine the Church was ever exposed to, and welcomed Rome's and the Inquisition's intervention as necessary and justified.

The word Quietism comes from the biblical *quies*, and means the peace Jesus promised his disciples, the peace the world cannot give. French and Italian Quietism came from the great mystics—pseudo-Dionysius, Tauler, John of the Cross, Teresa of Avila, who taught of a divine darkness, a *docta ignorantia*, a dark night of the soul, a "cloud of unknowing". But Quietism was by nature something more primitive, it can be taken as a sort of popular offshoot of higher mysticism, the most elementary stage of mystical prayer, the bottom rung, as it were. In France as elsewhere it arose in reaction to too systematic pious exercises, the Jesuits' in particular, and the discursive meditations based on the Exercises of Ignatius. Religious and laymen alike spent a daily half-hour or hour in the morning meditating on religious truths, and every day there might be two long examinations of conscience, while every year, or even every month, days of recollection and retreat took place. For communities profoundly affected by the prevalent unrest due to the wars of religion, and lacking firm foundations, such a method was undoubtedly very profitable.

But churchmen soon observed unusual phenomena that were cropping up here and there; devout and cultured ladies would declare that during their quiet hour of meditation or contemplation they could grasp nothing at all, getting no spiritual clarity, no moral impulse, no comprehensible conception of the divine and felt themselves slipping into a void, a sort of sleep. If this happened only to rather weak or superficial people, there would be nothing to worry about. But often very exalted souls complained of these depressing experiences.

The Jesuits worked out an elaborate system of individual prayer-exercises, analysing the various possible attitudes of the soul before God; they knew exactly what had to be done at every turning-point. For many simple people this was a little too involved, and distressing sterility was still liable to result: nothing happened, nothing positive, the soul remained as hungry and unsatisfied as ever.

This is where Quietism came in: no need to take pains or make an effort, it was enough to be still and attentive to God. Prayer was passive, patient and receptive: no need for theological thoughts about Christ or the Trinity or the Christian dogmas and other divine matters. If God spoke to the passively attentive soul, well and good. If not, there was no use in trying to approach Him on one's own. Man could do nothing of himself. It was enough to give oneself to God sincerely, once for all—no need to spend a lifetime anxiously straining for ideas about Him. If temptation came, it too came from God's omnipotence, and resistance was vain.

Now the greater mystics, St. John of the Cross for instance, tell us that after a certain amount of hard going, the soul reaches a state where thought is absent. Those mystics neither feared nor rejected this condition. In Quietism we find the same thing, quite independently of John of the Cross; devout people by-passed the intellectual and discursive method to attain to a state of pure listening in passivity, or resignation as it was called, and found themselves face to face with the divine, without apparently having to make any effort. The opponents of Quietism rejected this type of passive prayer.

Yet the conviction was widespread in France and Italy that here was a pure and primary form of prayer, consisting in the soul's utter submission, in order to receive as God's gift a new capacity for prayer and love, remote from the intellect. St. François de Sales, the great popular teacher of the Christian way of life, was himself familiar with this form of prayer.

There were of course progressive stages: Henri Brémond distinguished them as follows: "In ascetic or active Quietism you recollect yourself; in passive Quietism . . . you do not recollect yourself: there God intervenes."

The soul's "annihilation" goes step by step with God's take-over; passivity is only apparent—it is rather a higher form of activity. On the surface there is intellect and discursiveness, in the depths, the "actual presence of God". Naturally, passive Quietism is never found in a pure state—"through a thousand underground rifts the supra-discursive current forces its way back into the channels of thought". But the essential thing is that God represses a man's own efforts, teaching him by a deeper and more direct way what no exercise can do, to know God and love Him. It is God alone who is at work—but within man, giving him a new purpose, a new outlook.

Brémond asked ironically how a doctrine like this could possibly harm anyone; every Catholic subscribes to the dogma of sanctifying grace, and "is not all knowledge of the objects of our faith infused, and therefore passive?"

Blind Malaval of Marseilles found a very apt way of making it clear: we can give ourselves to God, he said, simply by contemplating one of His attributes, or a mystery, or heaven, or simply a flower . . . but then the soul abandons the original object, rises above the field of analysis, thought, meditation and meets God directly in a non-pictorial, supra-intellectual contemplation. Such experience was current through most of the seventeenth century, a reaction, as we pointed out, to over-systematic religious exercises and the prevailing moralistic tone.

But inherent in Quietism were certain grave dangers. Once the soul had capitulated it became defenceless, and a feeling of being protected and filled by God might or might not be genuine. The key-words of Quietism—annihilation, passivity, resignation, quiet, peace—were equated by wary confessors and experienced priests with slackness, indolence, inadequate spiritual discipline, arrogance and selfishness. Towards the end of the century, the famous controversy between the two French spiritual giants, Bossuet and Fénelon, ended with Fénelon's defeat. Immediately before this tragic finale, another act was played out in Rome, of which the outcome explains in large measure the astounding severity with which Bossuet and the Church proceeded against a high-ranking and greatly revered lady like Mme de Guyon, as well as against Fénelon.

In earlier books about Christina, the important part played by the Swedish queen in the Italian act of this tragedy was never dealt with, though it left its mark on her. For it was not until she came in contact with Quietism that she acquired a personal religion. In fact in the last years of her life mysticism is evident.

6. QUIETISM IN ITALY

Quietism had a long history in Italy. It was already in full flower before the new stimulus came from Spain. The Oratorian, Pier Petrucci, was early known as a convinced Quietist. In the sixteen-fifties, and still more in the two following decades, the Church had to deal with various kinds of quietist errors. In 1675 legal proceedings against a priest, Lombardi, were concluded; he taught that external penance and verbal prayers were meaningless and could be dispensed with. But Quietism had a good many supporters among the clergy, even among the higher clergy. In 1676 the Bishop of Savona received a useful piece of information from the Inquisition, to the effect that it did not condemn quietist prayer as such, but only the view that penance, traditional verbal prayer and other spiritual exercises recommended by the Church were useless, even dangerous. As a matter of fact, the Quietists had by then gained the sympathy of the cardinals and the Pope himself.

A Spanish priest, Miguel Molinos (1627–96), was at work in Rome for many years. He was a much-loved confessor; Pope Innocent XI was friendly to him and saw to his advancement; so did Cardinal Azzolino. Molinos was widely regarded as a saintly man, and in 1675 he published a book, *Guida spirituale* (spiritual guide) which had an exceptionally large circulation. This man was "theologian" to Queen Christina.

Molinos was ordained a priest in Valencia at the age of eighteen. Among his teachers was the Mercedarian, Juan Falconi, who was regarded as a saint, and a singular Mexican ascetic, Gregorio Lopez: in 1663, or perhaps 1665, Molinos came to Rome to put forward a case for the latter's canonization. In this he was unsuccessful, but he soon made himself beloved in Rome and remained there. Nuns, priests, abbots, higher prelates—all wanted to make his acquaintance and profit from his experience. He found enthusiastic followers in the highest circles, including Princess Ludovisi, Princess Borghese, Queen Christina of Sweden, Cardinals Azzolino, Ricci, Capizucchi, Cibo and the Pope's counsellors Favoriti and Casoni. His book went through three editions in Spanish and seven in Italian, and there were soon Latin, French, Dutch and German editions of it. When it was reissued in 1681, the Archbishop of Palermo, Jaime Palafox y Cardona, wrote a preface full of high praises for the author. In 1682, Pope Innocent XI thanked the archbishop for a letter warmly recommending Molinos and his book, but suggested that damage might be done if the book fell into inexperienced hands. Pier Petrucci, whom Innocent later made a cardinal, cannot perhaps be described as precisely a disciple of Molinos, but in his many works he took the same line, and he regarded him with respect and benevolence.

Thus Molinos represented a significant contemporary trend. In his travel book Bishop Burnet reports that in Naples alone the number of Molinos's supporters was reckoned at more than twenty thousand. He calls the first part of his work, "Of the spiritual darkness, dryness and trials by which God purifies the soul; of inner recollection or contemplation": we are drawn to what is evil because of our corrupt nature, other people's influence, bad example and the power of the devil. In prayer we sometimes discover that we are unable to think and do not feel God's presence. There are times when our horizon is limited and darkened. In this darkness, this dryness, it is important to safeguard peace of mind and to acquiesce in the providence of God. To be active in such a case is equivalent to self-love. A man of faith has to accept his lot with resignation. Through pure faith and perfect surrender the soul is open to inward recollection, and this passive prayer is true contemplation which cannot be broken into, so long as the soul avoids grave sin. Self-imposed chastisements and self-chosen ascetic exercises produce a false sense of security. God alone can purify the soul, God alone can enlighten it. Christ is the way, the truth and the life, as we know, but a soul whom God calls to this inward recollection has no need to meditate on the Gospel: silence before God's Majesty and fatherly goodness is the way of atonement with Him: These are in brief the basic ideas of the first book.

The second is entitled: "Of our spiritual Father; of the obedience we owe him; of thoughtless zealousness; of inward and outward penance." There are many confessors, we read, but only a few spiritual guides. To guide a soul spiritually, knowledge, experience and divine vocation are required. Most confessors have no experience of such recollection, silence, or knowledge of men. How many people make active efforts that are but self-love in disguise. The only sure way to elude the snares of the devil is submission to God. The more simply and rapidly this submission can occur, the more sure is the soul of its inward peace. Such obedience to God is specially necessary in times of trouble and trials. The frequent receiving of Communion is an effective means of attaining it. Exterior penitential exercises play a less important part than interior ones; penances chosen by ourselves are less important than those inspired by God. Everyday sins ought not to deprive us of peace: in most people they are unavoidable. Let us acknowledge our wretchedness and sinfulness and turn to God in all confidence.

Part Three is called: "Of the spiritual means used by God to purify the soul; of infused or passive contemplation, utter resignation, inner humility, divine wisdom, genuine annihilation and inward peace."—Between the inner and outer man there is a great difference. What gives peace is not consolation, which can be received through the senses, but the renunciation of self-concern. In its distress and trials, the soul must let go of itself and wait. In maturer souls this first mystery is followed by a second: a restless and vain search for God who remains hidden. Inward contrition, perfect renunciation and a conviction of our own wretchedness are essential if real peace is to be attained. It is easy to draw up rules to help us discover whether we possess this simplicity and humility of heart, but infused and passive contemplation depends on God and God alone. We may say: "God embraces, penetrates, raises and teaches the soul, which in the sight of the Lord enjoys Him and rests in Him." The mystical books tell of ecstasies, swoons, jubilations, unions, betrothals and spiritual marriage with God—but what really happens is nothing of the kind. "The gift of wisdom" consists of contemplation alone. Acknowledging our own corruption and God's majesty, we achieve "annihilation". And thus we attain to peace and union with God. But very few people have this experience.

Molinos's book is in no way original nor is it written in a very logical form. Its connection with earlier mystical literature is easy to perceive. Catherine of Siena, of instance, was full of the conviction that the soul can experience its own unworthiness and God's omnipotence—but she was an active mystic. The pages on darkness and dryness are traceable to Spanish mysticism—Teresa of Avila and John of the Cross. What was new and personal to Molinos was perhaps the lyrical warmth of his tone. The entire content of the work can be summed up roughly as follows:

1. Any form of activity is evil in origin. A man should not try to work at his own salvation—this would be an act of self-will, and self-will must be eradicated.

2. The proper attitude of the soul is passive resignation and silence. Resignation, too, in the sense that every fight against temptation—e.g. by means of flagellations—is worthless and only

leads to a false impression that the soul is capable of putting up its own defence—but that is self-will. Resignation in the face of our own sinfulness is the only proper and humble attitude for the soul.

3. Apart from Holy Communion, the soul has no special need of the second divine Person, the incarnate Christ.

4. All the high moments of mysticism as analysed in the manuals, culminating in spiritual marriage with God, are to be rejected: it does not matter whether the soul "feels" or "experiences" anything, all that is important is the eradication of self-esteem.

5. Caution is recommended towards the ordinary run of confessors and their counsels, with unconditional obedience only to quietist confessors.

All this may seem simple and innocuous enough. It is not really clear why it should have had such an appeal for anyone with so active and enterprising a nature, such determination and will-power, such incisive intellectual powers, such self-confidence and pride, as Queen Christina. In her younger days she would certainly have rejected it with scorn. But years had gone by, and she had her own experiences to reckon with.

7. THE CAMPAIGN AGAINST MOLINOS

In course of time Rome discovered that Molinos was dangerous. Reports were reaching the Inquisition from all over the country; wherever Molinos and Quietism led the way, distrust of priests and indifference towards the Church followed; people were behaving as though they no longer needed priests or sacraments. After careful preparation, the Inquisition struck. The driving force seems to have been that clever, ruthless Cardinal d'Estrées, with whom Queen Christina was often at loggerheads. There was not really much to be said against Molinos's book, which was prudently written. But his verbal utterances were apparently in a different key.

Many Religious in Italian monasteries could observe odd consequences arising out of quietist teaching: nuns discarded monastic rule, rejected holy water, closed their eyes at the elevation of the Host. Bartoli, a Jesuit, reported that some nuns had given up verbal prayer, scorned absolution and admitted to no sin when they failed to resist temptation. They received Communion without previous confession and ascribed all their sinful doings to the devil. Here and there the rosary fell into disuse; and whatever came into these women's minds was regarded as divine inspiration to be acted upon immediately.

Long before this, Molinos knew he would have to reckon with opposition to his teaching. But he thought he could rely on his good connections in the highest ecclesiastical circles, and the prospect did not trouble him. In 1676 he wrote letters in which his teaching was expressed in such prudent terms that not even his most determined opponents could have found anything to object to. But now the counter-blows began to fall. Gottardo Bellhuomo, novice-master and provincial of the Jesuit Order in the province of Venice, former professor of theology and philosophy, wrote a dissertation on prayer; he did not mention Malaval or Molinos by name but was evidently attacking their teaching.

Molinos then wrote a letter to the Jesuit General Oliva to explain his views. Oliva answered very politely, but was obviously in disagreement. Now another distinguished Italian priest joined the fray: Paolo Segneri, "the most revered Jesuit of the century", a missionary with a reputation for saintliness. His book appeared in 1680. But Molinos was still able to stand up for himself. A counter-move by Pier Petrucci was published, dedicated to Cardinal Cibo, secretary of State, and the author was made Bishop of Jesi soon after. Still more remarkable was the fact that in 1681, Segneri's and Bellhuomo's works were denounced by the Inquisition and put on the Index, though they were protected by other parties, e.g. the Grand Duke of Tuscany. Yet another attack on Molinos, with material collected by Alessandro Regio, suffered the same fate. It looked as though Molinos would carry the day with ease.

But his opponents stuck to their guns. On the suggestion of an Oratorian named Marchese, nearly all Roman confessors were sent a questionnaire to find out what they had discovered about the quietist movement. Marchese had the answers collected in a volume. Now among those who received the enquiry there was not a single Jesuit. At the end of his volume, Marchese placed the negative answers of a number of very distinguished Roman priests, showing it was by no means only the Jesuits who were against Molinos. In July 1682, the Inquisitor General in Brescia, Cecalti, a Dominican, issued a prohibition against all quietist assemblies. Although Maracci, the Pope's own confessor, was an opponent of Molinos, and old Cardinal Albizzi had raised objections in a work of his own, Molinos's position still seemed secure.

Finally, however, the opposition won: this was when reports on Molinos's private life reached the Inquisition.

Molinos had been in Rome since 1664. In 1681–2 he got the better of his critics, but on 18 July 1685 a troop of papal *sbirri* (police-spies) entered his house, not far from the church of San Lorenzo in Panisperma. He was alone with his servants. He started to argue with the *sbirri*, both indoors and out on the street, talking on and on in great excitement, calling heaven and earth to witness his innocence and begging the *sbirri* not to carry out their charge for fear of endangering his soul. He continued his defence all the way to the Inquisition prison—on the Tiber, near St. Peter's.

For several days (according to Cardinal d'Estrées) Rome talked of nothing else. The Spanish envoy reported to Madrid that some students of Molinos had spread a distorted version of his teaching, and when he disavowed them they accused him of unseemly behaviour—pure invention on their part. But other people expressed their astonishment that such a man had been able to enjoy a high degree of fame and honour for so long.

Cardinal d'Estrées too had a lot to report. The Pope, he said, was beside himself when he heard Molinos was under arrest. He termed him "a splendid man" and said that to attack him was to run a risk of grave error and serious consequences. The Queen of Sweden, said the cardinal, was very upset and sent messengers to the prison daily.

Molinos's arrest was due, the cardinal thought, to certain regrettable occurrences in connection with his teaching. The chief charge against him was his view that aberrations occurring during mystical experience in the "lower part of the soul" were not to be reckoned as sins, but at the most as temptations of the devil. This does not appear in so many words in Molinos's *Guida*, but his confidential advice to various people had that trend.

The proceedings lasted a long time. There were something like twenty thousand letters to sift, which had been confiscated from his home. According to Abbé de Servient, these included two hundred letters from Queen Christina, "which out of consideration for her were not scrutinized".

Finally, Molinos was accused of grave misdemeanour. He was said to have taken part in shameless acts, kisses, embraces, caresses, unchaste contacts, consorting with naked women; and also to have declared that such acts were by no means sinful.

At first glance one is inclined to dismiss it all as ill-intentioned gossip. How could so many outstanding people of high reputation, who knew Molinos well, have been so mistaken about his moral life? But after preliminary denials Molinos was confronted with one witness after another and was shown unequivocal evidence in letters; finally, he was, in the view of his judge, convicted of guilt.

The worst of it was, not so much the sins for which he was impeached as his own attempts to gloss them over. He admitted that the devil had irresistible power to mislead certain devout souls and prompt them to brutal actions, blasphemies, slanders, indecencies in word and deed, hatred and wrath; but he held the soul was guiltless and not responsible. Witnesses reported how he had slandered the Mother of God, broken up rosaries and done other things of the kind. Molinos even went so far as to say that under inspiration of the devil it might even come to physical union between man and woman without the parties concerned being held to account. Precisely on that subject he had written a whole dissertation which was read in Rome and elsewhere.

8. CHRISTINA, MALAVAL AND MOLINOS

Malaval too, the blind mystic of Marseilles, now came under suspicion, as was to be expected—his book had enjoyed a great success in Italy. Early in 1682, he wrote a long letter in defence of his work to the Index Congregation, for Bellhuomo and Segneri had thoroughly abused it. He declared himself ready to withdraw whatever might be found to be false: had certain errors crept in, he would be willing, should occasion arise, to sacrifice his own blood. In a letter to the Pope at about the same time, Malaval said he had asked Molinos to see Queen Christina on his behalf "for her Majesty has consented to be the protectress of the book which is dedicated to her".

Further he wrote a long letter to the queen herself. He spoke of the high esteem in which he had held her so for long, and of the "rare example of wisdom and piety she had given the whole world". He specially thanked her for giving his book and its dedication so friendly a welcome when it appeared in Italian translation. Now that his friend Cardinal Bona was dead, he begged her to help him. His friend Molinos had informed him how much Christina "was interested in our cause and what a positive view she took of our books, which are being opposed with such ardent hatred". He could only express the wish that Christina might be penetrated "by the Spirit of God", "whose cause she defended; may God teach her how elevating it is to contemplate Him constantly and to follow Him in love and faith". Before God, may the queen adopt the same attitude as ordinary people do before kings.

Then he made a personal appeal: she had shown such strong sympathy for quietist prayer that she must have "felt it within her", and "as it was essential to have complete readiness for renunciation if this blessed state was to be attained, no doubt she had long ago made the sacrifice of her reason to the living light of faith and caught sight of those eternal truths which one day would persuade many Protestant princes of the uselessness and wrongness of the modern faith, seeing that it cannot redeem them."

Christina's own achievement, he wrote, was threefold: she had revoked Protestantism, she had abdicated, and she had left Sweden. Malaval added that for his part he had given up Hermes Trismegistus and *les Platons* in favour of the Church Fathers, which seems to indicate that he had spoken to the queen about this, or knew her views. So there is nothing surprising, he continued, in that Christina should have rushed to the rescue of "so genuine, pure and coherent a doctrine". "Your approval is a seal that can seal the lips of our opponents." He positively rejoiced at the cruel persecutions to which Molinos and the Quietists in Italy were exposed, for they provided the opportunity for a thorough enquiry into a form of spiritual life that must be tested if its teaching was to be properly known: learning alone could not produce it; it humbled reason, silenced the sense-impressions, and was contrary to ordinary piety, always so busy drawing conclusions, producing ideas, speaking and acting. "I beg God to bring home to them [i.e. the persecutors] what it is they are opposing, and to oppose what they now applaud."

Molinos, whom Malaval regarded as "a great master of the spiritual life, utterly filled with the grace in which he participates", was, he said, by no means guilty of the heresies that are supposed to have been discovered in his writings. Even his own book was the object "of a new attack". It had been denounced to the Inquisition by a man whose own work, *Le sette illusioni*, only repeated old, no longer valid criticisms by the Jesuit Segneri. Finally Malaval begged Queen Christina to use her influence to obtain that a reprieve be granted him before the Inquisition pronounced on him: she could hardly refuse the request of an author whose book "had been read throughout the whole Christian world for fourteen years".

This letter is revealing as to Christina's own attitude: to Malaval it was clear that she was the great protectress and friend of Quietism, even though he knew she had not taken the final step and committed herself to the way of Quietism and to its utmost conclusion. No doubt his friend Molinos had passed on to him his own opinion of Christina's attitude: it agrees too with what we know about her from other sources, specially her own remarks on different occasions.

Christina got busy at once, writing a great number of letters in defence of the Quietists. For instance, in April 1862, she wrote to the Archbishop of Palermo, thanking him for his letter informing her of the case against Molinos, and declaring she was at her wit's end; she also thanked him for the support he had given Molinos, for which he would surely always be able to reckon with the help of the true and just God. "Thus our Molinos will never be beaten by his enemies, however much they persecute him . . . " She ended with an assurance that she would not cease to do all she could in defence of Molinos.

When the Archbishop of Palermo was appointed Archbishop of Seville, in November 1684, Christina wrote him a letter of congratulation to which she added a postscript to the effect that "our Molinos" felt "gratitude to and veneration for the archbishop", and she hoped an opportunity would arise for her to prove in deed as well as word how highly she valued him.

How close Christina really was to Molinos appears in a letter of Cardinal Pio's of 21 July 1685. It contains the remark that the number of Italians infected with Quietism was held to be considerable. Molinos was known as the "theologian" of the Queen of Sweden (religiously-inclined Italian princes often appointed a priest as court theologian, to come to their assistance in solving difficult theological or ecclesiastical problems). Cardinal Pio also reported that when the queen heard of Molinos's arrest she declared he was certain to be released and rehabilitated if he was innocent, but would be punished as he deserved if he was really guilty of the offence of which he was accused: she herself was convinced of his innocence.

This is also evident in Christina's letter of 17 November to the Archbishop of Seville, expressing the hope that Molinos would be acquitted by the high court before which he had to appear. According to other sources, Christina sent Molinos fruit and sweetmeats in prison and continued doing so demonstratively for two or three months after he had been condemned.

In a French report from Rome dealing in some detail with the Molinos scandal and its background, we read that Cardinal Azzolino introduced Molinos to the queen as "a sort of father confessor". According to this source, Molinos had a weekly discussion with her about his views. He used her carriage and seemed to be in her service, and thoroughly at home in her palace. According to Cardinal d'Estrées, Azzolino practised Jansenism and Quietism in order to cut the figure of a devout man in the Pope's eyes. That Azzolino had any sympathy for Jansenism is indeed quite incredible; on the other hand, for many years he was attracted to Quietism and did what he could to protect it—and so did Innocent XI. As we saw it, was Azzolino who drew Christina's attention to the first quietist book she came across. According to the French cardinal, Azzolino is supposed to have suggested to Christina to take up Molinos's cause herself, and—as he wrote —"it has been observed that the *quiete* religious movement is protected at this court by the most *inquiete* personality . . . "

This all helps to throw light on Christina's connection with the two Quietists, Malaval and Molinos. We still do not know her own inward reaction to their teaching. Before studying this, and how far Christina's views as evidenced in the maxims show quietist influence, let us take another look at her personal relations with Molinos. We can regard it as proven that she admired him, but she was by no means uncritical, she never completely capitulated.

The Vatican possesses documents in this connection of a most illuminating kind. A confessor of the queen's, a certain Father Tomasso, wrote an analysis of Quietism and also drew up a report on the two hundred and sixty-three points in which the Holy Office formulated its censure. Here is abundant material ready to hand. Not only Molinos's own writings are there, but also the confiscated letters and his replies at the trial. And it is all annotated copiously with marginal comments in the queen's hand. Finally there is a copy of a bill of indictment containing the entire charges and hearings of two whole years of legal proceedings, with commentaries in the left-hand margin on points raised and Molinos's objections to them. This is not in the queen's writing but a copy, though the notes are obviously hers, as we can tell from the vocabulary used and by comparing the text with others of hers, and there are corrections and additions to the copy in her own hand, with frequent use of a favourite expression of hers, *bachettoni* (priestlings).

The queen admired and appreciated Molinos as theologian and teacher, but as a man, and above all as father confessor and spiritual guide, she found a good deal to object to. It was fairly widely held in her day that Molinos was the queen's confessor for some considerable time. But quite what is meant is less clear: the main functions of the "theologians" the queen appointed—her friend the Duke of Parma did the same—seem to have been those of celebrating Mass and hearing the confessions of her household. They did of course come into contact with the queen herself, and would much have liked to be her spiritual guides, but all through her life Christina had a marked distaste for such things, as is clear from many of her maxims.

The same manuscript contains a number of outbursts against confessors and spiritual guides: "The profession of father-confessor is insufferable to me", and "One who wants none other than God needs no confessor." When the proceedings against Molinos had still not reached the point when it was clear he had misused his function, Christina remarked that he ought never to have consented to hear confessions. And when Molinos tried to defend himself before his judges and used the words "we confessors", Christina noted: "Anyone who has the affrontery to say 'we confessors' deserves the correction which Molinos has received and will further receive." But we have no right to conclude, from this or from a number of similar remarks, that the queen rejected confession as such. In fact she was to show her respect for it; in one of her maxims she said, what is difficult is not only to admit our evil deeds, but to repent of our "pleasures and passions too, and finally and for ever relinquish them"; but she added, "and yet God absolutely deserves this our greatest sacrifice". She also agreed that a Christian should punctually perform the penance laid on him by his father confessor. In the Vatican manuscript there is a note in the same spirit: "Really I have no pangs of conscience, but I will go to confession all the same."

In another respect too Christina was extremely critical of the man whom she otherwise spoke of with affection as *il nostro Molinos* or *il mio Molinos*, and whom she defended with all her might so long as it was still possible. In the record of the proceedings, the passage where Molinos declared he had an "inner voice" which always warned him when the devil came near, she noted: "Oh, how often he must have been deceived!" And to the passage about Molinos once advising someone to part from a painting because he loved it all too well, the queen, with her own love and understanding of art, jotted down one of her most characteristic remarks: "I would not condemn him for heresy but for blatant stupidity" (*bestialità* was the word she used).

Another document gives us insight into the queen's daily life and reveals a small difference of opinion between her and Molinos. It was about a letter Christina wrote him on 1 November 1684, half a year before his arrest. Here too she calls him *Molinos mio*, assuring him of her good will, but he had put it to her that she was hazarding her reputation by speaking too critically of the Pope. This Christina certainly did—her letters and notes are full of ironic phrases about Innocent XI; but here she argued strongly that she was not in the wrong, she merely praised what was worthy and criticized what was unworthy, and indeed she could keep silence too when necessary; if the Pope ever got into difficulties and was left high and dry by all the boot-lickers, she would risk her life and venture health and wealth in his cause. She refused to believe that Molinos wrote his letters under divine inspiration as he claimed: "God never inspires a man to write idiotic stuff." She would continue to honour and love Molinos as a saintly man, but she begged him to stop this nonsense; the power that inspired him to write that particular letter was not God, said Christina with conviction, but the devil—"a devil who is a blockhead and does not know me at all". She ended with the assurance that she wholeheartedly forgave Molinos and would not change her feelings towards him, but only on condition that he never raised the topic again.

So we see that Christina admired Molinos, but was not unduly dependent on him; when his advice did not suit her, she disdainfully rejected it. When he declared he spoke in the name of God, she made merciless fun of him and evidently had no high opinion of his religious illuminations.

There are a number of instances of her personal reactions to Molinos's teaching; she was passionately interested in his theology and went through his predictions point by point. She read with great thoroughness the many writs against him and filled the margins with her objections and excited comments. She followed the whole proceedings with the greatest attention, and probably with the help of Cardinal Azzolino, got hold of copies of all the acts of indictment, had commentaries on them done by a qualified theologian, and only reached her own conclusions after exhaustive investigation. One of the manuscripts gives very precise clues to her attitude to the more vulnerable aspects of quietist mysticism. It deals with Molinos's doctrine in twenty-four points, and she summarized some of them. Point 4: One must never allow oneself to think about the saints, the Holy Virgin, Christ or the Holy Trinity, divine grave, mercy, or other attributes of God.—But then God himself would not be known. To this crowning objection to Molinos, Christina's marginal note commented: "We know all these mysteries far more clearly in God himself and honour them in Him."

Point 6: Souls have to open to God in pure love, without knowing Him; if anyone tries to know God in any form whatever, it must be said he does not love the true God.—To which Christina commented: "God has neither form nor shape under which we can know Him; when he speaks of Himself in metaphors and similes, He is adapting Himself to our foolishness, our limited capacity."

Point 10: Every external perception that arises in our love of God, and every outward pious exercise, is supposed by Molinos to be a hindrance to true illumination and to any real progress on the way to perfection.—On this Christina remarked that it could not be very dangerous: "It is sufficient to set the end higher than the means."

Point 12: Flagellation should be forbidden.—Comment: "The world will not suddenly come to an end on account of that."

Point 15: Even in strong temptation the soul is in safety if only it remains with God—one of Molinos's cardinal sayings. Christina agreed: What can anyone fear who remains in contact with God?

Point 23: "Therefore the soul should not even try to find out if it loves God."—Christina concurred: "It is enough when God knows."

Point 26 is not far from Protestantism: people should stop appealing to the saints; a man who craves for nothing and remains in union with God needs no intermediary.—To which Christina remarked: "What else do the saints do but in a perfect manner desire what God desires?"

Point 29 concerns one of Molinos's most hazardous views: the soul should gradually become passive, and God will work in it without its co-operation as soon as it relinquishes the use of free will—a heresy to which Christina retorted ironically: "Truly a great misfortune! Happy he who finds himself in this happy position!"

Point 33: the view over which Molinos finally came to grief, that it did not matter if the devil drove a man to sin, if he had but relinquished his free will to God and held fast to God.—Christina countered with: "He who really lives in union with God can certainly not sin so long as he remains in this happy state."

It is hard to say when this manuscript came into existence: perhaps before the legal proceedings were started. But we know what Christina's attitude was during the trial, and we shall look at the important material dealing with this, too; first, however, quoting what she wrote on learning of Father Tomasso's criticism:

"In the persecution of poor Molinos, political motives play a larger part than factual ones. If he really said the stupid things we read in the records, he would have to be taken to a madhouse and not before the Holy Office; but I have a definite feeling we have to do with forged letters and false witnesses with a view to stifling the poor man's simple teaching, now that he is deprived of all human aid; but when all else fails, a man still has God, who helps everyone with his holy grace." In these difficult matters, she wrote, ignorance was not in a position to judge: some of the accusations were absolutely and incontestably correct, we could not disregard them without casting judgment on nearly all our great saints and serious Catholic authors, while other things have been misinterpreted and misunderstood, whether with evil intent or in ignorance: she, Christina, could not help wondering in some dismay whether in this case truth and innocence had not fallen victims to hypocrisy and self-interest.

Again and again during the trial she insisted that Molinos

could not have said any such thing—"Jesuits and monks" had invented most of it. "Anyone who regards Molinos as a sort of master of ceremonies is utterly mistaken."—"Never can Molinos have said such idiotic things, whatever the witnesses may declare." The margins were bespattered with her scorn: *gerghi di bacchetone*—(pious twaddle) . . .

So that in principle, at least so long as the trial had not completely demolished its victim, Christina was on his side. And she displayed such familiarity with the mystical world that she could quote the classic mystics from memory, as well as the Latin New Testament. Mystical prayer was nothing new, it already existed in the Old Testament and was later recommended and practised by Christ and the Apostles. She seized upon the word *rassegnazione*, resignation, so characteristic of Quietism, and paid homage to it: *Niente, niente, niente fuor che il consensu e la rassegnazione* (Nothing, nothing, nothing but acceptance and resignation). Molinos's insistence on complete passivity and his mistrust of any attempt to improve ourselves by our own efforts, she regarded with sympathetic approval. She rejected all pious exercises and said that a *Pater noster* and a *Miserere* were enough for her: adding mockingly that Church prayers were "an infallible sleeping-dose", and recalling contemptuously how the disciples fell asleep on the Mount of Olives. Molinos was reported to have said: "In a state of ineffability, we know and do not know, believe and do not believe, believe all or believe nothing", and Christina remarked: "That is true, in the highest degree true."

The vulnerable point in Molinos's theology was his view that in this exalted state the soul must relinquish its free will and pass into a condition of non-responsibility. Christina had pondered over this a good deal; she rejected the notion that will-power was not necessary: "It is necessary." Molinos was right when he taught that a man must relinquish his will unconditionally, but as Christina said, that did not mean he had the right to forget his duties to his neighbour: "This sacrifice, which is the one necessary sacrifice, must not prevent a man from performing his duties to the world in general, nor make him give himself to God exclusively." So on that point Christina did not accept Molinos's teaching. Molinos said the soul should not worry about heaven and hell. Christina remarked: "In all circumstances an interest in paradise is justified, and God can forgive those who have it." When Molinos quoted Bernard of Clairvaux, *Causa diligendi Deum Deus est* (the reason for loving God is God himself), Christina concurred: "This remarkable statement is perfectly correct but does not exclude our ardent longing for salvation."

On the other hand, Christina fully endorsed Molinos's censure of the Jesuits' schematism and the Church's external pomp. But she had no wish to be rid of the Mass, not even those splendid baroque musical Masses. When Molinos said that Masses with music and singing were wearisome worldly distractions, unbecoming for devout souls, Christina remarked: "These Masses are the most beautiful on earth. I think they are of a kind to make anyone listening to them believe."

Molinos's theology also contained the doctrine of "mystical death". This Christina could not accept: "I think mystical death is sheer fantasy"; "with this kind of death I cannot feel at home. . . ." She had no belief in perfect peace in this life. "I care not for this peace, this imperturbability." She turned down "all that talk about perfection": "Who of us is not a sinner?"—"Perfection is not to be found here on earth."

Christina took an even stronger line on another extremely important point, rejecting not only what the Inquisition read into it, but Molinos's own plain teaching: observing that the soul that rids itself of will-power is specially exposed to violent attacks from the devil. Molinos concluded that not even very severe sins committed by utterly God-forsaken people were to be regarded as sins, but were rather to be compared to the blasphemies which Job, that man of God, hurled at Him in his despair, or the deeds of which St. Paul speaks—that we do them without wishing to. With that characteristic, not unattractive, sobriety of hers, Christina commented: "The poor devil is not to blame here."

According to the records, Molinos was said to have defended blatant sexual lapses of otherwise devout people. Christina was sceptical: "Such things do not often happen, and I do not believe it is due to attacks of the devil but to something quite natural. . . .

Such 'violence' might occur, but to my mind it is as rare as a miracle!" Indeed there is much realism and good sense in the observations made by the queen in the last years of her life. She seems to have had personal experience in spiritual matters and was convinced that the spiritual world was accessible to the human soul, even though it be sinful; she never hesitated to express her gratitude for Molinos's advice, but she steered clear of any over-emphasis and was indeed much dismayed that Molinos's doctrine might have serious consequences affecting both his own life and that of his credulous followers.

Here we will quote a few more of Christina's sayings, earnest ones that evidently sprang from her very heart.

"God's unspeakable and inconceivable beauty carries all before it and consumes all, the soul forgets all, even itself, and loses itself in an inexhaustible sea of blessedness"—words reminiscent of St. Catherine of Genoa, whom she venerated.

She also wrote: "Faith believes in God, but love sees Him, for it possesses Him: this vision of God does not, however, appear to our bodily eyes but is mystical and therefore indescribable."

But we look in vain for any mention of Christ. Here and there is a mention of the Incarnation of God's Son, but it is to a remarkable degree impersonal; Christina's religion consisted in a belief in God which hardly felt the need for belief in the Incarnation. "If we let God act, how good it would be for everyone who harkens to Him and obeys, praises and adores Him—what miracles would God not work within us and outside of us!"

Certain clues to her own character are here revealed: "Anger and arrogance are things I know all too well. Envy is remote from me, thank God." She had gone through too much to be left with any conceit at all: "Self-esteem I do not need to confess. I have come so far that I can only admire in myself what is God's gift, myself I cannot admire." Of the saints she said in her racy way: "For my part I believe these people behaved just like others did; but the others did not do all that the saints did."

In conclusion, throughout the proceedings against Molinos Christina was sceptical as to the objectivity of the judges and the trustworthiness of the witnesses, and that was why she took

Molinos under her protection; but she really rejected a good deal of his teaching, specially his claim to be a spiritual guide. She evidently became more and more uneasy and critical as the trial proceeded and accusations accumulated. A lot of it was quite new to her—she had no idea of the life Molinos led: it did not seem compatible with her earlier impressions of the man. She found herself compelled to admit that the Inquisition's criticisms were justified, and she could but agree with the judges' verdict on the more serious deviations in the theology of Quietism. To the very last she held fast to what Molinos taught in his book—indeed it was utterly harmless, even in the eyes of the Inquisition; but she completely dissociated herself from the incontestable transgressions and errors that the trial brought to light, both in him and his followers.

Finally she admitted she had been mistaken in what mattered most: Molinos could only be described as a charlatan. Once again she had fallen victim to an illusion.

9. THE VERDICT

On 23 September 1687—two years before Christina's death—the last phase of the Molinos trial was staged in the church of Santa Maria sopra Minerva. Molinos renounced all his errors and the verdict was read. There are two sketches showing what happened: both by Arnald van Westerhout, who did a portrait of Molinos during the trial too. A stand in three tiers was erected in the church, in the boxes there sat members of high Roman society, foreign and Italian diplomatists and the Roman aristocracy; exactly opposite the *padre commissario* of the Inquisition sat the whole college of cardinals. In the same drawing Molinos is shown at two different stages of the drama: first standing on a high platform with the penitent's candle alight in his right hand, then kneeling before the Inquisition *commissario* in the yellow penitential tunic with a red cross on the back. The only distinguished personality of Rome *not* present was the Queen of Sweden. Her absence was very significant. Everyone knew her attitude to Molinos: it was believed that the Inquisition confiscated more than two hundred of her letters to Molinos, but as we said, they were not mentioned at the trial.

For a whole year, the Pope, who liked Quietism, refused to take part in the proceedings, but finally he appeared. He was in a very difficult position. According to French reports, until the very last moment he regarded Molinos as a man of honour, even though his teaching on certain matters seemed to be dubious and vulnerable. He had raised a Quietist, Pier Petrucci, to be bishop, then cardinal: if Molinos was condemned, there was bound to be an indictment against the cardinal who defended him, and this was personally distasteful to the Pope.

In the presence of this glittering assembly, as well as a seething mass of the populace, the verdict was finally read out. The crowd shouted: "To the scaffold with Molinos!" or, "Into the Tiber with Molinos!" When he was taken away from the church there was even an attempt to lynch him. But we know that Molinos was able to spend the rest of his life in a monastery.

How Christina took the verdict we do not know. She is said to have held a huge *autodafé* in her palace of all papers and books concerning Molinos. The persecution of the Quietists continued in the following years; one of Cardinal Azzolino's theologians fell a victim to it. The Archbishop of Seville changed his views and in a pastoral letter declared Molinos to be a hypocrite who with diabolical cunning had managed to keep his abominations secret; Segneri's work was allowed to reappear.

It was a painful situation for Cardinal Pier Petrucci, who remained well disposed towards Molinos to the very end. He had inveighed against Segneri too. During the proceedings it emerged that many of the suspects had had contact with Cardinal Petrucci or were among his followers. Among letters addressed to Molinos were some from Petrucci asking for advice about the violent ways of the devil—though he indicated that he did not quite agree with Molinos. In May 1687, the Inquisition decided to examine Cardinal Petrucci's written works—and legal proceedings were taken against him. On 19 June all his books were prohibited; forty-five passages were extracted and declared to be unequivocally or partially heretical.

And how did Christina's old friend Malaval take the terrible news from Rome? To this blind man of God, ambition and arrogance were utterly foreign. He soon heard what had happened to his friend Molinos, and his own book was drawn into the vortex and placed on the Index. Malaval quietly accepted his humiliation. In a letter he withdrew his book and surrendered the sixty-eight theses that had been denounced. Bossuet received this letter, it was submitted to him as to all other French bishops. When Malaval heard Bossuet was writing a book of his own on the nature of prayer, he wrote to him again. Bossuet wrote he would have justice done him, but in fact his verdict was annihilating. In 1698, when a new edition of Malaval's *Pratique facile* was due to appear, Malaval wrote to King Louis XIV's spiritual adviser, the Jesuit Father La Chaise, and explained he had nothing at all to do with the new edition. So Malaval submitted completely and without apparent difficulty.

There are a number of different opinions about the trial itself. The French Jesuit, Père Dudon, the man with the best knowledge of the material, came to the conclusion that Molinos was an out-and-out swindler—and in fact almost a sexual criminal—all in a very exaggerated style. Some Protestant writers, for instance Heinrich Heppe and Carl Emil Scharling, published works in defence of Molinos. But their deductions are worthless for they had no access to the documents. Surprisingly enough, a modern Swedish historian, Professor Sten Carlsson, is quite definitely of the opinion that the trial was rigged: "The pontifical (?) proceedings against him are reminiscent of the modern Bolshevik trials of disgraced marshals and police chiefs." But this is a purely subjective view without factual backing. The same author speaks of "Christina in her old age betraying her quietist chaplain", this too is unfounded; we know Christina followed the proceedings very closely and was only very reluctantly convinced by the evidence that caused Molinos's downfall.

These views are significant of the inadequate historical foundations on which opinion has been formed about Christina and her times. But some individual scholars put a question-mark to the whole proceedings and maintain that although Molinos was proved to have committed a number of offences against decency, these were not as scandalous as rumour would have it. It all depends on what standards are applied. Molinos scarcely ventured to deny what he was accused of; when the judge asked him whether certain things mentioned in letters and witnesses' statements really occurred, he usually assented, but excused himself on the grounds that they were pardonable offences because they concerned people who had given over their free will to God, and therefore were not, in the ordinary sense, responsible for their actions.

Molinos was never racked or tortured, he admitted at once everything he was charged with. He does really seem to have been in some way sexually pathological. Perhaps he began in good faith and really believed what he taught; but spoilt by success and the admiration of thousands of hysterical women, he side-slipped and committed almost unmentionable acts.

Yet the Holy Office is not there in the first place to watch over morals. Sexual aberrations might have been forgiven if he had truly repented of them. The Inquisition was much more concerned with his theology, which had created a veritable state of moral chaos among the devout, throughout great parts of Italy, and specially in many religious houses. And Molinos defended his theology to the bitter end. Finally he did formally withdraw it and declared it was all error. But after the verdict he is said to have told someone that one day, at the Last Judgement, it would be seen who was right.... Apparently he never did properly realize what absurdities his muddled brain had hatched. Today it is possible to study the Inquisition's proceedings in great detail; their moderate discreet and quiet tone amazes us. In fact Molinos really pronounced his own verdict by always admitting his follies and justifying them.

10. CONCLUSION

For Christina, quietist mysticism was evidently a liberating force. She was not aware of the distortions it underwent. What Molinos did for her, all in all, must have meant a lot to her. He passed on to her something of the riches of his own masters, John of the Cross and Teresa of Avila. Though she attended ordinary

Church services regularly and saw that her household did so too, with routine confession, Christina found nothing very elevating in this practice and was often subject to a depressing sense of dryness and emptiness; then she suddenly discovered that this very dryness and emptiness might be a sign of God's presence. She was told that most confessors had no idea of the hidden side of spiritual life and she herself should not expect any out-of-the-ordinary experiences or moral victories: all she need do was to give in, yield herself to God, and with eyes closed, throw herself into the arms of everlasting Love.

This rescued her from the bigotry she so much despised. It gave her the possibility of making more progress than she could along the lines of traditional religious exercises. And perhaps it settled something else—a more problematical and deeper matter—her relationship with Christ; I have tried to show that it did not really exist at all, till then at least. Spanish-Italian Quietism was founded on the great Spanish mystics; reading St. John of the Cross, one realizes how strongly Christo-centric his whole way of life was: as he wrote, he always saw Christ alive before him. But when people like Malaval and Molinos, for instance, attempted to simplify their mysticism and spread it abroad in a very primitive form, they ran the risk of by-passing Christ altogether. Higher mysticism was above all concerned with "pure Love", leading straight to God. In the *Ascent of Mount Carmel* and the *Dark Night of the Soul*, Christ is given as Example and Redeemer, but is not mentioned very frequently. An authority in these matters tells us that if John of the Cross did not pay much attention to Christology in his works, it was because he was writing for readers who already had experience in spiritual matters, mainly monks, nuns and other members of the clergy, for whom it was familiar and basic. As his mystical teaching spread, its main trend was sometimes misunderstood; it looked as though the master believed there was a more direct way, a short cut, leaving aside the Church, Christ, and Mary, to move by way of "pure Love" straight into the arms of God. There was no doubt about it in the case of Molinos's followers, and on that point he fell.

At a very early stage, Christina was sceptical about the Incarnation of the Son of God: she always avoided mentioning Christ, or the Incarnation, or the Redemption. In Quietism she found exactly what she had hitherto sought in vain, a genuinely Christian way of life that disregarded all the things she found so distasteful: pious gestures, pious exercises, a too ecclesiastical mentality and perhaps even the Second Person of the Trinity. This heterodoxy was neither consistent nor deliberate. But her total silence on the subject of Jesus Christ in her religious writings is hard to explain otherwise, as is her attraction to a man who like Molinos—though presumably unintentionally at first—spread gravely erroneous doctrine on this very subject.

CHAPTER NINE

Christina as Author

I. THE MANUSCRIPT OF THE MAXIMS

CHRISTINA had strong literary ambitions. She gathered a whole staff of writers around her—Filicaia, Guidi, Menzini, Lemene, gladly accepting their dedications and allotting generous subsidies. She also took an interest in the purity of the Italian language, for she abhorred mannerisms and artifice. Once in a letter to a writer of whom we know nothing, she criticized a book he had sent her adding:

> Please do not be annoyed with me for pointing out some things in your book that do not please me. Then I want to mention another fault: your language has an all-too-Tuscan ring. Do not forget you are living and writing in a century in which Boccaccio is no longer read and understood in Italy, and Dante hardly at all. You know how highly I prize those writers, but I know too that we have to read them in disregard of their language, for their Tuscan turns of phrase give an impression of pedantry; they have an old-fashioned air which is intolerable to people of taste. Our century has a very refined taste and the language spoken at the Roman Court is purer, more natural and far finer. As it appears to me, there is between the old and new way of writing the same difference as between Lucretius' or Virgil's or Cicero's style and that of writers two centuries earlier; exactly the same difference exists today between our Cardinal Azzolino and other contemporary or earlier writers.

We note in passing that in Christina's eyes, Cardinal Azzolino, already comparable to the heroes of antiquity, was also a wonderful stylist: no one else seems to have noticed it.

Christina herself wrote essays in French on Caesar and Alexander; she planned a larger scientific work, but her favourite literary exercise was composing maxims and aphorisms. In

Sweden, Bourdelot ran her academy and collected her *Apothegms*. After her death a vast quantity of maxims were found among her papers—in a surprising number of copies. Some of them have been published and even translated into various languages, but they have never been properly appreciated because they were not rightly understood, they seemed odd and full of contradictions. Proudly analytical passages on princes and great men were found alongside Christian and even mystical maxims, burning with a quite different ardour. Many bear witness to Christina's stoical belief in man, others again reflect an exactly contrary attitude—seeing man as helpless and dependent on the grace of God.

The manuscripts are scattered among libraries at Montpellier and Stockholm, in France and England, and do not convey much at first glance. The largest batch is at Montpellier and is bound—but the binder took not the slightest account of the sequence of the pages. . . . To bring order into this chaos, and indeed to understand the maxims at all, they must be re-sorted and some attempt be made to discover when they were written. By dint of scrutinizing alterations made in the queen's own hand, then copied out afresh only to be corrected again with additional remarks, it is possible in the long run to put them all in chronological order. And this method produces an *inner* chronology, so that relations in sequence between individual manuscripts can be established. But of course this does not tell us what the absolute chronology should be.

We are surprised to find that many copies bear the same heading: "Begun on 29 September 1680." It is unthinkable that all these papers were begun on one and the same day, or even that all the copies began then, so the date must mean something else. Evidently Christina's secretary started to write down the final versions under her direction and noted on a number of manuscripts that this work started on 29 September 1680: but why? The only possible reason seems to be that she wanted to keep these papers apart from another batch, presumably of an earlier date. Here and there the manuscripts contain remarks that are themselves chronological clues, for instance in one maxim—crossed out later on—we read: "What is said here is valid up to the year 1670; since then the world has altered so much that . . . " So we assume that Christina was already writing maxims in 1670, that is, ten years earlier than the final copy. From other sources too we know she was jotting down maxims in the seventies, in the margins of books and manuscripts she had at hand, or in the form of topics for discussion at her academy, inaugurated in 1674. In fact we know from notes in a book by Erasmus (published 1665) that she was writing maxims even earlier, and if we admit that her marginal entries in books that interested her were made soon after they appeared, as indeed they were, and that she took steps to obtain them immediately upon publication, as she did, we have some justification in assuming that as early as the middle sixties, that is to say, ten years after her arrival in Rome, she was already writing maxims.

The copies we have naturally provide no reliable clues as to their respective seniority. The only sure method of discovering this is to adopt a different viewpoint and come to a decision in relation to Christina's religious and intellectual development, returning to the maxims to check how they can then be fitted into her life. This mode of reconstruction is not difficult; we well know Christina's youthful philosophy and how long she remained ignorant of Christian teaching on man's dependence; and thanks to dated jottings, for example on Molinos's trial, but also from theological manuscripts among her posthumous papers, we know *when* the new challenge of Quietism, and for instance Catherine of Genoa's mysticism, came her way.

This is what we mean by *inner* chronology: though we cannot say with complete accuracy when certain stoical maxims were written, we are certainly entitled to assume they date back further than the Christian and mystical ones that obviously belong to the period after she became acquainted with Quietism. Thus it is very unlikely that in the eighties Christina wrote both stoical and mystical maxims, or even allowed the earlier ones to retain their validity and therefore had them copied too: this would amount to saying she subscribed to two diametrically opposite views of life at one and the same time, a preposterous notion. The hypothesis is also untenable because a comparison of the different versions of the chronological series puts us in a position to decide which maxims came earlier and which later, which were struck out or corrected, and how she made her corrections. We find a systematic tendency to water down or cross out older maxims that asserted too great a trust in man, and replace them with Christian or purely mystical maxims. However, two facts are worth recording: first, the final versions were never completed—the whole work may have been broken off after Molinos's trial; too many of the maxims showed pronounced quietist influence which might have meant trouble with the Index. Secondly, Stoicism and Christian doctrine sometimes merge: stoical self-control is in some respects compatible with it, and all her life long Christina never entirely lost the human ideal of her young days—indeed it was the dominant ideal of her century; if we can trace a gradual obliteration of the stoical image in Christina, that too is a characteristic trend in the spiritual life of the times. As Jules Lemaître put it: "Racine's Christian pessimism replaced Corneille's stoical optimism." French literary historians have made detailed investigations as to how this came about.

2. THE AUTOBIOGRAPHY

In the mid-seventeenth century, particularly between 1655 and 1663, a favourite pastime for cultured ladies was the writing of little portraits of themselves and their friends. In 1659, as someone remarked: "The talk is all of portraits, all pens are busy with this craze." The best-known collection is entitled *Divers portraits recueillis en l'année 1659*; then came *Recueil des portraits et éloges en vers et prose, dédié à S.E.R. Mademoiselle*, published by Jean Regnault de Segrais, for many years secretary to *la grande Mademoiselle*, the king's niece. Of its fifty-nine portraits, *Mademoiselle* wrote sixteen herself. Copies of the collection were widely distributed.

Christina was well acquainted with this literary *genre:* she had among her papers a number of French portraits in verse and prose, in particular those done by Madame de la Suze who never failed to send her literary effusions to Queen Christina. But Christina was not in the least frivolous, she did not care for this sort of biography, of which a typical example is the Duchesse de Châtillon's self-portrait. It begins by telling us that her bearing was "one of the finest and most elegant, nothing could be more harmonious, supple and light. My demeanour is full of charm and all my movements are infinitely spirited. My face is rounded, an enchanting oval. . . . " The blue-blooded Abbess Marie Eléonore de Rohan, who usually wrote little devotional treatises for the edification of her nuns, produced the following self-portrait: "My face reveals a certain arrogance, but modesty as well. I have too large a nose, a not very appealing mouth, harmonious lips and teeth that are neither beautiful nor ugly. . . . " With equal complacency she then proceeds to trace her character.

Christina began her autobiography in the years she spent in Hamburg, but she adopted a totally different style, and compared with these ridiculous amateurish efforts, hers was well written. She opens by calling God to witness: "You know that in my century all biographies are either panegyrics or cruel satires . . . You have not given me the strength to receive such impertinences with indifference, I feel such overwhelming repugnance I cannot control it. I have no wish to expose myself either to envy or to flattery. . . . I wish to follow Your Light and walk in the footsteps of the great men to whom You gave courage to speak of themselves without arrogance and without the slightest deviation from the truth."

Who were these "great men"? La Rochefoucauld and Pascal have been suggested, but this is hardly likely, for Pascal wrote no autobiography and La Rochefoucauld left but a short sketch for his. Christina doubtless had other models in mind; a closer scrutiny of her book will reveal what they were. However, the autobiography remained unfinished, consisting only of nine rather short chapters. The first is her great appeal to God—which would have appeared ridiculous in *Mademoiselle*'s salon. Christina describes herself as conscious of being one of God's creatures to whom He had shown great favour. She regarded it as her duty to describe the great gifts with which He had endowed her, for the benefit of posterity. Here we have a bold theme that belongs to quite a different category from the frivolous French portraits: God gave Christina "a heart that nothing could satisfy."—"Nothing can fulfil me, nothing can satisfy me, but You." God had endowed her with such greatness that she could not have been satisfied had He given her sovereignty over the whole world. And in order that her autobiography should start off on the right lines, she begged God to remove from her heart "all complacency and all pride". Her purpose in writing was "to acknowledge her responsibility before the whole world". She dedicated her work to God for He was "her sole and honoured Principle": "You who are my honoured and only End, and will for ever remain so."—"Into your infinitely deep abyss I hurl my whole ignorance and all my sins, solely and alone my own, and all my gifts and qualities, if any, which are Yours."

In the next chapters too, her descriptions are again interrupted by invocations to God. As a young woman she had often failed: "I was neither capable of thanking You as I should nor did I beg for Your help. . . ." Though somewhat clumsily, she did attempt to account for her shortcomings and put her trust in God as Judge. This sort of autobiography, dedicated to God the Father and constantly invoking Him, written to show God's action on a refractory soul, had no place in contemporary French salon literature; the current French portraits concentrated chiefly on physical traits, appearance, habits and the art of living, in a wholly exterior sense. Those who had real experience of life—Pascal, François de Sales, Vincent de Paul—wrote no books about it.

Christina found her model elsewhere, she must certainly have known St. Augustine's Confessions, his invocation to God, his eagerness to show that a self-engrossed man who turned away from God would never find rest, his realization that man's capacity for loving could never be satisfied by man, but only by eternal God: it was he who compared creation, wretched as it was, to its Creator, and he wrote down his life, not in order to show what was remarkable in it, but as an example, for "all that is created threatens to sink back into the void out of which it was raised by God's creative power". So Christina wrote: "God is all and I am nothing", and she felt it was her duty to let posterity know what grace God had bestowed on her. St. Augustine declared he was dust and ashes and worth nothing—and yet he had to speak, for it was to God's mercy he turned, not to a man with no compassion; "Let my soul not grow weary under Your lash, let me not shrink from acknowledging the mercy with which You set me free from all the wrongful ways of my wickedness". This was the underlying theme of Christina's autobiography too, though she often forgot it and preferred to write of her prerogatives and majesty.

As literature, Christina's writings cannot of course be compared to the great religious works of the times, those of a Pascal or a Bossuet for instance. But this we should not expect. She was far superior to the *précieux* portrait-writers, and presumably under the influence of St. Augustine, she attained to a certain greatness in her autobiography, though only in the grandiloquent manner of the baroque period. Her self-knowledge was seriously deficient, she seems to have had no idea of the shortcomings in herself that were so patent to posterity: her egocentricity, coldness and lack of true objectivity. But the work as it stands has a pathetic disposition to greatness and a gravity which puts it on a different plane from the petty portraits that were then the fashion.

CHAPTER TEN

Approaching Death

I. PORTRAITS OF CHRISTINA

THE story of Christina's evolution can be read in the many portraits that were painted of her: the reserved, solitary girl in the Stockholm palace, pondering over the secrets of her body and her dangerous maternal legacy (Sébastien Bourdon best conveys her tortured restlessness); the Athene pictures which she herself gave away, and then, portraits by artists who dared tell the truth about her. No fewer than three portraits of her were for a long time considered to be caricatures, but on closer inspection they turn out not to be so: in none of them is the face caricatured, and none were done in order to make fun of her. This strengthens our conviction that the painters were giving a true account not only of her face but of her figure and clothes too. Of particular interest is the remarkable sketch in which she has a hand firmly placed on her hip and is shown with a crooked shoulder. This is, as far as I know, the only picture of Christina that points to a fact well known from other sources, that she had "only one shoulder" or "only one breast", as the malicious ladies of the French Court declared. Christina herself believed that as a very small child she was thrown on the floor or dropped on purpose because she was not a boy, her own mother being responsible. We need not believe this: it may be that Christina was damaged at birth, or it might be the effect of rickets that one side of her ribs was bent in or slightly deformed. At all events she was aware of it and always tried to hide it—by raising the lower shoulder. This gave her an odd stance and made her gait look positively like a waddle. When she was in Paris she once attended a ball and was laughed at for her ungainly movements; she noticed it and withdrew with hurt feelings.

The pictures—which were not done in her lifetime—reveal very well why she was not attractive to men; no one ever thought of trying to court her. When a girl she possessed a certain androgynous charm—as Chanut's character-study shows (Descartes said it was the work of a man in love): in particular her large eyes (which Bourdon made even larger than they really were) seem to have made an impression with their deep earnest look. And like many other women in whom masculine traits predominate, Christina looked old early in life. So she will have looked very much as the pictures show her at the time she wrote her glowing love-letters to Cardinal Azzolino from Hamburg, letters he answered with such pitiless coldness.

It is interesting to compare the three portraits we have mentioned with the descriptions of her appearance given by passing visitors. A Swedish traveller, Mårten Törnhielm, who saw her in Rome in 1688, reported: "The queen spoke good pure Swedish and after asking me one thing and another about Sweden, she sat with me near the window, leant her hand on the window-sill and remained silent for a while, sunk in thought, her eyes cast to the ground. Finally she held out her hand for me to kiss and wished me a happy journey home. The queen was dressed in black, she wore her hair in waves over her head but with no ribbon to adorn it, she was fairly corpulent and full in the face, and not particularly tall."

Another description that comes even nearer to the pictures was given by a French visitor, a few years before her death:

> She is over sixty years of age, definitely small, very stout and dumpy. Her skin, voice and features appear mannish: large nose, large blue eyes, light eyebrows, a double chin with traces of beard and a prominent lower lip. Her hair is light brown, a span in length, powdered and uncombed. Her expression is friendly and her manner very forthcoming. Her dress consists of a close-fitting man's coat of black satin, reaching to the knees and buttoned all the way down. She wears a very short black skirt showing her mannish shoes. A very wide black ribbon takes the place of a neckerchief. A waist-band over her dress-coat holds in her stomach, strongly emphasizing its roundness.

This description is as near to the pictures as could be. So we can easily imagine what the queen looked like in the last years of her life, and what impression she made on people. We know too that she looked very much the same in the sixties and dressed in the same way.

Nicodemus Tessin the younger, who twice visited the queen in Rome, once in the seventies and again a year before her death—and to whom we owe so many valuable, sometimes coloured, drawings of her theatre, banquets and entertainments—drew her too, as she sat enthroned in her seat of honour in St. Peter's—not during Mass but during the choir-prayers of the cathedral canons. When this rather small picture is enlarged, we recognize how skilfully Tessin has caught her marked profile. But he never did a larger picture of her. In his old age, Tessin described certain small traits of the queen's to his son, who reported: "My father, who daily had the honour of paying his respects to Queen Christina in Rome, often told me that she did not mind raising her skirts in the presence of gentlemen and warming her feet. And, he added, her skin was unusually dark . . . "

What was meant by "dark" can be variously interpreted. Perhaps Tessin only wanted to say that the queen had a dark skin, but possibly he was indicating that her hygienic habits were not of the best, a thing other observers noticed too, nor was it unusual in those days. A Frenchman said that the queen, who as a rule had very little use for hats and gloves, was "black" and looked "like a gypsy". Here "black" evidently means sun-tanned, and one might well imagine Tessin was simply referring to her dark complexion, which struck others too.

2. THE LAST OUTBURST OF FURY

In her Swedish days, Queen Christina had fallen very ill—and it was the Frenchman Bourdelot who cured her, for which she remained grateful all her life; right into old age she wrote him cheerful letters to Paris and showed great interest in all his plans. At the beginning of 1689, she felt she was seriously ill again and called her doctors. On 13 February she fell unconscious; after a while she recovered consciousness but had high fever; the doctors were also struck by the fact that her legs were swollen. It had happened twice before. Three days later she lost consciousness again. Her death was regarded as imminent, she was brought the sacrament for the sick and received it quietly.

Then she began to think what would happen after her death. On 1 March she dictated her will, naming Cardinal Azzolino her universal heir—but with the proviso that he paid her debts, and they were indeed no small matter. She also wanted to make her peace with Pope Innocent XI and drew up a letter of apology herself, humbly begging for his consideration and pardon. Innocent, who was ill, was much touched, and sent a cardinal to tell her he wanted to blot out all the past and to forgive her. And he would send to Bologna for a famous doctor named Malpini. The viceroy of Naples, Don Lorenzo Colonna, also wrote that he wanted to send her three good doctors.

In those days something occurred that is almost a short story in itself: Carl Bildt has very cleverly pieced it together from printed and unprinted sources. Among the singers employed by the queen, the two sisters, Angelina and Barbara Georgini, attracted some attention. The elder in particular was a striking beauty and was courted by many suitors, among them the French sculptor Théodon, who represented the director of the Academy of French Art in Rome: it was then being inaugurated and still exists to this day. Angelina's beauty and the quality of her singing aroused so much interest that her mother had the greatest difficulty in chaperoning her. As it became increasingly impossible, she entrusted her daughter to Queen Christina who gave her a bedroom immediately above her own. The suitors did not lose heart; among the more fiery cavaliers was a certain "abbé" Vanini who spotted the girl at a concert of the queen's in the grounds of the palazzo Riario. He had already cast eyes on other pretty girls in the queen's entourage, one of them had died in mysterious circumstances, and the queen believed the reckless Vanini was responsible. At all events she hated him.

Vanini did not, however, give up hope. The mother of lovely Angelina, Catarina Georgini, lived with her two daughters in the queen's palace, and he knew the mother was not averse to giving the wooer a helping hand so long as he behaved with moderation; he even succeeded in obtaining from her the key to Angelina's room. At the time (it was March 1689) the queen lay very ill in bed—a fact which acted as a spur to the suitor's audacity. Angelina watched by the sick queen's bedside, and then went up to her room. To her amazement she found the table laid for a party and in addition to her mother and a few other attendants of the queen's, there was Abbé Vanini, whom she could not bear. She screamed out in alarm. The abbé fell on his knees and entreated her to stop, but in vain. Meanwhile the others crept away and left them alone. The girl's cries could not be heard in the huge palace, but in the course of the disturbance chairs and tables were overthrown and the noise penetrated to the floor below, waking the queen. One of her gentlemen-in-waiting dashed upstairs shouting for help as he ran; among those who joined him was the French painter Théodon, who immediately hurled himself upon Vanini and would have strangled him if the others had not come to the rescue. Then they went to find Cardinal Azzolino's nephew Pompeio. He knew that Vanini was in the good books of several influential ecclesiastics and let him escape: he fled first to Cardinal d'Este. To the queen's anxious questions only evasive answers were given, in the room over hers the cats had chased one another round and round. . . . Angelina was seriously affected and had to keep to her bed for some time.

Meanwhile the queen's health improved. For a time she believed she was out of danger. On 12 March she wrote a business letter to her banker Texeira: "Thanks to a miracle and the powerful constitution God endowed me with, I have remained alive. I may say that medical art did its share, for my doctor, and the able gentlemen who were called in, performed veritable miracles. May it last as long as it pleases God."

To her trusty servant Olivekrante she wrote: "Quite against my expectations, God has snatched me from death; I had fully prepared myself for the last journey and considered it to be inevitable. Nevertheless, thanks to a miracle of grace, nature and medical science, I was so basically strong that health and life were given me afresh. But the strength of my temperament has abated somewhat since my illness: formerly it would have sufficed to strangle twenty Hercules. I am improving, grace has so surprisingly strengthened this temperament of mine that all doctors are amazed. I have given instructions to draw up a report of my illness. . . ."

Everyone was glad at her recovery. King Karl XI of Sweden wrote her a dutiful letter and wished her well.

And now the queen remembered lovely Angelina. One day she enquired why she no longer waited on her; she was given evasive answers—the girl was ill. But finally it came out that she was perfectly well but stayed away for another reason. The queen sent for her, and kneeling before her in tears the girl told her the whole story. Then the queen sent for a disreputable fellow named Merola and ordered him to find Vanini and kill him. Merola was a Neapolitan and had a lot to answer for. He had entered the queen's service in order to escape punishment for several murders committed in Naples; moreover, in Rome he had struck down some papal *sbirri* with remarkable sangfroid. He promised to do the deed. But after thinking it over he decided it was better to tell the terrified Vanini he would be wise to leave Rome at once, and that is what happened: Vanini gave Merola a large sum of money and disappeared. The queen was informed that the rascal had been stabbed—which gave her great satisfaction. But soon after she learnt that Vanini was alive and well in Subiaco. Then she lost her temper, first because it was in her palace that the brazen assault was made, an attempt to seduce one of her ladies-in-waiting in a room immediately above her own; then because someone had the audacity to lie to her. In a fury she rose from her armchair and went towards the terrified Merola with hands outstretched and fingers crooked, ready to strangle him—but fell unconscious to the ground. That was on 14 April 1689.

3. THE SEER OF LYONS

Christina's papers include an extensive correspondence—letters received and copies of her answers. The sheets are covered with her impulsive corrections and marginal remarks. But a letter belonging to the last year of her life has no marginal comments, though Christina evidently read it; it is from a man who called himself the Seer of Lyons (*le devin de Lyon*), obviously a madman. He commanded the queen to destroy all the pictures in the palazzo Riario immediately, to hew down all shameful statues (meaning the naked ones) in the grounds on the slopes of the Janiculum. If she took no notice of his orders she would die that very year. St. Bridget had always had the crucifix before her eyes, "but you possess objects of unmistakable shamelessness." Bridget's crucifix was "an instrument of God to foretell the future," whereas Christina's art collection—the letter mentioned Raphael, Andrea Sacchi and Titian—was "a work of the devil for the corruption of souls".

This was written in 1689. Christina felt old and knew she was ill. In earlier days, so stupid and presumptuous a missive would have been peppered with furious scornful comments; now she could no longer defend herself. She had had so many distressing experiences, nothing more could surprise her. As recently as December she had been in humiliating financial straits again, servants and friends alike had cheated her, half the world accused her of living an immoral life and of murdering her lover Monaldesco. She never became queen of either Naples or Poland. Her candidate for the papal throne, Cardinal Azzolino, never became pope. She set her final hopes on Quietism, thinking that at last she had found real security, but here too was illusion; Molinos turned out to be a charlatan, and she was convinced that the Inquisition's verdict was just. She was seized with disgust with a world that used to enchant her, holding her spellbound and flattering her pride and will-to-power. She was no longer capable of putting up any defence against fresh injuries. Wearily she let the stupid insulting letter from the Seer of Lyons lie among her papers. She had something more important to come to terms with.

4. DEATH

As late as 14 April Christina tried in her fury to hurl herself upon Merola. She had only a few more days to live. We know little of her last hours. No Swede was at her bedside, her last father-confessor was Father Slavata of Bohemia, who spoke Latin, French and German with her. Cardinal Azzolino was himself very ill and died soon after but he watched by her bedside loyally—knowing that the poor old woman loved him more than anyone else in the world. At six o'clock in the morning of 19 April 1689, the queen raised her left hand to her neck as though to soothe a pain: at that moment she fell asleep.

Her body was laid out in the palazzo Riario for four days. On Friday 22 April it was borne by torchlight, on an open carriage surrounded by her bodyguard, to the church of Santa Maria in Vallicella, which Cardinal Azzolino administered. The next day, in the presence of the entire college of cardinals, a Requiem Mass was sung there. Then Christina was carried in a great procession to her last resting-place in St. Peter's. At its head walked schoolboys and children from the almshouses, after that, no fewer than sixty members of fraternities in foot-length cassocks, then monks from fifteen Roman religious houses, five abreast, all bearing crosses, banners and wax candles alight; then came the priests of her own parish of Santa Dorotea, the choir, priests of St. Peter's, then the bier borne high, covered with gold brocade embroidered with a crown and the Vasa arms. There lay the queen, visible to all, with crown and sceptre, wrapped in a white robe stitched with gold, and a purple ermine-trimmed cloak. The bier was carried shoulder-high by her own retinue, surrounded by her court and officers. At its head walked a poor Vasa cousin, Count Vesenau, and her latest favourite, Robert Dudley, Earl of Warwick, Duke of Northumberland. Behind, the commandant of the Swiss papal guard rode on horseback with six soldiers, papal heralds, masters of ceremonies, lords of the chamber, bishops, ecclesiastics of various ranks and many others. Ten of the queen's own carriages closed the procession.

In St Peter's she was laid in a cypress coffin, with crown and sceptre, and also some of her finest medallions; this coffin was placed in a leaden one with her name and coat of arms in relief, and then in a further wooden coffin which was deposited in the main nave of the crypt, in the so-called *grotte vecchie*. There it stands against the wall to this day, covered with bits of fallen mortar, unadorned but for this inscription:

D.O.M.
CORPUS CHRISTINAE ALEXANDRAE
GOTHORUM SUECORUM VANDALORUMQUE REGINAE
OBIIT DIE XIX APRILIS MDCLXXXIX

In her will Christina had decreed:

"We wish our body to be buried wrapped in a white cloth in the church of *La Rotunda* (the Pantheon) or another church chosen by our heirs; the body should not be displayed and we forbid all funeral pomp and suchlike vanities. The epitaph should consist of a simple stone with the following inscription: D.O.M. Vixit Christina annos LXIII. This is what we wish, neither more nor less." But she was dead; there was no need to respect her wishes any longer.

CHAPTER ELEVEN

Conclusion

FOR all too long Christina was regarded as from an early age complete and entire, with hardly any subsequent development. My purpose has chiefly been to trace phases of her intellectual and spiritual evolution during a life that was anything but tranquil. In doing so I have had to meet and parry two misconceptions.

First, that of popular literature: founded on lampoons and forged letters of her time, painting Christina as an unbridled adventuress, a voluptuous, hysterical, utterly frivolous woman with no real purpose in life. While I was writing this book, fresh material of this sort has come to my notice.

The other misconception is the one for which Curt Weibull is responsible: heroic and unhistorical, idealizing Christina as though she were an integrated personality, and overlooking her shortcomings, for instance her propensity to lying and Machiavellian dissimulation, for which ample evidence is provided in papers published by Arckenholtz in mid-eighteenth century; Weibull had no idea of her real motives in the abdication crisis, nor of the facts of her life as a woman, nor of her contacts with the libertines.

Neither of these misconceptions takes into account the last act of her life—the quietist episode. That is not to say that Christina's life is now an open book for all to read; there is still a good deal of research to be done; but the main lines of her spiritual evolution now seem to emerge.

To our contemporaries it may be puzzling that such a dominating woman as Christina could possibly have been so strongly drawn to the Catholic and Christian doctrine of self-denial, love of others, and mercy. She remained for a long time stubbornly addicted to her natural arrogance, ruthless prejudices, scorn of her fellows and self-idolization. But almost the same problem arises in other seventeenth-century characters. The century itself is a fascinating one in its complexity, and so are some of its notable people: Louis XIV for instance, with his icy cynicism, his cold-blooded betrayal of Christian Europe (plotting with the Turks and so on); his depravity on the one hand and his undoubted religious leanings on the other—how hard it is to grasp, and how inexplicable it all is.

For young Christina, anxious about her physical constitution, shrinking from marriage, afflicted with a neurosis due to her strange temperament and inept upbringing, there were doubtless many obstacles in the way of a Christian life. All the same it cannot be denied that at all times she set out resolutely to find God and religion. Over the years, this religious yearning in her culminated in a decisive acceptance of redemption through Jesus Christ. She never stopped longing for God inwardly, that is evident. In memorable words, Chanut described her love of honour and duty; in her autobiography she gave touching expression to her longing for closeness to God that occupied her lonely nights in the Stockholm palace.

Christina was always solitary from the very beginning—without a father, and to all intents and purposes without a mother—for the State council parted them once and for all. Her education was typical of the times she lived in and imbued her with a strong, absolute sense of duty; how accountable is that arrogance of hers, encouraged as she was to regard herself as the focus of all things! Everything contributed to foster in her a stoical cult of virtue, a stoical scorn for femininity, an almost inhuman ideal of perfection, a deeply ingrained conception of the anointed monarch as God's representative and image, exposed as she was to the flattery, hypocrisy and lip-service of the Court. Truly the life of the Swedish queen was a tragic one. All contributing elements, inheritance, environment, circumstances and upbringing, combined to enclose her in shining armour in which she was bound to suffocate sooner or later.

Her character was inhibited and introverted to a remarkable degree. She had no feeling for nature, no sense of joy in belonging to a springtime world—a joy evident in all the foremost figures of devout humanism, e.g. the Jesuit Louis Richeome with his love of all creatures, or Yves de Paris with his delight in the miracle of man and nature, or François de Sales with that lovely merging of faith in man and yearning for the transcendental. It seems as though Christina never had her attention caught by anything outside herself or without some relation to herself; as though she could never forget herself—her dignity, greatness, majesty, her privileged position; her anxieties, restlessness, physical infirmities and unsatisfied love always got in her way. Never, or only extremely seldom, did she come positively and selflessly to terms with any social obligation, any natural phenomenon, or any fellow human-being. A social conscience and sympathy for the poor and oppressed are as conspicuously absent in her as in the tyrant, Louis XIV.

Twice, in despair, Christina sought to break loose from her bonds. Her adoption of Catholicism I do not regard as an honest search for liberation but rather an attempt at evasion, a desire to elude the demands of the religious life and find a more tolerant and comfortable form of culture in which she could without hindrance continue to give full play to her sceptical, free-thinking, arrogant habits.

In her love for Cardinal Azzolino she made a real attempt to break free from her shackles for the first time. How often had she referred to her inability to accept submission or indeed to admit any form of dependence, or obligations involving the exercise of discretion, as human society requires—and now she was pathetically begging to be allowed to be the slave of a man who was not outstanding in any way, but whom she idealized beyond all bounds. Such an over-excited attempt at escape was foredoomed to failure: the object of her veneration was nothing real, but a surrogate, a phantasy. The true Azzolino was quite different.

This experience might have been of great value to her, she could have reaped much benefit from her defeat and disappointment, it might have given the deathblow to her arrogance, her intractable habit of regarding herself as a miracle of creation, God's great masterpiece. Perhaps she would then have discovered something that the rest of us have less difficulty in perceiving—that she was by no means an exalted, noble and good person but a small-minded, selfish, warped woman, though possessing strong will-power and considerable intelligence.

Then came her second attempt at escape. She broke with her confessor, the Franciscan Lars Skytte, a Swede of noble family, and adopted Molinos's Quietism. She took this step very seriously, three hours a week she discussed mystical theology with Molinos, and her maxims show how strongly she was under the influence of his doctrine. She discovered in it totally new elements—a lightening of her burden, a release, a beginning of peace.

But unknowingly she was once more on a false track. Molinos distorted the Gospel, disregarding the most important part of it, the Person of Christ; instead of helping her to find her true Redeemer and submit her wretchedness to his loving care, he armed her with theological arguments of a kind to make her even more shy of Christ, and useless to her in overcoming her stubborn subconscious efforts to cling to her pride, arrogance and self-adulation. So this hypercritical, always mistrustful woman, who once remarked that whatever people said of her seemed suspect and that she never believed anything she had not first doubted for a long time, now adopted a doctrine that brought her great clarity and helped to purge her soul, but ultimately led her astray.

Her last great disappointment was that the very man whom she believed had saved her, who taught "pure love of God", free of ecclesiastical formalism, was had up for trial, discovered to be a heretic and condemned to lifelong imprisonment; moreover he ended by recanting his own teaching. We can follow step by step the tragedy it was to her, in her marginal jottings in the records of the trial. First she was up in arms and offered all her support to Molinos. For a long time she was convinced he had been put on trial by unscrupulous political opponents. But like Azzolino and Innocent XI, she had to revise her views. It is distressing to trace how, gradually, the truth dawned on her. But there was no alternative when poor Molinos, as his mind gave way, readily admitted his follies and sexual aberrations and tried to give them extravagant doctrinal justification. Those who say Christina "betrayed" her spiritual guide do not know the facts; through the accuracy of her information during the course of this exemplary trial, which does highest credit to the Inquisition, she came to a better understanding.

Christina's maxims reveal her attitude in old age. She had to get along without Molinos, but she by no means gave up all she had learnt from him in his good days, things she found endorsed by better teachers. Catherine of Genoa, as we know, affected her profoundly. In the last phase of her life, the world and its doings positively repelled her, and she longed for the great adventure we all have to submit to when we cross the pitiless threshold of death. Now at last she knew that no reliance can be placed in anything human: "All that has an end can be borne, the insignificant duration of our life can and should help us through all the evil that this world has in store for us."—"All that is visible and tangible has a bitter taste which some notice earlier, others later." The world no longer attracted this once active woman with her formerly unquenchable eagerness for deeds, intrigues, plans, and her urge to get the better of her fellows and opponents. Not only power and grandeur had lost their attraction, but life itself; the whole splendour of life, so intoxicating to the sovereigns of the baroque world, was now extinguished.

Not till her last maxims did Christina speak from true experience and a real knowledge of life: "All these dream-pictures of fatherland, freedom, honour, happiness and pride, which have inspired so many outstanding men to perform great and noble deeds, are in truth no more than human day-dreams." And in her autobiography she wrote, as in the presence of God:

> Quench with Your hand all that does not come from You; of Your goodness and for Your glory complete Your work. Let Your goodness overcome my ingratitude and weakness. Protect me from myself as You used to protect me from my enemies. By You and through You I long for You. Do not be unmoved by the immense burning longing You have lit in my heart, for I look upon it as the greatest grace You have bestowed on me. Make me worthy to possess You in that blind and utter renunciation that I owe You, for

no one can withhold it from You without courting eternal unhappiness. Detach me from my secret bonds, however fair and guileless they may be. Help me to dedicate my work, my life and my death to You alone for ever and ever.

Index